Contents

Introduction, Electronic Resources, Acknowledgments and Authors

AS Unit 1
Introduction to Financial Accounting

AS Unit 2
Financial and Management Accounting

Introduction

AS Accounting for AQA has been written to provide a study resource for students taking the Assessment and Qualifications Alliance's AS examinations in Accounting. The AS course is structured into two equally-weighted Units, as follows:

Unit 1 **Introduction to Financial** **Accounting**	**Unit 2** **Financial and Management** **Accounting**

Unit 1 is designed as a foundation for the course and covers double-entry procedures as applied to the accounting systems of sole traders.

Unit 2 provides the opportunity to develop knowledge and understanding of financial accounting and introduces some of the ways in which financial accounting can provide valuable information for measuring and monitoring business performance and for planning future business operations.

Each Unit is assessed externally by a written examination of 1 hour 30 minutes.

Full details of the Units, together with past examination papers, can be found on AQA's website, www.aqa.org.uk

AS Accounting for AQA has been designed to be user-friendly and contains:

* clear explanations and numerous worked examples
* chapter summaries to help with revision
* a wide range of questions, many from past AQA examinations
* answers to selected questions, set out in full at the end of the book
* full coverage of the ICT content of Unit 2

For those questions where answers are not given in the book, separate **tutor support material** provides the answers, together with a range of photocopiable layouts, a web directory and various electronic resources (see next page). Contact the Osborne Books Sales Office on 01905 748071 for details of how to obtain this tutor support material.

David Cox, Michael Fardon

Spring 2008

Electronic Resources

The Osborne Books website – www.osbornebooks.co.uk – is constantly developing its range of facilities for students and tutors. There are a number of resources which support this text:

Online Multiple Choice Tests for each chapter

At the beginning of the questions at end of each chapter you will see the following screen:

visit
www.osbornebooks.co.uk
to take an online test

This indicates that an additional 'True or False' multiple choice test is available online to test understanding of the chapter. These tests, which are also useful for revision, can be accessed in the Resources section of www.osbornebooks.co.uk

Downloadable Documents

Also available in the Resources section of www.osbornebooks.co.uk are downloadable pdf files which will help with the practice questions in this book. These include:

- ledger accounts
- sole trader trading and profit and loss account and balance sheet
- limited company trading and profit and loss account and balance sheet
- accounting ratios
- cash budget

Resources for teachers

Further electronic resources are available for teachers who adopt this book as a class text. They include:

- PowerPoint presentations on subjects such as the principles of double-entry
- Excel spreadsheets set up for cash budgets

Contact the Osborne Books Sales Office on 01905 748071 for details of how to obtain these resources.

More electronic resources?

If you have suggestions about further electronic resources that you would like to use to support this text, please email books@osbornebooks.co.uk with details.

Acknowledgments

The publisher wishes to thank Jean Cox, Mike Gilbert and Jon Moore for their help with the reading and production of this book. Particular thanks go to Roger Petheram of Worcester College of Technology for his technical editorial work.

AQA examination materials are reproduced by kind permission of the Assessment and Qualifications Alliance (AQA). Thanks are also due to Sage (UK) Limited for their permission to use screen images within the text. It should be noted that Osborne Books Limited is a company which operates completely independently of Sage (UK) Limited.

Authors

David Cox is a Certified Accountant with more than twenty years' experience teaching accountancy students over a wide range of levels. Formerly with the Management and Professional Studies Department at Worcester College of Technology, he now lectures on a freelance basis and carries out educational consultancy work in accountancy studies. He is author and joint author of a number of textbooks in the areas of accounting, finance and banking.

Michael Fardon has extensive teaching experience of a wide range of banking, business and accountancy courses at Worcester College of Technology. He now specialises in writing business and financial texts and is General Editor at Osborne Books. He is also an educational consultant and has worked extensively in the areas of vocational business curriculum development.

AS Accounting Unit 1

Introduction to Financial Accounting

This Unit for AQA AS Accounting is designed as a foundation for the course, and covers:

- double-entry procedures, business documents

- verification of accounting records, including correction of errors

- use of the trial balance

- trading and profit and loss accounts, and balance sheets

The Unit focuses on the accounting systems of sole traders. A sole trader is a person in business on his or her own, not involving partners and avoiding the costs of forming a limited company. In AS Unit 2 we will compare the advantages and disadvantages of the different types of business organisation – sole traders, partnerships and limited companies.

1 WHAT IS FINANCIAL ACCOUNTING?

Accounting – known as 'the language of business' – is essential to the recording and presentation of business activities in the form of accounting records and financial statements. Financial accounting involves:

● recording business transactions in financial terms

● reporting financial information to the owner of the business and other interested parties

● advising the owner – and other stakeholders – how to use the financial reports to assess the past performance of the business, and to make decisions for the future

Throughout AS Units 1 and 2 we will see how the three main elements of the definition – recording, reporting and advising – are carried out. First though, in this chapter we will look at an outline of the financial accounting system.

---

an important note about VAT

As you will know, many of the goods and services that we buy are subject to Value Added Tax (VAT), which is a tax on sales. The specifications for AS Accounting Unit 1 state that you "will **not** be required to understand the VAT system or make accounting records of VAT." Although this will simplify your study of accounting, it does mean that some documents and layouts in this book and in examination questions will differ slightly from those you will see in day-to-day use by individuals and businesses.

THE FINANCIAL ACCOUNTING SYSTEM

Businesses need to record transactions in the financial accounting system for very practical purposes:

• to quantify items such as sales, expenses and profit

• to present the accounts in a meaningful way so as to measure the success of the business

• to provide information to the owner of the business and to other stakeholders (eg the bank manager, who may be providing a loan)

Business accounting records can be complex, and one of the problems that you face as a student is having difficulty in relating what you are learning to the financial accounting system of the business as a whole. In this chapter we will summarise how a typical business records and presents financial information in the form of accounts. The process follows a number of distinct stages which are illustrated in the diagram on the next page.

the financial accounting system

SOURCE DOCUMENTS
invoices
credit notes
cash receipts
till rolls
bank paying-in slip counterfoils
cheque counterfoils
information from bank statements

sources of accounting information

SUBSIDIARY BOOKS
sales day book
purchases day book
sales returns day book
purchases returns day book
general journal
main cash book

gathering and summarising accounting information

DOUBLE-ENTRY BOOK-KEEPING
sales ledger – accounts of debtors

purchases ledger – accounts of creditors

general (nominal) ledger
- 'nominal' accounts for sales, purchases, expenses, capital, loans etc
- 'real' accounts for items, eg fixed assets, cash, bank balance

recording the dual aspect of accounting transactions in the ledger accounts

TRIAL BALANCE
a summary of the balances of all the accounts at the end of the accounting period

arithmetic checking of double-entry book-keeping

FINAL ACCOUNTS
- trading and profit and loss account

  and

- balance sheet

statement measuring profit (or loss) for an accounting period

statement of assets, liabilities and capital at the end of an accounting period

The financial accounting system can be summarised as follows:

source documents	processing of source documents relating to accounting transactions
↓	
subsidiary books	recording of accounting transactions in subsidiary books (also known as books of prime entry)
↓	
double-entry accounts	transfer from the subsidiary books into the double-entry book-keeping system of accounts contained in 'the ledger'
↓	
trial balance	extraction of figures from all the double-entry accounts to check their accuracy in the form of a trial balance
↓	
final accounts	production of a trading and profit and loss account, and a balance sheet – collectively known as the final accounts

Over the next few chapters we will look at these stages – the financial accounting system – in detail. If you should at any time lose sight of where your studies are taking you, refer back to this chapter, and it should help to place your work in context.

Before summarising each stage in the accounting system we will first examine what form accounting records can take.

ACCOUNTING RECORDS

Accounting records are usually kept in one of two forms: handwritten records or computer records.

written accounting records

This is the traditional form of keeping 'the books', particularly for the smaller business. The main record is the ledger which, at one time, would be a large leather-bound volume, neatly ruled, in which the book-keeper would enter each business transaction in immaculate copperplate handwriting into individual accounts. In modern times, the handwritten ledger is still used, and stationery shops sell ledgers and other accounting books, designed especially for the smaller business.

computer accounting records

Nowadays, computers are relatively cheap so that they can be afforded by most businesses. With computer accounting, business transactions are input into the computer and stored on disk. The major advantage of computer accounting is that it is a very accurate method of recording business transactions; the disadvantage is that it may be expensive and time-consuming to set up, particularly for the smaller business. Interestingly, the word 'ledger' has survived into the computer age but, instead of being a bound volume, it is represented by data files held on a computer disk.

Whether business transactions are recorded by hand, or by using a computer, the basic principles remain the same. The first few chapters of this book concentrate on these basic principles; the impact of computers in accounting is looked at in more detail in AS Unit 2 (Chapter 20).

practical points

When maintaining financial accounts you should bear in mind that they should be kept:

*   accurately
*   up-to-date
*   confidentially, ie not revealed to unauthorised people outside the business

Maintaining financial accounts is a discipline, and you should develop disciplined accounting skills as you study with this book. Your studies will involve you in working through many questions and practical examples. These will require you to apply logical thought to the skills you have learned. In particular, when attempting questions you should:

*   be neat in the layout of your work
*   use ink (in accounting, the use of pencil shows indecision)
*   use correcting fluid in moderation (it is preferable to cross through errors neatly with a single line and write the correct version on the line below)

The reason for using correcting fluid only in moderation in handwritten accounts is because the accounts will often be audited (checked by accountants); correcting fluid may hide errors, but it can also conceal fraudulent transactions and will raise the suspicions of auditors.

SOURCE DOCUMENTS

Business transactions generate documents. In this section we will relate them to the type of transaction involved and also introduce other accounting terminology which is essential to your studies.

sale and purchase of goods and services – the invoice

When a business buys or sells goods or a service, it is the seller who prepares an invoice stating

*   the amount owing
*   when it should be paid
*   details of the goods sold or service provided

An invoice is illustrated on page 45.

cash sales and credit sales – debtors

An invoice is prepared by the seller for

- **cash sales** – where payment is immediate, whether in cash, by cheque, by debit card, by credit card, or by bank transfer. (Note that not all cash sales will require an invoice to be prepared by the seller – shops, for instance, normally issue a **cash receipt** for the amount paid and record the sale on their **till roll**.)
- **credit sales** – where payment is to be made at a later date (often 30 days later)

A debtor is an individual or a business who owes you money when you sell on credit.

Note that, in accounting, the term 'sales' is used for the sale of goods – whether on credit or for cash – in which the business trades; for example, a shoe shop will record as its sales the money amounts of shoes sold.

cash purchases and credit purchases – creditors

To the business buying goods

- **cash purchases** are where goods are bought and paid for immediately, whether in cash, by cheque, by debit card, by credit card, or by bank transfer
- **credit purchases** are where goods are bought with payment to be made at a later date (often 30 days later)

A creditor is an individual or a business to whom you owe money when you buy on credit.

Note that, in accounting, the term 'purchases' is used for goods bought – whether on credit or for cash – which are intended to be resold later.

return of goods – the credit note

If the buyer returns goods which are bought on credit (they may be faulty or incorrect) the seller will prepare a credit note (see page 47 for an example) which is sent to the buyer, reducing the amount of money owed. The credit note, like the invoice, states the money amount and the goods or services to which it relates.

banking transactions – paying-in slips, cheques, BACS transfers

Businesses, like anyone else with a bank account, need to pay in money, and draw out cash and make payments. Paying-in slip counterfoils, cheque counterfoils and information from bank statements are used frequently as source documents for bank account transactions.

further reading

The subject of business documents is covered in detail in Chapter 4, while Chapters 7 and 8 deal with the use of information from bank statements.

RECORDING OF TRANSACTIONS – SUBSIDIARY BOOKS

Many businesses issue and receive large quantities of invoices, credit notes and banking documents, and it is useful for them to list these in summary form, during the course of the working day. These summaries are known as subsidiary books (or books of prime entry.). These include:

- **sales day book** – a list of credit sales made, compiled from invoices issued
- **purchases day book** – a list of credit purchases made, compiled from invoices received
- **sales returns day book** – a list of returns inwards, ie goods returned by customers, compiled from credit notes issued
- **purchases returns day book** – a list of returns outwards, ie goods returned by the business to suppliers, compiled from credit notes received
- **main cash book** – the business' record of the bank account and the amount of cash held, compiled from cash receipts, till rolls, paying-in slip counterfoils, cheque counterfoils and information from bank statements
- **general journal** – a record of non-regular transactions, which are not recorded in any other subsidiary book

The subsidiary books are explained in detail in Chapter 6. The point you should bear in mind is that they provide the information for the double-entry book-keeping system.

DOUBLE-ENTRY ACCOUNTS – THE LEDGER

The basis of the accounting system is the double-entry book-keeping system which is embodied in a series of records known as the **ledger**. This is divided into a number of separate accounts.

double-entry book-keeping

Double-entry book-keeping involves making two entries in the accounts for each transaction: for instance, if you are paying wages by cheque you will make an entry in bank account and an entry in wages account. The reasoning behind this procedure and the rules involved are explained in detail in Chapters 2 and 3. If you are operating a manual accounting system you will make the two entries by hand, if you are operating a computer accounting system you will make one entry on the keyboard, but indicate to the machine where the other entry is to be made by means of a code.

accounts

The sources for the entries you make are the subsidiary books. The ledger into which you make the entries is normally a bound book (in a non-computerised system) divided into separate accounts, eg a separate account for sales, purchases, each type of business expense, each debtor, each creditor, and so on. Each account will be given a specific name, and a number for reference purposes (or input code, if you use a computer system).

division of the ledger

Because of the large number of accounts involved, the ledger has traditionally been divided into a number of sections. These same sections are used in computer accounting systems.

- **sales ledger** – personal accounts of debtors, ie customers to whom the business has sold on credit

- **purchases ledger** – personal accounts of creditors, ie suppliers to whom the business owes money

- **general (or nominal) ledger** – the remainder of the accounts: nominal accounts, eg sales, purchases, expenses, and real accounts for items owned by the business, eg fixed assets, cash, bank balance

trial balance

Double-entry book-keeping, because it involves making two entries for each transaction, is open to error. What if the book-keeper writes in £45 in one account and £54 in another? The trial balance – explained in full in Chapter 5 – effectively checks the entries made over a given period and will pick up most errors. It sets out the balances of all the double-entry accounts, ie the totals of the accounts for a certain period. It is, as well as being an arithmetic check, the source of valuable information which is used to help in the preparation of the final accounts of the business.

FINAL ACCOUNTS

The final accounts of a business comprise the profit statement and the balance sheet.

profit statement

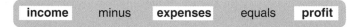

income   minus   **expenses**   equals   **profit**

The profit statement of a business comprises the trading and profit and loss account. The object of this statement is to calculate the profit (or loss) due to the owner of the business after the deduction of cost of sales to give gross profit, and also after the deduction of all expenses (overheads) to give net profit

The figures for these calculations – sales, purchases, expenses of various kinds – are taken from the double-entry system. The layout of profit statements is explained in Chapter 9.

balance sheet

The double-entry system also contains figures for:

assets   items the business owns, which can be

- fixed assets – items bought for use in the business, eg premises, vehicles, computers
- current assets – items used in the everyday running of the business, eg stock, debtors (money owed by customers), cash, and money in the bank

liabilities   items that the business owes, eg bank loans and overdrafts, and creditors (money owed to suppliers)

capital   money or assets introduced by the owner of the business; capital is in effect owed by the business to the owner

The balance sheet is so called because it balances in numerical (money) terms:

assets	minus	**liabilities**	equals	**capital**
what a business owns		what a business owes		how the business has been financed

The layout of balance sheets is explained in Chapter 9.

the accounting equation

The balance sheet illustrates a concept important to accounting theory, known as the accounting equation. This equation is illustrated in the diagram above, namely

$$\text{Assets} - \text{Liabilities} = \text{Capital}$$

Every business transaction will change the balance sheet and the equation, as each transaction has a dual effect on the accounts. However, the equation will always balance.

Consider the following transactions made through the business bank account:

	Transaction	**Effect on equation**
1.	Business pays a creditor	decrease in asset (bank)
		decrease in liability (money owed to creditor)
2.	Business buys a computer	increase in asset (computer)
		decrease in asset (bank)
3.	The owner introduces new capital by paying a cheque into the bank	increase in asset (bank)
		increase in capital (money owed by the business to owner)

How is the equation affected by these particular transactions?

1. Assets and liabilities both decrease by the amount of the payment; capital remains unchanged.

2. Assets remain the same because the two transactions cancel each other out in the assets section: value is transferred from the asset of bank to the asset of computer.

3. Both sides of the equation increase by the amount of the capital introduced.

In short, the equation always balances, as will the balance sheet of a business.

In conclusion, every transaction has a dual aspect, as two entries are involved: this is the basis of the theory of double-entry book-keeping, which will be described in detail in Chapters 2 and 3.

ACCOUNTING CONCEPTS

Accounting concepts are broad assumptions which underlie the preparation of all accounting reports. For the moment, we will consider two very important aspects:

- business entity
- money measurement

Business entity means that the accounts record and report on the financial transactions of a particular business: for example, the accounts of J Smith Limited – a limited company – record and report on that business only. The problem is that, when a business is run by a sole trader, the owner's personal financial transactions can be sometimes mixed in with the business' financial transactions; the two should be kept entirely separate.

Money measurement means that the accounting system uses money as the common denominator in recording and reporting all business transactions. Thus, it is not possible to record, for example, the loyalty of a firm's workforce or the quality of a product, because these cannot be reported in money terms.

WHO USES FINANCIAL ACCOUNTS?

Before answering the question of who uses the accounts, and why, it is important to draw a distinction between the processes of book-keeping and accounting.

Book-keeping is the basic recording of business transactions in financial terms – literally 'keeping the books of account'. This task can be carried out by anyone – the owner, or by a full-time or part-time book-keeper. The book-keeper should be able to record transactions, and extract a trial balance (see Chapter 5).

Accounting involves the financial accountant taking the information recorded by the book-keeper and presenting it in the form of financial reports to the business owner or managers. Such reports either look back at what has already happened:

- profit statement and balance sheet

or they are forward looking:

- forecast, or budgeted, accounts

In each case, these reports help the owner or managers – who are stakeholders in the business – to monitor the financial progress of the business, and to make decisions for the future.

information for the owner or managers

The accounting system will be able to give information about:

- purchases of goods (for resale) to date
- turnover (cash and credit sales) to date
- expenses and overheads to date
- debtors – both the total amount owed to the business, and also the names of individual debtors and the amount owed by each
- creditors – both the total owed by the business, and the amount owed to each creditor
- assets owned by the business
- liabilities, eg bank loans, owed by the business
- profit made by the business during a particular time period

The owner will want to know how profitable the business is, and what it may be worth.

information for outsiders

As well as the owner and managers, other stakeholders interested in the accounts of a business include:

- the providers of finance, eg the bank manager if the business wants to borrow from the bank
- suppliers, who wish to assess the likelihood of receiving payment from the business
- customers, who wish to ensure that the business has the financial strength to continue selling the goods and services that they buy
- employees and trade unions, who wish to check on the financial prospects of the business
- the tax authorities, who will wish to see that tax due by the business on profits and for Value Added Tax has been paid
- competitors, who wish to assess the profitability of the business
- potential investors in the business
- the local community and national interest groups, who may be seeking to influence business policy
- government and official bodies, eg Companies House who need to see the final accounts of limited companies

Clearly not all of these will be interested in smaller businesses – such as those run by sole traders. However, when we study limited companies in AS Unit 2, we will see how a wider range of stakeholders has an interest in the activities of companies.

ACCOUNTING TERMS

In the course of this chapter a number of specific accounting terms have been introduced. You should now study this section closely to ensure that you are clear about these definitions:

accounts   financial records, where business transactions are entered

ledger   the set of accounts of a business

assets	items owned by a business
liabilities	items owed by a business
capital	the amount of the owner's stake in the business
debtors	individuals or businesses who owe money in respect of goods or services supplied by the business
creditors	individuals or businesses to whom money is owed by the business
purchases	goods bought – whether on credit or for cash – which are intended to be resold later
credit purchases	goods bought, with payment to be made at a later date
cash purchases	goods bought, with immediate payment made in cash, by cheque, by debit card, by credit card, or by bank transfer
sales	the sale of goods – whether on credit or for cash – in which the business trades
credit sales	goods sold, with payment to be received at an agreed date in the future
cash sales	goods sold, with immediate payment received in cash, by cheque, by debit card, by credit card, or by bank transfer
turnover	the total of sales, both cash and credit, for a particular time period
sales returns	goods returned by customers; also known as returns inwards
purchases returns	goods returned by the business to suppliers; also known as returns outwards

CHAPTER SUMMARY

- Accounting is known as 'the language of business'.

- The accounting system comprises a number of specific stages of recording and presenting business transactions:
  - source documents
  - subsidiary books
  - double-entry system of ledgers
  - trial balance
  - final accounts

- Accounting records call for the development of skills of accuracy and neatness.

- The balance sheet uses the accounting equation:
  Assets – Liabilities = Capital

- Two basic accounting concepts which apply to all business accounts are:
  - business entity
  - money measurement

- Financial accounts are used both by the owner and managers of the business and also by outside bodies.

- Accounting involves the use of very specific terminology which should be learned.

In the next chapter we will look at some transactions that are to be found in most financial accounts. By studying these we will begin to understand the principles of double-entry book-keeping.

QUESTIONS

visit
www.osbornebooks.co.uk
to take an online test

An asterisk (*) after the question number means that the answer is given at the end of this book.

1.1* Fill in the missing words from the following sentences:

(a) The set of double-entry accounts of a business is called the ....

(b) A .... is a person who owes you money when you sell on credit.

(c) A .... is a person to whom you owe money when you buy on credit.

(d) The .... is a list of sales made, compiled from invoices issued.

(e) The business' record of bank account and amount of cash held is kept in the main ....

(f) Accounts such as sales, purchases, expenses are kept in the ....

(g) The accounting equation is:
.... minus ....equals ....

(h) Accounts record and report on the financial transactions of a particular business: this is the application of the .... concept.

1.2 State three purposes of accounting.

1.3 Describe the main stages in the financial accounting system. State five pieces of information that can be found from the accounting system that will be of interest to the owner of the business.

1.4 As well as the owner and managers of the business, other stakeholders have an interest in the accounting information. Select any *four* of these other stakeholders, and briefly explain the interest they will have.

1.5 Explain the accounting concepts of:

    (a) business entity

    (b) money measurement

1.6 Distinguish between:

- assets and liabilities
- debtors and creditors
- purchases and sales
- credit purchases and cash purchases

1.7 Show the dual aspect, as it affects the accounting equation (assets – liabilities = capital), of the following transactions for a particular business:

- owner starts in business with capital of £8,000 in the bank
- buys a computer for £4,000, paying by cheque
- obtains a loan of £3,000 by cheque from a friend
- buys a van for £6,000, paying by cheque

1.8* Fill in the missing figures:

Assets	Liabilities	Capital
£	£	£
20,000	0	....
15,000	5,000	....
16,400	....	8,850
....	3,850	10,250
25,380	....	6,950
....	7,910	13,250

1.9* The table below sets out account balances from the books of a business. The columns (a) to (f) show the account balances resulting from a series of transactions that have taken place over time.

You are to compare each set of adjacent columns, ie (a) with (b), (b) with (c), and so on and state, with figures, what accounting transactions have taken place in each case.

	(a)	(b)	(c)	(d)	(e)	(f)
	£	£	£	£	£	£
Assets						
Office equipment	–	2,000	2,000	2,000	2,000	2,000
Van	–	–	–	10,000	10,000	10,000
Bank	10,000	8,000	14,000	4,000	6,000	3,000
Liabilities						
Loan	–	–	6,000	6,000	6,000	3,000
Capital	10,000	10,000	10,000	10,000	12,000	12,000

2 DOUBLE-ENTRY BOOK-KEEPING: FIRST PRINCIPLES

As we have seen in Chapter 1, book-keeping is the basic recording of business transactions in financial terms. Before studying financial accounting in detail it is important to study the principles of double-entry book-keeping, as these form the basis of much that we shall be doing in the rest of the book.

In the previous chapter we looked briefly at the dual aspect of accounting – each time there is a business transaction there are two effects on the accounting equation. This chapter shows how the dual aspect is used in the principles of book-keeping. In particular, we shall be looking at accounts for:

- bank
- cash
- capital
- fixed assets
- expenses
- income
- drawings
- loans

LEDGER ACCOUNTS

Double-entry book-keeping, as its name suggests, recognises that each transaction has a dual aspect. Once the dual aspect of each transaction has been identified, the two book-keeping entries can be made in the ledger accounts of the accounting system. An account is kept in the ledger to record each different type of transaction. In a handwritten book-keeping system, the ledger will consist either of a bound book, or a series of separate sheets of paper – each account in the ledger will occupy a separate page; in a computerised system, the ledger will consist of a computer file, divided into separate accounts. Whether a handwritten or computerised system is being used, the principles remain the same.

A commonly-used layout for an account is set out on the next page. Entries in ledger accounts always include dates. Please note that dates used in this book, for the sake of simplicity, are often expressed as 20-8, 20-9, etc, unlike in a real business where the actual year date is shown (ie 2008, 2009, etc). Occasionally in this book 20-9 is followed by 20-0, ie when the decade changes from 2009 to 2010.

Debit (Dr) **Name of the account, eg Wages Account** **Credit (Cr)**

Date	Details	Reference	£ p	Date	Details	Reference	£ p
date of the trans-action	name of the other account	page or reference number of the other account	amount of the trans-action	date of the trans-action	name of the other account	page or reference number of the other account	amount of the trans-action

Note the following points about the layout of this account:

- the name of the account is written at the top
- the account is divided into two identical halves, separated by a central double vertical line
- the left-hand side is called the debit side (debit is abbreviated to 'Dr' – short for DebtoR)
- the right-hand side is called the credit (or Cr) side
- the date, details and amount of the transaction are entered in the account
- in the details column is entered the name of the other account involved in the book-keeping transaction
- the reference column is used as a cross-referencing system to the other entry of the double-entry book-keeping transaction

In practice, each account would occupy a whole page in a handwritten book-keeping system but, to save space when doing exercises, it is usual to put several accounts on a page. In future, in this book, the account layout will be simplified to give more clarity as follows:

Dr	**Wages Account**	Cr
20-1	£	20-1	£

This layout is often known in accounting jargon as a 'T' account; it will be used extensively in this book because it separates in a simple way the two sides – debit and credit – of the account. An alternative style of account has three money columns: debit, credit and balance. This type of account is commonly used for bank statements, building society passbooks and computer accounting statements. Because the balance of the account is calculated after every transaction, it is known as a running balance account (see page 24).

DEBITS AND CREDITS

The principle of double-entry book-keeping is that for every business transaction:

• one account is debited, and

• one account is credited

Debit entries are on the left-hand side of the appropriate account, while credit entries are on the right. The rules for debits and credits are:

• **debit entry** – the account which gains value, or records an asset, or an expense

• **credit entry** – the account which gives value, or records a liability, or an income item

This is illustrated as follows:

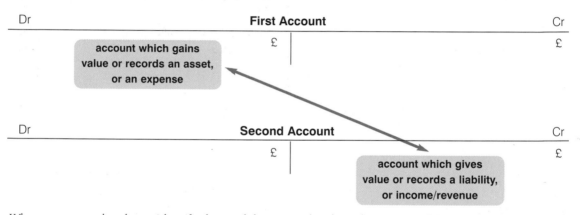

When one entry has been identified as a debit or credit, the other entry will be on the opposite side of the other account.

EXAMPLE TRANSACTIONS

In order to put the theory of double-entry book-keeping into practice, we will look at some financial transactions undertaken by a new business which has just been set up by Jayne Hampson in 20-1:

1 September	Started in business with capital of £5,000, a cheque paid into the bank
4 September	Bought office equipment £2,500, paying by cheque
7 September	Paid rent of office £500, by cheque
10 September	Received commission of £100, by cheque
12 September	Withdrew £250 from the bank for own use (drawings)
16 September	Received a loan of £1,000 from James Henderson by cheque

All of these transactions involve the bank, and the business will enter them in its bank account. The bank account records money in the form of bank receipts and payments, ie cheques, standing orders, direct debits, credit transfers, credit card transactions, and debit card transactions. Many businesses use a separate cash account to record transactions which involve money in the form of cash and, in practice, the separate bank account and cash account are brought together in the main cash book – see Chapter 7.

With both bank account and cash account, the rules for debit and credit are:

- money in is recorded on the debit side
- money out is recorded on the credit side

Using these rules, the bank account of Jayne Hampson's business, after entering the transactions listed on the previous page, appears as:

Dr				Bank Account		Cr
20-1		£	20-1			£
1 Sep	Capital	5,000	4 Sep	Office equipment		2,500
10 Sep	Commission	100	7 Sep	Rent paid		500
16 Sep	J Henderson: loan	1,000	12 Sep	Drawings		250
		Money in		Money out		

Note: the bank account shows the firm's record of how much has been paid into, and drawn out of, the bank - it is not exactly the same as the record of receipts and payments kept by the bank (we will compare the two in the form of a bank reconciliation statement in Chapter 8).

To complete the double-entry book-keeping transactions we need to:

- identify on which side of the bank account the transaction has been recorded – debit (money in), or credit (money out)
- record the other double-entry transaction on the opposite side of the appropriate account
- note that business transactions involving cash will be entered in the cash account

The other accounts involved can now be recorded, and over the next few pages we shall look at the principles involved for each transaction.

CAPITAL

Capital is the amount of money invested in the business by the owner. The amount is owed by the business back to the owner, although it is unlikely to be repaid immediately as the business would cease to exist. A capital account is used to record the amount paid into the business; the book-keeping entries are:

● **capital introduced**

–   debit bank account, as in the case of Jayne Hampson, (or cash account, or a fixed asset account, where cash or fixed assets have been introduced by the owner as part of the capital)

–   credit capital account

Example transaction

1 Sep 20-1   Started in business with capital of £5,000, a cheque paid into the bank.

Dr		**Capital Account**		Cr
20-1	£	20-1		£
		1 Sep Bank		5,000

Note: the dual aspect is that bank account has gained value and has been debited (see account on page 19); capital account records a liability (an amount owed to the owner) and is credited. Remember that the business is a separate entity (see Chapter 1, page 10), and this book-keeping entry looks at the transaction from the point of view of the business. The introduction of capital into a business is often the very first business transaction entered into the books of account.

FIXED ASSETS

Fixed assets are items purchased by a business for use on a long-term basis. Examples are premises, motor vehicles, machinery and office equipment. All of these are bought by a business with the intention that they will be used over a long period of time. Without fixed assets, it would be difficult to continue in business, eg without machinery it would prove difficult to run a factory; without delivery vans and lorries it would be difficult to transport the firm's products to its customers.

When a business buys fixed assets, the expenditure is referred to as **capital expenditure**. This means that items have been bought for use in the business for some years to come. By contrast, **revenue expenditure** is where the items bought will be used by the business quite quickly. For example, the purchase of a car is capital expenditure, while the cost of fuel for the car is revenue expenditure.

fixed assets and double-entry book-keeping

When fixed assets are bought, a separate account for each type of fixed asset is used, eg premises account, motor vehicles account, machinery account, etc. The book-keeping entries are:

● **purchase of a fixed asset**

–   debit fixed asset account (using the appropriate account)

–   credit bank account (or cash account)

Example transaction

4 Sep 20-1   Bought office equipment £2,500, paying by cheque.

Dr		Office Equipment Account			Cr
20-1		£	20-1		£
4 Sep	Bank	2,500			

The other part of the dual aspect of this transaction is a credit to bank account: this has been entered already (see account on page 19).

Expenses

Businesses pay various running expenses (overheads), such as rent, wages, electricity, telephone, and vehicle running expenses. These day-to-day expenses of running the business are termed **revenue expenditure**. A separate account is used in the accounting system for each main class of revenue expenditure, eg rent account, wages account, and so on.

The book-keeping entries are:

● **payment of an expense**
   – debit expense account (using the appropriate account)
   – credit bank account (or cash account)

Example transaction

7 Sep 20-1   Paid rent of office £500, by cheque.

Dr		Rent Account			Cr
20-1		£	20-1		£
7 Sep	Bank	500			

Note: the accounting rules followed are that we have debited the account which has gained value (rent paid – the business has had the use and benefit of the office for a certain period of time). The account which has given value (bank) has already been credited (see page 19).

INCOME

From time-to-time a business may receive amounts of income, eg rent, commission, or fees. These are recorded in separate accounts for each category of income, eg rent received account, commission income account. The book-keeping entries are:

● **receipt of income**

   – debit bank account (or cash account)

   – credit income account (using the appropriate account)

Example transaction

10 September 20-1   Received commission of £100, by cheque.

Dr			**Commission Income Account**		Cr
20-1		£	20-1		£
			10 Sep Bank		100

Note: We have already debited the account which has gained value (bank – see page 19) and credited the account which has given value (commission income).

OWNER'S DRAWINGS

Drawings is the term used when the owner takes money, in cash or by cheque (or sometimes goods), from the business for personal use. A drawings account is used to record such amounts; the book-keeping entries for withdrawal of money are:

● **owner's drawings**

   – debit drawings account

   – credit bank account (or cash account)

Example transaction

12 Sep 20-1   Withdrew £250 from the bank for own use.

Dr			**Drawings Account**		Cr
20-1		£	20-1		£
12 Sep Bank		250			

The other part of the dual aspect of this transaction is a credit to bank account: this has been entered already (see page 19).

LOANS

When a business receives a loan, eg from a relative or the bank, it is the cash account or bank account which gains value, while a loan account (in the name of the lender) records the liability.

● **loan received**

 – debit bank account (or cash account)

 – credit loan account (in name of the lender)

> **Example transaction**
>
> 16 September 20-1   Received a loan of £1,000 from James Henderson by cheque

Dr			James Henderson: Loan Account		Cr
20-1		£	20-1		£
			16 Sep Bank		1,000

The debit entry has already been made in bank account (see page 19).

FURTHER TRANSACTIONS

Using the accounts which we have seen already, here are some further transactions:

● **loan repayment**

 – debit loan account

 – credit bank account (or cash account)

● **sale (disposal) of a fixed asset**

 – debit bank account (or cash account)

 – credit fixed asset account

Note: accounting for the disposal of fixed assets is dealt with fully in AS Unit 2, Chapter 15.

● **withdrawal of cash from the bank for use in the business**

 – debit cash account

 – credit bank account

● **payment of cash into the bank**

 – debit bank account

 – credit cash account

RUNNING BALANCE ACCOUNTS

The layout of accounts that we have used has a debit side and a credit side. Although this layout is very useful when learning the principles of book-keeping, it is not always appropriate for practical business use. Most 'real-life' accounts have three money columns: debit transactions, credit transactions, and balance. A familiar example of this type of account is a bank statement. With a three-column account, the balance is calculated after each transaction has been entered – hence the name running balance accounts. For handwritten accounts, it would be rather tedious to calculate the balance after each transaction (and a potential source of errors) but, using computer accounting, the calculation is carried out automatically.

The following is the bank account used earlier in this chapter (page 19), set out in 'traditional' format:

Dr				**Bank Account**		Cr
20-1		£	20-1			£
1 Sep	Capital	5,000	4 Sep	Office equipment		2,500
10 Sep	Commission	100	7 Sep	Rent paid		500
16 Sep	J Henderson: loan	1,000	12 Sep	Drawings		250

The account does not show the balance, and would need to be balanced (see Chapter 5).

In 'running balance' layout, the account appears as:

Bank Account

20-1		Debit	Credit	Balance
		£	£	£
1 Sep	Capital	5,000		5,000 Dr
4 Sep	Office equipment		2,500	2,500 Dr
7 Sep	Rent paid		500	2,000 Dr
10 Sep	Commission	100		2,100 Dr
12 Sep	Drawings		250	1,850 Dr
16 Sep	J Henderson: loan	1,000		2,850 Dr

With a running balance account, it is necessary to state after each transaction whether the balance is debit (Dr) or credit (Cr). Note that the bank account in the books of this business has a debit balance, ie there is money in the bank – an asset.

In your studies you will normally use the traditional 'T' account format.

CHAPTER SUMMARY

- Every business transaction has a dual aspect.

- Business transactions are recorded in ledger accounts using double-entry book-keeping principles.

- Each double-entry book-keeping transaction involves a debit entry and a credit entry.

- Entries in the bank account and cash account are:
    - debit money in
    - credit money out

- Capital is the amount of money invested in the business by the owner. Capital introduced is recorded as:
    - debit bank account or cash account (or an asset account if an asset is introduced)
    - credit capital account

- Fixed assets are items purchased by a business for use on a long-term basis, eg premises, motor vehicles, machinery and office equipment. The purchase of such items is called capital expenditure.

- The purchase of fixed assets is recorded in the business accounts as:
    - debit fixed asset account
    - credit bank account (or cash account)

- Running expenses or overheads of a business, such as rent paid, wages, electricity, etc are called revenue expenditure.

- Expenses are recorded in the business accounts as:
    - debit expense account
    - credit bank account (or cash account)

- Receipt of income, eg rent received, commission received, fees received, is recorded as:
    - debit bank account (or cash account)
    - credit income account

- Drawings is where the owner takes money (or goods) from the business for personal use. The withdrawal of money is recorded as:
    - debit drawings account
    - credit bank account (or cash account)

- When a business receives a loan, it is recorded as:
    - debit bank account (or cash account)
    - credit loan account in the name of the lender

In the next chapter we will continue with double-entry book-keeping and look at regular business transactions for purchases, sales and returns.

QUESTIONS

An asterisk (*) after the question number means that the answer is given at the end of this book.

2.1 James Anderson has kept his bank account up-to-date, but has not got around to the other double-entry book-keeping entries. Rule up the other accounts for him, and make the appropriate entries.

Dr				**Bank Account**			Cr
20-1			£	20-1			£
1 Feb	Capital		7,500	6 Feb	Computer		2,000
14 Feb	Bank loan		2,500	8 Feb	Rent paid		750
20 Feb	Commission received		145	12 Feb	Wages		425
				23 Feb	Drawings		200
				25 Feb	Wages		380
				28 Feb	Van		6,000

2.2* The following are the business transactions of Tony Long for the month of May 20-2:
20-2

1 May	Started a business with capital of £6,000 in the bank
4 May	Bought a machine for £3,500, paying by cheque
6 May	Bought office equipment for £2,000, paying by cheque
10 May	Paid rent £350, by cheque
12 May	Obtained a loan of £1,000 from a friend, Lucy Warner, and paid her cheque into the bank
15 May	Paid wages £250, by cheque
17 May	Received commission £150, by cheque
20 May	Drawings £85, by cheque
25 May	Paid wages £135, by cheque

You are to:

(a) Write up Tony Long's bank account

(b) Complete the double-entry book-keeping transactions

2.3 Enter the following transactions into the double-entry book-keeping accounts of Jean Lacey:
20-5

1 Aug	Started in business with capital of £5,000 in the bank
3 Aug	Bought a computer for £1,800, paying by cheque
7 Aug	Paid rent £100, by cheque
10 Aug	Received commission £200, in cash

12 Aug	Bought office fittings £2,000, paying by cheque
15 Aug	Received a loan, £1,000 by cheque, from a friend, Sally Orton
17 Aug	Drawings £100, in cash
20 Aug	Returned some of the office fittings (unsuitable) and received a refund cheque of £250
25 Aug	Received commission £150, by cheque
27 Aug	Made a loan repayment to Sally Orton of £150, by cheque

2.4* Tom Griffiths has recently set up in business. He has made some errors in writing up his bank account. You are to set out the bank account as it should appear, rule up the other accounts for him, and make the appropriate entries.

Dr				Bank Account			Cr
20-2			£	20-2			£
4 Mar	Office equipment		1,000	1 Mar	Capital		6,500
12 Mar	Drawings		175	5 Mar	Bank loan		2,500
				7 Mar	Wages		250
				8 Mar	Commission received		150
				10 Mar	Rent paid		200
				15 Mar	Van		6,000

2.5 Enter the following transactions into the double-entry book-keeping accounts of Caroline Yates:

20-7

1 Nov	Started in business with capital of £75,000 in the bank
3 Nov	Bought a photocopier for £2,500, paying by cheque
7 Nov	Received a bank loan of £70,000
10 Nov	Bought office premises £130,000, paying by cheque
12 Nov	Paid rates of £3,000, by cheque
14 Nov	Bought office fittings £1,500, paying by cheque
15 Nov	Received commission of £300, in cash
18 Nov	Drawings in cash £125
20 Nov	Paid wages £250, by cheque
23 Nov	Paid £100 of cash into the bank
25 Nov	Returned some of the office fittings (unsuitable) and received a refund cheque for £200
28 Nov	Received commission £200, by cheque

2.6 Write up the bank account from Question 2.5 in the form of a 'running balance' account.

2.7 You are the book-keeper at Wyvern Electronics. A trainee has just joined the firm and is helping you with the recording of business transactions. Write down the guidance you will give her which explains the principles of double-entry book-keeping.

3 DOUBLE-ENTRY BOOK-KEEPING: FURTHER TRANSACTIONS

This chapter continues with the principles of double-entry book-keeping and builds on the skills established in the previous chapter. We shall be looking at the dual aspect and the book-keeping required for the business transactions of:

- cash purchases
- cash sales
- credit purchases
- credit sales
- returns
- carriage

PURCHASES AND SALES

Common business transactions are to buy and sell goods. These transactions are recorded in purchases account and sales account respectively. These two accounts are used to record the purchase and sale of the goods in which the business trades. For example, a shoe shop buys shoes from the manufacturer and records this in purchases account; as shoes are sold, the transactions are recorded in sales account. Note that the book-keeping system does not use a 'goods account' – instead, when buying goods, a purchases account is used; when selling goods, a sales account is used. In this way, a business knows the amount of its purchases and sales.

The normal entry on a purchases account is on the debit side – the account has gained value, ie the business has bought goods for resale. The normal entry on a sales account is on the credit side – the account has given value, ie the business has sold goods.

When a business buys an item for use in the business, eg a computer, this is debited to a separate account, because a fixed asset – see Chapter 2, page 20 – has been purchased. Likewise, when a fixed asset is sold (disposed of), it is not entered in the sales account.

WORKED EXAMPLE: PURCHASES AND SALES

In order to put the theory of double-entry book-keeping for purchases and sales into practice, we will use as an illustration some financial transactions undertaken by Temeside Traders, a business which started trading on 1 October 20-1:

1 October	Started in business with capital of £7,000 paid into the bank
2 October	Bought goods for £5,000, paying by cheque
3 October	Sold some of the goods for £3,000, a cheque being received
5 October	Bought computer for £700, paying by cheque
10 October	Bought goods for £2,800, paying by cheque
12 October	Sold some of the goods for £5,000, a cheque being received
15 October	Paid rent £150, by cheque

These transactions are entered into the book-keeping system of Temeside Traders as follows:

Dr			**Bank Account**			Cr
20-1		£		20-1		£
1 Oct	Capital	7,000		2 Oct	Purchases	5,000
3 Oct	Sales	3,000		5 Oct	Computer	700
12 Oct	Sales	5,000		10 Oct	Purchases	2,800
				15 Oct	Rent paid	150

Dr		**Capital Account**			Cr
20-1		£	20-1		£
			1 Oct	Bank	7,000

Dr		**Purchases Account**		Cr
20-1		£	20-1	£
2 Oct	Bank	5,000		
10 Oct	Bank	2,800		

Dr		**Sales Account**			Cr
20-1		£	20-1		£
			3 Oct	Bank	3,000
			12 Oct	Bank	5,000

Dr		**Computer Account**		Cr
20-1		£	20-1	£
5 Oct	Bank	700		

Dr		**Rent Paid Account**		Cr
20-1		£	20-1	£
15 Oct	Bank	150		

---

notes to worked example

- Only one purchases account and one sales account is used to record the purchases and sales of the goods in which a business trades.

- The computer is a fixed asset, so its purchase is entered to a separate computer account.

- The purchases and sales made in the transactions above are called cash purchases and cash sales, because payment is immediate.

CREDIT TRANSACTIONS

In the previous section, we looked at the book-keeping for cash purchases and cash sales (here 'cash' means 'where payment is made immediately' - involving either notes and coins or bank payments). However, in business, many transactions for purchases and sales are made on credit, ie the goods are bought or sold now, with payment (for example, in cash, or by cheque) to be made at a later date. It is an important aspect of double-entry book-keeping to record the credit transaction as a purchase or a sale, and then record the second entry in an account in the name of the creditor or debtor, ie to record the amount owing by the firm to a creditor, or to the firm by a debtor.

Note that the term 'credit transactions' does not refer to the side of an account. Instead, it means the type of transaction where money is not paid at the time of making the sale but will be made at a later date.

credit purchases

Credit purchases are goods or services obtained from a supplier, with payment to take place at a later date. From the buyer's viewpoint, the supplier is a creditor.

The book-keeping entries are:

● **credit purchase**

- debit purchases account

- credit creditor's (supplier's) account

When payment is made to the creditor the book-keeping entries are:

● **payment made to creditor**

- debit creditor's account

- credit bank account or cash account

credit sales

With credit sales, goods or services are sold to a customer who is allowed to settle the account at a later date. From the seller's viewpoint, the customer is a debtor.

The book-keeping entries are:

- **credit sale**
  - debit debtor's (customer's) account
  - credit sales account

When payment is received from the debtor the book-keeping entries are:

- **payment received from debtor**
  - debit bank account or cash account
  - credit debtor's account

WORKED EXAMPLE: CREDIT TRANSACTIONS

A local business, Wyvern Wholesalers, has the following transactions in the year 20-1:

18 Sep	Bought goods, £250, on credit from Malvern Manufacturing Co, with payment to be made in 30 days' time
20 Sep	Sold goods, £175, on credit to Strensham Stores, payment to be made in 30 days' time
18 Oct	Paid £250 by cheque to Malvern Manufacturing Co
20 Oct	Received a cheque for £175 from Strensham Stores

These transactions will be recorded in the book-keeping system of Wyvern Wholesalers (previous transactions on accounts, if any, not shown) as follows:

Dr			**Purchases Account**		Cr
20-1		£	20-1		£
18 Sep	Malvern Manufacturing Co	250			

Dr			**Sales Account**		Cr
20-1		£	20-1		£
			20 Sep	Strensham Stores	175

Dr			**Malvern Manufacturing Co**		Cr
20-1		£	20-1		£
18 Oct	Bank	250	18 Sep	Purchases	250

Dr		Strensham Stores		Cr
20-1	£	20-1		£
20 Sep Sales	175	20 Oct Bank		175

Dr		Bank Account		Cr
20-1	£	20-1		£
20 Oct Strensham Stores	175	18 Oct Malvern Manufacturing Co		250

Note: the name of the other account involved has been used in the details column as a description.

balancing off accounts

In the example above, after the transactions have been recorded in the books of Wyvern Wholesalers, the accounts of Malvern Manufacturing Co and Strensham Stores have the same amount entered on both debit and credit side. This means that nothing is owing to Wyvern Wholesalers, or is owed by it, ie the accounts have a 'nil' balance. In practice, as a business trades, there will be a number of entries on both sides of such accounts, and we shall see in Chapter 5 how accounts are 'balanced off' at regular intervals.

fixed assets bought on credit

Fixed assets are often purchased on credit terms. As with the purchase of goods for resale, an account is opened in the name of the creditor, as follows:

- **purchase of a fixed asset on credit**
    - debit fixed asset account, eg computer account
    - credit creditor's (supplier's) account

When payment is made to the creditor the book-keeping entries are:

- **payment made to a creditor**
    - debit creditor's account
    - credit bank account or cash account

PURCHASES RETURNS AND SALES RETURNS

From time-to-time goods bought or sold are returned, perhaps because the wrong items have been supplied (eg wrong type, size or colour), or because the goods are unsatisfactory. We will now see the book-keeping entries for returned goods.

- **Purchases returns** (or returns out) is where a business returns goods to a creditor (supplier).

  The book-keeping entries are:

  – debit creditor's (supplier's) account

  – credit purchases returns (or returns out) account

  Purchases returns are kept separate from purchases, ie they are entered in a separate purchases returns account rather than being credited to purchases account.

- **Sales returns** (or returns in) is where a debtor (customer) returns goods to the business.

  The book-keeping entries are:

  – debit sales returns (or returns in) account

  – credit debtor's (customer's) account

Sales returns are kept separate from sales, ie they are entered in a separate sales returns account rather than being debited to sales account.

WORKED EXAMPLE: PURCHASES RETURNS AND SALES RETURNS

Hightown Stores has the following transactions during the year 20-1:

7 October	Bought goods, £280, on credit from B Lewis Ltd
10 October	Returned unsatisfactory goods, £30, to B Lewis Ltd
11 October	Sold goods, £125, on credit to A Holmes
17 October	A Holmes returned goods, £25
26 October	Paid the amount owing to B Lewis Ltd by cheque
29 October	A Holmes paid the amount owing in cash

The transactions will be recorded in the book-keeping system of Hightown Stores (previous transactions on accounts, if any, not shown) as follows:

Dr		Purchases Account			Cr
20-1		£	20-1		£
7 Oct	B Lewis Ltd	280			

Dr		B Lewis Ltd			Cr
20-1		£	20-1		£
10 Oct	Purchases Returns	30	7 Oct	Purchases	280
26 Oct	Bank	250			

Dr		Purchases Returns Account			Cr
20-1		£	20-1		£
			10 Oct	B Lewis Ltd	30

Dr		Sales Account			Cr
20-1		£	20-1		£
			11 Oct	A Holmes	125

Dr		A Holmes			Cr
20-1		£	20-1		£
11 Oct	Sales	125	17 Oct	Sales Returns	25
			29 Oct	Cash	100

Dr		Sales Returns Account			Cr
20-1		£	20-1		£
17 Oct	A Holmes	25			

Dr		Bank Account			Cr
20-1		£	20-1		£
			26 Oct	B Lewis Ltd	250

Dr		Cash Account			Cr
20-1		£	20-1		£
29 Oct	A Holmes	100			

CARRIAGE INWARDS AND CARRIAGE OUTWARDS

When goods are bought and sold, the cost of transporting the goods is referred to as 'carriage'.

Carriage inwards is where the buyer pays the carriage cost of purchases, eg an item is purchased by mail order, and the buyer has to pay the additional cost of delivery (and possibly packing also).

Carriage outwards is where the seller pays the carriage charge, eg an item is sold to the customer and described as 'delivery free'.

Both carriage inwards and carriage outwards are expenses and their cost should be debited to two separate accounts, carriage inwards account and carriage outwards account respectively.

GENERAL PRINCIPLES OF DEBITS AND CREDITS

By now you should have a good idea of the principles of debits and credits. From the transactions we have considered in this and the previous chapter, the 'rules' can be summarised as follows:

Debits include

- purchases of goods for resale
- sales returns (or returns in) when goods previously sold are returned to the business
- purchase of fixed assets for use in the business
- expenses and overheads incurred by the business
- debtors where money is owed to the business
- money received through cash account or bank account
- drawings made by the owner of the business
- loan repayment, where a loan liability is reduced/repaid

Credits include

- sales of goods by the business
- purchases returns (or returns out) of goods previously bought by the business
- sale of fixed assets
- income received by the business
- creditors where money is owed by the business
- money paid out through cash account or bank account
- capital introduced into the business by the owner
- loan received by the business

It is important to ensure, at an early stage, that you are clear about the principles of debits and credits. They are important for an understanding of book-keeping, and are essential for your later studies in financial accounting.

To summarise the double-entry book-keeping 'rules':

- **debit entry** – the account which gains value, or records an asset, or an expense
- **credit entry** – the account which gives value, or records a liability, or an income item

TYPES OF ACCOUNT

Within a book-keeping system there are different types of account: a distinction is made between personal and impersonal accounts. Personal accounts are in the names of people or businesses, eg the accounts for debtors and creditors. Impersonal accounts are the other accounts; these are usually divided between real accounts, which represent things such as cash, bank, computers, vehicles, stock, etc, and nominal accounts, which record income and expenses such as sales, purchases, wages, etc.

These distinctions are shown in the diagram below.

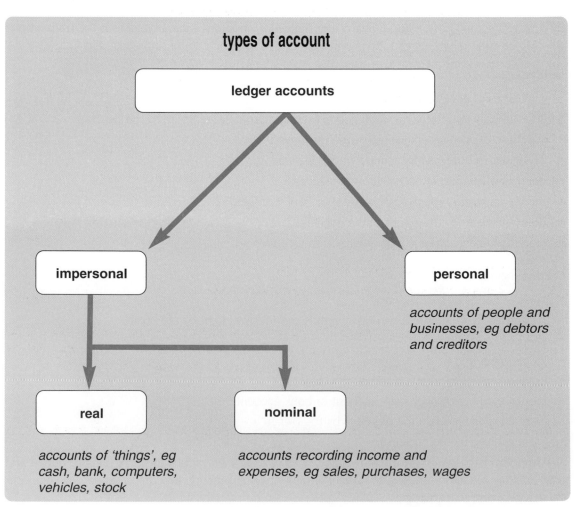

CHAPTER SUMMARY

● Purchases account is used to record the purchase of goods in which the business trades: the normal entry is on the debit side.

● Sales account is used to record the sale of goods in which the business trades: the normal entry is on the credit side.

● The purchase of goods is recorded as:
  – debit purchases account
  – credit bank/cash account or, if bought on credit, creditor's account

● The sale of goods is recorded as:
  – debit bank/cash account or, if sold on credit, debtor's account
  – credit sales account

● Purchases returns (or returns out) are recorded as:
  – debit creditor's account
  – credit purchases returns (or returns out) account

● Sales returns (or returns in) are recorded as:
  – debit sales returns (or returns in) account
  – credit debtor's account

● 'Carriage' is the expense of transporting goods:
  – carriage inwards is the cost of carriage paid on purchases
  – carriage outwards is the cost of carriage paid on sales

● Accounts are divided between personal (the accounts of people, firms, eg debtors and creditors; also capital account), and impersonal accounts; impersonal accounts are sub-divided between real (the accounts of things), and nominal (the accounts of income and expenses).

In the next chapter we will look at the business documents used when goods are sold to another business.

QUESTIONS

An asterisk (*) after the question number means that the answer is given at the end of this book.

3.1

The following are the business transactions of Evesham Enterprises for the month of October 20-2:

1 Oct	Started in business with capital of £2,500 in the bank
2 Oct	Bought goods, £200, paying by cheque
4 Oct	Sold goods, £150, a cheque being received
6 Oct	Bought goods, £90, paying by cheque
8 Oct	Sold goods, £125, a cheque being received
12 Oct	Received a loan of £2,000 from J Smithson by cheque
14 Oct	Bought goods, £250, paying by cheque
18 Oct	Sold goods, £155, a cheque being received
22 Oct	Bought a secondhand delivery van, £4,000, paying by cheque
25 Oct	Paid wages, £375, by bank giro credit
30 Oct	Sold goods, £110, a cheque being received

You are to:

(a)   Write up the firm's bank account

(b)   Complete the double-entry book-keeping transactions

3.2*

The following are the business transactions of Oxford Trading Company for the month of February 20-1:

1 Feb	Started in business with capital of £3,000 in the bank
2 Feb	Sold goods, £250, a cheque being received
3 Feb	Bought goods, £100, paying by cheque
5 Feb	Paid wages, £150, by bank giro credit
7 Feb	Sold goods, £300, a cheque being received
12 Feb	Bought goods, £200, paying by cheque
15 Feb	Received a loan of £1,000 from James Walters by cheque
20 Feb	Bought a computer for £1,950, paying by cheque
25 Feb	Sold goods, £150, a cheque being received
27 Feb	Paid wages, £125, by bank giro credit

You are to:

(a)   Write up the firm's bank account

(b)   Complete the double-entry book-keeping transactions

3.3* Write up the bank account from Question 3.2 in the form of a 'running balance' account.

3.4* The following are the business transactions of Pershore Packaging for the month of January 20-1:

4 Jan	Bought goods, £250, on credit from AB Supplies Ltd
5 Jan	Sold goods, £195, a cheque being received
7 Jan	Sold goods, £150, cash being received
10 Jan	Received a loan of £1,000 from J Johnson by cheque
15 Jan	Paid £250 to AB Supplies Ltd by cheque
17 Jan	Sold goods, £145, on credit to L Lewis
20 Jan	Bought goods, £225, paying by cheque
22 Jan	Paid wages, £125, in cash
26 Jan	Bought office equipment, £160, on credit from Mercia Office Supplies Ltd
29 Jan	Received a cheque for £145 from L Lewis
31 Jan	Paid the amount owing to Mercia Office Supplies Ltd by cheque

You are to record the transactions in the books of account.

3.5 The following are the business transactions for April 20-2 of William King, who runs a food wholesaling business:

2 Apr	Bought goods, £200, on credit from Wyvern Producers Ltd
4 Apr	Bought goods, £250, on credit from A Larsen
5 Apr	Sold goods, £150, on credit to Pershore Patisserie
7 Apr	Sold goods, £175, a cheque being received
9 Apr	Returned goods, £50, to Wyvern Producers Ltd
12 Apr	Sold goods, £110, a cheque being received
15 Apr	Pershore Patisserie returned goods, £25
17 Apr	Bought a weighing machine for use in the business £250, on credit from Amery Scales Limited
20 Apr	Paid Wyvern Producers Ltd £150, by cheque
22 Apr	Pershore Patisserie paid the amount owing by cheque
26 Apr	Returned goods, £45, to A Larsen
28 Apr	Sold goods, £100, cash received
29 Apr	Paid wages in cash, £90
30 Apr	Paid the amount owing to Amery Scales Ltd by cheque

You are to record the transactions in the books of account.

3.6 The following are the business transactions for June 20-3 of Helen Smith who trades as 'Fashion Frocks':

2 Jun	Bought goods, £350, on credit from Designs Ltd
4 Jun	Sold goods, £220, a cheque being received
5 Jun	Sold goods, £115, cash received
6 Jun	Returned goods, £100, to Designs Ltd
7 Jun	Bought goods, £400, on credit from Mercia Knitwear Ltd
10 Jun	Sold goods, £350, on credit to Wyvern Trade Supplies
12 Jun	Sold goods, £175, a cheque being received
15 Jun	Wyvern Trade Supplies returned goods, £50
17 Jun	Returned goods, £80, to Mercia Knitwear Ltd
18 Jun	Paid the amount owing to Designs Ltd by cheque
20 Jun	Sold goods, £180, cash received
23 Jun	Bought goods, £285, on credit from Designs Ltd
26 Jun	Paid rent in cash, £125
28 Jun	Received a cheque from Wyvern Trade Supplies for the amount owing

You are to record the transactions in the books of account.

3.7 For each transaction below, complete the table on the next page to show the names of the accounts which will be debited and credited:

(a)	Bought goods, paying by cheque
(b)	Cheque received for sales
(c)	Bought goods on credit from Teme Traders
(d)	Sold goods on credit to L Harris
(e)	Returned unsatisfactory goods to Teme Traders
(f)	L Harris returns unsatisfactory goods
(g)	Received a loan from D Perkins, by cheque
(h)	Withdrew cash from the bank for use in the business

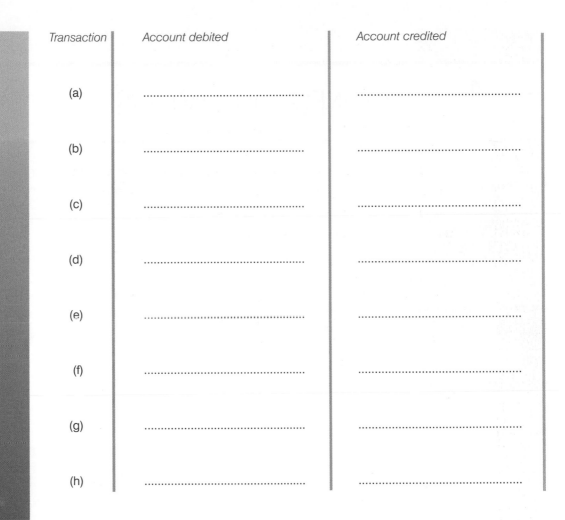

Transaction	Account debited	Account credited
(a)	....	....
(b)	....	....
(c)	....	....
(d)	....	....
(e)	....	....
(f)	....	....
(g)	....	....
(h)	....	....

3.8

You are the book-keeper at Wyvern Electronics. Today your trainee has been working on recording sales and purchases transactions in the double-entry system. She asks you to explain the following points:

- Why do we use separate accounts for purchases and sales? Surely a combined account – called 'goods' – would be better?

- I can't see why purchases should go on the debit side and sales on the credit side of their respective accounts.

- Why can't I record the purchase of a new delivery van for use in the business in purchases account?

- I can't see the logic of purchases returns and sales returns.

- Why do I need separate accounts for carriage inwards and carriage outwards? Surely an account called 'carriage' would do just as well?

Write the answers you will give to the trainee.

4 BUSINESS DOCUMENTS

In this chapter we look at the main business documents which are used when goods are bought and sold. Two of these documents are 'source documents' which are used to update the book-keeping records. We cover the following:

- purchase order
- delivery note
- invoice (a source document)
- credit note (a source document)
- statement of account
- other source documents

We will also see how cash discount – an allowance off the invoice price for quick settlement – is recorded in the book-keeping system.

DOCUMENTS FOR A CREDIT TRANSACTION

You will see that the documents to be explained involve credit transactions, ie selling or buying with payment to be made at a later date. The normal stages in a credit transaction are:

1 buyer prepares
    – purchase order

2 seller prepares
    – delivery note
    – invoice
    – statement of account

3 buyer sends payment by
    – cheque, or
    – bank transfer

If some or all of the goods are unsatisfactory and are returned, the seller prepares a credit note.

The flow of these documents is shown in the diagram on the next page.

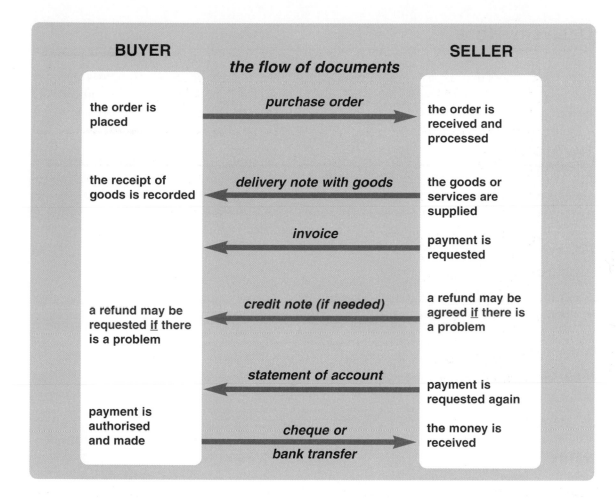

PURCHASE ORDER

A purchase order is prepared by the buyer, and is sent to the seller. Details normally found on a purchase order include:

- reference number of purchase order
- name and address of buyer
- name and address of seller
- full description of the goods, reference numbers, quantity required and unit price
- date of issue
- signature of person authorised to issue the order

In order to keep control over purchases many businesses authorise certain people as buyers. In this way, purchases are controlled so that duplicate or unauthorised goods are not ordered.

Delivery Note

When the business that is selling the goods despatches them to the buyer, a delivery note is prepared. This accompanies the goods and gives details of what is being delivered. When the goods are received by the buyer, a check can be made by the buyer to ensure that the correct goods have been delivered.

Invoice

The invoice (see next page) is the most important document in a business transaction. It is prepared by the seller and is sent to the buyer who uses it as a **source document** for book-keeping transactions. The invoice gives details of the goods supplied, and states the money amount to be paid by the buyer. The information to be found on an invoice includes:

- invoice number (serially numbered)
- name and address of seller
- name and address of buyer
- date of sale
- date that goods are supplied, including reference numbers, quantity supplied and unit price
- details of trade discount allowed (if any)
- total amount of money due
- terms of trade

value added tax

Where the seller is registered for Value Added Tax (VAT), tax must be charged at the appropriate rate on all sales subject to VAT. However, the specification for AS Accounting Unit 1 states that you "will **not** be required to understand the VAT system or make accounting records of VAT." Accordingly, there is no calculation of VAT on any of the documents in this chapter, nor is it including in transactions.

terms of trade

The terms of trade are stated on an invoice to indicate the date by which the invoice amount is to be paid. The term 'net' on an invoice means that the invoice total is the amount to be paid; 'net 30 days' means that the amount is payable within 30 days of the invoice date.

Other terms include 'carriage paid' and 'E & OE', which stands for 'errors and omissions excepted'. This means that if there is an error or something left off the invoice by mistake, resulting in an incorrect final price, the supplier has the right to correct the mistake and demand the correct amount.

trade discount

Trade discount is the amount sometimes allowed as a reduction:

- to businesses, often in the same trade (but not normally to the general public)

INVOICE

TREND FASHION DESIGNS LIMITED

Unit 45 Elgar Estate, Broadfield, BR7 4ER
Tel 01908 765314 Fax 01908 765951

invoice to

Zing Fashions
4 Friar Street
Broadfield
BR1 3RF

invoice no	**787923**
account	**3993**
your reference	**47609**

deliver to

as above

date	**01 10 -5**

product code	description	quantity	unit price £	unit	total £	trade discount %	net £
45B	**Trend tops (black)**	**40**	**12.50**	**each**	**500.00**	**10**	**450.00**

TOTAL	**450.00**

terms
Net 30 days
Carriage paid
E & OE

– for buying in bulk, ie large quantities (this discount is also known as bulk discount)

– by wholesalers as a discount off list price to retailers

In the invoice shown above, trade discount of 10%, amounting to £50, is allowed on clothes supplied to Zing Fashions, a shop. Note that trade discount is never shown in the accounts – only the amount after deduction of trade discount is recorded. Here this amount is £450.

cash discount

Cash discount (also known as settlement discount) is an allowance off the invoice amount for quick settlement. It is indicated on the invoice, eg 2% cash discount for settlement within seven days. The buyer can choose whether to take up the cash discount by paying promptly, or whether to take longer to pay, perhaps thirty days from the invoice date, without cash discount. When cash discount is taken, it needs to be recorded in the accounts – see page 52.

Compare the amounts to be paid in the following example where the terms of trade are "2% cash discount for full settlement within seven days, otherwise net 30 days."

	No cash discount taken – full settlement between 8 and 30 days	Cash discount of 2% taken – full settlement within 7 days
	£	£
Invoice amount	1,000	1,000
Cash discount at 2%	–	20
Amount paid	1,000	980

format of invoices

Invoices (like other business documents) can be handwritten or typed on printed forms, or input and printed out on a computer. Invoicing is an ideal function for computerised accounting (see Chapter 20) and, for this purpose, pre-printed invoices are available, either in the form of continuous stationery or as separate sheets. Also, increasingly nowadays, invoices can be sent electronically as part of the paperless EDI (electronic data interchange) system which integrates the ordering, invoicing and payment processes. EDI is commonly used by larger retailers to order stock.

CREDIT NOTE

If a buyer returns goods for some reason (eg faulty goods supplied), or requires a reduction in the amount owed (the buyer may have been overcharged) the seller prepares a credit note (see next page) to record the amount of the allowance made to the buyer. The credit note is the **source document** for recording returned goods in the book-keeping system.

STATEMENT OF ACCOUNT

At regular intervals, often at the end of each month, the seller sends a statement of account (see page 48) to each debtor. This gives a summary of the transactions that have taken place since the previous statement and shows how much is currently owed. The details on a statement are:

——————————— CREDIT NOTE ———————————

TREND FASHION DESIGNS LIMITED

Unit 45 Elgar Estate, Broadfield, BR7 4ER
Tel 01908 765314 Fax 01908 765951

to

Zing Fashions	
4 Friar Street	
Broadfield	
BR1 3RF	

credit note no	12157
account	3993
your reference	47609
our invoice	787923
date	10 10 -5

product code	description	quantity	unit price £	unit	total £	trade discount %	net £
45B	**Trend tops (black)**	**2**	**12.50**	**each**	**25.00**	**10**	**22.50**

Reason for credit
2 tops received damaged
(Your returns note no. R/N 2384)

TOTAL	22.50

- name and address of seller
- name and address of the debtor (buyer)
- date of the statement
- details of transactions, eg invoices, debit notes, credit notes, payments
- balance currently due

Most statements have three money columns: debit, credit and balance.

The debit column is used to record the money amount of invoices and debit notes sent to the debtor; the credit column is for payments received and credit notes issued; the balance column shows the amount due, and is prepared on the 'running balance' (see page 24) basis, ie a new balance is shown after each transaction. The balance is usually a debit balance, which indicates that the buyer is a debtor in the seller's accounting records.

Some statements of account also incorporate a remittance advice as a tear-off slip; this is returned to the seller together with the payment.

STATEMENT OF ACCOUNT

TREND FASHION DESIGNS LIMITED

Unit 45 Elgar Estate, Broadfield, BR7 4ER
Tel 01908 765314 Fax 01908 765951

TO

Zing Fashions
4 Friar Street
Broadfield
BR1 3RF

account   **3993**

date   **31 10 -5**

date	details	debit £	credit £	balance £
01 10 -5	Invoice 787923	450.00		450.00
10 10 -5	Credit note 12157		22.50	427.50

AMOUNT NOW DUE		427.50

PAYMENT

Before payment is made to the seller, the buyer must check that the goods have been received and are as ordered. The payment can then be authorised by an appointed employee and made by means of either a cheque (sent by post) or a bank credit transfer which passes the money from the buyer's bank account to the seller's account. Most bank credit transfers nowadays are made by BACS (Bankers Automated Clearing Services) computer transfer. If a cheque is posted to the seller, it is sent with a remittance advice, which shows the amount of the payment, and the transactions to which it relates. If a payment is sent through the bank BACS system, a separate remittance advice will be mailed, faxed, or emailed.

OTHER SOURCE DOCUMENTS

cash receipts

Often when payment is made to the seller, a receipt is given; this can take the form of a machine-produced receipt, such as is given in a shop, or a handwritten receipt. The copy of these receipts – in the form of a till roll/till summary and receipt book – form the **source documents** for the seller. The originals are the **source documents** for the buyer. Look at these examples:

Everest Sports	◄———————	retailer
15 High St Mereford	◄———————	address
08 10 -5 15.05	◄———————	date and time of transaction
Salesperson Tina	◄———————	salesperson
Tennis balls 5.99	◄———————	goods purchased
Shin guards 8.99	◄———————	goods purchased
TOTAL 14.98	◄———————	total due
CASH 20.00	◄———————	£20 (probably a £20 note) given by the customer
CHANGE 5.02	◄———————	change given
Thank you for your custom	◄———————	personal message to help public relations
Please retain this receipt in case of any query	◄———————	advice to retain receipt in case of a problem with the goods

a till receipt

ENIGMA MUSIC LIMITED   *receipt*   958

13 High Street, Mereford MR1 2TF

Customer ....*R V Williams*...date .....*3 Oct 20-5*.......

'Golden Oldies' by J Moore	*£20.00*
Total	*£20.00*

a hand-written receipt

Note that, although the above documents are often described as 'cash receipts', they are issued whatever payment method is used – cash, cheque, credit card, debit card.

banking documents

Most businesses have a bank account into which they pay money using a paying-in slip, and make payments by cheque and other bank transfers. The paying-in slip counterfoils (below) and cheque counterfoils (on the next page) form **source documents** for the accounting system. At regular intervals a bank sends a statement of account to its customers – the statement may show other receipts and payments – for example, standing orders, direct debits, credit transfers and bank charges.

We will be looking further at bank statements and banking transactions in Chapters 7 and 8 when we deal with the main cash book and prepare bank reconciliation statements.

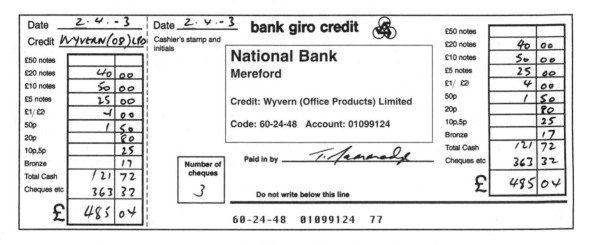

counterfoil	paying-in slip (front)

counterfoil	paying-in slip (back)

paying-in slip counterfoils

In a paying-in book, which is issued by the bank to business customers, the counterfoil is the part that is retained by the customer and stamped as a receipt by the bank cashier for the amount being paid in. A completed paying-in slip and counterfoil is illustrated on the previous page.

cheque counterfoils

In cheque books the counterfoil is the part retained by the payer when the cheque is sent off to the payee (the person who is being paid). The counterfoil gives information as to the date of the cheque, the payee, and the amount being paid; it also has the cheque number printed along the bottom. A completed cheque and counterfoil are illustrated below

counterfoil   cheque

information from bank statements

A bank sends statements to its customers in the same way that a business will send statements of account to its customers. In addition to entries for cheques paid in and out, a bank statement shows a number of other receipts and payments which need to be recorded in the book-keeping system:

* standing orders, for regular payments – eg hire purchase – made automatically by the bank on the instructions of the customer
* direct debits, for fixed or variable amounts – eg telephone bills – where the payment is requested by the receiver (beneficiary) of the payment through the banking system
* credit transfers, where money has been received through the banking system by BACS and credited to a seller's account, eg where the seller's customers have paid the amounts they owe
* bank charges, where the bank makes a charge for providing banking services; the charge may be calculated by reference to the number of transactions that have taken place on the bank account

These items are explained in more detail in Chapter 7, page 98.

RECORDING CASH DISCOUNT IN THE BOOK-KEEPING SYSTEM

We saw earlier (page 46) that cash discount (or settlement discount) is an allowance deducted from the invoice amount for quick settlement, eg 2% cash discount for settlement within seven days. A business can be involved with cash discount in two ways:

- discount allowed to debtors
- discount received from creditors

Note that, although the terms 'discount allowed' and 'discount received' do not use the word 'cash', they do refer to cash discount.

discount allowed

When cash discount is taken by a debtor it is entered into the accounts as shown by the following transactions:

10 October 20-2	Sold goods, £100, on credit to P Henry, allowing her a cash discount of 2% for settlement within seven days
15 October 20-2	P Henry pays £98 by cheque

Dr			Sales Account			Cr
20-2			£	20-2		£
				10 Oct	P Henry	100

Dr			P Henry			Cr
20-2			£	20-2		£
10 Oct	Sales		100	15 Oct	Bank	98
				15 Oct	Discount allowed	2
			100			100

Dr			Bank Account			Cr
20-2			£	20-2		£
15 Oct	P Henry		98			

Dr			Discount Allowed Account			Cr
20-2			£	20-2		£
15 Oct	P Henry		2			

Notes

- The amount of the payment received from the debtor is entered in the bank account.
- The amount of discount allowed is entered in both the debtor's account and discount allowed account:
  - debit discount allowed account
  - credit debtor's account
- Discount allowed is an expense of the business, because it represents the cost of collecting payments more speedily from the debtors.
- The account of P Henry has been totalled to show that both the debit and credit money columns are the same – thus her account now has a nil balance (the method of balancing accounts is looked at in the next chapter).

discount received

With cash discount received, a business is offered cash discount for quick settlement by its creditors. The following transactions give an example of this:

20 October 20-2	Bought goods, £200, on credit from B Lewis Ltd; 2.5% cash discount is offered for settlement by the end of October
30 October 20-2	Paid B Lewis Ltd £195 by cheque

Dr			Purchases Account			Cr
20-2		£		20-2		£
20 Oct	B Lewis Ltd	200				

Dr			B Lewis Ltd			Cr
20-2		£		20-2		£
30 Oct	Bank	195		20 Oct	Purchases	200
30 Oct	Discount received	5				
		200				200

Dr			Bank Account			Cr
20-2		£		20-2		£
				30 Oct	B Lewis Ltd	195

Dr			Discount Received Account			Cr
20-2		£		20-2		£
				30 Oct	B Lewis Ltd	5

Notes

- The business is receiving cash discount from its creditor, and the amount is entered as:
  - debit creditor's account
  - credit discount received account
- Discount received account is an income account.
- The money columns of the account of B Lewis Ltd have been totalled to show that the account now has a nil balance.

revision summary

- Cash discount – when taken – is recorded in the debtors' and creditors' accounts.
- Both discount allowed (an expenses account) and discount received (an income account) store up information until the end of the financial year, when it is used in the firm's profit and loss account – see Chapter 9.
- The main cash book (see Chapter 7) is usually used for listing the amounts of discount received and allowed – transfers are then made at the end of each month to the discount accounts.
- Trade discount is never recorded in the double-entry accounts; only the net amount of an invoice is recorded after trade discount has been deducted.

CHAPTER SUMMARY

- Correct documentation is important for businesses to be able to record accurately buying and selling transactions.
- There are a number of documents involved – the two most important source documents for book-keeping transactions are the invoice and the credit note.
- An invoice is a source document prepared by the seller and states the value of goods sold and the amount to be paid by the buyer.
- Trade discount is often deducted when goods are sold to other businesses.
- Bulk discount may be given for buying in large quantities.
- Cash discount (or settlement discount) is an allowance off the invoice amount for quick settlement.
- A credit note is a source document which shows that the buyer is entitled to a reduction in the amount charged by the seller; it is used, for example, if:
  - some of the goods delivered were faulty, or incorrectly supplied
  - the price charged on the invoice was too high
- Statements of account are sent out regularly to each debtor of a business to show the amount currently due.
- Other source documents include cash receipts, till rolls, cheque counterfoils, paying-in slip counterfoils.

● Information from bank statements gives details of standing orders, direct debits, BACS, credit transfers, bank charges.

● Cash discount allowed is entered in the accounts as:
  – debit discount allowed account
  – credit debtor's account

● Cash discount received is entered as:
  – debit creditor's account
  – credit discount received account

This chapter has explained business documents; the next chapter concentrates on double-entry book-keeping and shows how accounts are balanced, and a trial balance is extracted.

QUESTIONS

An asterisk (*) after the question number means that the answer is given at the end of this book.

> **free download from website** www.osbornebooks.co.uk
> Blank financial documents for use in these questions are available for free download from the Resources section of the Osborne Books website.

4.1* Fill in the missing words from the following sentences:

(a) A .... is prepared by the buyer and sent to the seller and describes the goods to be supplied.

(b) The seller prepares the ...., which gives details of the goods supplied, and states the money amount to be paid by the buyer.

(c) .... is a deduction made in the price if the purchaser pays within a stated time.

(d) When the purchaser is in business, an amount of ....

.... is sometimes allowed as a reduction in the price.

(e) The term .... on an invoice means that the invoice total is the amount to be paid.

(f) If a buyer returns goods, the seller prepares a ....

(g) At regular intervals the seller sends a summary of transactions to the buyer in the form of a ....

4.2

You work for Jane Smith, a wholesaler of fashionwear, who trades from Unit 21, Eastern Industrial Estate, Wyvern, Wyvernshire, WY1 3XJ. A customer, Excel Fashions of 49 Highland Street, Longtown, Mercia, LT3 2XL, orders the following:

> 5 dresses at £30 each
>
> 3 suits at £45.50 each
>
> 4 coats at £51.50 each

A 2.5 per cent cash discount is offered for full settlement within 14 days.

You are to prepare invoice number 2451, under today's date, to be sent to the customer. What amount will be paid by Excel Fashions if they pay the invoice in full within 14 days?

4.3

You work for Deansway Trading Company, a wholesaler of office stationery, which trades from The Model Office, Deansway, Rowcester, RW1 2EJ. A customer, The Card Shop of 126 The Cornbow, Teamington Spa, Wyvernshire, WY33 0EG, orders the following:

> 5 boxes of assorted rubbers at £5 per box
>
> 100 shorthand notebooks at £4 for 10
>
> 250 ring binders at 50p each

A 2.5 per cent cash discount is offered for full settlement within 14 days.

You are to prepare invoice number 8234, under today's date, to be sent to the customer. What amount will be paid by The Card Shop if they pay the invoice in full within 14 days?

4.4

Enter the following transactions into the double-entry book-keeping accounts of Sonya Smith:

20-4

2 Feb	Bought goods £200, on credit from G Lewis
4 Feb	Sold goods £150, on credit to L Jarvis
7 Feb	Sold goods £240, on credit to G Patel
10 Feb	Paid G Lewis the amount owing by cheque, after deducting a cash discount of 5%
12 Feb	L Jarvis pays the amount owing by cheque, after deducting a cash discount of 2%
16 Feb	Bought goods £160, on credit from G Lewis
20 Feb	G Patel pays the amount owing by cheque, after deducting a cash discount of 2.5%
24 Feb	Paid G Lewis the amount owing by cheque, after deducting a cash discount of 5%

4.5 Trend Fashion Designs Limited has partially prepared the following invoice from a delivery note:

─────── **INVOICE** ───────

TREND FASHION DESIGNS LIMITED

Unit 45 Elgar Estate, Broadfield, BR7 4ER
Tel 01908 765314 Fax 01908 765951

invoice to

Fashion Shop **48 High Street** **Wyvern** **WV1 2AJ**	

invoice no	**7878106**
account	**2667**
your reference	**54208**

deliver to

as above

date **10 11 -5**

product code	description	quantity	unit price £	unit	total £	trade discount %	net £
45B	**Trend tops (black)**	**30**	**12.50**	**each**		**10**	
35W	**Trend trousers (white)**	**20**	**25.00**	**each**		**10**	

terms
5% cash discount for full settlement
within 7 days
Net 30 days

TOTAL	

REQUIRED

(a) Complete the invoice to show the total amount due.

(b) Explain the following terms:
- trade discount
- cash discount

(c) What amount will be paid by the Fashion Shop if they pay the invoice in full within seven days?

4.6* Kingston Traders is seeking to attract new customers and has decided to offer trade and cash discounts.

REQUIRED

(a)   Explain the circumstances under which they would give:

     (i)   Trade discount

     (ii)   Cash discount

(b)   Kingston Traders supply goods to a customer, Queenstown Retail, on the following terms:

     Selling price   £500

     Trade discount   20%

     Cash discount   5% (for full settlement within 14 days)

     Calculate the total of the invoice for these goods. Show your workings.

(c)   What amount will be paid by Queenstown Retail if they pay the invoice in full within 14 days?

4.7 (a)   What is meant by the term source documents?

(b)   Describe the purpose of (i) an invoice, and (ii) a credit note, as source documents.

(c)   State *three* further source documents used in book-keeping.

4.8 You work in the accounts department of Alpha Office Furniture Limited. Part of your job involves checking invoices before they are sent to customers.

The invoice, shown on the next page, to Wyvern Products Limited, has been prepared by a new member of staff. The purchase order, number 5915, from Wyvern Products to Alpha Office Furniture was for the following:

- 5 computer desks, product code CD, at £65 each

- 10 office chairs, product code OC, at £20 each

The terms of trade offered to Wyvern Products are for 10% trade discount, and 5% cash discount for full settlement within 14 days, otherwise net 30 days.

Today's date is 6 April 20-5.

─────── INVOICE ───────

ALPHA OFFICE FURNITURE LIMITED

Unit 1, Ashtree Estate, Mereford, MR3 7JG
Tel 01907 334482 Fax 01907 334493

invoice to

Wyvern Products Limited	
Wyvern Business Park	
Wyvern	
WV1 8TQ	

invoice no	234061
account	3571
your reference	5915

deliver to

as above

date	**06 04 20-5**

product code	description	quantity	unit price £	unit	total £	trade discount %	net £
CD	**Computer desks**	10	70.00	each	350.00	10	350.00
OC	**Office chairs**	5	20.00	each	200.00	10	20.00

terms
5% cash discount for full settlement
within 14 days
Net 30 days

TOTAL	370.00

REQUIRED

(a)   Check the invoice using the information available to you, and list any errors that you find.

(b)   Prepare a corrected invoice.

(c)   What amount will be paid by Wyvern Products Limited if they pay the invoice in full within 14 days

5 BALANCING ACCOUNTS – THE TRIAL BALANCE

With the 'traditional' form of account – a 'T' account – that we have used so far, it is necessary to calculate the balance of each account from time-to-time, according to the needs of the business, and at the end of each financial year.

The balance of an account is the total of that account to date, eg the amount of wages paid, the amount of sales made. In this chapter we shall see how this balancing of accounts is carried out.

We shall then use the balances from each account in order to check the double-entry book-keeping by extracting a trial balance, which is a list of the balances of ledger accounts.

BALANCING THE ACCOUNTS

At regular intervals, often at the end of each month, accounts are balanced in order to show the amounts, for example:

- owing to each creditor
- owing by each debtor
- of sales
- of purchases
- of sales returns (returns in)
- of purchases returns (returns out)
- of expenses incurred by the business
- of fixed assets, eg premises, machinery, etc owned by the business
- of capital and drawings of the owner of the business
- of other liabilities, eg loans

We have already noted earlier that, where running balance accounts (see page 24) are used, there is no need to balance each account, because the balance is already calculated – either manually or by computer – after each transaction.

METHOD OF BALANCING ACCOUNTS

Set out below is an example of an account which has been balanced at the month-end:

Dr			**Bank Account**			Cr
20-1		£	20-1			£
1 Sep	Capital	5,000	2 Sep	Computer		1,800
5 Sep	J Jackson: loan	2,500	6 Sep	Purchases		500
10 Sep	Sales	750	12 Sep	Drawings		100
			15 Sep	Wages		200
			30 Sep	Balance c/d		5,650
		8,250				8,250
1 Oct	Balance b/d	5,650				

The steps involved in balancing accounts are:

Step 1

The entries in the debit and credit money columns are subtotalled and either recorded on the account, or noted on a separate piece of paper. In the example above, the debit side totals £8,250, while the credit side is £2,600.

Step 2

The difference between the two totals is the balance of the account and this is entered on the account:

- on the side of the smaller total
- on the next available line
- with the date of balancing (often the last day of the month)
- with the description 'balance c/d', or 'balance carried down'

In the bank account above, the balance carried down is £8,250 – £2,600 = £5,650, entered in the credit column.

Step 3

Both sides of the account are now totalled, including the balance which has just been entered, and the totals (the same on both sides) are entered on the same line in the appropriate column, and bold or double underlined. The bold underline indicates that the account has been balanced at this point using the figures above the total: the figures above the underline should not be added in to anything below the underline.

In the bank account above, the totals on each side of the account are £8,250.

Step 4

As we are using double-entry book-keeping, there must be an opposite entry to the 'balance c/d' calculated in Step 2. The same money amount is entered on the other side of the account below the bold underlined totals entered in Step 3. We have now completed both the debit and credit entry. The date is usually recorded as the next day after 'balance c/d', ie often the first day of the following month, and the description can be 'balance b/d' or 'balance brought down'.

In the example above, the balance brought down on the bank account on 1 October 20-1 is £5,650 debit; this means that, according to the firm's accounting records, there is £5,650 in the bank.

a practical point

When balancing accounts, use a pen and not a pencil. If any errors are made, cross them through neatly with a single line, and write the corrected version on the line below. Use correcting fluid in moderation; at best it conceals errors, at worst it conceals fraudulent transactions.

FURTHER EXAMPLES OF BALANCING ACCOUNTS

Dr			Wages Account		Cr
20-1		£	20-1		£
9 Apr	Bank	750	30 Apr	Balance c/d	2,250
16 Apr	Bank	800			
23 Apr	Bank	700			
		2,250			2,250
1 May	Balance b/d	2,250			

The above wages account has transactions on one side only, but is still balanced in the same way. This account shows that the total amount paid for wages is £2,250.

Dr			B Lewis Ltd		Cr
20-1		£	20-1		£
10 Apr	Purchases Returns	30	7 Apr	Purchases	280
26 Apr	Bank	250			
		280			280

This account in the name of a creditor has a 'nil' balance after the transactions for April have taken place. The two sides of the account are totalled and, as both debit and credit side are the same amount, there is nothing further to do, apart from entering the bold or double underlined total.

Dr		A Holmes			Cr
20-1		£	20-1		£
1 Apr	Balance b/d	105	10 Apr	Bank	105
11 Apr	Sales	125	11 Apr	Sales Returns	25
			30 Apr	Balance c/d	100
		230			230
1 May	Balance b/d	100			

This is the account of a debtor and, at the start of the month, there was a debit balance of £105 brought down from March. After the various transactions for April, there remains a debit balance of £100 owing at 1 May.

Dr		Office Equipment Account		Cr
20-1		£	20-1	£
12 Apr	Bank	2,000		

This account has just the one transaction and, in practice, there is no need to balance it. It should be clear that the account has a debit balance of £2,000, which is represented by the asset of office equipment.

Dr		Malvern Manufacturing Co			Cr
20-1		£	20-1		£
29 Apr	Bank	250	18 Apr	Purchases	250

This creditor's account has a 'nil' balance, with just one transaction on each side. All that is needed here is to bold or double underline the amount on both sides.

EXTRACTING A TRIAL BALANCE

The book-keeper extracts a trial balance from the accounting records in order to check the arithmetical accuracy of the double-entry book-keeping, ie that the debit entries equal the credit entries.

A trial balance is a list of the balances of every account forming the ledger, distinguishing between those accounts which have debit balances and those which have credit balances.

A trial balance is extracted at regular intervals – often at the end of each month.

example of a trial balance

Trial balance of A-Z Suppliers as at 31 January 20-1

Name of account	Dr £	Cr £
Purchases	750	
Sales		1,600
Sales returns	25	
Purchases returns		50
J Brown (debtor)	155	
T Sweet (creditor)		110
Rent paid	100	
Wages	150	
Heating and lighting	125	
Office equipment	500	
Machinery	1,000	
Cash	50	
Bank	455	
J Williams – loan		800
Capital		1,000
Drawings	250	
	3,560	3,560

Notes

- The debit and credit columns have been totalled and are the same amount. Thus the trial balance proves that the accounting records are arithmetically correct. (A trial balance does not prove the complete accuracy of the accounting records – see page 66.)

- The heading for a trial balance gives the name of the business whose accounts have been listed and the date it was extracted, ie the end of the accounting period.

- The balance for each account transferred to the trial balance is the figure brought down after the accounts have been balanced.

- As well as the name of each account, it is quite usual to show in the trial balance the account number. Most accounting systems give numbers to accounts and these can be listed in a separate reference column.

DEBIT AND CREDIT BALANCES – GUIDELINES

Certain accounts always have a debit balance, while others always have a credit balance. You should already know these, but the lists set out below will act as a revision guide, and will also help in your understanding of trial balances.

debit balances include:

- cash account
- purchases account
- sales returns account (returns in)
- fixed asset accounts, eg premises, motor vehicles, machinery, office equipment, etc
- expenses and overheads accounts, eg wages, telephone, rent paid, carriage outwards, carriage inwards, discount allowed
- drawings account
- debtors' accounts (often, for the purposes of a trial balance, the balances of individual debtors' accounts are totalled, and the total is entered in the trial balance as debtors)

credit balances include:

- sales account
- purchases returns account (returns out)
- income accounts, eg rent income, commission income, discount received
- capital account
- loan account
- creditors' accounts (often a total is entered in the trial balance, rather than the individual balances of each account)

Note: bank account can be either debit or credit – it will be debit when the business has money in the bank, and credit when it is overdrawn.

IF THE TRIAL BALANCE DOESN'T BALANCE . . .

If the trial balance fails to balance, ie the two totals are different, there is an error (or errors):

- either in the addition of the trial balance
- and/or in the double-entry book-keeping

The procedure for finding the error(s) is as follows:

- check the addition of the trial balance

- check that the balance of each account has been correctly entered in the trial balance, and under the correct heading, ie debit or credit
- check that the balance of every account in the ledger has been included in the trial balance
- check the calculation of the balance on each account
- calculate the amount that the trial balance is wrong, and then look in the accounts for a transaction for this amount: if one is found, check that the double-entry book-keeping has been carried out correctly
- halve the amount by which the trial balance is wrong, and look for a transaction for this amount: if it is found, check the double-entry book-keeping
- if the amount by which the trial balance is wrong is divisible by nine, then the error may be a reversal of figures, eg £65 entered as £56, or £45 entered as £54
- if the trial balance is wrong by a round amount, eg £10, £100, £1,000, the error is likely to be in the calculation of the account balances
- if the error(s) is still not found, it is necessary to check the book-keeping transactions since the date of the last trial balance, by going back to the source documents and the subsidiary books

ERRORS NOT SHOWN BY A TRIAL BALANCE

As mentioned earlier, a trial balance does not prove the complete accuracy of the accounting records. There are six types of errors that are not shown by a trial balance.

error of omission

Here a business transaction has been completely omitted from the accounting records, ie both the debit and credit entries have not been made.

reversal of entries

With this error, the debit and credit entries have been made in the accounts but on the wrong side of the two accounts concerned. For example, a cash sale has been entered wrongly as debit sales account, credit cash account – this should have been entered as a debit to cash account, and a credit to sales account.

mispost/error of commission

Here, a transaction is entered to the wrong person's account. For example, a sale of goods on credit to A T Hughes has been entered as debit A J Hughes' account, credit sales account. Here, double-entry book-keeping has been completed but, when A J Hughes receives a statement of account, he or she will soon complain about being debited with goods not ordered or received.

error of principle

This is when a transaction has been entered in the wrong type of account. For example, the cost of petrol for vehicles has been entered as debit motor vehicles account, credit bank account. The error is that motor vehicles account represents fixed assets, and the transaction should have been debited to the expense account for motor vehicle running expenses.

error of original entry (or transcription)

Here, the correct accounts have been used, and the correct sides: what is wrong is that the amount has been entered incorrectly in both accounts. This could be caused by a 'bad figure' on an invoice or a cheque, or it could be caused by a 'reversal of figures', eg an amount of £45 being entered in both accounts as £54. Note that both debit and credit entries need to be made incorrectly for the trial balance still to balance; if one entry has been made incorrectly and the other is correct, then the error will be shown.

compensating error

This is where two errors cancel each other out. For example, if the balance of purchases account is calculated wrongly at £10 too much, and a similar error has occurred in calculating the balance of sales account, then the two errors will compensate each other, and the trial balance will not show the errors.

Correction of errors is covered fully in Chapter 10.

IMPORTANCE OF THE TRIAL BALANCE

A business will extract a trial balance on a regular basis to check the arithmetic accuracy of the book-keeping. However, the trial balance is also used as the starting point in the production of the final accounts of a business. These final accounts, which are produced once a year (often more frequently) comprise:

- **trading account**
- **profit and loss account**
- **balance sheet**

The final accounts show the owner how profitable the business has been, what the business owns, and how the business is financed. The preparation of final accounts is an important aspect of your studies and one which we shall be coming to in later chapters. For the moment, we can say that extraction of a trial balance is an important exercise in the accounting process: it proves the book-keeper's accuracy, and also lists the account balances which form the basis for the final accounts of a business.

CHAPTER SUMMARY

- The traditional 'T' account needs to be balanced at regular intervals – often at the month-end.

- When balancing accounts, the book-keeper must adhere strictly to the rules of double-entry book-keeping.

- When each account in the ledger has been balanced, a trial balance can be extracted.

- A trial balance is a list of the balances of every account forming the ledger, distinguishing between those accounts which have debit balances and those which have credit balances.

- A trial balance does not prove the complete accuracy of the accounting records; errors not shown by a trial balance are:
  - error of omission
  - reversal of entries
  - mispost/error of commission
  - error of principle
  - error of original entry
  - compensating error

- The trial balance is used as the starting point for the preparation of a business' final accounts.

In the next chapter we will look at the division of the ledger into manageable sections, and we will see how an expanding accounting system uses subsidiary books to cope with large numbers of routine transactions.

QUESTIONS

visit
www.osbornebooks.co.uk
to take an online test

An asterisk (*) after the question number means that the answer is given at the end of this book.

5.1

The following are the business transactions of Andrew Johnstone, a retailer of computer software, for the months of January and February 20-9:

Transactions for January

1 Jan	Started in business with £10,000 in the bank
4 Jan	Paid rent on premises £500, by cheque
5 Jan	Bought shop fittings £1,500, by cheque
7 Jan	Bought stock of computer software £5,000, on credit from Comp Supplies Limited
11 Jan	Software sales £1,000 paid into bank

12 Jan	Software sales £1,250 paid into bank
16 Jan	Software sales £850 on credit to Rowcester College
20 Jan	Paid Comp Supplies Limited £5,000 by cheque
22 Jan	Software sales £1,450 paid into bank
25 Jan	Bought software £6,500 on credit from Comp Supplies Limited
27 Jan	Rowcester College returns software £100

Transactions for February

2 Feb	Paid rent on premises £500 by cheque
4 Feb	Software sales £1,550 paid into bank
5 Feb	Returned faulty software, £150 to Comp Supplies Limited
10 Feb	Software sales £1,300 paid into bank
12 Feb	Rowcester College pays the amount owing by cheque
15 Feb	Bought shop fittings £850 by cheque
19 Feb	Software sales £1,600 paid into bank
22 Feb	Paid Comp Supplies Limited the amount owing by cheque
24 Feb	Bought software £5,500 on credit from Comp Supplies Limited
25 Feb	Software sales £1,100 paid into bank
26 Feb	Software sales £1,050 on credit to Rowcester College

You are to:

(a) record the January transactions in the books of account, and balance each account at 31 January 20-9

(b) draw up a trial balance at 31 January 20-9

(c) record the February transactions in the books of account, and balance each account at 28 February 20-9

(d) draw up a trial balance at 28 February 20-9

5.2   Produce the trial balance of Jane Greenwell as at 28 February 20-1. She has omitted to open a capital account.

	£
Bank overdraft	1,250
Purchases	850
Cash	48
Sales	730
Purchases returns	144
Creditors	1,442
Equipment	2,704
Van	3,200
Sales returns	90
Debtors	1,174
Wages	1,500
Capital	?

5.3*

The book-keeper of Lorna Fox has extracted the following list of balances as at 31 March 20-2:

	£
Purchases	96,250
Sales	146,390
Sales returns	8,500
Administration expenses	10,240
Wages	28,980
Telephone	3,020
Interest paid	2,350
Travel expenses	1,045
Premises	125,000
Machinery	40,000
Debtors	10,390
Bank overdraft	1,050
Cash	150
Creditors	12,495
Loan from bank	20,000
Drawings	9,450
Capital	155,440

You are to:

(a) Produce the trial balance at 31 March 20-2.

(b) Take any three debit balances and any three credit balances and explain to someone who does not understand accounting why they are listed as such, and what this means to the business.

5.4*

Fill in the missing words from the following sentences:

(a) "You made an error of .... when you debited the cost of diesel fuel for the van to vans account."

(b) "I've had the book-keeper from D Jones Limited on the 'phone concerning the statements of account that we sent out the other day. She says that there is a sales invoice charged that she knows nothing about. I wonder if we have done a .... and it should be for T Jones' account?"

(c) "There is a 'bad figure' on a purchases invoice – we have read it as £35 when it should be £55. It has gone through our accounts wrongly so we have an error of .... to put right."

(d) "Although the trial balance balanced last week, I've since found an error of £100 in the calculation of the balance of sales account. We will need to check the other balances as I think we may have a .... error."

(e) "Who was in charge of that trainee last week? He has entered the payment for the electricity bill on the debit side of the bank and on the credit side of electricity – a .... of ...."

(f) "I found this purchase invoice from last week in amongst the copy letters. As we haven't put it through the accounts we have an error of ...."

5.5 *"A trial balance does not prove the complete accuracy of the accounting records."*

You are to describe *four* types of error that are not shown by a trial balance.

Give an example of each type of error.

6 DIVISION OF THE LEDGER – THE USE OF SUBSIDIARY BOOKS

As we saw in Chapter 1, the double-entry system involves the recording of transactions in accounts in the ledger. In this chapter we will learn how, in order to cope with an expanding book-keeping system, the ledger is divided into separate sections. This is called the division of the ledger.

We will also examine how a business makes use of subsidiary books to summarise business transactions before they are entered into the double-entry system.

DIVISION OF THE LEDGER

Double-entry book-keeping involves, as we have seen, making two entries in the ledger accounts for each business transaction. The traditional meaning of a ledger is a weighty leather-bound volume into which each account was entered on a separate page. With such a hand-written book-keeping system, as more and more accounts were opened, the point was reached where another ledger book was needed. Finally, in order to sort the accounts into a logical order, the accounting system was divided into main sections or divisions, and this practice continues today:

- sales ledger, containing the accounts of debtors
- purchases ledger, containing the accounts of creditors
- general (or nominal) ledger, containing the nominal accounts (expenses, etc) and the real accounts (fixed assets, cash, bank, etc)

These three divisions comprise the ledger, and are illustrated in full on the opposite page. Most computer accounting programs (see AS Unit 2, Chapter 20) use these divisions of the ledger.

USE OF THE DIVISIONS OF THE LEDGER

To understand how the divisions of the ledger are used, we will examine a number of business transactions and see which ledgers are used and in which accounts the transactions are recorded:

purchase of goods on credit
- general ledger – debit purchases account
- purchases ledger – credit the account of the creditor (supplier)

DIVISION OF THE LEDGER

sales ledger

Sales ledger contains the accounts of debtors, and records:

- sales made on credit to customers of the business
- sales returns (returns in) by customers
- payments received from debtors
- cash discount allowed for prompt settlement
- bad debts written off (see page 210)

Sales ledger does not record cash sales.

Sales ledger contains an account for each debtor and records the transactions with that debtor. A sales ledger control account (see Chapter 11) is often used to summarise the transactions on the accounts of debtors.

purchases ledger

Purchases ledger contains the accounts of creditors, and records:

- purchases made on credit from suppliers of the business
- purchases returns (returns out) made by the business
- payments made to creditors
- cash discount received for prompt settlement

Purchases ledger does not record cash purchases.

Purchases ledger contains an account for each creditor and records the transactions with that creditor. A purchases ledger control account (see Chapter 11) may be used to summarise the creditor account transactions.

general (nominal) ledger

The general (nominal) ledger contains the other accounts of the business:

Nominal Accounts

- sales account (cash and credit sales), sales returns
- purchases account (cash and credit purchases), purchases returns
- expenses and income, loans, capital, drawings
- profit and loss

Real Accounts

- fixed assets, eg computers, vehicles
- main cash book*, which records all transactions for bank account and cash account
- stock

*   note that in some accounting systems the main cash book is kept as a separate division of the ledger

purchase of goods by cheque

- general ledger – debit purchases account
- general ledger – credit bank account

sale of goods on credit

- sales ledger – debit the account of the debtor (customer)
- general ledger – credit sales account

sale of goods for cash

- general ledger – debit cash account
- general ledger – credit sales account

purchase of a computer for use in the business, paying by cheque

- general ledger – debit computer account (fixed asset)
- general ledger – credit bank account

Note that in some accounting systems the main cash book is kept as a separate division of the ledger.

SUBSIDIARY BOOKS

The place where a business transaction is recorded for the first time, prior to entry in the ledger, is known as the subsidiary book (or book of prime entry). These comprise:

- sales day book (or sales journal)
- purchases day book (or purchases journal)
- sales returns, or returns in, day book (or sales returns journal)
- purchases returns, or returns out, day book (or purchases returns journal)
- main cash book (see Chapter 7)
- general journal (see Chapter 10)

In the rest of this chapter we will see how the first four of these – the day books – fit into the accounting system. The other two subsidiary books will be looked at in more detail in later chapters. We have already used cash account and bank account which, together, make up a business' cash book. In the next chapter (Chapter 7), we will see how the two accounts are brought together in one main cash book. Cash book is the subsidiary book for receipts and payments in the forms of cash or cheque. General journal (often known more simply as the journal) is covered in Chapter 10.

SALES DAY BOOK

The sales day book (which can also be called a sales journal, or sales book) is used by businesses that have a lot of separate sales transactions. The day book is simply a list of transactions, the total of which, at the end of the day, week, or month, is transferred to sales account. (When used as a weekly or monthly record, it is still called a day book.) Note that the day book is not part of double-entry book-keeping, but is used as a subsidiary book to give a total which is then entered into the accounts. By using a day book for a large number of transactions in this way, there are fewer transactions passing through the double-entry accounts. Also, the work of the accounts department can be divided up – one person can be given the task of maintaining the day book, while another can concentrate on keeping the ledger up-to-date.

The most common use of a sales day book is to record credit sales from invoices issued.

example transactions	
3 Jan 20-1	Sold goods, £80, on credit to E Doyle, invoice no 901
8 Jan 20-1	Sold goods, £200, on credit to A Sparkes, invoice no 902
12 Jan 20-1	Sold goods, £80, on credit to T Young, invoice no 903
18 Jan 20-1	Sold goods, £120, on credit to A Sparkes, invoice no 904

The sales day book is written up as follows:

Sales Day Book				
Date	Details	Invoice	Reference	Amount
20-1				£
3 Jan	E Doyle	901	SL 58	80
8 Jan	A Sparkes	902	SL 127	200
12 Jan	T Young	903	SL 179	80
18 Jan	A Sparkes	904	SL 127	120
31 Jan	Total for month			480

Notes
- Total credit sales for the month are £480, and this amount is credited to sales account in the general ledger.

- The credit sales transactions are debited in the personal accounts of the firm's debtors in the sales ledger.
- The sales day book incorporates a reference column which cross-references each transaction to the personal account of each debtor. In this way, an audit trail is created so that a particular transaction can be traced from source document (invoice), through the subsidiary book (sales day book), to the debtor's ledger account.
- Where control accounts are in use (see Chapter 11), the total for the month, £480, is debited to the sales ledger control account.
- When businesses are registered for Value Added Tax (VAT), they incorporate a VAT money column into their sales – and other – day books and operate a VAT account. However, for AS Accounting Unit 1, you do not need to make accounting records for VAT.

The accounts to record the above transactions are:

GENERAL LEDGER

Dr				Sales Account			Cr
20-1			£	20-1			£
				31 Jan	Sales Day Book		480

SALES LEDGER

Dr				E Doyle (account no 58)			Cr
20-1			£	20-1			£
3 Jan	Sales		80				

Dr				A Sparkes (account no 127)			Cr
20-1			£	20-1			£
8 Jan	Sales		200				
18 Jan	Sales		120				

Dr				T Young (account no 179)			Cr
20-1			£	20-1			£
12 Jan	Sales		80				

revision summary

Sales day book fits into the accounting system in the following way:

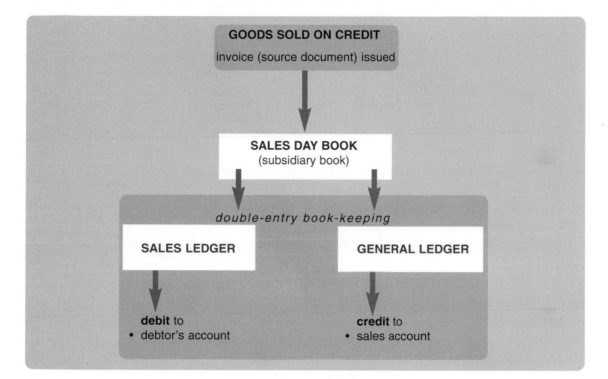

PURCHASES DAY BOOK

This subsidiary book is used by businesses that have a lot of separate purchases transactions. The purchases day book lists the transactions for credit purchases from invoices received and, at the end of the day, week or month, the total is transferred to purchases account.

example transactions

2 Jan 20-1	Bought goods, £80, on credit from P Bond, his invoice no 1234
11 Jan 20-1	Bought goods, £120, on credit from D Webster, her invoice no A373
16 Jan 20-1	Bought goods, £160, on credit from P Bond, his invoice no 1247

The purchases day book is written up as follows:

Purchases Day Book				
Date	Details	Invoice	Reference	Amount
20-1				£
2 Jan	P Bond	1234	PL 525	80
11 Jan	D Webster	A373	PL 730	120
16 Jan	P Bond	1247	PL 525	160
31 Jan	Total for month			360

Notes

- Total credit purchases for the month are £360, and this amount is debited to purchases account in the general ledger.
- The credit purchases transactions are credited in the personal accounts of the firm's debtors in the purchases ledger.
- The reference column gives a cross-reference to the creditors' accounts and provides an audit trail.
- Where control accounts are in use (see Chapter 11), the total for the month, £360, is credited to the purchases ledger control account
- As noted earlier, businesses registered for VAT incorporate a VAT money column into their day books and operate a VAT account. However, for AS Accounting Unit 1, you do not need to make accounting records for VAT.

The accounts to record the above transactions are:

GENERAL LEDGER

Dr			Purchases Account			Cr
20-1		£	20-1			£
31 Jan	Purchases Day Book	360				

PURCHASES LEDGER

Dr			P Bond (account no 525)			Cr
20-1		£	20-1			£
			2 Jan	Purchases		80
			16 Jan	Purchases		160

Dr			D Webster (account no 730)			Cr
20-1		£	20-1			£
			11 Jan	Purchases		120

revision summary

Purchases day book fits into the accounting system in the following way:

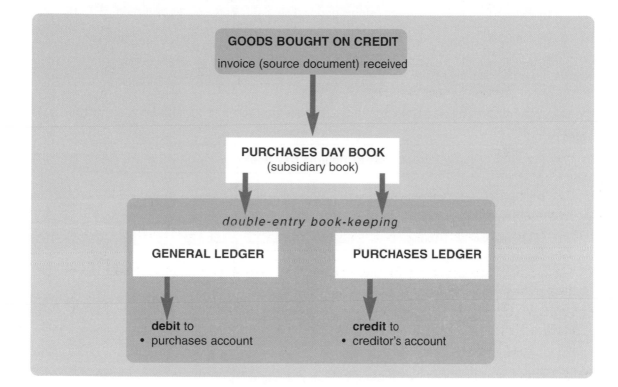

RETURNS DAY BOOKS

Where a business has a sufficient number of sales returns and purchases returns each day, week or month, it will make use of the two returns books:

- **Sales Returns (or Returns In) Day Book** – for goods previously sold on credit and now being returned to the business by its customers

- **Purchases Returns (or Returns Out) Day Book** – for goods purchased on credit by the business, and now being returned to the suppliers

The two returns day books operate in a similar way to the other day books: they are used to store information about returns until such time as it is transferred to the appropriate returns account. Note that, like all day books, the transactions are recorded from source documents (credit notes issued for sales returns, and credit notes received for purchases returns). The returns day books are subsidiary books and do not form part of the double-entry book-keeping system: the information from the day book must be transferred to the appropriate account in the ledger.

---

example transactions

6 Jan 20-1	Returned goods, £40, to P Bond, credit note no 406 received
15 Jan 20-1	T Young returns goods, £40, credit note no CN702 issued
20 Jan 20-1	Returned goods, £40, to D Webster, credit note no 123 received
25 Jan 20-1	A Sparkes returns goods, £120, credit note no CN703 issued

The sales returns (returns in) day book and purchases returns (returns out) day book are written up as follows:

Sales Returns Day Book				
Date	Details	Credit Note	Reference	Amount
20-1				£
15 Jan	T Young	CN702	SL 179	40
25 Jan	A Sparkes	CN703	SL 127	120
31 Jan	Total for month			160

Purchases Returns Day Book				
Date	Details	Credit Note	Reference	Amount
20-1				£
6 Jan	P Bond	406	PL 525	40
20 Jan	D Webster	123	PL 730	40
31 Jan	Total for month			80

Notes

- Total net sales returns and net purchases returns are debited to the sales returns account and credited to the purchases returns account respectively in the general ledger.
- The amounts of sales returns are credited to the debtors' personal accounts in the sales ledger; purchases returns are debited to the creditors' accounts in the purchases ledger.
- Where control accounts are in use (see Chapter 11), the total for the month of sales returns, £160, is credited to sales ledger control account, and the total for the month of purchases returns, £80, is debited to purchases ledger control account.

- As noted earlier, businesses registered for VAT incorporate a VAT money column into their day books and operate a VAT account. However, for AS Accounting Unit 1, you do not need to make accounting records for VAT.

The accounts to record the above transactions (including any other transactions already recorded on these accounts) are:

GENERAL LEDGER

Dr		£		Sales Returns Account	Cr		£
20-1				20-1			
31 Jan	Sales Returns Day Book	160					

Dr		£		Purchases Returns Account	Cr		£
20-1				20-1			
				31 Jan	Purchases Returns Day Book		80

SALES LEDGER

Dr		£	A Sparkes (account no 127)		Cr	£
20-1			20-1			
8 Jan	Sales	200	25 Jan	Sales Returns		120
18 Jan	Sales	120				

Dr		£	T Young (account no 179)		Cr	£
20-1			20-1			
12 Jan	Sales	80	15 Jan	Sales Returns		40

PURCHASES LEDGER

Dr		£	P Bond (account no 525)		Cr	£
20-1			20-1			
6 Jan	Purchases Returns	40	2 Jan	Purchases		80
			16 Jan	Purchases		160

Dr		£	D Webster (account no 730)		Cr	£
20-1			20-1			
20 Jan	Purchases Returns	40	11 Jan	Purchases		120

revision summary

The two returns day books fit into the accounting system as follows:

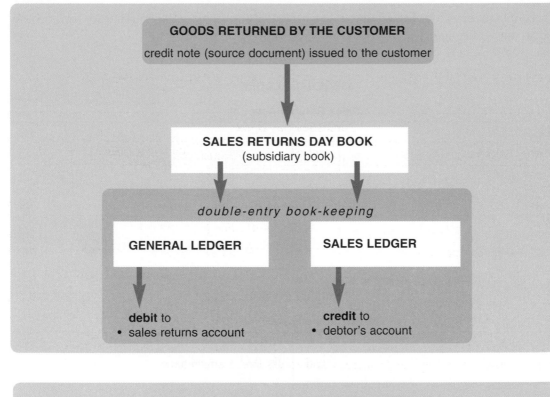

GOODS RETURNED BY THE CUSTOMER

credit note (source document) issued to the customer

SALES RETURNS DAY BOOK
(subsidiary book)

double-entry book-keeping

GENERAL LEDGER

SALES LEDGER

debit to
• sales returns account

credit to
• debtor's account

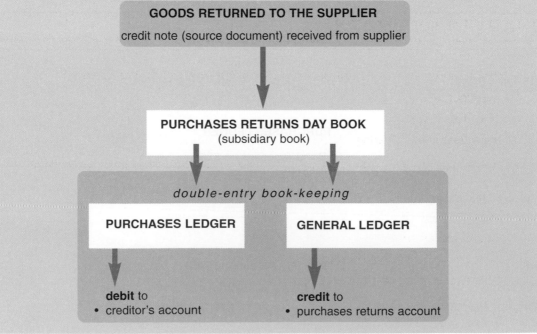

GOODS RETURNED TO THE SUPPLIER

credit note (source document) received from supplier

PURCHASES RETURNS DAY BOOK
(subsidiary book)

double-entry book-keeping

PURCHASES LEDGER

GENERAL LEDGER

debit to
• creditor's account

credit to
• purchases returns account

ANALYSED DAY BOOKS

An analysed day book is used whenever a business needs to split its purchases, sales or returns between different categories of products, between different departments, or between different geographical areas, eg southern division, northern division.

For example, a paint and wallpaper shop may decide to write up its purchases day book as follows:

Purchases Day Book						
Date	Details	Invoice	Reference	Paint	Wallpaper	Total
20-1				£	£	£
8 Jan	DIY Wholesalers Ltd	5478	PL 210	75	125	200
12 Jan	Luxor Paints Ltd	A869	PL 360	120	-	120
16 Jan	Bond Supplies	9740	PL 150	180	100	280
22 Jan	Southern Manufacturing Co	2162	PL 450	60	100	160
31 Jan	Totals for month			435	325	760

By using analysed day books, a business can keep track of the purchases, sales, etc between different products, departments, geographical areas, and assess their performance.

CHAPTER SUMMARY

- Division of the ledger means that the accounts are divided between three sections:
  - sales ledger
  - purchases ledger
  - general (or nominal) ledger

  In some accounting systems the main cash book is kept as a separate division of the ledger.

- Subsidiary books include:
  - sales day book
  - purchases day book
  - sales returns, or returns in, day book
  - purchases returns, or returns out, day book
  - main cash book
  - general journal

● A day book is a listing device which is used to take pressure off the main double-entry book-keeping system, and also allows the work of the accounts department to be split up amongst staff.

● Most businesses use day books for credit transactions only.

● An analysed day book is used when a business needs to know the purchases, sales, etc made by different products, departments, geographical areas of the business.

In the next chapter, we will look at the main cash book – which is the subsidiary book for all cash and bank transactions.

QUESTIONS

An asterisk (*) after the question number means that the answer is given at the end of this book.

6.1* Lucinda Lamille operates a clothes wholesaling business. During February 2006, the following credit transactions took place:

20-6

1 Feb	Purchased goods from Flair Clothing Co for £520
2 Feb	Sold goods to Wyvern Fashions for £200
4 Feb	Purchased goods from Modernwear for £240
10 Feb	Sold goods to Zandra Smith for £160
15 Feb	Sold goods to Just Jean for £120
18 Feb	Purchased goods from Quality Clothing for £800
23 Feb	Sold goods to Zandra Smith for £320
24 Feb	Sold goods to Wyvern Fashions for £80
26 Feb	Sold goods to Mercian Models for £320
28 Feb	Purchased goods from Flair Clothing Co for £200

You are to:

(a)   enter the above transactions in Lucinda Lamille's subsidiary books, and total the columns for the month

(b)   record the accounting entries in Lucinda Lamille's purchases ledger, sales ledger and general ledger

6.2

James Scriven started in business as a furniture wholesaler on 1 February 20-2. During the first month of business, the following credit transactions took place:

1 Feb Purchased furniture for resale and received invoice no 961 from Softseat Ltd, £320

2 Feb Purchased furniture for resale and received invoice no 068 from PRK Ltd, £80

8 Feb Sold furniture and issued invoice no 001 to High Street Stores, £440

14 Feb Sold furniture and issued invoice no 002 to Peter Lounds Ltd, £120

15 Feb Purchased furniture for resale and received invoice no 529 from Quality Furnishings, £160

18 Feb Sold furniture and issued invoice no 003 to Carpminster College, £320

19 Feb Purchased furniture for resale and received invoice no 984 from Softseat Ltd, £160

25 Feb Sold furniture and issued invoice no 004 to High Street Stores, £200

You are to:

(a) enter the above transactions in James Scriven's subsidiary books, and total the columns for the month

(b) record the accounting entries in James Scriven's purchases ledger, sales ledger and general ledger

6.3

Anne Green owns a shop selling paint and decorating materials. She has two suppliers, Wyper Ltd (account no 301) and M Roper & Sons (account no 302). During the month of May 20-2 Anne received the following business documents from her suppliers:

2 May Invoice no 562 from M Roper & Sons for £190

4 May Invoice no 82 from Wyper Ltd for £200

10 May Invoice no 86 from Wyper Ltd for £210

18 May Invoice no 580 from M Roper & Sons for £180

18 May Credit note no 82 from M Roper & Sons for £30

21 May Invoice no 91 from Wyper Ltd for £240

23 May Credit note no 6 from Wyper Ltd for £40

25 May Invoice no 589 from M Roper & Sons for £98

28 May Credit note no 84 from M Roper & Sons for £38

You are to:

(a)   enter the above transactions in the appropriate day books which are to be totalled at the end of May

(b)   enter the transactions in the appropriate accounts in Anne Green's ledgers. (The credit balances of Wyper Ltd and M Roper & Sons at the beginning of the month were £100 and £85 respectively.)

(c)   balance each account and bring down a balance on 1 June 20-2

6.4* Lorna Pratt runs a computer software business, specialising in supplies to educational establishments. At the beginning of January 20-2 the balances in her ledgers were as follows:

Sales ledger	Mereford College (account no 201)	£705.35 debit
	Carpminster College (account no 202)	£801.97 debit
Purchases ledger	Macstrad plc (account no 101)	£1,050.75 credit
	Amtosh plc (account no 102)	£2,750.83 credit

During the course of the month the following business documents are issued:

2 Jan	Invoice from Macstrad plc, M1529	£2,900.00
3 Jan	Invoice from Amtosh plc, A7095	£7,500.00
5 Jan	Invoice to Mereford College, 1093	£3,900.00
7 Jan	Invoice to Carpminster College, 1094	£8,500.00
10 Jan	Credit note from Macstrad plc, MC105	£319.75
12 Jan	Credit note from Amtosh plc, AC730	£750.18
13 Jan	Credit note to Mereford College, CN109	£850.73
14 Jan	Invoice to Carpminster College, 1095	£1,800.50
14 Jan	Invoice to Mereford College, 1096	£2,950.75
18 Jan	Invoice from Macstrad plc, M2070	£1,750.00
19 Jan	Invoice from Amtosh plc, A7519	£5,500.00
20 Jan	Invoice to Carpminster College, 1097	£3,900.75
22 Jan	Invoice to Mereford College, 1098	£1,597.85
23 Jan	Credit note from Macstrad plc, MC120	£953.07
27 Jan	Credit note to Mereford College, CN110	£593.81

You are to:

(a)   enter the above transactions in the appropriate day books which are to be totalled at the end of January

(b)   record the accounting entries in Lorna Pratt's sales ledger, purchases ledger and general ledger

6.5   Malik Importers has partially prepared the following invoice from the delivery note.

━━━ INVOICE ━━━
MALIK IMPORTERS
Unit 2B, Brookside Estate, Wyvern, WV3 8PT
Tel 01927 493841 Fax 01927 493822

invoice to

Flair Fashions
18B Retail Arcade
Porthperran
TR10 0BX

invoice no	**45762**
account no	**F28**
your order no	**0347**
delivery note no	**0175**
date	**15 March 20-7**

product code	quantity	details	unit price (£)	unit	total amount (£)
X24	**96**	**Trend tops**	**8.50**	**each**	
Y36	**20**	**Jeans**	**15**	**each**	
				trade discount 20%	
				total	

terms
5% cash discount for full settlement within 7 days
Net 30 days

---

question continued on the next page . . .

question continued from the previous page . . .

REQUIRED

(a)   Complete the total amount column of the invoice.

(b)   This invoice will be used as a source document by both Flair Fashions and Malik
        Importers. Which subsidiary book will be used for the entry:

        (i)   in the books of Flair Fashions ....

                    ....

        (ii)   in the books of Malik Importers ....

                    ....

(c)   Explain the terms:

        (i)   trade discount ....

                    ....

                    ....

                    ....

        (ii)   cash discount ....

                    ....

                    ....

                    ....

                    ....

6.6*

In the catalogue of Wyvern Plumbers Merchants is part number B321 which has a list price of £50.00, less a trade discount of 20%.

Russell The Plumber, a customer, who is allowed trade discount and a cash discount of 5% for payment in 7 days, returned 8 units of part B321, which were faulty.

REQUIRED

(a)   What document will Wyvern Plumbers Merchants prepare and send to Russell The Plumber?

....

(b)   Calculate the amount to be recorded on the document, clearly showing your calculations.

....

....

....

....

....

....

....

(c)   What subsidiary book is used by Wyvern Plumbers Merchants for the returned parts and show the amount to be entered.

....

6.7* Complete the following table by giving the source document and the subsidiary book (or book of prime entry) to be used for the transactions.

	Transaction	Source Document	Subsidiary Book
(a)	Goods purchased on credit from a supplier		
(b)	Goods sold on credit to a customer		
(c)	Faulty goods returned to a supplier		
(d)	Payment made by cheque to a supplier		
(e)	Purchase of a new machine for use in the factory on credit		
(f)	Faulty goods returned by a customer		
(g)	Cheque received from a customer and paid into the bank		

6.8 Complete the following table by giving for each source document:

- the subsidiary book
- the account to be debited
- the account to be credited

The first item has been completed as an example.

Source Document	Subsidiary Book	Account to be debited	Account to be credited
Invoice for goods sold on credit to V Singh	*Sales Day Book*	*V Singh*	*Sales*
(a) Invoice received for goods bought on credit from Okara Limited			
(b) Credit note issued to S Johnson			
(c) Credit note received from Roper & Company			

6.9* For each transaction shown below, state

- the source document
- the subsidiary book
- the account to be debited
- the account to be credited

(a) purchased goods on credit from A Cotton

(b) sold goods on credit to D Law

(c) cheque received for cash sales

(d) returned damaged goods to A Cotton

(e) paid gas bill by cheque

(f) D Law returns damaged goods

Set up your answer in the form of a table.

7 THE MAIN CASH BOOK

The main cash book brings together the separate cash and bank transactions of a business into one 'book'.

The main cash book is used to record the book-keeping transactions which involve the receipt and payment of money, for example cash, cheques and bank transfers.

The main cash book forms part of the double-entry system.

Control of cash and money in the bank is very important for all businesses. A shortage of money may mean that wages and other day-to-day running expenses cannot be paid as they fall due. This could lead to the failure of the business.

THE MAIN CASH BOOK IN THE ACCOUNTING SYSTEM

For most businesses, control of cash takes place in the main cash book which records:

- receipts and payments in cash
- receipts and payments by cheque and bank transfer

The main cash book combines the roles of a subsidiary book and double-entry book-keeping. The main cash book is:

- a subsidiary book for cash and bank transactions
- the double-entry accounts for cash and bank

Within the division of the ledger (Chapter 6), the main cash book is usually located in the general ledger. However, in some accounting systems, the main cash book is kept as a separate division of the ledger.

Note that, as well as the main cash book, businesses often have a petty cash book which is used for low-value expense payments. However, your AS course does not require you to study the petty cash book.

USES OF THE MAIN CASH BOOK

We have already used a separate cash account and bank account for double-entry book-keeping transactions. These two accounts are, in practice, brought together into one book under the title of the main cash book. This cash book is, therefore, used to record the money side of book-keeping transactions and is part of the double-entry system. The main cash book is used for:

- **cash transactions**
  - all receipts in cash
  - most payments for cash, except for low-value expense payments
- **bank transactions**
  - all receipts by cheque and bank transfer (or payment of cash into the bank)
  - all payments by cheque or bank transfer (or withdrawal of cash from the bank)

The main cash book is usually controlled by a **cashier** who:

- records receipts and payments by cheque and in cash
- makes cash payments, and prepares cheques and BACS payments for signature and authorisation
- pays cash and cheques received into the bank
- has control over the firm's cash, either in a cash till or cash box
- checks the accuracy of the cash and bank balances at regular intervals

It is important to note that transactions passing through the cash book must be supported by **documentary evidence**. In this way an audit trail is established which provides a link that can be checked and followed through the accounting system:

- source document
- subsidiary book
- double-entry accounts

Such an audit trail is required both as a security feature within the business (to help to ensure that fraudulent transactions cannot be made), and also for taxation purposes.

The **cashier** has an important role to play within the accounting function of a business – most business activities will, at some point, involve cash or cheque transactions. Thus the main cash book and the cashier are at the hub of the accounting system. In particular, the cashier is responsible for:

- issuing receipts for cash (and sometimes cheques) received
- making authorised payments in cash and by cheque against documents received (such as invoices and statements) showing the amounts due

At all times, payments can only be made by the cashier when authorised to do so by the appropriate person within the organisation, eg the accountant or the purchasing manager.

With so many transactions passing through the main cash book, accounting procedures must include:

- security – of cash and cheque books, correct authorisation of payments
- confidentiality – that all cash/bank transactions, including cash and bank balances, are kept confidential

If the cashier has any queries about any transactions, he or she should refer them to the accounts supervisor.

LAYOUT OF THE MAIN CASH BOOK

Although a cash book can be set out in many formats to suit the requirements of a particular business, a common format is the columnar cash book. This is set out like other double-entry accounts, with debit and credit sides, but there may be several money columns on each side. An example of a three column cash book (three money columns on each side) is shown below:

Dr					Cash Book						Cr
Date	Details	Ref	Discount allowed	Cash	Bank	Date	Details	Ref	Discount received	Cash	Bank
			£	£	£				£	£	£

Note the following points:

- The debit side is used for receipts.
- The credit side is used for payments.
- On both the debit and credit sides there are separate money columns for cash receipts/payments and bank receipts/payments.
- A third money column on each side is used to record cash discount (that is, an allowance offered for quick settlement of the amount due, eg 2% cash discount for settlement within seven days).
- The discount column on the debit side is for discount allowed to customers.
- The discount column on the credit side is for discount received from suppliers.
- The discount columns are not part of the double-entry book-keeping system – they are used in the cash book as a listing device or memorandum column. As we will see in the worked example which follows, the discount columns are totalled at the end of the week or month, and the totals are then transferred into the double-entry system.
- The reference column is used to cross-reference to the other entry in the ledger system.

WORKED EXAMPLE: TRANSACTIONS IN THE MAIN CASH BOOK

We will now look at some example transactions and then see how the three-column cash book is balanced at the month-end. The year is 20-7.

The transactions to be entered in the cash book are:

1 April	Balances at start of month: cash £300, bank £550
4 April	Received a cheque from S Wright for £98 – we have allowed her £2 cash discount
7 April	Paid a cheque to S Crane for £145 – he has allowed £5 cash discount
11 April	Paid wages in cash £275
14 April	Paid by cheque the account of T Lewis £120, deducting 2.5% cash discount
17 April	J Jones settles in cash her account of £80, deducting 5% cash discount
21 April	Withdrew £100 in cash from the bank for use in the business
23 April	Received a cheque for £45 from D Whiteman in full settlement of her account of £48
28 April	Paid cash of £70 to S Ford in full settlement of our account of £75

All cheques are banked on the day of receipt.

The main cash book records these transactions (as shown below) and, after they have been entered, is balanced on 30 April. (The other part of each double-entry book-keeping transaction is not shown here, but has to be carried out in order to record the transactions correctly.)

Dr						**Cash Book**					Cr
Date	Details	Ref	Discount allowed	Cash	Bank	Date	Details	Ref	Discount received	Cash	Bank
			£	£	£				£	£	£
20-7						20-7					
1 Apr	Balances b/d			300	550	7 Apr	S Crane		5		145
4 Apr	S Wright		2		98	11 Apr	Wages			275	
17 Apr	J Jones		4	76		14 Apr	T Lewis		3		117
21 Apr	Bank	C		100		21 Apr	Cash	C			100
23 Apr	D Whiteman		3		45	28 Apr	S Ford		5	70	
						30 Apr	Balances c/d			131	331
			9	476	693				13	476	693
1 May	Balances b/d			131	331						

Note that the transaction on 21 April (£100 withdrawn from the bank for use in the business) involves a transfer of money between cash and bank. As each transaction is both a receipt and a payment within the cash book, it is usual to indicate both of them in the reference column with a 'C' – this stands for 'contra' and shows that both parts of the transaction are in the same book.

BALANCING THE MAIN CASH BOOK

We saw in Chapter 5 how accounts are balanced. The main cash book is the ledger for cash account and bank account, and the procedure for balancing these is exactly the same as for other ledger accounts.

The cash book in the worked example on the previous page is balanced in the following way:

- subtotal the two cash columns (ie £476 in the debit column, and £345 in the credit column)
- deduct the lower total from the higher (payments from receipts) to give the balance of cash remaining (£476 – £345 = £131)
- the higher total is recorded at the bottom of both cash columns in a totals 'box' (£476)
- the balance of cash remaining (£131) is entered as a balancing item above the totals box (on the credit side), and is brought down underneath the total on the debit side as the opening balance for next month (£131)
- the two bank columns are dealt with in the same way (£693 – £362 = £331)

Notice that, in the cash book shown above, the cash and bank balances have been brought down on the debit side. It may happen that the balance at bank is brought down on the credit side: this occurs when payments exceed receipts, and indicates a bank overdraft. It is very important to appreciate that the bank columns of the cash book represent the firm's own records of bank transactions and the balance at bank – the bank statement may well show different figures (see the next chapter, Chapter 8).

A cash balance can only be brought down on the debit side, indicating the amount of cash held.

At the end of the month, each discount column is totalled separately – no attempt should be made to balance them. At this point, amounts recorded in the columns and the totals are not part of the double-entry system. However, the two totals are transferred to the double-entry system as follows:

- the total on the debit side (£9 in the example above) is debited to discount allowed account in the general (or nominal) ledger
- the total on the credit side (£13 in the example) is credited to discount received account, also in the general (or nominal) ledger

The opposite book-keeping entries will have already been entered in the debtors' and creditors' accounts respectively (see Chapter 4). The accounts appear as follows:

Dr		Discount Allowed Account			Cr
20-7		£	20-7		£
30 Apr	Cash Book	9			

Dr		Discount Received Account			Cr
20-7		£	20-7		£
			30 Apr	Cash Book	13

The two discount accounts represent an expense and income respectively and, at the end of the firm's financial year, the totals of the two accounts will be used in the calculation of profit. Where control accounts (see Chapter 11) are in use, the total of discount allowed is credited to the sales ledger control account, while the total of discount received is debited to the purchases ledger control account.

THE MAIN CASH BOOK AS A SUBSIDIARY BOOK

The main cash book performs two functions within the accounting system:

- it is a subsidiary book for cash/bank transactions
- it forms part of the double-entry book-keeping system

The diagram below shows the flow involving:

- source documents – cash and bank receipts and payments
- the cash book as a subsidiary book
- double-entry book-keeping, involving cash book and other ledgers (note that the main cash book is located in the general ledger)

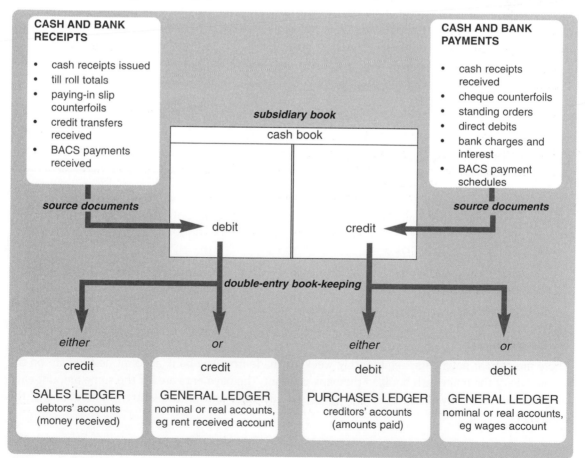

CHECKING THE MAIN CASH BOOK

As the cash book forms such an integral part of a firm's book-keeping system, it is essential that transactions are recorded accurately and that balances are calculated correctly at regular intervals, eg weekly or monthly – depending on the needs of the business. How can the cash book be checked for accuracy?

cash columns

To check the cash columns is easy. It is simply a matter of counting the cash in the cash till or box, and agreeing it with the balance shown by the cash book. In the example in the worked example on page 95, there should be £131 in the firm's cash till at 30 April 20-7. If the cash cannot be agreed in this way, the discrepancy needs to be investigated urgently.

bank columns

How are these to be checked? We could, perhaps, enquire at the bank and ask for the balance at the month-end, or we could arrange for a bank statement to be sent to us at the end of each month. However, the balance of the account at the bank may well not agree with that shown by the bank columns of the cash book. There are several reasons why there may be a difference: for example, a cheque that has been written out recently to pay a bill may not yet have been recorded on the bank statement, ie it has been entered in the cash book, but is not yet on the bank statement. To agree the bank statement and the bank columns of the cash book, it is usually necessary to prepare a bank reconciliation statement, and this topic is dealt with fully in the next chapter, Chapter 8.

BANK RECEIPTS AND PAYMENTS

In writing up the receipts and payments columns of the cash book we come across a number of banking terms that are commonly used (and also commonly examined!). These are:

- standing orders
- direct debits
- credit transfers
- bank charges

standing orders

There are regular payments – eg monthly, weekly – made from the bank account (ie they are on the credit side of the main cash book, in the bank column). The payments are for the same amount each time and are made by the bank on behalf of the customer and on the written instructions of the customer.

direct debits

These are payments (ie credit side of the cash book, in the bank column) made from the bank for the customer. It is the payee, or beneficiary, who originates the payment on the written instructions of the customer. Direct debits are often used where money amounts to be paid vary, and where the payments dates alter.

credit transfers

These can be either receipts or payments – ie the debit and credit side of the cash book (bank columns) respectively. Receipts are from customers who have paid the amount due, through the banking system, directly into the bank account of the payee. Payments are to suppliers, or to employees for wages, and go into the bank account of the payees. Most credit transfers are made by BACS (Bankers Automated Clearing Services) computer transfer. In order to make these payments, it is necessary to have the bank account details – account number, sort code of bank – of the payee.

bank charges and interest

Bank charges are made by the bank for services provided. Charges are usually calculated in relation to the number of transactions – eg cheques written, amounts paid in – during the period. As a payment from bank account, bank charges are on the credit side of the cash book.

In addition to bank charges, a bank will make a separate charge for interest on overdrafts and loans which have been provided to the customer.

The source document for bank charges and interest is the bank statement.

CHAPTER SUMMARY

- The main cash book records receipts (debits) and payments (credits) both in cash (except for low-value expense payments) and by cheque.

- A basic layout for a cash book has money columns for cash transactions and bank transactions on both the debit and credit sides, together with a further column on each side for discounts.

- In the discount columns are recorded cash discounts: discounts allowed (to customers) on the debit side, and discounts received (from suppliers) on the payments side.

- Banking terms commonly used are: standing orders, direct debits, credit transfers and bank charges.

In the next chapter we will see how bank reconciliation statements are prepared in order to agree the balance of the bank columns in the cash book with the bank statement balance.

QUESTIONS

visit
www.osbornebooks.co.uk
to take an online test

An asterisk (*) after the question number means that the answer is given at the end of this book.

7.1* You work as the cashier for Wyvern Publishing, a company which publishes a wide range of travel and historical books. As cashier, your main responsibility is for the firm's cash book. Explain to a friend what your job involves and the qualities required of a cashier.

7.2* Walter Harrison is a sole trader who records his cash and bank transactions in a three-column cash book. The following are the transactions for June 20-2:

1 June	Balances: cash £280; bank overdraft £2,240
3 June	Received a cheque from G Wheaton for £195, in full settlement of a debt of £200
5 June	Received cash of £53 from T Francis, in full settlement of a debt of £55
8 June	Paid the amount owing to F Lloyd by cheque: the total amount due is £400 and Harrison takes advantage of a 2.5% per cent cash discount
10 June	Paid wages in cash £165
12 June	Paid A Morris in cash, £100 less 3 per cent cash discount
16 June	Withdrew £200 in cash from the bank for use in the business
18 June	Received a cheque for £640 from H Watson in full settlement of a debt of £670
20 June	Paid R Marks £78 by cheque
24 June	Paid D Farr £65 by cheque, in full settlement of a debt of £67
26 June	Paid telephone account £105 in cash
28 June	Received a cheque from M Perry in settlement of his account of £240 – he has deducted 2.5% per cent cash discount
30 June	Received cash £45 from K Willis

You are to:

(a) enter the above transactions in Walter Harrison's three column cash book, balance the cash and bank columns, and carry the balances down to 1 July

(b) total the two discount columns and transfer them to the appropriate accounts

7.3

On 1 August 20-7, the balances in the cash book of Metro Trading Company were:

Cash £276 debit
Bank £4,928 debit

Transactions for the month were:

1 Aug Received a cheque from Wild & Sons Limited, £398

5 Aug Paid T Hall Limited a cheque for £541 in full settlement of a debt of £565

8 Aug Paid wages in cash £254

11 Aug Withdrew £500 in cash from the bank for use in the business

12 Aug Received a cheque for £1,755 from A Lewis Limited in full settlement of their account of £1,775

18 Aug Paid F Jarvis £457 by cheque

21 Aug Received a cheque for £261 from Harvey & Sons Limited

22 Aug Paid wages in cash £436

25 Aug Paid J Jones a cheque for £628 in full settlement of a debt of £661

27 Aug Paid salaries by cheque £2,043

28 Aug Paid telephone account by cheque £276

29 Aug Received a cheque for £595 from Wild & Sons Limited in full settlement of their account of £610

29 Aug Withdrew £275 in cash from the bank for use in the business

All cheques are banked on the day of receipt.

REQUIRED

• Enter the above transactions in the three column cash book of Metro Trading Company.

• Balance the cash and bank columns at 31 August, and carry the balances down to September 1st.

• Total the two discount columns.

7.4

Tom Singh keeps a three-column cash book for his business. The following information relates to the month of March 20-5:

20-5

1 March Balances of cash and bank were £106 and £3,214 respectively

2 March Drew cheque no 10674 for rent of £250

3 March Sales £1,050. Banked £950 of this on the same day

5 March Paid cleaning expenses of £35 from cash

8 March   Sales banked £1,680

9 March   Drew cheque no 10675 for purchases costing £1,200

11 March   Drew cheque no 10676 for £150, to replenish cash in hand

13 March   Sales banked £1,800

16 March   Paid postage of £50 from cash

18 March   Drew cheque no 10677 for £168, to pay a telephone bill

20 March   Paid Stationery of £128 from cash

22 March   Drew cheque no 10678 for £150, to replenish cash in hand

25 March   Sales banked £2,108

26 March   Paid miscellaneous expenses of £70 from cash

27 March   Drew cheque no 10679 for £2,000, to pay wages

29 March   Sales £2,200. Banked £2,000 of this on the same day

30 March   Drew cheque no 10680 for £106, to pay an electricity bill

31 March   Drew cheque no 10681 for £855 payable to Evans & Co, in settlement of a debt of £900

31 March   Drew cheque no 10682 for £494 payable to A Bennett, in settlement of a debt of £520

31 March   Received cheque for £720 from Hobbs Ltd, in settlement of an amount of £750

31 March   Received cheque for £1,160 from Pratley & Co, in settlement of an amount of £1,210

REQUIRED

Write up the three-column cash book, bringing down the balances at 1 April 20-5.

7.5* The following items have yet to be recorded in the cash book of J A Summerfield for the first week in January 2002:

		£	
1 January	Balance in cash account	50.00	
1 January	Overdrawn bank balance	263.67	
	Cheque counterfoils show:	£	
3 January	J B Smith Ltd (cash discount taken – £4.00)	120.00	cheque amount
4 January	A E Evans Ltd	146.59	cheque amount
5 January	K L M Spares (cash discount taken – £3.96)	127.45	cheque amount
6 January	PCB Limited	45.67	cheque amount
	Paying-in counterfoils show:		
3 January	M S Supplies	136.98	amount banked
4 January	J O Jones (cash discount taken – £4.67)	246.89	amount banked

The following additional items should also be recorded in the cash book:

	£
The bank statement shows:	
Direct debit payment Shop Insurances plc	100.00
Credit transfer received ABC Traders	120.56
Bank charges	23.98
Bank interest paid	46.97
The week's till rolls show:	
Cash receipts total of	467.23
There were cash payments of:	
Part time wages	40.00
Postage stamps	27.00

It is the business's policy to retain a cash float of £50 at the end of each week and pay the rest of the cash into the bank. This was done on 7 January 2002.

REQUIRED

(a)   Record this information in the cash book below and balance the cash book at 7 January 2002.

Dr					Cash Book of J A Summerfield					Cr
Date	Details	Disc't allowed £	Cash £	Bank £	Date	Details	Disc't rec'd £	Cash £	Bank £	
2002					2002					
Jan					Jan					

(b)   What method or technique can be used to verify:

(i)   the cash balance ....

....

(ii)   the bank balance* ....

....

* see Chapter 8

Assessment and Qualifications Alliance (AQA), 2002

7.6

Explain the meaning of the following items which have been found in the bank statement received by R Masters for his business and give the ledger entries for them.

(i)   Standing order

Explanation ....

....

....

....

Account to be debited ....

Account to be credited ....

(ii)   Credit transfer for payment by a customer

Explanation ....

....

....

....

Account to be debited ....

Account to be credited ....

Assessment and Qualifications Alliance (AQA), 2002

7.7*

Complete the following table by filling in the blank boxes. The first entry has been completed as an example.

	Source document	Subsidiary book	Ledger account to be debited	Ledger account to be credited
Sold goods on credit to a customer	Sales invoice	Sales day book	Debtors/Sales ledger control account*	Sales
Faulty goods returned to the supplier		Purchases returns day book	Creditors/Purchases ledger control account*	Purchases returns
Cash sales paid into the bank		Cash book		
Charges made by the bank		Cash book	Bank charges	
Purchase of office stationery, paid for by cheque				

* see Chapter 11

7.8 Usman Khan uses a three-column cash book as part of his double-entry bookkeeping system. The following details relate to January 2006.

January		£
1	Balance in cash account	50
	Overdrawn bank balance	1,236
2	Cheque paid to Bilton Office Supplies in settlement of an invoice for £167	164
6	Cheque from R Reed paid into bank	567
11	Paid rent by cheque	450
13	Cheque from B Brown paid into bank. Discount of £4 had been taken by the customer	366
14	Cash sales	752
27	Paid wages of part-time employee in cash	75
28	Cash sales	642

A bank statement received on 28 January revealed the following additional items.

20	Standing order to British Gas	200
21	Interest charged by bank	28
24	Credit transfer from C Denton and Co Ltd	248

On 31 January, all cash in hand, except a float of £50, was paid into the bank.

REQUIRED

(a) Prepare the cash book, below, for the month of January 2006 from the information provided above.

(b) Balance the cash book at the end of the month and bring down the balances at 1 February 2006.

(c) Post the discounts to the general ledger accounts shown on the next page.

Dr	Usman Khan Cash Book									Cr
Date 2006	Details	Discount £	Cash £	Bank £	Date 2006	Details		Discount £	Cash £	Bank £

Dr	Discounts Allowed Account				Cr
Date 2006	Details	£	Date 2006	Details	£

Dr	Discounts Received Account				Cr
Date 2006	Details	£	Date 2006	Details	£

Assessment and Qualifications Alliance (AQA), 2006

8 BANK RECONCILIATION STATEMENTS

Bank reconciliation statements form the link between the balance at bank shown in the main cash book of a firm's book-keeping system and the balance shown on the bank statement received from the bank.

The reasons why the cash book and bank statement may differ are because:
● there are timing differences caused by:
  – unpresented cheques, ie the time delay between writing out (drawing) a cheque and recording it in the cash book, and the cheque being entered on the bank statement
  – outstanding lodgements, ie amounts paid into the bank, but not yet recorded on the bank statement
● the cash book has not been updated with items which appear on the bank statement and which should also appear in the cash book, eg bank charges

Assuming that there are no errors, both cash book and bank statement are correct, but need to be reconciled with each other, ie the closing balances need to be agreed.

TIMING DIFFERENCES

The two main timing differences between the bank columns of the main cash book and the bank statement are:

* **unpresented cheques**, ie cheques issued, not yet recorded on the bank statement
* **outstanding lodgements**, ie amounts paid into the bank, not yet recorded on the bank statement

The first of these – unpresented cheques – is caused because, when a cheque is written out, it is immediately entered on the payments side of the cash book, even though it may be some days before the cheque passes through the bank clearing system and is recorded on the bank statement. Therefore, for a few days at least, the cash book shows a lower balance than the bank statement in respect of this cheque. When the cheque is recorded on the bank statement, the difference will disappear. We have looked at only one cheque here, but a business will often be issuing many cheques each day, and the difference between the cash book balance and the bank statement balance may be considerable.

With the second timing difference – outstanding lodgements – the firm's cashier will record a receipt in the cash book as he or she prepares the bank paying-in slip. However, the receipt may not be recorded by the bank on the bank statement for a day or so, particularly if it is paid in late in the day (when the bank will put it into the next day's work), or if it is paid in at a bank branch other than the one at which the account is maintained. Until the receipt is recorded by the bank the cash book will show a higher bank account balance than the bank statement. Once the receipt is entered on the bank statement, the difference will disappear.

These two timing differences are involved in the calculation known as the bank reconciliation statement. The business cash book must not be altered for these because, as we have seen, they will correct themselves on the bank statement as time goes by.

UPDATING THE MAIN CASH BOOK

Besides the timing differences described above, there may be other differences between the bank columns of the cash book and the bank statement, and these do need to be entered in the main cash book to bring it up-to-date. For example, the bank might make an automatic standing order payment on behalf of a business – such an item is correctly debited by the bank, and it might be that the bank statement acts as a reminder to the business cashier of the payment: it should then be entered in the main cash book.

Examples of items that show in the bank statement and need to be entered in the main cash book include:

receipts

- credit transfers (BACS – Bankers Automated Clearing Services) amounts received by the bank, eg payments from debtors (customers)
- dividend amounts received by the bank
- interest credited by the bank

payments

- standing order and direct debit payments
- bank charges and interest
- unpaid cheques debited by the bank (ie cheques from debtors paid in by the business which have 'bounced' and are returned by the bank marked 'refer to drawer')

For each of these items, the cashier needs to check to see if they have been entered in the main cash book; if not, they need to be recorded (provided that the bank has not made an error). If the bank has made an error, it must be notified as soon as possible and the incorrect transactions reversed by the bank in its own accounting records.

THE BANK RECONCILIATION STATEMENT

This forms the link between the balances shown in the main cash book and the bank statement.

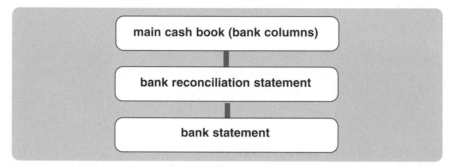

Upon receipt of a bank statement, reconciliation of the two balances is carried out in the following way:

- tick off the items that appear in both cash book and bank statement
- the unticked items on the bank statement are entered into the bank columns of the cash book to bring it up-to-date (provided none are errors made by the bank)
- the bank columns of the main cash book are now balanced to find the revised figure
- the remaining unticked items from the cash book will be the timing differences
- the timing differences are used to prepare the bank reconciliation statement, which takes the following format (with example figures):

XYZ TRADING LTD
Bank Reconciliation Statement as at 31 October 20-1

		£	£
Balance at bank as per cash book			525
Add: unpresented cheques			
J Lewis	cheque no. 0012378	60	
ABC Ltd	cheque no. 0012392	100	
Eastern Oil Company	cheque no. 0012407	80	
			240
			765
Less: outstanding lodgements		220	
		300	
			520
Balance at bank as per bank statement			245

Notes:

- The layout shown on the opposite page starts from the cash book balance, and works towards the bank statement balance. A common variation of this layout is to start with the bank statement balance and to work towards the cash book balance (see page 114).

- If a bank overdraft is involved, brackets should be used around the numbers to indicate this for the cash book or bank statement balance. The timing differences are still added or deducted, as appropriate.

- Once the bank reconciliation statement agrees, it should be filed because it proves that the cash book (bank columns) and bank statement were reconciled at a particular date. If, next time it is prepared, it fails to agree, the previous statement is proof that reconciliation was reached at that time.

WORKED EXAMPLE: BANK RECONCILIATION STATEMENT

The cashier of Severn Trading Co has written up the firm's main cash book for the month of February 20-2, as follows (the cheque number is shown against payments):

Dr					**Cash Book**					Cr
Date	Details		Cash	Bank	Date	Details		Cash	Bank	
20-2			£	£	20-2			£	£	
1 Feb	Balances b/d		250.75	1,340.50	3 Feb	Appleton Ltd 123456			675.25	
7 Feb	A Abbott			208.50	5 Feb	Wages		58.60		
10 Feb	Sales		145.25		12 Feb	Rent 123457			125.00	
13 Feb	Sales		278.30		14 Feb	Transfer to bank	C	500.00		
14 Feb	Transfer from cash	C		500.00	17 Feb	D Smith & Co 123458			421.80	
20 Feb	Sales		204.35		24 Feb	Stationery		75.50		
21 Feb	D Richards Limited			162.30	25 Feb	G Christie 123459			797.55	
26 Feb	Sales		353.95		27 Feb	Transfer to bank	C	500.00		
27 Feb	Transfer from cash	C		500.00	28 Feb	Balances c/d		98.50	954.00	
28 Feb	P Paul Limited			262.30						
			1,232.60	2,973.60				1,232.60	2,973.60	
1 Mar	Balances b/d		98.50	954.00						

The cash balance of £98.50 shown by the cash columns on 1 March has been agreed with the cash held in the firm's cash box.

The bank statement for February 20-2, which has just been received, is shown on the next page.

National Bank plc

Branch ..Bartown..............

TITLE OF ACCOUNT ...Severn Trading Company.................

ACCOUNT NUMBER ..67812318.........................

STATEMENT NUMBER 45

DATE	PARTICULARS	PAYMENTS	RECEIPTS	BALANCE
20-2		£	£	£
1 Feb	Balance brought forward			1340.50 CR
8 Feb	Credit		208.50	1549.00 CR
10 Feb	Cheque no. 123456	675.25		873.75 CR
17 Feb	Credit		500.00	1373.75 CR
17 Feb	Cheque no. 123457	125.00		1248.75 CR
24 Feb	Credit		162.30	1411.05 CR
24 Feb	BACS credit: J Jarvis Ltd		100.00	1511.05 CR
26 Feb	Cheque no. 123458	421.80		1089.25 CR
26 Feb	Direct debit: A-Z Finance	150.00		939.25 CR
28 Feb	Credit		500.00	1439.25 CR
28 Feb	Bank charges	10.00		1429.25 CR

Note that the bank statement is prepared from the bank's viewpoint: thus a credit balance shows that the customer is a creditor of the bank, ie the bank owes the balance to the customer. In the customer's own cash book, the bank is shown as a debit balance, ie an asset.

As the month-end balance at bank shown by the cash book, £954.00, is not the same as that shown by the bank statement, £1,429.25, it is necessary to prepare a bank reconciliation statement. The steps are:

1   Tick off the items that appear in both cash book and bank statement.

2   The unticked items on the bank statement are entered into the bank columns of the cash book to bring it up-to-date. These are:

-   receipt   24 Feb   BACS credit, J Jarvis Limited £100.00
-   payments   26 Feb   Direct debit, A-Z Finance £150.00
                              28 Feb   Bank Charges, £10.00

In double-entry book-keeping, the other part of the transaction will need to be recorded in the accounts, eg in J Jarvis Ltd's account in the sales ledger, etc.

3   The cash book is now balanced to find the revised balance:

Dr		Cash Book (bank columns)			Cr
20-2		£	20-2		
	Balance b/d	954.00	26 Feb	A-Z Finance	150.00
24 Feb	J Jarvis Ltd	100.00	28 Feb	Bank Charges	10.00
			28 Feb	Balance c/d	894.00
		1,054.00			1,054.00
1 Mar	Balance b/d	894.00			

4 The remaining unticked items from the cash book are used in the bank reconciliation statement:

- receipt 28 Feb – P Paul Limited £262.30
- payment 25 Feb – G Christie (cheque no 123459) £797.55

These items are timing differences, which should appear on next month's bank statement.

5 The bank reconciliation statement is now prepared, starting with the re-calculated cash book balance of £894.00.

SEVERN TRADING CO.

Bank Reconciliation Statement as at 28 February 20-2

	£
Balance at bank as per cash book	894.00
Add: unpresented cheque, no. 123459	797.55
	1,691.55
Less: outstanding lodgement, P Paul Limited	262.30
Balance at bank as per bank statement	1,429.25

With the above, a statement has been produced which starts with the amended balance from the cash book, and finishes with the bank statement balance, ie the two figures are reconciled.

Notes:

- The unpresented cheque is added back to the cash book balance because, until it is recorded by the bank, the cash book shows a lower balance than the bank statement.
- The outstanding lodgement is deducted from the cash book balance because, until it is recorded by the bank, the cash book shows a higher balance than the bank statement.

PREPARING A BANK RECONCILIATION STATEMENT

In order to help you with the questions at the end of the chapter, here is a step-by-step summary of the procedure. Reconciliation of the cash book balance with that shown in the bank statement should be carried out in the following way:

1 From the bank columns of the main cash book tick off, in both cash book and bank statement, the receipts that appear in both.

2 From the bank columns of the main cash book tick off, in both cash book and bank statement, the payments that appear in both.

3 Identify the items that are unticked on the bank statement and enter them in the cash book on the debit or credit side, as appropriate. If, however, the bank has made a mistake and debited or credited an amount in error, this should not be entered in the cash book, but should be notified to the bank for them to make the correction. The amount will need to be entered on the bank reconciliation statement – see section below, dealing with unusual items on bank statements: bank errors.

4   The bank columns of the cash book are now balanced to find the up-to-date balance.

5   Start the bank reconciliation statement with the balance brought down figure shown in the cash book.

6   In the bank reconciliation statement add the unticked payments shown in the cash book – these will be unpresented cheques.

7   In the bank reconciliation statement, deduct the unticked receipts shown in the cash book – these are outstanding lodgements.

8   The resultant money amount on the bank reconciliation statement is the balance of the bank statement.

The layout which is often used for the bank reconciliation statement is that shown on page 110. The layout starts with the cash book balance and finishes with the bank statement balance. However, there is no reason why it should not commence with the bank statement balance and finish with the cash book balance. With this layout it is necessary to:

*   deduct unpresented cheques

*   add outstanding lodgements

The bank reconciliation statement of Severn Trading Company (see previous page) would then appear as:

SEVERN TRADING COMPANY
Bank Reconciliation Statement as at 28 February 20-2

	£
Balance at bank as per bank statement	1,429.25
Less: unpresented cheque, no 123459	797.55
	631.70
Add: outstanding lodgement, P Paul Limited	262.30
Balance at bank as per cash book	894.00

DEALING WITH UNUSUAL ITEMS ON BANK STATEMENTS

The following are some of the unusual features that may occur on bank statements. As with other accounting discrepancies and queries, where they cannot be resolved they should be referred to a supervisor for guidance.

out-of-date cheques

These are cheques that are more than six months' old. Where a business has a number of out-of-date – or 'stale' – cheques which have not been debited on the bank statement, they will continue to appear on the bank reconciliation statement. As the bank will not pay these cheques, they can be written back in the cash book, ie debit cash book (and credit the other double-entry account involved).

returned cheques

A cheque received by a business is entered as a receipt in the cash book and then paid into the bank, but it may be returned ('bounced') by the drawer's bank because:

- the drawer (the issuer) has instructed the bank to 'stop' the cheque
- the cheque has been returned by the bank, either because the drawer has no money (a 'dishonoured' cheque) or because there is a technical problem with the cheque, eg it is not signed

A cheque returned ('bounced') in this way should be entered in the book-keeping system:

- as a payment in the cash book on the credit side
- as a debit to the debtor's account in the sales ledger (if it is a credit sale), or sales account if it is a cash sale

bank errors

Errors made by the bank can include:

- A cheque deducted from the bank account which has not been issued by the business – look for a cheque number on the bank statement that is different from the current cheque series. Care should be taken, however, as it could be a cheque from an old cheque book.
- A BACS payment (or other credit) shown on the bank statement for which the business is not the correct recipient. If in doubt, the bank will be able to give further details of the sender of the credit.
- Standing orders and direct debits paid at the wrong time or for the wrong amounts. A copy of all standing order and direct debit mandates sent to the bank should be kept by the business for reference purposes.

When an error is found, it should be queried immediately with the bank. The item and amount should not be entered in the firm's cash book until the issue has been resolved. If, in the meantime, a bank reconciliation statement is to be prepared, the bank error should be shown separately:

- if working from the cash book balance to the bank statement balance, deduct payments and add receipts that the bank has applied to the account incorrectly
- if working from the bank statement balance to the cash book balance, add payments and deduct receipts that the bank has applied to the account incorrectly

bank charges and interest

From time-to-time the bank will debit business customers' accounts with an amount for:

- service charges, ie the cost of operating the bank account
- interest, ie the borrowing cost when the business is overdrawn

Banks usually notify customers in writing before debiting the account.

reconciliation of opening cash book and bank statement balances

If you look back to the example on page 111, you will see that both the cash book (bank columns) and the bank statement balance both started the month with the same balance: 1 February 20-2 £1,340.50.

In reality, it is unlikely that the opening cash book and bank statement balances will be the same. It will be necessary, in these circumstances, to prepare an opening bank reconciliation statement in order to prove that there are no errors between cash book and bank statement at the start of the month.

This is set out in the same format as the end-of-month bank reconciliation statement, and is best prepared immediately after ticking off the items that appear in both cash book and bank statement. The earliest unpresented cheques drawn and outstanding lodgements will comprise the opening bank reconciliation statement. Of course, where last month's bank reconciliation statement is available, such as in business, there is no need to prepare an opening reconciliation.

In your AS examination there will be no need to prepare a formal opening bank reconciliation statement, unless the question calls for one. Any discrepancy in opening balances can be resolved quickly by checking the bank statement for the earliest receipts and payments.

IMPORTANCE OF BANK RECONCILIATION STATEMENTS

- A bank reconciliation statement is important because, in its preparation, the transactions in the bank columns of the main cash book are compared with those recorded on the bank statement. In this way, any errors in the cash book or bank statement will be found and can be corrected (or advised to the bank, if the bank statement is wrong).

- The bank statement is an independent accounting record, therefore it will assist in deterring fraud by providing a means of verifying the cash book balance.

- By writing the cash book up-to-date, the organisation has an amended figure for the bank balance to be shown in the trial balance.

- Unpresented cheques over six months old – out-of-date cheques – can be identified and written back in the cash book (any cheque dated more than six months' ago will not be paid by the bank).

- It is good practice to prepare a bank reconciliation statement each time a bank statement is received. The reconciliation statement should be prepared as quickly as possible so that any queries – either with the bank statement or in the firm's cash book – can be resolved. Many firms will specify to their accounting staff the timescales for preparing bank reconciliation statements – as a guideline, if the bank statement is received weekly, then the reconciliation statement should be prepared within five working days.

CHAPTER SUMMARY

● A bank reconciliation statement is used to agree the balance shown by the bank columns of the main cash book with that shown by the bank statement.

● Certain differences between the two are timing differences. The main timing differences are:
  – unpresented cheques
  – outstanding lodgements

  These differences will be corrected by time and, most probably, will be recorded on the next bank statement.

● Certain differences appearing on the bank statement need to be entered in the cash book to bring it up-to-date. These include:

  Receipts   – credit transfers (BACS) amounts received by the bank
              – dividend amounts received by the bank
              – interest credited by the bank

  Payments   – standing order and direct debit payments
              – bank charges and interest
              – unpaid cheques debited by the bank

● The bank reconciliation statement makes use of the timing differences.

● Once prepared, a bank reconciliation statement is proof that the bank statement and the cash book (bank columns) were agreed at a particular date.

In the next chapter we will see how the general journal is used as a subsidiary book, including recording the book-keeping transfers to correct errors.

QUESTIONS

visit
www.osbornebooks.co.uk
to take an online test

An asterisk (*) after the question number means that the answer is given at the end of this book.

8.1* The bank columns of Tom Reid's cash book for December 20-7 are as follows:

20-7	Receipts		£	20-7	Payments		£
1 Dec	Balance b/d		280	9 Dec	W Smith	345123	40
12 Dec	P Jones		30	12 Dec	Rent	345124	50
18 Dec	H Homer		72	18 Dec	Wages	345125	85
29 Dec	J Hill		13	19 Dec	B Kay	345126	20
				31 Dec	Balance c/d		200
			395				395

He then received his bank statement which showed the following transactions for December 20-7:

BANK STATEMENT		Payments	Receipts	Balance
20-7		£	£	£
1 Dec	Balance brought forward			280 CR
12 Dec	Credit		30	310 CR
15 Dec	Cheque no. 345123	40		270 CR
17 Dec	Cheque no. 345124	50		220 CR
22 Dec	Credit		72	292 CR
23 Dec	Cheque no. 345125	85		207 CR

You are to prepare a bank reconciliation statement which agrees with the bank statement balance.

8.2 The bank columns of P Gerrard's cash book for January 20-7 are as follows:

20-7	Receipts	£	20-7	Payments		£
1 Jan	Balance b/d	800.50	2 Jan	A Arthur Ltd	001351	100.00
6 Jan	J Baker	495.60	10 Jan	C Curtis	001352	398.50
31 Jan	G Shotton Ltd	335.75	13 Jan	Donald & Co	001353	229.70
			14 Jan	Bryant & Sons	001354	312.00
			23 Jan	P Reid	001355	176.50
			31 Jan	Balance c/d		415.15
		1,631.85				1,631.85

He received his bank statement which showed the following transactions for January 20-7:

BANK STATEMENT		Payments	Receipts	Balance
20-7		£	£	£
1 Jan	Balance brought forward			800.50 CR
6 Jan	Cheque no. 001351	100.00		700.50 CR
6 Jan	Credit		495.60	1,196.10 CR
13 Jan	BACS credit: T K Supplies		716.50	1,912.60 CR
20 Jan	Cheque no. 001352	398.50		1,514.10 CR
23 Jan	Direct debit: Omni Finance	207.95		1,306.15 CR
24 Jan	Cheque no. 001353	229.70		1,076.45 CR

You are to:

(a)   write the cash book up-to-date at 31 January 20-7

(b)   prepare a bank reconciliation statement at 31 January 20-7

8.3

The bank columns of Jane Doyle's cash book for May 20-7 are as follows:

20-7	Receipts	£	20-7	Payments		£
1 May	Balance b/d	300	2 May	P Stone	867714	28
7 May	Cash	162	14 May	Alpha Ltd	867715	50
16 May	C Brewster	89	29 May	E Deakin	867716	110
23 May	Cash	60				
30 May	Cash	40				

She received her bank statement which showed the following transactions for May 20-7:

	BANK STATEMENT			
		Payments	Receipts	Balance
20-7		£	£	£
1 May	Balance brought forward			400 CR
2 May	Cheque no 867713	100		300 CR
5 May	Cheque no. 867714	28		272 CR
7 May	Credit		162	434 CR
16 May	Standing order: A-Z Insurance	25		409 CR
19 May	Credit		89	498 CR
20 May	Cheque no. 867715	50		448 CR
26 May	Credit		60	508 CR
31 May	Bank Charges	10		498 CR

You are to:

(a)   write the cash book up-to-date at 31 May 20-7

(b)   prepare a bank reconciliation statement at 31 May 20-7

8.4* On 4 June Milestone Motors received a bank statement which showed the following transactions for May 20-4:

BANK STATEMENT		Paid out	Paid in	Balance
20-4		£	£	£
1 May	Balance brought forward			3,652 C
10 May	Cheque no 451762	751		2,901 C
11 May	Cheque no 451763	268		2,633 C
13 May	Cheque no 451765	1,045		1,588 C
14 May	BACS credit: Perran Taxis		2,596	4,184 C
18 May	Direct debit: Wyvern Council	198		3,986 C
20 May	Direct debit: A1 Insurance	1,005		2,981 C
25 May	Direct debit: Okaro and Company	254		2,727 C
25 May	Bank charges	20		2,707 C
D = Debit C = Credit				

The cash book of Milestone Motors as at 31 May 20-4 is shown below:

CASH BOOK

Date	Details	Bank	Date	Cheque no	Details	Bank
20-4		£	20-4			£
1 May	Balance b/f	3,652	4 May	451762	Smith and Company	751
26 May	J Ackland	832	4 May	451763	Bryant Limited	268
28 May	Stamp Limited	1,119	7 May	451764	Curtis Cars	1,895
			7 May	451765	Parts Supplies	1,045

You are to:

(a) check the items on the bank statement against the items in the cash book

(b) update the cash book as needed

(c) total the cash book and show clearly the balance carried down at 31 May and brought down at 1 June

(d) prepare a bank reconciliation statement at 31 May 20-4 which agrees the bank statement balance with the cash book balance

8.5

When reconciling bank statements the adjustments will include entries in the cash book for standing orders, direct debits and credit transfers.

REQUIRED

(a)   Explain what each of these terms means and whether they will be **debited** or **credited** to the bank account in the business's books.

(i)   Standing orders

....

....

....

(ii)   Direct debits

....

....

....

(iii)   Credit transfers

....

....

....

The bank statement received by A Smith and Co shows a debit balance of £600 at 31 March 2001. The accountant checks it against the cash book and makes the following discoveries:

(1)   The bank statement shows the following items **not** shown in the cash book:

•   a standing order for £230 in favour of Planet Insurance;

•   a direct debit payable to Electric Supplies £420;

•   a credit transfer has been received from The Best Co for £540;

•   a cheque for £265 is debited on the bank statement, which A Smith and Co are querying;

•   bank charges of £46 have been levied.

(2)   The cash book has an overdrawn balance of £378 and shows the following items **not** shown on the bank statement:

•   unpresented cheques amounting to £469;

•   uncleared bankings of £270.

REQUIRED

(b)   Make any necessary entries in the cash book.

Dr		**Cash Book – Bank Account**	Cr
	£		£

(c)   Prepare a bank reconciliation as at 31 March 2001.

Assessment and Qualifications Alliance (AQA), 2001

8.6*   Kingdom Carpet Fitters received a bank statement showing the following transactions in their account during December 2005.

Bank Statement

Date	Details	Dr £	Cr £	Balance £
Dec 1	Balance			430 Cr
6	Cheque to F Banks	250		180 Cr
7	Cash and cheques paid in		380	560 Cr
12	Standing order: British Gas	200		360 Cr
18	Credit transfer from J Ball		240	600 Cr
22	Cash and cheques paid in		300	900 Cr
23	Cheque to H Wilton	470		430 Cr
30	Bank charges	20		410 Cr
30	Dishonoured cheque: B Brown	150		260 Cr

REQUIRED

(a)   Update the cash book below with the relevant items from the bank statement, and bring down the balance at the end of the month.

Dr			**Cash Book**			Cr
Date	Details	£	Date	Details		£
Dec 1	Balance b/d	430	Dec 2	F Banks		250
7	Sales banked	380	18	H Wilton		470
22	Sales banked	300	29	M Wall		140
31	Sales banked	560	30	Wages		100

(b)   Prepare a bank reconciliation statement as at 31 December 2005.

(c)   Explain the term 'dishonoured cheque' shown in the bank statement.

Assessment and Qualifications Alliance (AQA), 2006

8.7 On the next page there is a bank statement for the month of November 2003 which has been received by James Jolly and Co. A junior clerk has checked the cash against the bank statement, and has ticked (√) the items that appear in both.

REQUIRED

(a) Update the following cash book on 30 November with any necessary entries and calculate the new balance.

			Cash Book				
Date 2003	Details	Bank £ p		Date 2003	Details	Cheque number	Bank £ p	
Nov 1	Balance b/d	2,459.35		Nov 1	Banks Ltd	11346	134.37	√
Nov 3	Toys for You	234.00	√	Nov 1	Books & Paints	11347	276.89	√
Nov 5	B J Patel	3,219.00	√	Nov 10	Wages	11348	92.50	√
Nov 5	Dolls & Things	1,142.00	√	Nov 12	Jones and Son	11349	3,781.95	√
Nov 23	J A Smith Ltd	560.00	√	Nov 23	Smith and Son	11350	139.43	√
Nov 26	Cash banked	340.00		Nov 25	HGF Finance	11351	256.00	
				Nov 25	Toy Designs	11352	1,245.98	
				Nov 30	Balance c/d		2,027.23	
		7,954.35					7,954.35	
Nov 30	Balance b/d	2,027.23						

WESTBANK LTD   27-43-56

WESTOWN BRANCH   Account 4569823

James Jolly and Co

STATEMENT OF ACCOUNT

Date	Details	Payments		Receipts		Balance
2003		£		£		£
Nov 1	Balance b/f					2,659.35
2	Cheque 345	200.00	√			2,459.35
3	Counter credit			234.00	√	2,693.35
4	Cheque 346	134.37	√			2,558.98
4	Cheque 347	276.89	√			2,282.09
5	Counter credit			4,361.00	√	6,643.09
9	Cr. tfr. J Black Ltd			246.98		6,890.07
12	s/o Business rates	547.90				6,342.17
15	Cheque 349	3,781.95	√			2,560.22
18	s/o Proper Ins Co	145.65				2,414.57
23	Counter credit			560.00	√	2,974.57
23	Bank charges	45.89				2,928.68
27	Cheque 350	139.43	√			2,789.25
27	Cheque 348	92.50	√			2,696.75

Note:
Cr. tfr. = credit transfer
s/o = standing order

(b)   Prepare a bank reconciliation statement as at 30 November 2003.

Assessment and Qualifications Alliance (AQA), 2004

9 INTRODUCTION TO FINAL ACCOUNTS

For most businesses, the final accounts, which are produced at the end of each financial year, comprise:

- trading account, which shows gross profit
- profit and loss account, which shows net profit
- balance sheet, which shows the assets and liabilities of the business at the year-end

This chapter provides an introduction to final accounts, explaining how they fit in with the double-entry book-keeping system. Final accounts will be studied further – both in this Unit (Chapter 12) and in AS Unit 2.

FINAL ACCOUNTS AND THE TRIAL BALANCE

So far we have described the format of financial accounts and the recording of different types of transactions. All that we have covered is usually carried out by the book-keeper. We will now explain how the financial accountant takes to a further stage the information prepared by the book-keeper. The financial accountant will use the information from the accounting system, which is summarised in the trial balance (see Chapter 5), in order to produce the final accounts of a business.

The final accounts can be produced more often than once a year in order to give information to the owner on how the business is progressing. However, it is customary to produce annual or final accounts for the benefit of the tax authorities, the bank and other stakeholders.

The starting point for preparing final accounts is the trial balance prepared by the book-keeper. All the figures recorded on the trial balance are used in the final accounts. The trading account and the profit and loss account are both 'accounts' in terms of double-entry book-keeping. This means that amounts recorded in these accounts must also be recorded elsewhere in the book-keeping system. By contrast, the balance sheet is not an account, but is simply a statement of account balances remaining after the trading and profit and loss accounts have been prepared.

To help us with the preparation of final accounts we will use the trial balance, shown on the next page, of Wyvern Wholesalers, a sole trader business. This has been produced by the book-keeper at the end of the financial year of the business.

TRIAL BALANCE OF WYVERN WHOLESALERS AS AT 31 DECEMBER 20-1

	Dr £	Cr £
Sales		250,000
Purchases	156,000	
Sales returns	5,400	
Purchases returns		7,200
Discount received		2,500
Discount allowed	3,700	
Stock at 1 January 20-1	12,350	
Salaries	46,000	
Electricity and gas	3,000	
Rent and rates	2,000	
Sundry expenses	4,700	
Premises	100,000	
Equipment	30,000	
Debtors	23,850	
Bank overdraft		851
Cash	125	
Creditors		12,041
Capital		113,475
Drawings	10,442	
Long-term loan		11,500
	397,567	397,567

Note: stock at 31 December 20-1 was valued at £16,300

You will see that the trial balance includes the stock value at the start of the year, while the end-of-year valuation is noted after the trial balance. For the purposes of financial accounting, the stock of goods for resale is valued by the business (and may be verified by an auditor who checks the accounts) at the end of each financial year, and the valuation is entered into the book-keeping system (see page 135). We will set out the final accounts

- before adjustments for items such as accruals and prepayments of expenses, depreciation of fixed assets, and bad debts written off (each of which will be dealt with in Chapter 12)
- in vertical presentation, ie in columnar form

On page 135 we will illustrate the double-entry book-keeping for amounts entered in the trading and profit and loss accounts.

TRADING ACCOUNT

The main activity of a trading business is to buy goods at one price and then to sell the same goods at a higher price. The difference between the two prices represents a profit known as **gross profit**. Instead of calculating the gross profit on each item bought and sold, we have seen how the book-keeping system stores up the totals of transactions for the year in either purchases account or sales account. Further, any goods returned are recorded in either purchases returns account or sales returns account.

At the end of the financial year (which can end at any date – it does not have to be the calendar year) the totals of purchases and sales accounts, together with purchases returns and sales returns, are used to form the trading account. It is also necessary to take note of the value of stock of goods for resale held at the beginning and end of the financial year.

The trading account is set out in a columnar form as follows:

TRADING ACCOUNT OF WYVERN WHOLESALERS
FOR THE YEAR ENDED 31 DECEMBER 20-1

	£	£	£
Sales			250,000
Less Sales returns			5,400
Net sales (or turnover)			244,600
Opening stock (1 January 20-1)		12,350	
Purchases	156,000		
Carriage in	–		
Less Purchases returns	7,200		
Net purchases		148,800	
		161,150	
Less Closing stock (31 December 20-1)		16,300	
Cost of sales			144,850
Gross profit			99,750

*Note that, when using the columnar form, the right-hand column is the total column. Other columns for showing figures used in sub-totals – these other columns do **not** represent debit and credit.*

notes on trading account

- **Sales and purchases** only include items in which the business trades – items to be kept for use in the business, such as machinery, are not included in sales and purchases but are classified as fixed assets.
- **Adjustments** are made for the value of stock in the store or warehouse at the beginning and end of the financial year. The opening stock is added to the purchases because it has been sold during

the year. The closing stock is deducted from purchases because it has not been sold; it will form the opening stock for the next financial year, when it will be added to next year's figure for purchases.

- The figure for **cost of sales** (or cost of goods sold) represents the cost to the business of the goods which have been sold in this financial year. Cost of sales is:

  opening stock
  + purchases
  + carriage in (see below)
  − purchases returns
  − closing stock
  = cost of sales (or cost of goods sold)

- **Gross profit** is calculated as:

  sales
  − sales returns
  = net sales
  − cost of sales
  = gross profit

  If cost of sales is greater than net sales, the business has made a *gross loss*.

- **Carriage in** is the expense to the business of having purchases delivered (eg if you buy from a mail order company, you often have to pay the post and packing – this is the 'carriage in' cost). The cost of carriage in is added to purchases.

- **Net sales** (often described as turnover) is:

  sales
  − sales returns
  = net sales

- **Net purchases** is:

  purchases
  + carriage in
  − purchases returns
  = net purchases

PROFIT AND LOSS ACCOUNT

In the profit and loss account are listed the various expenses (overheads) of running the business. The total of expenses is deducted from gross profit to give **net profit** for the year. Net profit is an important figure: it shows the profitability of the business after all expenses, and how much has been earned by the business for the owner. It is on this profit, after certain adjustments, that the tax liability will be based.

The profit and loss account follows on from the trading account and is set out as follows:

PROFIT AND LOSS ACCOUNT OF WYVERN WHOLESALERS
FOR THE YEAR ENDED 31 DECEMBER 20-1

	£	£	£
Gross profit			99,750
Add Discount received			2,500
			102,250
Less expenses:			
Discount allowed		3,700	
Salaries		46,000	
Electricity and gas		3,000	
Rent and rates		2,000	
Sundry expenses		4,700	
			59,400
Net profit			42,850

Notes:

• The various expenses (overheads) shown in the profit and loss account can be listed to suit the needs of a particular business: the headings used here are for illustrative purposes only.

• Amounts of income are also included in profit and loss account, eg discount received in the example; these are added to gross profit.

• The net profit is the amount the business earned for the owner(s) during the year; it is important to note that this is not the amount by which the cash/bank balance has increased during the year.

• If the total of expenses exceeds gross profit (and other income), the business has made a net loss.

• Drawings by the owner are not listed as an overhead in profit and loss account – instead, they are deducted from capital (see balance sheet on page 132).

• If the owner of the business has taken goods for his or her own use, the amount should be deducted from purchases and added to drawings.

The trading account and the profit and loss account are usually combined together, rather than being shown as separate accounts, as shown at the top of the next page.

The trading and profit and loss account forms part of the double-entry book-keeping system (see page 135).

service sector businesses

You should note that when preparing the final accounts of a service sector business – such as a secretarial agency, a firm of solicitors, an estate agency, a doctors' practice – a trading account will not be prepared because, instead of trading in goods, the business supplies services. Thus the final accounts will consist of a profit and loss account and balance sheet. The profit and loss account, instead of starting with gross profit, will commence with the income from the business activity, such as 'fees', 'income from clients', 'charges', 'work done'. Other items of income, such as discount received, are added, and the expenses are then listed and deducted to give the net profit, or net loss, for the accounting period. An example is shown at the bottom of the next page.

TRADING AND PROFIT AND LOSS ACCOUNT OF WYVERN WHOLESALERS
FOR THE YEAR ENDED 31 DECEMBER 20-1

	£	£	£
Sales			250,000
Less Sales returns			5,400
Net sales			244,600
Opening stock (1 January 20-1)		12,350	
Purchases	156,000		
Carriage in	–		
Less Purchases returns	7,200		
Net purchases		148,800	
		161,150	
Less Closing stock (31 December 20-1)		16,300	
Cost of sales			144,850
Gross profit			99,750
Add Discount received			2,500
			102,250
Less expenses:			
Discount allowed		3,700	
Salaries		46,000	
Electricity and gas		3,000	
Rent and rates		2,000	
Sundry expenses		4,700	
			59,400
Net profit			42,850

PROFIT AND LOSS ACCOUNT OF WYVERN SECRETARIAL AGENCY
FOR THE YEAR ENDED 31 DECEMBER 20-1

	£	£
Income from clients		110,000
Less expenses:		
Salaries	64,000	
Heating and Lighting	2,000	
Telephone	2,000	
Rent and Rates	6,000	
Sundry Expenses	3,000	
		77,000
Net profit		33,000

BALANCE SHEET

The trading and profit and loss account shows two types of profit – gross profit and net profit – for the financial year (or such other time period as may be chosen by the business). A balance sheet, by contrast, shows the state of the business at one moment in time. It lists the assets and the liabilities at a particular date, but is not part of the double-entry book-keeping system.

The balance sheet of Wyvern Wholesalers, using the figures from the trial balance on page 127, is as follows:

BALANCE SHEET OF WYVERN WHOLESALERS
AS AT 31 DECEMBER 20-1

	£	£	£
Fixed Assets			
Premises			100,000
Equipment			30,000
			130,000
Current Assets			
Stock		16,300	
Debtors		23,850	
Cash		125	
		40,275	
Less Current Liabilities			
Creditors	12,041		
Bank overdraft	851		
		12,892	
Net Current Assets or Working Capital			27,383
			157,383
Less Long-term Liabilities			
Loan			11,500
NET ASSETS			145,883
FINANCED BY			
Capital			
Opening capital			113,475
Add net profit			42,850
			156,325
Less drawings			10,442
			145,883

notes on the balance sheet

● **assets**

Assets are items or amounts owned or owed to the business, and are normally listed in increasing order of liquidity, ie the most permanent assets are listed first.

Fixed assets are long-term assets purchased for use in the business and used over a long period (more than 12 months) to generate profits. They are divided between tangible fixed assets, which have material substance such as premises, equipment, machinery, vehicles, and intangible fixed assets, such as goodwill (see below).

Current assets are short-term assets held for less than 12 months. They change from day-to-day, such as stock (which will be sold and replaced with new stock), debtors (who will pay the amounts due and will be replaced by further amounts as credit sales are made), bank (if not overdrawn) and cash.

● **intangible fixed assets**

Intangible fixed assets (not shown in the balance sheet above) will appear on some balance sheets, and are listed before the tangible fixed assets. An intangible asset does not have material substance, but belongs to the business and has value. A common example of an intangible fixed asset is goodwill, which is where a business has bought another business and paid an agreed amount for the existing reputation and customer connections (the goodwill).

● **liabilities**

Liabilities are items or amounts owed by the business.

Current liabilities are amounts owing at the balance sheet date and due for repayment within 12 months or less (eg creditors, bank overdraft).

Long-term liabilities are where repayment is due in more than 12 months (eg loans, bank loans).

● **capital**

Capital is money owed by the business to the owner. It is usual practice to show on the balance sheet the owner's investment at the start of the year plus net profit for the year less drawings for the year; this equals the owner's investment at the end of the year, ie at the balance sheet date.

● **net current assets**

Net current assets – often referred to as working capital – is the excess of current assets over current liabilities. Without net current assets, a business cannot continue to operate.

significance of the balance sheet

The balance sheet shows the assets used by the business and how they have been financed:

	Fixed assets
	Fixed assets
plus	Net current assets
less	Long-term liabilities
equals	Net assets
equals	Capital

The columnar presentation balance sheet agrees the figure for net assets (£145,883), with capital.

PREPARATION OF FINAL ACCOUNTS FROM A TRIAL BALANCE

The trial balance contains the basic figures necessary to prepare the final accounts but, as we shall see in the next section, the figures are transferred from the double-entry accounts of the business. Nevertheless, the trial balance is a suitable summary from which to prepare the final accounts. The information needed for the preparation of each of the final accounts needs to be picked out from the trial balance in the following way:

- go through the trial balance and write against the items the final account in which each appears
- 'tick' each figure as it is used – each item from the trial balance appears in the final accounts once only
- the year end (closing) stock figure is not listed in the trial balance, but is shown as a note; the closing stock appears twice in the final accounts – firstly in the trading account, and secondly in the balance sheet (as a current asset).

If this routine is followed with the trial balance of Wyvern Wholesalers, it then appears as follows:

TRIAL BALANCE OF WYVERN WHOLESALERS AS AT 31 DECEMBER 20-1				
	Dr	Cr		
	£	£		
Sales		250,000	T	✔
Purchases	156,000		T	✔
Sales returns	5,400		T	✔
Purchases returns		7,200	T	✔
Discount received		2,500	P & L *(income)*	✔
Discount allowed	3,700		P & L *(expense)*	✔
Stock 1 January 20-1	12,350		T	✔
Salaries	46,000		P & L *(expense)*	✔
Electricity and gas	3,000		P & L *(expense)*	✔
Rent and rates	2,000		P & L *(expense)*	✔
Sundry expenses	4,700		P & L *(expense)*	✔
Premises	100,000		BS *(fixed asset)*	✔
Equipment	30,000		BS *(fixed asset)*	✔
Debtors	23,850		BS *(current asset)*	✔
Bank overdraft		851	BS *(current liability)*	✔
Cash	125		BS *(current asset)*	✔
Creditors		12,041	BS *(current liability)*	✔
Capital		113,475	BS *(capital)*	✔
Drawings	10,442		BS *(capital)*	✔
Long-term loan		11,500	DS *(long term liability)*	✔
	397,567	397,567		
Stock at 31 December 20-1 was valued at £16,300			T	✔
			BS *(current asset)*	✔

Note: T = trading account; P & L = profit and loss account; BS = balance sheet

DOUBLE-ENTRY BOOK-KEEPING AND THE FINAL ACCOUNTS

We have already noted earlier in this chapter that the trading and profit and loss account forms part of the double-entry book-keeping system. Therefore, each amount recorded in this account must have an opposite entry elsewhere in the accounting system. In preparing the trading and profit and loss account we are, in effect, emptying each account that has been storing up a record of the transactions of the business during the course of the financial year and transferring it to the trading and profit and loss account.

trading account

In the trading account of Wyvern Wholesalers the balance of purchases account is transferred as follows (debit trading account; credit purchases account):

Dr			Purchases Account			Cr
20-1		£	20-1			£
31 Dec	Balance b/d (ie total for year)	156,000	31 Dec	Trading account		156,000

The account now has a nil balance and is ready to receive the transactions for next year.

The balances of sales, sales returns, and purchases returns accounts are cleared to nil in a similar way and the amounts transferred to trading account, as debits or credits as appropriate.

Stock account, however, is dealt with differently. Stock is valued for financial accounting purposes at the end of each year (it is also likely to be valued more regularly in order to provide management information). Only the annual stock valuation is recorded in stock account, and the account is not used at any other time. After the book-keeper has extracted the trial balance, but before preparation of the trading account, the stock account appears as follows:

Dr			Stock Account		Cr
20-1		£	20-1		£
31 Dec	Balance b/d	12,350			

This balance, which is the opening stock valuation for the year, is transferred to the trading account to leave a nil balance, as follows (debit trading account; credit stock account):

Dr			Stock Account			Cr
20-1		£	20-1			£
31 Dec	Balance b/d	12,350	31 Dec	Trading account		12,350

The closing stock valuation for the year is now recorded on the account as an asset (debit stock account; credit trading account):

Dr			Stock Account		Cr
20-1		£	20-1		£
31 Dec	Balance b/d	12,350	31 Dec	Trading account	12,350
31 Dec	Trading account	16,300	31 Dec	Balance c/d	16,300
20-2					
1 Jan	Balance b/d	16,300			

The closing stock figure is shown on the balance sheet as a current asset, and will be the opening stock in next year's trading account.

profit and loss account

Expenses (overheads) and income items are transferred from the double-entry accounts to the profit and loss account. For example, the salaries account of Wyvern Wholesalers has been storing up information during the year and, at the end of the year, the total is transferred to profit and loss account (debit profit and loss account; credit salaries account):

Dr			Salaries Account		Cr
20-1		£	20-1		£
31 Dec	Balance b/d	46,000	31 Dec	Profit and loss account	46,000
	(ie total for year)				

The salaries account now has a nil balance and is ready to receive transactions for 20-2, the next financial year.

net profit

After the profit and loss account has been completed, the amount of net profit (or net loss) is transferred to the owner's capital account. The book-keeping entries are:

● **net profit**
  – debit profit and loss account
  – credit capital account

● **net loss**

   – debit capital account

   – credit profit and loss account

A net profit increases the owner's stake in the business by adding to capital account, while a net loss decreases the owner's stake.

drawings

At the same time the account for drawings, which has been storing up the amount of drawings during the year is also transferred to capital account:

   – debit capital account

   – credit drawings account

Thus the total of drawings for the year is debited to capital account.

capital account

When these transactions are completed, the capital account for Wyvern Wholesalers appears as·

Dr			Capital Account			Cr
20-1		£	20-1			£
31 Dec	Drawings for year	10,442	31 Dec	Balance b/d		113,475
31 Dec	Balance c/d	145,883	31 Dec	Profit and loss account		
				(net profit for year)		42,850
		156,325				156,325
20-2			20-2			
			1 Jan	Balance b/d		145,883

Note: It is the balance of capital account at the end of the year, ie £145,883, which forms the total for the capital section of the balance sheet. Whilst this figure could be shown on the balance sheet by itself, it is usual to show capital at the start of the year, with net profit for the year added, and drawings for the year deducted. In this way, the capital account is summarised on the balance sheet.

balance sheet

Unlike the trading and profit and loss account, the balance sheet is not part of the double-entry accounts. The balance sheet is made up of those accounts which remain with balances after the trading and profit and loss account transfers have been made. Thus it consists of asset and liability accounts, including capital.

A 'PRO-FORMA' LAYOUT OF FINAL ACCOUNTS

Many students studying final accounts for the first time find it helpful to be able to follow a set layout, or pro-forma – certainly in the early stages. A sample layout for final accounts is available as a free download from the Resources section at www.osbornebooks.co.uk. Note that there are some items included in these final account layouts that will be covered in the later chapters of AS Unit 2.

CHAPTER SUMMARY

● The final accounts of a business comprise:

- trading account, which shows gross profit
- profit and loss account, which shows net profit
- balance sheet, which shows the assets and liabilities of the business at the year-end

● The starting point for the preparation of final accounts is the summary of the information from the accounting records contained in the book-keeper's trial balance.

● Each item from the trial balance is entered into the final accounts once only.

● Any notes to the trial balance, such as the closing stock, affect the final accounts in two places.

● The trading account and profit and loss account form part of the double-entry book-keeping system – amounts entered must be recorded elsewhere in the accounts.

● The balance sheet is not part of the double-entry system; it lists the assets and liabilities at a particular date.

There is more material in connection with final accounts later in this book:
- adjustments to the accounts: accruals and prepayments, depreciation of fixed assets, bad debts and provision for doubtful debts (Chapters 12 and 15)
- accounting concepts (Chapter 14)
- specialist final accounts of limited companies (Chapter 17)
- the analysis and interpretation of final accounts – which gives the user of the accounts information about the financial state of the business (Chapter 18)

In the next chapter we will see how the general journal is used as a subsidiary book to record transfers to the final accounts, and for the correction of errors.

QUESTIONS

visit
www.osbornebooks.co.uk
to take an online test

An asterisk (*) after the question number means that the answer is given at the end of this book.

9.1*   The following information has been extracted from the business accounts of Matthew Lloyd for his first year of trading which ended on 31 December 20-8:

	£
Purchases	94,350
Sales	125,890
Stock at 31 December 20-8	5,950
Rates	4,850
Heating and lighting	2,120
Wages and salaries	10,350
Office equipment	8,500
Vehicles	10,750
Debtors	3,950
Bank balance	4,225
Cash	95
Creditors	1,750
Capital at start of year	20,000
Drawings for year	8,450

You are to prepare the trading and profit and loss account of Matthew Lloyd for the year ended 31 December 20-8, together with his balance sheet at that date.

9.2   Complete the table below for each item (a) to (g) indicating with a tick:

- whether the item would normally appear in the debit or credit column of the trial balance
- in which final account the item would appear at the end of the accounting period and whether as a debit or credit

	TRIAL BALANCE		FINAL ACCOUNTS			
			TRADING & P& L		BALANCE SHEET	
	Debit	Credit	Debit	Credit	Debit	Credit
(a) Salaries						
(b) Purchases						
(c) Debtors						
(d) Sales returns						
(e) Discount received						
(f) Vehicle						
(g) Capital						

9.3* You are to fill in the missing figures for the following businesses:

	Sales	Opening Stock	Purchases	Closing Stock	Gross Profit	Expenses	Net Profit/ (Loss)*
	£	£	£	£	£	£	£
Business A	20 000	5 000	10 000	3 000	....	4 000	....
Business B	35 000	8 000	15 000	5 000	....	....	10 000
Business C	....	6 500	18 750	7 250	18 500	11 750	....
Business D	45 250	9 500	....	10 500	20 750	....	10 950
Business E	71 250	....	49 250	9 100	22 750	24 450	....
Business F	25 650	4 950	13 750	....	11 550	....	(3 450)

* Note: a net loss is indicated in brackets

9.4* The following trial balance has been extracted by the book-keeper of John Adams at 31 December 20-7:

	Dr £	Cr £
Stock at 1 January 20-7	14,350	
Purchases	114,472	
Sales		259,688
Rates	13,718	
Heating and lighting	12,540	
Wages and salaries	42,614	
Vehicle expenses	5,817	
Advertising	6,341	
Premises	75,000	
Office equipment	33,000	
Vehicles	21,500	
Debtors	23,854	
Bank	1,235	
Cash	125	
Capital at 1 January 20-7		62,500
Drawings	9,903	
Loan from bank		35,000
Creditors		17,281
	374,469	374,469

Stock at 31 December 20-7 was valued at £16,280.

You are to prepare the trading and profit and loss account of John Adams for the year ended 31 December 20-7, together with his balance sheet at that date.

9.5 The following trial balance has been extracted by the book-keeper of Clare Lewis at 31 December 20-4:

	Dr £	Cr £
Debtors	18,600	
Creditors		12,140
Bank overdraft		5,820
Capital at 1 January 20-4		25,250
Sales		144,810
Purchases	96,318	
Stock at 1 January 20-4	16,010	
Salaries	18,465	
Heating and lighting	1,820	
Rent and rates	5,647	
Vehicles	9,820	
Office equipment	5,500	
Sundry expenses	845	
Vehicle expenses	1,684	
Drawings	13,311	
	188,020	188,020

Stock at 31 December 20-4 was valued at £13,735.

You are to prepare the trading and profit and loss account of Clare Lewis for the year ended 31 December 20-4, together with her balance sheet at that date.

9.6* The following balances are taken from the books of James Cadwallader showing totals for the year ended 31 December 2002.

	£
Sales	67,945
Purchases	34,981
Returns inwards	2,945
Returns outwards	1,367
Carriage inwards	679

Carriage outwards	386
Stock at 1 January 2002	5,780
Stock at 31 December 2002	6,590
Wages	12,056
Other expenses	4,650

REQUIRED

Prepare the profit and loss account for the year ended 31 December 2002.

Assessment and Qualifications Alliance (AQA), 2003

9.7 R Masters has completed his trading account for the year ended 31 March 2002.

REQUIRED

From the following information:

(a) (i) prepare the profit and loss account for the year ended 31 March 2002

	£
Gross profit	56,231
Wages	23,980
Discount received	350
Carriage outwards	3,600
Motor expenses	4,500
Bank charges	450
Drawings	12,500
Capital	36,790

(ii) prepare the capital account as at 31 March 2002

Dr **Capital Account** Cr

Date 2002	Details	£	Date 2002	Details	£

(b) Explain two possible causes of a change in the balance of the capital account over the course of a year's trading.

Assessment and Qualifications Alliance (AQA), 2002

9.8* From the following figures complete the balance sheet for A to Z Engineering Supplies as at 31 March 2003. Clearly show the fixed and current assets and long-term and current liabilities. To complete the balance sheet calculate the proprietor's capital.

	£
Net profit for the year	23,460
Stocks at 31 March 2003	14,905
Debtors	6,500
Creditors	4,590
Premises	50,000
Motor vehicles	14,560
Bank overdraft	3,400
Cash	56
Drawings	13,000
Mortgage on premises	25,000

Assessment and Qualifications Alliance (AQA), 2003

9.9 The subsidiary books of Amaryllis Trading show the following totals for the month of December 2001.

Totals for the month	Amount
	£
Sales day book	4,560.30
Returns inwards day book	236.91
Purchases day book	2,769.56
Returns outwards day book	127.50

The balances in the general ledger, made up of the totals for October and November 2001, are:

	£
Sales account	16,493.27
Returns inwards account	1,269.43
Purchases account	10,276.41
Returns outwards account	1,039.41

(a)   From the information given above enter the necessary data into the following accounts. The accounts need **not** be balanced.

Dr   **Sales Account**   Cr

Date	Details	£	p	Date	Details	£	p
2001				2001			

Dr   **Returns Inwards Account**   Cr

Date	Details	£	p	Date	Details	£	p
2001				2001			

Dr   **Purchases Account**   Cr

Date	Details	£	p	Date	Details	£	p
2001				2001			

Dr					**Returns Outwards Account**		Cr	
Date 2001	Details	£	p	Date 2001	Details		£	p

(b)   The following information is also given:

		£
Stocks on 1 October 2001		2,560.87
Stocks on 31 December 2001		2,640.96
Carriage inwards for the 3 months		871.26

Prepare the trading account for the three months ended 31 December 2001.

(c)   Using the figures from the trading account, state the totals of the following items:

		£
(i)	Cost of sales	
(ii)	Goods available for sale	
(iii)	Turnover	

Assessment and Qualifications Alliance (AQA), 2002

9.10   Mary Arbuthnot runs Mary's Doll Shop and is preparing her balance sheet but has problems with allocating four items.

Using the memorandum on the next page, advise her as to which section/sub-heading of the balance sheet the items should appear under. Give detailed reasons for your choice.

MEMORANDUM

Date ....

To ....

From ....

Subject ....

---

1.   Cost of new delivery van

       Section: ....

       Reasons: ....

       ....

       ....

       ....

       ....

2.   Stock of dolls for resale

       Section: ....

       Reasons: ....

       ....

       ....

       ....

       ....

continued on next page

3.   Telephone bill due to be paid in one month's time

Section: ....

Reasons: ....

....

....

....

....

4.   Drawings for the year

Section: ....

Reasons: ....

....

....

....

....

Assessment and Qualifications Alliance (AQA), 2003

10 THE GENERAL JOURNAL AND CORRECTION OF ERRORS

The general journal – or journal – is the subsidiary book for non-regular transactions, eg opening entries at the start of a business, purchase and sale of fixed assets on credit, correction of errors and end-of-year ledger transfers.

As a subsidiary book, the general journal is not part of double-entry book-keeping; instead the journal is used to list transactions before they are entered into the accounts. In this way, the journal completes the accounting system by providing the subsidiary book for non-regular transactions.

USES OF THE GENERAL JOURNAL

The general journal – or journal – completes the accounting system by providing the subsidiary book for non-regular transactions, which are not recorded in any other subsidiary book. The categories of such non-regular transactions include:

- opening entries at the start of a business
- purchase and sale of fixed assets on credit
- correction of errors
- year end ledger transfers

The reasons for using a journal are:

- to provide a subsidiary book for non-regular transactions
- to eliminate the need for remembering why non-regular transactions were put through the accounts – the journal acts as a notebook
- to reduce the risk of fraud, by making it difficult for unauthorised transactions to be entered in the accounting system
- to reduce the risk of errors, by listing the transactions that are to be put into the double-entry accounts
- to ensure that entries can be traced back to a source document, thus providing an audit trail for non-regular transactions

THE GENERAL JOURNAL – A SUBSIDIARY BOOK

The general journal is a subsidiary book; it is not, therefore, part of the double-entry book-keeping system. The journal is used to list the transactions that are then to be put through the accounts. The accounting system for non-regular transactions is as follows:

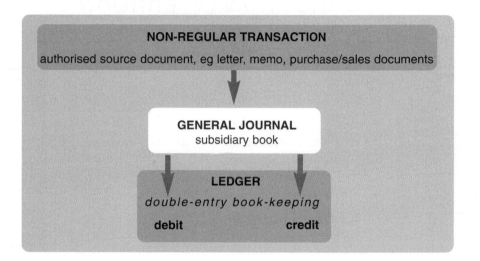

Study the way the journal is set out with a sample transaction, and then read the notes that follow.

Date	Details	Reference	Dr	Cr
20-1			£	£
1 Jan	Bank	GL	10,000	
	Capital	GL		10,000
	Opening capital introduced			

- the names of the accounts to be debited and credited in the book-keeping system are written in the details column; it is customary to show the debit transaction first
- the money amount of each debit and credit is stated in the appropriate columns
- the reference column cross-references to the division of the ledger where each account will be found – general ledger (GL), sales ledger (SL), purchases ledger (PL); an account number can also be included (note that the main cash book – containing bank account – is in the general ledger)
- a journal entry always balances, ie debit and credit entries are for the same amount or total
- it is usual to include a brief narrative explaining why the transaction is being carried out, and making reference to the source document whenever possible (when answering questions you should always include a narrative unless specifically told otherwise)
- each journal entry is complete in itself and is ruled off to separate it from the next entry

OPENING ENTRIES

These are the transactions which open the accounts at the start of a new business. For example, a first business transaction is:

1 Jan 20-1   Started in business with £10,000 in the bank

This non-regular transaction is entered in the journal as follows:

Date	Details	Reference	Dr	Cr
20-1			£	£
1 Jan	Bank	GL	10,000	
	Capital	GL		10,000
	Opening capital introduced			

After the journal entry has been made, the transaction can be recorded in the double-entry accounts.

Here is another opening entries transaction to be recorded in the journal:

1 Feb 20-2   Started in business with cash £100, bank £5,000, stock £1,000, machinery £2,500, creditors £850

The journal entry is:

Date	Details	Reference	Dr	Cr
20-2			£	£
1 Feb	Cash	GL	100	
	Bank	GL	5,000	
	Stock	GL	1,000	
	Machinery	GL	2,500	
	Creditors	PL		850
	Capital	GL		7,750
			8,600	8,600
	Assets and liabilities at the start of business			

Notes:

- Capital is in this example the balancing figure, ie assets minus liabilities.

- The journal is the subsidiary book for all opening entries, including cash and bank; however the normal subsidiary book for other cash/bank transactions is the cash book.

- The amounts from the journal entry will now need to be recorded in the double-entry accounts.

PURCHASE AND SALE OF FIXED ASSETS ON CREDIT

The purchase and sale of fixed assets are non-regular business transactions which are recorded in the journal as the subsidiary book. Only credit transactions are entered in the journal (because cash/bank transactions are recorded in the cash book as the subsidiary book). However, a business (or an examination question) may choose to journalise cash entries: strictly, though, this is incorrect as two subsidiary books are being used.

15 Apr 20-3   Bought a machine for £1,000 on credit from Machinery Supplies Limited, purchase order no 2341.

Date	Details	Reference	Dr	Cr
20-3			£	£
15 Apr	Machinery	GL	1,000	
	Machinery Supplies Limited*	PL		1,000
	Purchase of machine,			
	purchase order 2341			

20 May 20-4   Car sold for £2,500 on credit to Wyvern Motors Limited.

Date	Details	Reference	Dr	Cr
20-4			£	£
20 May	Wyvern Motors Limited*	SL	2,500	
	Disposals**	GL		2,500
	Sale of car, registration no VU54 XXX			

* Instead of entering these transactions in the purchases ledger and sales ledger, an alternative treatment would be to open general ledger accounts for the creditor (Machinery Supplies Limited) and the debtor (Wyvern Motors Limited). This would avoid confusion with trade creditors (in the purchases ledger) and trade debtors (in the sales ledger).

** Accounting for the disposal of fixed assets is dealt with in AS Unit 2 (Chapter 15).

CORRECTION OF ERRORS

In any book-keeping system there is always the possibility of an error. Ways to avoid errors, or ways to reveal them sooner, include:

- division of the accounting function between a number of people
- regular circulation of statements to debtors, who will check the transactions on their accounts and advise any discrepancies
- checking statements received from creditors
- extraction of a trial balance at regular intervals
- the preparation of bank reconciliation statements (see Chapter 8)
- checking cash balances against cash held
- the use of control accounts (see Chapter 11)
- the use of a computer accounting program (see Chapter 20)

Despite all these precautions, errors will still occur from time-to-time. In this chapter we will describe:

- correction of errors not shown by a trial balance
- correction of errors shown by a trial balance, using a suspense account
- the effect of correcting errors on profit and the balance sheet

errors not shown by a trial balance

In Chapter 5, page 66, we have already seen that some types of errors in a book-keeping system are not revealed by a trial balance. These are:

- error of omission
- reversal of entries
- mispost/error of commission
- error of principle
- error of original entry (or transcription)
- compensating error

Although these errors are not shown by a trial balance, they are likely to come to light if the procedures suggested in the introduction, above, are followed. For example, a debtor will soon let you know if her account has been debited with goods she did not buy. When an error is found, it needs to be corrected by means of a journal entry which shows the book-keeping entries that have been made.

We will now look at an example of each of the errors not shown by a trial balance, and will see how it is corrected by means of a journal entry. (A practical hint which may help in correcting errors is to write out the 'T' accounts as they appear with the error; then write in the correcting entries and see if the result has achieved what was intended.) Note that the journal narrative includes document details.

ERROR OF OMISSION

Credit sale of goods, £200 on invoice 4967 to H Jarvis completely omitted from the accounting system; the error is corrected on 12 May 20-8

Date	Details	Reference	Dr	Cr
20-8			£	£
12 May	H Jarvis	SL	200	
	Sales	GL		200
	Invoice 4967 omitted from the accounts.			

This type of error can happen in a very small business – often where the book-keeping is done by one person. For example, an invoice, when typed out, is 'lost' down the back of a filing cabinet. In a large business, particularly one using a computer accounting system, it should be impossible for this error to occur. Also, if documents are numbered serially, then none should be mislaid.

REVERSAL OF ENTRIES

A payment, on 3 May 20-8 by cheque of £50 to a creditor, S Wright, has been debited in the cash book and credited to Wright's account; this is corrected on 12 May 20-8

Date	Details	Reference	Dr	Cr
20-8			£	£
12 May	S Wright	PL	50	
	Bank	GL		50
	S Wright	PL	50	
	Bank	GL		50
			100	100
	Correction of £50 reversal of entries: cheque no. 93459			

To correct this type of error it is best to reverse the entries that have been made incorrectly (the first two journal entries), and then to put through the correct entries. This is preferable to debiting Wright £100 and crediting £100 to bank account: this is because there was never a transaction for £100 – the original transaction was for £50.

As noted earlier, it is often an idea to write out the 'T' accounts, complete with the error, and then to write in the correcting entries. As an example, the two accounts involved in this last error are shown with the error made on 3 May, and the corrections made on 12 May indicated by the shading (the opening credit balance of S Wright's account is shown as £50):

Dr			S Wright			Cr
20-8		£	20-8			£
12 May	Bank	50	1 May	Balance b/d		50
12 May	Bank	50	3 May	Bank		50
		100				100

Dr			Cash Book (bank columns)			Cr
20-8		£	20-8			£
3 May	S Wright	50	12 May	S Wright		50
			12 May	S Wright		50

The accounts now show a net debit transaction of £50 on S Wright's account, and a net credit transaction of £50 on bank account, which is how this payment to a creditor should have been recorded in order to clear the balance on the account.

MISPOST/ERROR OF COMMISSION

Credit sales of £47 have been debited to the account of J Adams, instead of the account of J Adams Ltd; the error is corrected on 15 May 20-8

Date	Details	Reference	Dr	Cr
20-8			£	£
15 May	J Adams Ltd	SL	47	
	J Adams	SL		47
	Correction of mispost of invoice 5327			

This type of error can be avoided, to some extent, by the use of account numbers, and by persuading the customer to quote the account number or reference on each transaction.

ERROR OF PRINCIPLE

The cost of diesel fuel, £30, has been debited to vehicles account; the error is corrected on 20 May 20-8

Date	Details	Reference	Dr	Cr
20-8			£	£
20 May	Vehicle running expenses	GL	30	
	Vehicles	GL		30
	Correction of error: voucher no. 647			

This type of error is similar to a mispost except that, instead of the wrong person's account being used, it is the wrong class of account. In this example, the vehicle running expenses must be kept separate from the cost of the asset (the vehicle), otherwise the expense and asset accounts will be incorrect, leading to profit for the year being overstated and the fixed asset being shown in the balance sheet at too high a figure.

ERROR OF ORIGINAL ENTRY (OR TRANSCRIPTION)

Postages of £45 paid by cheque entered in the accounts as £54; the error is corrected on 27 May 20-8

Date	Details	Reference	Dr	Cr
20-8			£	£
27 May	Bank	GL	54	
	Postages	GL		54
	Postages	GL	45	
	Bank	GL		45
			99	99
	Correction of error: postages of £45 entered into the accounts as £54; cheque no. 93617			

This error could have been corrected by debiting bank and crediting postages with £9, being the difference between the two amounts. However, there was no original transaction for this amount, and it is better to reverse the wrong transaction and put through the correct one. A reversal of figures either has a difference of nine (as above), or an amount divisible by nine. An error of original entry can also be a 'bad' figure on a cheque or an invoice, entered wrongly into both accounts.

COMPENSATING ERROR

Rates account is added up by £100 more than it should be (ie it is overadded or overcast); sales account is also overcast by the same amount; the error is corrected on 31 May 20-8

Date	Details	Reference	Dr	Cr
20-8			£	£
31 May	Sales	GL	100	
	Rates	GL		100
	Correction of overcast on rates account			
	and sales account			

Here, an account with a debit balance – rates – has been overcast; this is compensated by an overcast on an account with a credit balance – sales. There are several permutations on this theme, eg two debit balances, one overcast, one undercast; a debit balance undercast, a credit balance undercast.

important notes to remember

We have just looked at several journal entries in connection with the correction of errors. Remember that:

- The general journal is the subsidiary book for non-regular transactions. The journal entries must then be recorded in the book-keeping system.

- When a business uses control accounts (see Chapter 11), the transactions from the journal must be recorded in the sales ledger control account or purchase ledger control account as well as in the sales ledger or purchases ledger accounts of debtors or creditors.

TRIAL BALANCE ERRORS: USE OF SUSPENSE ACCOUNT

There are many types of errors revealed by a trial balance. Included amongst these are:

- omission of one part of the double-entry transaction
- recording two debits or two credits for a transaction
- recording a different amount for a transaction on the debit side from the credit side
- errors in the calculation of balances (not compensated by other errors)
- error in transferring the balance of an account to the trial balance
- error of addition in the trial balance

When errors are shown, the trial balance is 'balanced' by recording the difference in a suspense account, as shown in the worked example on the next page.

WORKED EXAMPLE: SUSPENSE ACCOUNT

The book-keeper of a business is unable to balance the trial balance on 31 December 20-1. As the error or errors cannot be found quickly the trial balance is balanced by recording the difference in a suspense account, as follows:

	Dr	Cr
	£	£
Trial balance totals	100,000	99,850
Suspense account		150
	100,000	100,000

A suspense account is opened in the general ledger with, in this case, a credit balance of £150:

Dr		Suspense Account		Cr
20-1	£	20-1		£
		31 Dec	Trial balance difference	150

A detailed examination of the book-keeping system is now made in order to find the errors. As errors are found, they are corrected by means of a journal entry. The journal entries will balance, with one part of the entry being either a debit or credit to suspense account. In this way, the balance on suspense account is eliminated by book-keeping transactions. Using the above suspense account, the following errors are found and corrected on 15 January 20-2:

- sales account is undercast by £100
- a payment to a creditor, A Wilson, for £65, has been recorded in the bank as £56
- telephone expenses of £55 have not been entered in the expenses account
- stationery expenses £48 have been debited to both the stationery account and the bank account

These errors are corrected by journal entries shown on the next page. Note that the journal narrative includes details of cheque numbers and dates taken from the records of the business.

Date	Details	Reference	Dr	Cr
20-2			£	£
15 Jan	Suspense	GL	100	
	Sales	GL		100
	Undercast on 23 December 20-1 now corrected			
15 Jan	Bank	GL	56	
	Suspense	GL		56
	Suspense	GL	65	
	Bank	GL		65
			121	121
	Payment to A Wilson for £65 (cheque no. 783726) on *30 December 20-1 entered in bank as £56 in error*			
15 Jan	Telephone expenses	GL	55	
	Suspense	GL		55
	Omission of entry in expenses account: *paid by cheque no 783734*			
15 Jan	Suspense	GL	48	
	Bank	GL		48
	Suspense	GL	48	
	Bank	GL		48
			96	96
	Correction of error: payment by cheque no 783736 *debited in error to bank account*			

After these journal entries have been recorded in the accounts, suspense account appears as:

Dr			**Suspense Account**			Cr
20-2		£	20-1			£
15 Jan	Sales	100	31 Dec	Trial balance difference		150
15 Jan	Bank	65	20-2			
15 Jan	Bank	48	15 Jan	Bank		56
15 Jan	Bank	48	15 Jan	Telephone expenses		55
		261				261

Thus all the errors have now been found, and suspense account has a nil balance.

Note that if final accounts have to be prepared after creating a suspense account but before the errors are found, the balance of suspense account is shown, depending on the balance, as either a current asset (debit balance) or a current liability (credit balance). Nevertheless, the error must be found at a later date and suspense account eliminated.

EFFECT ON PROFIT AND BALANCE SHEET

The correction of errors, whether shown by a trial balance or not, often has an effect on the profit figure calculated before the errors were found. For example, an undercast of sales account, when corrected, will increase gross and net profits and, of course, the profit figure shown in the balance sheet. Some errors, however, only affect the balance sheet, eg errors involving debtors' and creditors' accounts. The diagram that follows shows the effect of errors when corrected on gross profit, net profit and the balance sheet.

TRADING ACCOUNT

Correction of error	Gross profit	Net profit	Balance sheet
sales undercast/understated	increase	increase	net profit increase
sales overcast/overstated	decrease	decrease	net profit decrease
purchases undercast/understated	decrease	decrease	net profit decrease
purchases overcast/overstated	increase	increase	net profit increase
opening stock undervalued	decrease	decrease	net profit decrease
opening stock overvalued	increase	increase	net profit increase
closing stock undervalued	increase	increase	net profit increase / stock increase
closing stock overvalued	decrease	decrease	net profit decrease / stock decrease

PROFIT AND LOSS ACCOUNT

Correction of error	Gross profit	Net profit	Balance sheet
expense undercast/understated	-	decrease	decrease in net profit
expense overcast/overstated	-	increase	increase in net profit
income undercast/understated	-	increase	increase in net profit
income overcast/overstated	-	decrease	decrease in net profit

BALANCE SHEET

Correction of error	Gross profit	Net profit	Balance sheet
asset undercast/understated	-	-	increase asset
asset overcast/overstated	-	-	decrease asset
liability undercast/understated	-	-	increase liability
liability overcast/overstated	-	-	decrease liability

Some examination questions on correction of errors require the preparation of a statement showing the amended profit after errors have been corrected. We will look at the errors shown on page 158 and see how their correction affects the net profit (assume the net profit before adjustments is £10,000).

Statement of corrected net profit for the year ended 31 December 20-1

	£
Net profit (unadjusted)	10,000
Add sales undercast	100
	10,100
Less additional telephone expenses	55
Adjusted net profit	10,045

Note: the other two errors do not affect net profit.

The effect on the balance sheet of correcting the errors is:

• net profit increases £45

• bank balance reduces £105 (+£56, −£65, −£48, −£48)

• the credit balance of £150 in suspense account (shown as a current liability) is eliminated

The balance sheet will now balance without the need for a suspense account – the errors have been found and corrected.

YEAR END LEDGER TRANSFERS

Any other non-regular transactions or adjustments need to be recorded in the general journal. These usually take place at the end of a firm's financial year and are concerned with:

• transfers to the trading and profit and loss account

• expenses charged to the owner's drawings

• goods for the owner's use

• bad debts written off

transfers to trading and profit and loss account

As we have seen in the previous chapter, the trading and profit and loss account forms part of double-entry book-keeping. Therefore, each amount recorded in trading and profit and loss account must have an opposite entry in another account: such transfers are recorded in the journal as the subsidiary book, as shown by the entries which follow.

*31 Dec 20-1   Balance of sales account at the year end, £155,000, transferred to trading account
(debit sales account; credit trading account)*

Date	Details	Reference	Dr	Cr
20-1			£	£
31 Dec	Sales	GL	155,000	
	Trading	GL		155,000
	Transfer to trading account of sales for the year			

*31 Dec 20-1   Balance of purchases account at the year end, £105,000, transferred to trading
account (debit trading account; credit purchases account)*

Date	Details	Reference	Dr	Cr
20-1			£	£
31 Dec	Trading	GL	105,000	
	Purchases	GL		105,000
	Transfer to trading account of purchases for the year			

31 Dec 20-1   Closing stock has been valued at £12,500 and is to be entered into the accounts

Date	Details	Reference	Dr	Cr
20-1			£	£
31 Dec	Stock	GL	12,500	
	Trading	GL		12,500
	Stock valuation at 31 December 20-1 transferred to trading account			

Remember that the closing stock valuation for the year is recorded in stock account as an asset (*debit* stock account; *credit* trading account).

*31 Dec 20-1   Balance of wages account, £23,500, transferred to profit and loss account (debit
profit and loss account; credit wages account)*

Date	Details	Reference	Dr	Cr
20-1			£	£
31 Dec	Profit and loss	GL	23,500	
	Wages	GL		23,500
	Transfer to profit and loss account of expenditure for the year			

expenses charged to owner's drawings

Sometimes the owner of a business uses business facilities for private use, eg telephone, or car. The owner will agree that part of the expense shall be charged to him or her as drawings, while the other part represents a business expense. The book-keeping entry to record the adjustment is:

- debit drawings account

- credit expense account, eg telephone

31 Dec 20-1   The balance of telephone account is £600; of this, one-quarter is the estimated cost of the owner's private usage

The journal entry is:

Date	Details	Reference	Dr	Cr
20-1			£	£
31 Dec	Drawings	GL	150	
	Telephone	GL		150
	Transfer of private use to drawings account			

goods for the owner's use

When the owner of a business takes some of the goods in which the business trades for his or her own use, the double-entry book-keeping is:

- debit drawings account

- credit purchases account

15 Oct 20-1   Owner of the business takes goods for own use, £105

The journal entry is:

Date	Details	Reference	Dr	Cr
20-1			£	£
15 Oct	Drawings	GL	105	
	Purchases	GL		105
	Goods taken for own use by the owner			

bad debts written off

A bad debt is a debt owing to a business which it considers will never be paid.

One of the problems of selling goods and services on credit terms is that, from time-to-time, some customers will not pay. As a consequence, the balances of such debtors' accounts have to be written off when they become uncollectable. This happens when all reasonable efforts to recover the amounts owing have been exhausted, ie statements and letters have been sent to the debtor requesting payment, and legal action – where appropriate – or the threat of legal action has failed to obtain payment.

In writing off a debtor's account as bad, the business is bearing the cost of the amount due. The debtor's account is written off as bad and the amount (or amounts where a number of accounts are dealt with in this way) is debited to bad debts written off account.

Towards the financial year-end it is good practice to go through the debtors' accounts to see if any need to be written off. The book-keeping entries for this are:

– debit bad debts written off account

– credit debtor's account

15 Dec 20-1   Write off the account of T Hughes, which has a balance of £25, as a bad debt

The journal entry is:

Date	Details	Reference	Dr	Cr
20-1			£	£
15 Dec	Bad debts written off	GL	25	
	T Hughes	SL		25
	Account written off as a bad debt – see memo			
	dated 14 December 20-1			

Note that in Chapter 12 we will see how bad debts are dealt with in the final accounts.

MAKING JOURNAL ENTRIES

As we have seen in this chapter, the general journal is the subsidiary book for non-regular transactions. Because of the irregular nature of journal transactions, it is important that they are correctly authorised by the appropriate person – such as the accounts supervisor, the administration manager, the owner of the business. The authorisation will, ideally, be a source document – eg letter, memo, email or other document – but may well be verbal – eg "make the year end ledger transfers to profit and loss account", or "find the errors and put them right".

It is good practice to ensure that journal entries are checked by an appropriate person before they are entered into the double-entry book-keeping system. It is all too easy to get a journal entry the wrong way round resulting in an error becoming twice as much as it was in the first place!

CHAPTER SUMMARY

- The general journal is used to list non-regular transactions.
- The general journal is a subsidiary book – it is not a double-entry account.
- The general journal is used for:
  - opening entries at the start of a business
  - purchase and sale of fixed assets on credit
  - correction of errors
  - year end ledger transfers
- Correction of errors is always a difficult topic to put into practice: it tests knowledge of book-keeping procedures and it is all too easy to make the error worse than it was in the first place! The secret of dealing with this topic well is to write down – in account format – what has gone wrong. It should then be relatively easy to see what has to be done to put the error right.
- Errors not shown by a trial balance: error of omission, reversal of entries, mispost/error of commission, error of principle, error of original entry (or transcription), compensating error.
- Errors shown by a trial balance include: omission of one part of the book-keeping transaction, recording two debits/credits for a transaction, recording different amounts in the two accounts, calculating balances, transferring balances to the trial balance.
- All errors are non-regular transactions and need to be corrected by means of a journal entry: the book-keeper then needs to record the correcting transactions in the accounts.
- When error(s) are shown by a trial balance, the amount is placed into a suspense account. As the errors are found, journal entries are made which 'clear out' the suspense account.
- Correction of errors may have an effect on gross profit and net profit, and on the figures in the balance sheet. It may be necessary to restate net profit and to adjust the balance sheet.

In the next chapter we shall look at the use of control accounts which are used as a checking device for a section of the ledgers.

QUESTIONS

visit
www.osbornebooks.co.uk
to take an online test

An asterisk (*) after the question number means that the answer is given at the end of this book.

10.1* Lucy Wallis started in business on 1 May 20-8 with the following assets and liabilities:

	£
Vehicle	6,500
Fixtures and fittings	2,800
Opening stock	4,100
Cash	150
Loan from husband	5,000

You are to prepare Lucy's opening journal entry, showing clearly her capital at 1 May 20-8.

10.2 Show the journal entries for the following transfers which relate to Trish Hall's business for the year ended 31 December 20-8:

(a) Closing stock is to be recorded in the accounts at a valuation of £22,600.

(b) Telephone expenses for the year, amounting to £890, are to be transferred to profit and loss account.

(c) Motoring expenses account shows a balance of £800; one-quarter of this is for Trish Hall's private motoring; three-quarters is to be transferred to profit and loss account.

(d) Trish has taken goods for her own use of £175.

(e) The sales ledger account of N Marshall, which has a debit balance of £125, is to be written off as a bad debt.

10.3* Henry Lewis is setting up the book-keeping system for his new business, which sells office stationery. He decides to use the following subsidiary books:
- general journal (or journal)
- sales day book
- purchases day book
- sales returns day book
- purchases returns day book
- cash book

The following business transactions take place:

(a) He receives an invoice from Temeside Traders for £956 for goods supplied on credit

(b) He issues an invoice to Malvern Models for £176 of goods

(c) He buys a computer for use in his business for £2,000 on credit from A-Z Computers Limited

(d) He issues a credit note to Johnson Brothers for £55 of goods

(e) A debtor, Melanie Fisher, settles the balance of her account, £107, by cheque

(f) He makes cash sales of £25

(g) Henry Lewis withdraws cash £100 for his own use

(h) He pays a creditor, Stationery Supplies Limited, the balance of the account, £298, by cheque

(i) A debtor, Jim Bowen, with an account balance of £35 is to be written off as a bad debt

(j) A credit note for £80 is received from a creditor, Ian Johnson

You are to take each business transaction in turn and state:
- the name of the subsidiary book
- the name of the account to be debited
- the name of the account to be credited

10.4   The trial balance of Thomas Wilson balanced. However, a number of errors have been found in the book-keeping system:

(a)   Credit sale of £150 to J Rigby has not been entered in the accounts.

(b)   A payment by cheque for £125 to H Price Limited, a creditor, has been recorded in the account of H Prince.

(c)   The cost of a new delivery van, £10,000, has been entered to vehicle expenses account.

(d)   Postages of £55, paid by cheque, have been entered on the wrong sides of both accounts.

(e)   The totals of the purchases day book and the purchases returns day book have been undercast by £100.

(f)   A payment for £89 from L Johnson, a debtor, has been entered in the accounts as £98.

You are to take each error in turn and:

- state the type of error
- show the correcting journal entry

10.5*   Jeremy Johnson extracts a trial balance from his book-keeping records on 30 September 20-8. Unfortunately the trial balance fails to balance and the difference, £19 debit, is placed to a suspense account pending further investigation.

The following errors are later found:

(a)   A cheque payment of £85 for office expenses has been entered in the cash book but no entry has been made in the office expenses account.

(b)   A payment for photocopying of £87 by cheque has been correctly entered in the cash book, but is shown as £78 in the photocopying account.

(c)   The sales returns day book has been overcast by £100.

(d)   Commission received of £25 has been entered twice in the account.

You are to:

- make journal entries to correct the errors
- show the suspense account after the errors have been corrected

10.6 R Masters has drawn up a suspense account at 31 March 2002 following the discovery of errors.

REQUIRED

(a) Name two accounting techniques which may have been used to detect the presence of errors in the books.

....

....

(b) Make the necessary entries in the journal below to correct the following errors. Narratives are not required.

(1) The sales day book has been overcast by £270.

(2) The returns inwards has been entered as a credit of £500. In fact it only totalled £300.

(3) A discount received of £400 was entered in the cash book but omitted from the general ledger.

(4) A cheque paid to J Jones of £350 was entered in the account of A Jones in error.

JOURNAL

Account	Debit £	Credit £

Assessment and Qualifications Alliance (AQA), 2002

10.7* The trial balance of Fancy Goods Enterprises was drawn up as at 31 March 2001 but the totals did not agree. The following errors have been discovered.

1. The purchases account has been overcast by £4,500.

2. The debtors' total includes £650 which has been written off as a bad debt.

3. Discount received of £300 has been entered on the debit of the account.

4. A cheque for £673, payable to Sunshine Products Ltd, has been entered in the account of Sunmaster Products in error.

5. The credit balance in the rent payable account has been brought down as £990, it should have been £909.

REQUIRED

Make any necessary entries in the suspense account to correct these errors, and show the opening balance.

Dr		Suspense Account	Cr
Details	£	Details	£

Assessment and Qualifications Alliance (AQA), 2001

10.8 The trial balance of H G Patel, as at 30 April 2003, has been partially completed. The following balances have now to be included:

	£
Purchases	38,900
Sales	98,000
Returns outwards	3,698
Carriage inwards	367
Carriage outwards	450
Discount received	2,135
Drawings	6,900

REQUIRED

(a) Complete the trial balance.

(b) Total the trial balance and enter any difference in the suspense account.

H G Patel: Trial Balance as at 30 April 2003

Account	Debit £	Credit £
Wages	23,890	
Administration costs	6,000	
Capital		60,000
Premises	65,000	
Motor vehicles	5,000	
Motor expenses	1,650	
Purchases		
Sales		
Returns outwards		
Carriage inwards		
Carriage outwards		
Discount received		
Drawings		
Suspense		
TOTAL		

(c) There are many reasons for the error(s) giving rise to the suspense account.

From the following list of book-keeping errors, tick the Yes or No box to indicate whether or not the error could be responsible for the difference in the trial balance.

An example has been given.

Error	Yes	No
A balance has been entered in the wrong column of the trial balance.	✓	
An error of principle has occurred.		
The sales account has been totalled incorrectly.		
An invoice has been omitted from the books.		
A cheque has been debited in the cash book as £150 but credited in the customer's account as £105.		

Assessment and Qualifications Alliance (AQA), 2003

10.9* The totals of John Wilson's trial balance on 31 March 2005 did not agree.

The totals were:

Debit   £46,250   Credit   £45,416

He entered the difference in a suspense account. On checking his books, he discovered the following errors.

1. The sales account was undercast by £230.

2. Postage of £154, entered in the cash book, had been omitted from the expense account.

3. The wages of £600 paid for the month ended 31 March had been debited twice in the wages account.

4. Discount received of £79 had been entered on the debit side of the discount received account.

REQUIRED

(a)   Enter the trial balance difference in the suspense account below. Make the entries necessary to correct the errors.

Dr					Suspense Account		Cr
Date 2005	Details		£	Date 2005	Details		£

(b)   Explain clearly, using an example, why some types of error are not revealed by a trial balance.

(c)   Explain two benefits that could be obtained by preparing a monthly bank reconciliation statement.

Assessment and Qualifications Alliance (AQA), 2005

10.10   On 30 April 2004 the owner of China Products prepared a trial balance. The trial balance totals did not agree. A suspense account was opened.

The following errors have been discovered.

1.   The sales account had been overcast by £200.

2.   A purchase invoice for £500 had been entered in both the supplier's account and the purchases account as £50.

3.   Rent paid of £650 had been correctly entered in the cash book, but had been entered in the rent account as £400.

REQUIRED

(a)   Make appropriate entries in the suspense account. Show the opening balance.

Dr			**Suspense Account**		**Cr**
Date 2004	Details	£	Date 2004	Details	£

(b)   Give an example of an error of commission. Explain why it will not be revealed by a trial balance.

Example: ....

....

Explanation: ....

....

....

(c)   Which account should you prepare to discover if there are errors in the debtors' accounts?*

....

*   see chapter 11

Assessment and Qualifications Alliance (AQA), 2004

10.11 Jonathon Smith had prepared his profit and loss account for 30 November 2004 which showed a profit of £26,790. His accountant then discovered the following errors:

1. The sales account had been undercast by £450.

2. Discount allowed of £140 had been entered on the credit of the discount allowed account.

3. Wages of £2,500 had been completely omitted from the books of account.

4. The cost of a fixed asset £9,500 had been included in the purchases account.

5. A payment from B A Jones of £1,200 had been entered in the account of C A Jones.

6. The closing stock had been entered as £2,400; it was actually £2,500.

REQUIRED

Calculate the corrected profit. Show clearly whether each adjustment is added, subtracted or has no effect on the total.

Adjustment 1 has been completed as an example.

Jonathon Smith

Corrected Profit for the year ended 30 November 2004

		£
Profit calculated by Jonathon		26,790
1. Sales undercast	*add*	*450*
....		
....		
....		
....		
....		
....		

Assessment and Qualifications Alliance (AQA), 2005

11 CONTROL ACCOUNTS

Control accounts are used as 'master' accounts which control a number of subsidiary ledger accounts (see the diagram below).

A control account (also known as a totals account) is used to record the totals of transactions passing through the subsidiary accounts.

In this way, the balance of the control account will always be equal (unless an error has occurred) to the total balances of the subsidiary accounts.

Two commonly-used control accounts are:

- sales ledger control account – the total of the debtors
- purchases ledger control account – the total of the creditors

In this chapter we shall look at:

- the concept of control accounts
- the layout of sales ledger and purchases ledger control accounts
- the use of control accounts as an aid to the management of a business

THE CONCEPT OF CONTROL ACCOUNTS

The illustration above shows how a control account acts as a master account for a number of subsidiary accounts. The principle is that, if the total of the opening balances for subsidiary accounts is known, together with the total of amounts increasing these balances, and the total of amounts decreasing these balances, then the total of the closing balances for the subsidiary accounts can be calculated.

For example:

	£
Total of opening balances	50,000
Add increases	10,000
	60,000
Less decreases	12,000
Total of closing balances	48,000

The total of the closing balances can now be checked against a separate listing of the subsidiary accounts to ensure that the two figures agree. If so, it proves that the ledgers within the section are correct (subject to any errors such as misposts and compensating errors). Let us now apply this concept to one of the divisions of the ledger – sales ledger.

The diagram on the next page shows the personal accounts which form the entire sales ledger of a particular business (in practice there would, of course, be more than four accounts involved). The sales ledger control account acts as a totals account, which records totals of the transactions passing through the individual accounts which it controls. Notice that transactions appear in the control account on the same side as they appear in the individual accounts. It follows that the control account acts as a checking device for the individual accounts which it controls. Thus, control accounts act as an aid to locating errors: if the control account and subsidiary accounts agree, then the error is likely to lie elsewhere. In this way the control account acts as an intermediate checking device – proving the arithmetical accuracy of the ledger section.

Normally the whole of a ledger section is controlled by one control account, eg sales ledger control account and purchases ledger control account. However, it is also possible to have a number of separate control accounts for subdivisions of the sales ledger and purchases ledger, eg sales ledger control account A-K, purchases ledger control account S-Z, etc. It is for a business – the user of the accounting system – to decide what is most suitable, taking into account the number of accounts in the sales and purchases ledger, together with the type of book-keeping system – manual or computerised.

In the diagram on the next page the balances on the sales ledger control account and subsidiary accounts are agreed at the beginning and end of the month, as follows:

Reconciliation of sales ledger control account with debtor balances		
	1 January 20-1 £	31 January 20-1 £
A Ackroyd	100	150
B Barnes	200	200
C Cox	50	180
D Douglas	150	150
Sales ledger control account	500	680

Note: The business will decide how often to reconcile the control account with the subsidiary accounts – weekly, monthly, quarterly or annually. Any discrepancy should be investigated immediately and the error(s) traced.

Dr				SALES LEDGER CONTROL ACCOUNT		Cr
20-1			£	20-1		£
1 Jan	Balance b/d		500	31 Jan	Bank	443
31 Jan	Sales		700	31 Jan	Discount allowed	7
				31 Jan	Sales returns	70
				31 Jan	Balance c/d	680
			1,200			1,200
1 Feb	Balance b/d		680			

Dr				A Ackroyd		Cr
20-1			£	20-1		£
1 Jan	Balance b/d		100	10 Jan	Bank	98
6 Jan	Sales		150	10 Jan	Discount allowed	2
				31 Jan	Balance c/d	150
			250			250
1 Feb	Balance b/d		150			

Dr				B Barnes		Cr
20-1			£	20-1		£
1 Jan	Balance b/d		200	13 Jan	Bank	195
6 Jan	Sales		250	13 Jan	Discount allowed	5
				27 Jan	Sales returns	50
				31 Jan	Balance c/d	200
			450			450
1 Feb	Balance b/d		200			

Dr				C Cox		Cr
20-1			£	20-1		£
1 Jan	Balance b/d		50	20 Jan	Bank	50
15 Jan	Sales		200	29 Jan	Sales returns	20
				31 Jan	Balance c/d	180
			250			250
1 Feb	Balance b/d		180			

Dr				D Douglas		Cr
20-1			£	20-1		£
1 Jan	Balance b/d		150	30 Jan	Bank	100
20 Jan	Sales		100	31 Jan	Balance c/d	150
			250			250
1 Feb	Balance b/d		150			

SALES LEDGER CONTROL ACCOUNT

The layout of a sales ledger control account (or debtors' control account) is shown below. Study the layout carefully and then read the text which explains the additional items.

Dr	Sales Ledger Control Account		Cr
	£		£
Balance b/d		Cash/cheques received from debtors	
Credit sales		Cash discount allowed	
Returned cheques		Sales returns	
Interest charged to debtors		Bad debts written off	
		Set-off/contra entries	
		Balance c/d	
Balance b/d			

● **Balance b/d**

The figure for balance b/d on the debit side of the control account represents the total of the balances of the individual debtors' accounts in the sales ledger. This principle is illustrated in the diagram on the opposite page. Remember that, at the end of the month (or other period covered by the control account), the account must be balanced and carried down (on the credit side) on the last day of the month, and then brought down (on the debit side) on the first day of the next month.

Note that it is possible for a debtor's account to have a credit balance, instead of the usual debit balance – see page 182. This may come about, for example, because the debtor has paid for goods and then returned them, or has overpaid in error: the business owes the amount due, ie the debtor has a credit balance for the time being.

● **Credit sales**

Only credit sales – and not cash sales – are entered in the control account because it is this transaction that is recorded in the debtors' accounts. The total sales of the business will comprise both credit and cash sales.

● **Returned (dishonoured) cheques**

If a debtor's cheque is returned unpaid by the bank, ie the cheque has 'bounced', then entries have to be made in the book-keeping system to record this. These entries are:

– debit debtor's account
– credit cash book (bank columns)

As a transaction has been made in a debtor's account, then the amount must also be recorded in the sales ledger control account – on the debit side.

● **Interest charged to debtors**

Sometimes a business will charge a debtor for slow payment of an account. The entries are:

– debit debtor's account

– credit interest received account

As a debit transaction has been made in the debtor's account, so a debit entry must be recorded in the control account.

● **Bad debts written off**

The book-keeping entries for writing off a bad debt (see Chapter 10) are:

– debit bad debts written off account

– credit debtor's account

As you can see, a credit transaction is entered in a debtor's account. The control account 'masters' the sales ledger and so the transaction must also be recorded as a credit transaction in the control account.

● **Set-off/contra entries**

See page 181.

PURCHASES LEDGER CONTROL ACCOUNT

The specimen layout for the purchases ledger control account (or creditors' control account) is shown below. Study the format and read the notes which follow.

Dr		Purchases Ledger Control Account		Cr
	£			£
Cash/cheques paid to creditors		Balance b/d		
Cash discount received		Credit purchases		
Purchases returns		Interest charged by creditors		
Set-off/contra entries				
Balance c/d	____			____
	▬▬	Balance b/d		▬▬

● **Balance b/d**

The figure for balance b/d on the credit side of the control account represents the total of the balances of the individual creditors' accounts in the purchases ledger. This principle is illustrated in the diagram on the next page.

Note that it is possible for a creditor's account to have a debit balance, instead of the usual credit balance – see page 183. This may come about, for example, if the creditor has been paid and then goods are returned, or if the creditor has been overpaid.

● **Credit purchases**

Only credit purchases – and not cash purchases – are entered in the control account. However, the total purchases of the business will comprise both credit and cash purchases.

● **Interest charged by creditors**

If creditors charge interest because of slow payment, this must be recorded on both the creditor's account and the control account.

● **Set-off/contra entries**

See page 181.

reconciliation of purchases ledger control account

The diagram on the next page shows how a purchases ledger control account acts as a totals account for the creditors of a business.

Reconciliation of the balances on the purchases ledger control account and subsidiary accounts is made as follows:

Reconciliation of purchases ledger control account with creditor balances		
	1 January 20-1	31 January 20-1
	£	£
F Francis	100	200
G Gold	200	350
H Harris	300	500
I Ingram	400	900
Purchases ledger control account	1,000	1,950

Dr	PURCHASES LEDGER CONTROL ACCOUNT		Cr	
20-1		£	20-1	£
31 Jan	Purchases returns	150	1 Jan Balances b/d	1,000
31 Jan	Bank	594	31 Jan Purchases	1,700
31 Jan	Discount received	6		
31 Jan	Balance c/d	1,950		
		2,700		2,700
			1 Feb Balance b/d	1,950

Dr	F Francis		Cr	
20-1		£	20-1	£
17 Jan	Bank	98	1 Jan Balance b/d	100
17 Jan	Discount received	2	3 Jan Purchases	200
31 Jan	Balance c/d	200		
		300		300
			1 Feb Balance b/d	200

Dr	G Gold		Cr	
20-1		£	20-1	£
15 Jan	Purchases returns	50	1 Jan Balance b/d	200
28 Jan	Bank	100	9 Jan Purchases	300
31 Jan	Balance c/d	350		
		500		500
			1 Feb Balance b/d	350

Dr	H Harris		Cr	
20-1		£	20-1	£
28 Jan	Purchases returns	100	1 Jan Balance b/d	300
30 Jan	Bank	200	17 Jan Purchases	500
31 Jan	Balance c/d	500		
		800		800
			1 Feb Balance b/d	500

Dr	I Ingram		Cr	
20-1		£	20-1	£
22 Jan	Bank	196	1 Jan Balance b/d	400
22 Jan	Discount received	4	27 Jan Purchases	700
31 Jan	Balance c/d	900		
		1,100		1,100
			1 Feb Balance b/d	900

SET-OFF/CONTRA ENTRIES

These entries occur when the same person or business has an account in both sales ledger and purchases ledger, ie they are both buying from, and selling to, the business whose accounts we are preparing. For example, M Patel Ltd has the following accounts in the sales and purchases ledgers:

SALES LEDGER

Dr		A Smith		Cr
		£		£
Balance b/d		200		

PURCHASES LEDGER

Dr		A Smith		Cr
		£		£
			Balance b/d	300

From these accounts we can see that:

• A Smith owes M Patel Ltd £200 (sales ledger)

• M Patel Ltd owes A Smith £300 (purchases ledger)

To save each having to make a payment and send it to the other, it is possible (with A Smith's agreement) to set-off one account against the other, so that they can settle their net indebtedness with one payment. The book-keeping entries for this contra transaction in M Patel's books will be:

– debit A Smith (purchases ledger) £200

– credit A Smith (sales ledger) £200

The accounts will now appear as:

SALES LEDGER

Dr		A Smith		Cr
		£		£
Balance b/d		200	Set-off: purchases ledger	200

PURCHASES LEDGER

Dr		A Smith		Cr
		£		£
Set-off: sales ledger		200	Balance b/d	300

The net result is that M Patel Ltd owes A Smith £100. The important point to note is that, because transactions have been recorded in the personal accounts, an entry needs to be made in the two control accounts:

- debit purchases ledger control account with the amount set-off
- credit sales ledger control account with the amount set-off

Set-off transactions should be appropriately documented with a general journal entry authorised by the accounts supervisor.

SALES LEDGER CREDIT BALANCES AND PURCHASES LEDGER DEBIT BALANCES

sales ledger

The normal account balance of debtors in the sales ledger is debit, ie the amount is owing to the business by the debtors. As noted earlier in the chapter (page 177), it can sometimes happen that a debtor's account has a credit balance. This comes about, for example, when a debtor has paid for goods and then returns them, or has overpaid in error.

The following example shows a debtor's account with a credit balance at the end of the month:

SALES LEDGER

Dr					S Johnson			Cr
20-1			£	20-1				£
1 Jan	Balance b/d		100	20 Jan	Bank			300
3 Jan	Sales		200	30 Jan	Sales returns			200
31 Jan	Balance c/d		200					
			500					500
				1 Feb	Balance b/d			200

This debtor's account has a credit balance at the end of January – not what we would expect to find on an account in sales ledger. Assuming that this is the only such balance, for sales ledger control account the credit balance is shown on the same side as in the debtor's account:

Dr				Sales Ledger Control Account			Cr
20-1			£	20-1			£
31 Jan	Balance c/d		200				
				1 Feb	Balance b/d		200

All other aspects of the sales ledger control account are the same as before. If there should, by chance, be more than one such credit balance in sales ledger, then they will be added together for the control account. Also note that, in a trial balance, any such credit balances must be shown on the credit side, ie separate from the main debit balances of sales ledger.

purchases ledger

In purchases ledger the normal account balance of creditors is credit, ie the amount the business owes to its creditors. As noted on page 179, it is possible for a creditor's account to have a debit balance – for example, if a creditor has been paid and then goods are returned, or if the creditor has been overpaid.

The following example shows a creditor's account with a debit balance at the end of the month.

PURCHASES LEDGER

Dr				**T Singh**			Cr
20-1			£	20-1			£
10 Jan	Bank		300	1 Jan	Balance b/d		200
20 Jan	Purchases returns		100	4 Jan	Purchases		100
				31 Jan	Balance c/d		100
			400				400
1 Feb	Balance b/d		100				

The debit balance on a creditor's account in purchases ledger is shown in purchases ledger control account as it appears on the account (assuming that this is the only such balance at the end of January):

Dr			**Purchases Ledger Control Account**			Cr
20-1		£	20-1			£
			31 Jan	Balance c/d		100
1 Feb	Balance b/d	100				

All other aspects of purchases ledger control account are the same as before. If there is more than one such debit balance, then they will be added together for the control account. Note that, in a trial balance, any such debit balances must be shown on the debit side, ie separate from the main credit balances of sales ledger.

SOURCES OF INFORMATION FOR CONTROL ACCOUNTS

Control accounts use totals (remember that their other name is totals accounts) for the week, month, quarter or year – depending on what time period is decided upon by the business. The totals come from a number of sources in the accounting system:

sales ledger control account

- total credit sales – from the sales day book
- total sales returns – from the sales returns day book
- total cash/cheques received from debtors – from the main cash book
- returned cheques – from the main cash book
- total discount allowed – from the discount allowed column of the main cash book, or from discount allowed account
- bad debts – from the general journal, or bad debts written off account
- set-off/contra entries – from the general journal

purchases ledger control account

- total credit purchases – from the purchases day book
- total purchases returns – from the purchases returns day book
- total cash/cheques paid to creditors – from the main cash book
- total discount received – from the discount received column of the main cash book, or from discount received account
- set-off/contra entries – from the general journal

Note that when using a computer accounting system, relevant transactions are automatically recorded on the control account

CONTROL ACCOUNTS AS AN AID TO MANAGEMENT

- **instant information**

  When the manager of a business needs to know the figure for debtors or creditors – important information for the manager – the balance of the appropriate control account will give the information immediately. There is no need to add up the balances of all the debtors' or creditors' accounts. With a computer accounting system, the control accounts can be printed at any time.

- **prevention of fraud**

  The use of a control account makes fraud more difficult – particularly in a manual accounting system. If a fraudulent transaction is to be recorded on a personal account, the transaction must also be entered in the control account. As the control account will be either maintained by a supervisor, and/or checked regularly by the manager, the control account adds another level of security within the accounting system.

● **location of errors**

We have already seen in this chapter how control accounts can help in locating errors. However, a control account can only indicate that there is an error within a ledger section – it will not pinpoint where the error has occurred. Also, a control account only demonstrates the arithmetical accuracy of the accounts which it controls – there could still be errors, such as misposts and compensating errors, within the ledger section.

● **preparation of final accounts**

A further use of control accounts is to help with the preparation of final accounts when a business has not kept double-entry accounts and a trial balance cannot be extracted. This aspect of accounting – known as 'incomplete records' – is covered at A2 level.

● **limitation of control accounts**

Whilst control accounts can help in locating errors, they do have the limitation that not all errors will be revealed by them. As noted above, such errors include:

– omission, where a transaction has been completely omitted from the accounting records

– mispost/error of commission, where a transaction is entered in the wrong person's account, but within the same ledger section

– original entry, where the wrong money amount has been entered into the accounting system, eg a 'bad' figure on a cheque received from a debtor is entered wrongly in both cash book and sales ledger

– compensating error, where one error is cancelled out by another error within the same ledger section, eg the balance of one account in purchases ledger is calculated at £1,000 too much, while another account in the same ledger is calculated at £1,000 too little

CONTROL ACCOUNTS AND BOOK-KEEPING

A business must decide how to use control accounts in its book-keeping system. One way of doing this is to keep the control accounts as memorandum records only, ie they are not part of the double-entry system.

The control accounts, therefore, do not form part of the double-entry system, but are used as a 'checking device' for the ledger section which they control. The personal accounts of debtors and creditors – in the sales ledger and purchases ledger respectively – continue to be part of the double-entry system. From time-to-time, the balances of the memorandum control accounts are agreed with the balances of the personal accounts in the sales ledger and purchases ledger.

The diagrams on the next two pages show how the sales ledger control account and the purchases ledger control account are kept as memorandum accounts, while the personal accounts of debtors and creditors are part of the double-entry system – in the sales ledger and purchases ledger.

continued on page 188

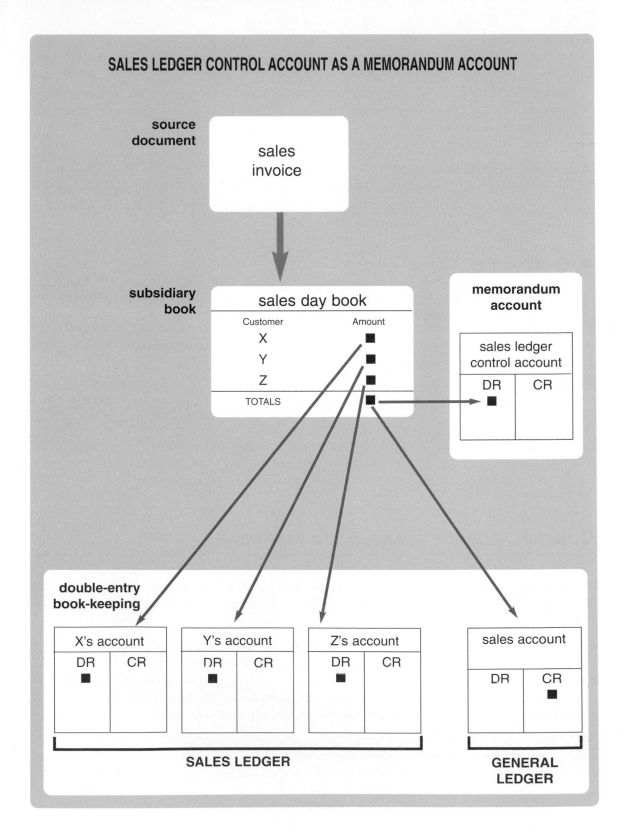

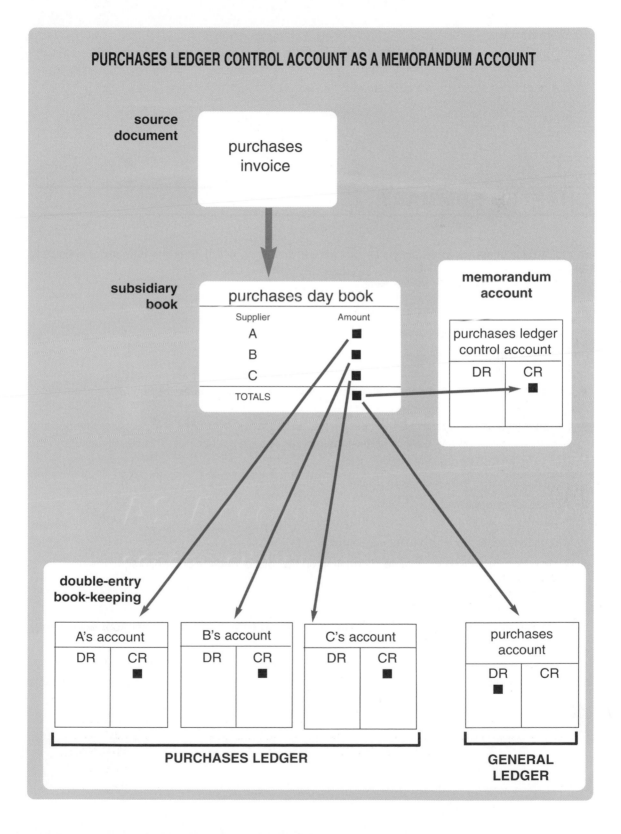

An alternative way – often used by computer accounting programs – is for the control accounts to be incorporated into the double-entry book-keeping, with the individual debtors' and creditors' accounts being kept as memorandum accounts. However, the specifications for AS Accounting Unit 1 state that control accounts will be memorandum accounts only.

CHAPTER SUMMARY

- Control accounts (or totals accounts) are 'master' accounts, which control a number of subsidiary accounts.

- Two commonly used control accounts are:
  - sales ledger control account
  - purchases ledger control account

- Transactions are recorded on the same side of the control account as on the subsidiary accounts.

- Set-off/contra entries occur when one person has an account in both sales and purchases ledger, and it is agreed to set-off one balance against the other to leave a net balance. This usually results in the following control account entries:
  - debit purchases ledger control account
  - credit sales ledger control account

- Control accounts are an aid to management:
  - in giving immediate, up-to-date information on the total of debtors or creditors
  - by making fraud more difficult
  - in helping to locate errors
  - in assisting with the preparation of final accounts when a business has not kept double-entry accounts

- The specifications for AS Accounting Unit 1 state that control accounts will be memorandum accounts only.

QUESTIONS

visit
www.osbornebooks.co.uk
to take an online test

An asterisk (*) after the question number means that the answer is given at the end of this book.

11.1* Prepare a sales ledger control account for the month of June 20-1 from the following information:

20-1		£
1 Jun	Sales ledger balances	17,491
30 Jun	Credit sales for month	42,591
	Sales returns	1,045
	Payments received from debtors	39,024
	Cash discount allowed	593
	Bad debts written off	296

The debtors figure at 30 June is to be entered as the balancing figure.

11.2* Prepare a purchases ledger control account for the month of April 20-2 from the following information:

20-2		£
1 Apr	Purchases ledger balances	14,275
30 Apr	Credit purchases for month	36,592
	Purchases returns	653
	Payments made to creditors	31,074
	Cash discount received	1,048
	Transfer of credit balances to sales ledger	597

The creditors figure at 30 April is to be entered as the balancing figure.

11.3 The sales ledger of Rowcester Traders contains the following accounts on 1 February 20-8:

Arrow Valley Retailers	balance £826.40 debit
B Brick (Builders) Limited	balance £59.28 debit
Mereford Manufacturing Company	balance £293.49 debit
Redgrove Restorations	balance £724.86 debit
Wyvern Warehouse Limited	balance £108.40 debit

The following transactions took place during February:

3 Feb	Sold goods on credit to Arrow Valley Retailers £338.59, and to Mereford Manufacturing Company £127.48
7 Feb	Redgrove Restorations returned goods £165.38
15 Feb	Received a cheque from Wyvern Warehouse Limited for the balance of the account after deduction of 2.5% cash discount
17 Feb	Sold goods on credit to Redgrove Restorations £394.78, and to Wyvern Warehouse Limited £427.91
20 Feb	Arrow Valley Retailers settled an invoice for £826.40 by cheque after deducting 2.5% cash discount
24 Feb	Mereford Manufacturing Company returned goods £56.29
28 Feb	Transferred the balance of Mereford Manufacturing Company's account to the company's account in the purchases ledger
28 Feb	Wrote off the account of B Brick (Builders) Limited as a bad debt

You are to:

(a) write up the personal accounts in the sales ledger of Rowcester Traders for February 20-8, balancing them at the end of the month

(b) prepare a sales ledger control account for February 20-8, balancing it at the end of the month

(c) reconcile the control account balance with the debtors' accounts at 1 February and 28 February 20-8.

Note: day books are not required.

11.4* (a) Advise Wholesale Car Spares of **two** benefits they would gain from keeping control accounts.

Benefit 1 ....

....

Benefit 2 ....

....

The sales ledger control account for the month ended 31 October 2000 did not agree with the sales ledger balances list total.

The following errors have been discovered.

1.   The sales day book was undercast by £540.

2.   The return inwards day book includes £100 which is actually for returns outwards.

3.   A discount allowed of £37 has been omitted from the books completely.

4.   A cheque received from J C Cross Garages for £1,479 was entered in the account of A B Cross Ltd in error.

5.   The opening balance brought down should have been £25,080.

(b)   Enter the necessary corrections in the control account. Balance the account.

Dr		£	2000		£
2000					
31 Oct	Balance b/d	25,800			

Sales Ledger Control Account — Cr

(c)   Explain the main limitation of control accounts using two examples to illustrate your answer.

Assessment and Qualifications Alliance (AQA), 2001

11.5 The following figures have been drawn from the books of Kings Products for the month ended 31 March 2001:

	£
Balances at 1 March 2001:	
Credit balances	23,437
Debit balances	465
Balances at 31 March 2001:	
Purchases on credit for the month	245,897
Returns to suppliers of credit purchases	4,679
Cash purchases	25,679
Purchase ledger balances set off against sales ledger	475
Cash paid to suppliers	236,498
Discounts received	3,674
Cash refunds from credit suppliers	450
Debit balance on the purchase ledger	749
Credit balances on the purchase ledger	?

Selecting from the above information, complete the control account for the month ended 31 March 2001 and calculate the credit balance at that date.

Dr	Purchase Ledger Control Account				Cr
Date 2001	Details	£	Date 2001	Details	£

Assessment and Qualifications Alliance (AQA), 2001

11.6 The following is the sales ledger control account of Wyvern Supplies for January 20-5:

Dr		**Sales Ledger Control Account**			Cr
20-5		£	20-5		£
1 Jan	Balance b/d	44,359	31 Jan	Bank	23,045
31 Jan	Sales	26,632	31 Jan	Discount allowed	1,126
31 Jan	Returned cheque	275	31 Jan	Sales returns	2,347
			31 Jan	Balance c/d	44,748
		71,266			71,266
1 Feb	Balance b/d	44,748			

The following errors have been discovered.

1. the sales day book total has been undercast by £1,000

2. the sales returns day book total should be £2,964

3. a contra entry with the purchases ledger of £247 has been omitted

4. a cheque for £685 received from a debtor, J Hampton, has been credited in error to the account of Hampton Limited

You are to redraft the sales ledger control account making the entries necessary to show the correct balance to be brought down on 1 February 20-5.

11.7 (a) From the following list of balances extracted from the books of BJ Patel on 30 November 2003 complete the sales and purchases ledger control accounts. Bring down the balance on each account.

	£
Sales on credit	26,500
Purchases on credit	19,600
Returns inwards	590
Returns outwards	450
Amounts received from customers	18,900
Amounts paid to suppliers	16,300
A debit balance set off from the sales ledger to the purchases ledger (contra)	400

Debit   **Sales Ledger Control Account**   Credit

2003	Details	£	2003	Details	£
Nov 1	Balance b/d	5,476			

Debit   **Purchases Ledger Control Account**   Credit

2003	Details	£	2003	Details	£
			Nov 1	Balance b/d	2,960

(b) Explain how control accounts are used to verify the balances in the sales ledger and purchase ledger accounts.

(c) What is the main limitation of using a control account to verify these ledger accounts?

Assessment and Qualifications Alliance (AQA), 2004

11.8* The following information has been extracted from the books of account of Alpha Engineering at 30 April 2007.

	£
Debtors at 1 April 2007	44,267
Sales day book total	93,882
Sales returns day book total	884
Receipts from credit customers entered in the cash book	95,501
Debit balance in sales ledger transferred to purchase ledger	235
Cash sales	2,276
Bad debt written off on 20 April 2007	150
Discount allowed	1,788
Customer's dishonoured cheque	107

You discover the following:

(a) A sales invoice totalling £545 was entered in the sales day book as £554.

(b) The sales returns day book total had been undercast by £100.

(c) A cheque received from a customer on 30 April 2007 for £2,339 had not yet been entered in the cash book.

REQUIRED

(a) Taking account of all of the above information, prepare a sales ledger control account for the month of April 2007.

Dr			**Sales Ledger Control Account**			Cr
Date	Details	£	Date	Details		£

(b) Control accounts can help in identifying some errors. Explain two other benefits to the management of a business from preparing a sales ledger control account.

(c) State and explain two types of error that would not be revealed by a control account.

Assessment and Qualifications Alliance (AQA), Specimen Paper for 2009

12 ADJUSTMENTS TO FINAL ACCOUNTS

In Chapter 9 we prepared the final accounts – trading and profit and loss account, and balance sheet. There are, however, a number of adjustments which are made to the final accounts at the year end in order to show a more relevant and reliable view of the state of the business.

This chapter is concerned with adjustments for accruals and prepayments of expenses, bad debts and depreciation.

Also covered in this chapter are the treatment of the owner's private expenses and goods for the owner's use.

The difference between income and expenditure accounting and receipts and payments accounting is discussed towards the end of the chapter.

INTRODUCTION TO ADJUSTMENTS TO FINAL ACCOUNTS

By making adjustments to final accounts we can improve the relevance and reliability of accounts in determining the income and expenditure, and showing the profit, and the assets and liabilities of the business.

The adjustments to final accounts covered in this chapter are as follows:

- **closing stock** – incorporating the value of stock held at the financial year end into the final accounts (this adjustment has been made already in the final accounts we have prepared in Chapter 9)
- **adjusting for accruals of expenses** – expenses due in an accounting period which have not been paid for at the end of that period (see page 197)
- **adjusting for prepayments of expenses** – payments of expenses made in advance of the accounting period to which they relate (see page 200)
- **depreciation of fixed assets** – writing down the value of fixed assets over their useful economic lives (see page 204)
- **bad debts written off** – removing from the sales ledger the accounts of debtors who will not pay, or cannot pay (see page 210)

Each of these adjustments is based on a number of accounting concepts – which we will look at in more detail in AS Unit 2 (Chapter 14). For the moment, we can say that the two main accounting concepts which form the basis of these adjustments are:

- the **accruals concept** – which is the matching of expenses and income to the same goods or services and the same time period – applies to closing stock, accruals, prepayments, depreciation
- the **prudence concept** – which requires that final accounts should always, where there is any doubt, report a conservative (ie lower) figure for profit or the valuation of assets – applies to depreciation and bad debts written off

To illustrate the effect of adjustments on final accounts we shall be referring to the final accounts of Wyvern Wholesalers, a sole trader business, which are shown on the next two pages (the trial balance – if you wish to refer to it – is on page 127).

ACCRUAL OF EXPENSES

An accrual is an amount due in an accounting period which is unpaid at the end of that period.

In the final accounts, accrued expenses are:

- added to the expense in the trial balance before listing it in the profit and loss account
- shown as a current liability in the year end balance sheet

The reason for dealing with accruals in this way is to ensure that the profit and loss account records the expense that has been incurred for the year, instead of simply the amount that has been paid. In other words, the expense is adjusted to relate to the time period covered by the profit and loss account. The year end balance sheet shows a liability for the amount that is due, but unpaid.

example of an accrual expense

The trial balance of Wyvern Wholesalers (see page 127) shows a debit balance for electricity and gas of £3,000. Before preparing the final accounts, an electricity bill for £250 is received on 1st January 20-2, ie on the first day of the new financial year. As this bill is clearly for electricity used in 20-1, an adjustment needs to be made in the final accounts for 20-1 to record this accrued expense.

In the profit and loss account, the total cost of £3,250 (ie £3,000 from the trial balance, plus £250 accrued) is recorded as an expense. In the balance sheet, £250 is shown as a separate current liability of 'accruals'.

accruals – the book-keeping records

In the double-entry records, accruals must be shown as an amount owing at the end of the financial year. Thus the account for electricity and gas in the records of Wyvern Wholesalers will appear as shown at the top of page 200.

continued on page 200

TRADING AND PROFIT AND LOSS ACCOUNT OF WYVERN WHOLESALERS
FOR THE YEAR ENDED 31 DECEMBER 20-1

	£	£	£
Sales			250,000
Less Sales returns			5,400
Net sales			244,600
Opening stock (1 January 20-1)		12,350	
Purchases	156,000		
Carriage in	–		
Less Purchases returns	7,200		
Net purchases		148,800	
		161,150	
Less Closing stock (31 December 20-1)		16,300	
Cost of sales			144,850
Gross profit			99,750
Add Discount received			2,500
			102,250
Less expenses:			
Discount allowed		3,700	
Salaries		46,000	
Electricity and gas		3,000	
Rent and rates		2,000	
Sundry expenses		4,700	
			59,400
Net profit			42,850

BALANCE SHEET OF WYVERN WHOLESALERS
AS AT 31 DECEMBER 20-1

	£	£	£
Fixed Assets			
Premises			100,000
Equipment			30,000
			130,000
Current Assets			
Stock		16,300	
Debtors		23,850	
Cash		125	
		40,275	
Less Current Liabilities			
Creditors	12,041		
Bank overdraft	851		
		12,892	
Net Current Assets or Working Capital			27,383
			157,383
Less Long-term Liabilities			
Loan			11,500
NET ASSETS			145,883
FINANCED BY			
Capital			
Opening capital			113,475
Add net profit			42,850
			156,325
Less drawings			10,442
			145,883

Dr		Electricity and Gas Account			Cr
20-1		£	20-1		£
31 Dec	Balance b/d (trial balance total)	3,000	31 Dec	Profit and loss account	3,250
31 Dec	Balance c/d	250			
		3,250			3,250
20-2			20-2		
			1 Jan	Balance b/d	250

Notes:

- The book-keeper's trial balance showed the debit side balance brought down of £3,000
- As £250 is owing for electricity at the end of the year, the transfer to profit and loss account is the expense that has been incurred for the year – this amounts to £3,250
- The balance remaining on the account – a credit balance of £250 – is the amount of the accrual, which is listed on the balance sheet at 31 December 20-1 as a current liability
- Later on, for example on 5 January, the electricity bill is paid by cheque and the account for 20-2 now appears as:

Dr		Electricity and Gas Account			Cr
20-2		£	20-2		£
5 Jan	Bank	250	1 Jan	Balance b/d	250

The effect of the payment on 5 January is that the account now has a 'nil' balance and the bill received on 1 January will not be recorded as an expense in the profit and loss account drawn up at the end of 20-2.

effect on profit

Taking note of the accrual of an expense has the effect of reducing a previously reported net profit. As the expenses have been increased, net profit is less (but there is no effect on gross profit). Thus, the net profit of Wyvern Wholesalers reduces by £250 from £42,850 to £42,600.

PREPAYMENT OF EXPENSES

A prepayment is a payment made in advance of the accounting period to which it relates.

A prepayment is, therefore, the opposite of an accrual: with a prepayment of expenses, some part of the expense has been paid in advance of the next accounting period.

In the final accounts, prepaid expenses are:

- deducted from the expense in the trial balance before listing it in the profit and loss account
- shown as a current asset in the year end balance sheet

As with accruals, the reason for dealing with prepaid expenses in this way is to ensure that the profit and loss account records the expense incurred for the year, and not the amount that has been paid – the profit and loss account expense relates to the time period covered by the profit and loss account. The year end balance sheet shows an asset for the amount that has been prepaid.

example of a prepaid expense

The owner of Wyvern Wholesalers tells you that the trial balance figure for rent and rates of £2,000, includes £100 of rent paid in advance for January 20-2. An adjustment needs to be made in the final accounts for 20-1 to record this prepaid expense.

In the profit and loss account, the cost of £1,900 (ie £2,000 from the trial balance, less £100 prepaid) is recorded as an expense. In the balance sheet, £100 is shown as a separate current asset of 'prepayments'.

prepayments – the book-keeping records

In the double-entry records, prepayments must be shown as an asset at the end of the financial year. Thus the account for rent and rates in the records of Wyvern Wholesalers will appear as follows:

Dr			**Rent and Rates Account**		Cr
20-1		£	20-1		£
31 Dec	Balance b/d (trial balance total)	2,000	31 Dec	Profit and loss account	1,900
			31 Dec	Balance c/d	100
		2,000			2,000
20-2					
1 Jan	Balance b/d	100			

Notes:

- The trial balance total for rent and rates is £2,000
- As £100 is prepaid at the end of the year, the transfer to profit and loss account is the expense that has been incurred for the year of £1,900
- The balance remaining on the account – a debit balance of £100 – is the amount of the prepayment, which is listed on the balance sheet at 31 December 20-1 as a current asset
- The debit balance of £100 on 1 January 20-2 will be included in the expenses for rent and rates for the year and will be transferred to profit and loss account on 31 December 20-2

effect on profit

Taking note of the prepayment of an expense has the effect of increasing a previously reported net profit – expenses have been reduced, so net profit is greater.

stocks of office supplies

At the end of a financial year most businesses have stocks of office supplies which have been recorded as expenses during the year, such as stationery, postage stamps (or a balance held in a franking machine). Technically, at the end of each year, these items should be valued and treated as a prepayment for next year, so reducing the expense in the current year's profit and loss account. However, in practice, this is done only when the stock of such items is substantial enough to affect the accounts in a material way. The firm's accountant will decide at what level the prepayment will apply.

To give an example of office stocks, the trial balance total for postages of a business at the year-end is £1,050; stocks of postage stamps at the same date are £150. The business will record an expense of £900 (£1,050, less £150) in the profit and loss account, while £150 is listed on the balance sheet as a current asset 'stocks of postage stamps'.

ACCRUALS AND PREPAYMENTS IN THE FINAL ACCOUNTS

We have looked at the separate effect of dealing with accruals and prepayments of expenses. Let us now see how they are presented in the final accounts of Wyvern Wholesalers. Remember that we are taking note of the following items at 31 December 20-1:

* electricity accrued £250
* rent prepaid £100

trading and profit and loss account

As there is no effect on gross profit, the details of the trading account are not shown here. The profit and loss section appears as shown below. Note that the calculations for accruals and prepayments do not appear in the final accounts; they are presented here for illustrative purposes only.

PROFIT AND LOSS ACCOUNT OF WYVERN WHOLESALERS FOR THE YEAR ENDED 31 DECEMBER 20-1			
		£	£	£
Gross profit				99,750
Add Discount received				2,500
				102,250
Less overheads (expenses):				
Discount allowed			3,700	
Salaries			46,000	
Electricity and gas	3,000 + 250		3,250	
Rent and rates	2,000 – 100		1,900	
Sundry expenses			4,700	
				59,550
Net profit				42,700

The effect of taking note of accruals and prepayments of expenses is to alter net profit:

	£
Net profit (before adjustments)	42,850
Add rent prepaid	100
	42,950
Less electricity accrued	250
Net profit (after adjustments)	42,700

balance sheet

The balance sheet is shown below with the accruals and prepayments of expenses shaded for illustrative purposes. These items do appear in the final accounts, (but not the shading).

BALANCE SHEET OF WYVERN WHOLESALERS
AS AT 31 DECEMBER 20-1

	£	£	£
Fixed Assets			
Premises			100,000
Equipment			30,000
			130,000
Current Assets			
Stock		16,300	
Debtors		23,850	
Prepayment of expenses		100	
Cash		125	
		40,375	
Less Current Liabilities			
Creditors	12,041		
Accrual of expenses	250		
Bank	851		
		13,142	
Net Current Assets or Working Capital			27,233
			157,233
Less Long-term Liabilities			
Loan			11,500
NET ASSETS			145,733
FINANCED BY			
Capital			
Opening capital			113,475
Add net profit			*42,700
			156,175
Less drawings			10,442
			145,733

* see net profit calculations at top of page

DEPRECIATION OF FIXED ASSETS

Depreciation is a measure of the amount of the fall in value of fixed assets over a time period.

Most fixed assets fall in value over time and, in accounting, it is necessary, in order to present a realistic view of the business, to measure the amount of the fall in value. This is done by showing an expense – called 'depreciation of fixed assets' – in the profit and loss account, and recording the asset at a lower value than cost price in the balance sheet. The expense of depreciation is an estimate of both the fall in value of the fixed asset and the time period; the estimate is linked usually to the cost price of the asset. Depreciation is an application of the accruals concept because we are recognising the timing difference between payment for the fixed asset and the asset's fall in value, and the prudence concept because we are estimating the fall in value of the asset and reporting a more reliable value for the asset on the balance sheet.

The main factors which cause fixed assets to depreciate are:

- wearing out through use, eg vehicles, machinery, etc
- passage of time, eg the lease on a building
- using up, eg extraction of stone from a quarry
- economic reasons
    - obsolescence, eg a new design of machine which does the job better and faster makes the old machine obsolete
    - inadequacy, eg a machine no longer has the capacity to meet the demand for its goods

Fixed assets – even buildings – are depreciated over their useful economic life. The only exception is freehold land which, because it is a non-wasting asset, does not normally depreciate (unless it is a quarry or a mine, when it will have a limited useful economic life). Land and buildings are sometimes increased in value from time-to-time, ie a revaluation takes place, and this is recorded in the accounts (see AS Unit 2, Chapter 17).

calculating depreciation

There are several different ways in which we can allow for the fall in value of fixed assets. All of these are estimates, and it is only when the asset is sold or scrapped that we will know the accuracy of the estimate, and adjustments can be made. The two most common methods of calculating depreciation are:

- straight line method
- reducing balance method (see AS Unit 2, Chapter 15)

For AS Unit 1 we are only concerned with the first of these methods – straight-line depreciation.

For the calculation of depreciation amounts we will use the following data:

MACHINE	
Cost price on 1 January 20-1	£2,000
Estimated life	4 years
Estimated scrap value at end of four years	£400

With the straight-line method of calculating depreciation, a fixed percentage is written off the original cost of the asset each year. For this example, twenty-five per cent will be written off each year by the straight-line method. The depreciation amount (ignoring for the moment any residual or scrap value) for each year is:

$$£2,000 \times 25\% = £500 \text{ per year}$$

The depreciation percentage will be decided by a business on the basis of what it considers to be the useful economic life of the asset. Thus, twenty-five per cent each year gives a useful economic life of four years (assuming a nil residual value at the end of its life).

Different classes of fixed assets are often depreciated at different rates, eg motor vehicles may be depreciated at a different rate to office equipment. It is important that, once a particular method and rate of depreciation has been selected, depreciation should be applied consistently, ie methods and rates are not changed from year-to-year without good reason.

The method of calculating straight-line depreciation, taking into account the asset's estimated sale proceeds at the end of its useful economic life, is:

$$\frac{\text{cost of asset} - \text{estimated residual (scrap or salvage) sale proceeds}}{\text{number of years' expected use of asset}}$$

For example, the machine is expected to have a residual (scrap or salvage) value of £400, so the depreciation amount will be:

$$\frac{£2,000 - £400}{4 \text{ years}} = £400 \text{ per year (ie 20\% per annum on cost)}$$

depreciation and final accounts

profit and loss account

The depreciation amount calculated for each class of asset is listed amongst the expenses as the allowance for depreciation for that particular class of asset. For example, for the machine we have just depreciated by the straight-line method, the profit and loss account will show 'depreciation: machinery £400' as an expense for each of the years 20-1 to 20-4.

balance sheet

Each class of fixed asset should be shown at cost price (or revaluation – see AS Unit 2, Chapter 17), less the amount of provision* for depreciation to date (ie this year's depreciation, plus depreciation from previous years if any). The resulting figure is the net book value (NBV) of the fixed asset.

* Note that a provision is an amount of profits set aside to meet a known expense, but where the amount can only be estimated for the time being; thus provision for depreciation is an estimate of the fall in value of fixed assets and, as we will see in the balance sheet extracts which follow, may well comprise depreciation amounts for more than one year.

The usual way of setting out depreciation amounts in a balance sheet (using the first year figures for the machine being depreciated by the straight-line method) is:

Balance sheet (extract) as at 31 December 20-1

	£	£	£
	Cost	Prov for dep'n	Net book value
Fixed Assets			
Machinery	2,000	400	1,600
Vehicles, etc	X	X	X
	X	X	X

Where there is only one class of fixed asset, eg machinery, the balance sheet extract can be set out in a simpler layout, as follows:

Balance sheet (extract) as at 31 December 20-1

	£
Fixed Assets	
Machinery at cost	2,000
Less provision for depreciation	400
Net book value	1,600

At the end of the second year, the machine is shown in the balance sheet as follows:

Balance sheet (extract) as at 31 December 20-2

	£	£	£
	Cost	Prov for dep'n	Net book value
Fixed Assets			
Machinery	2,000	800	1,200
Vehicles, etc	X	X	X
	X	X	X

Notice, from the above, how provision for depreciation increases with the addition of each further year's depreciation. At the same time, the net book value figure reduces – it is this net book value figure which is added to the other fixed assets to give a sub-total for this section of the balance sheet.

trial balance figures

When preparing final accounts from a trial balance, the trial balance often gives separate figures for the cost of an asset and its provision for depreciation at the start of the year. For example:

Trial Balance as at 31 December 20-3

	Dr £	Cr £
Machinery at cost	2,000	
Provision for depreciation: machinery		800

If a note to the trial balance then says, for example, to "depreciate machinery for the year at twenty per cent on cost", this indicates that the trial balance figure is at the start of the year. Accordingly, depreciation of £400 for 20-3 must be calculated and shown as an expense in profit and loss account.

The balance sheet will then show:

Balance sheet (extract) as at 31 December 20-3

	£ Cost	£ Prov for dep'n	£ Net book value
Fixed Assets			
Machinery	2,000	1,200	800
Vehicles, etc	X	X	X
	X	X	X

depreciation policies of a business

In examination questions, information will be given – where it is needed – on the depreciation policies of the business whose accounts you are preparing. In particular, the information will be given on what to do when a fixed asset is bought part of the way through a firm's financial year. The choices here will be to allocate depreciation for the part of the year that it is owned; alternatively the firm may choose to provide for depreciation for the whole year on assets held at the end of the year.

DEPRECIATION IN THE FINAL ACCOUNTS

We will now focus on how the depreciation amounts are shown in the profit and loss account and balance sheet. We will continue with the final accounts of Wyvern Wholesalers (see pages 202 and 203) and include depreciation for the year of:

* premises: 2 per cent straight-line, ie £2,000 depreciation
* equipment: 10 per cent straight-line, ie £3,000 depreciation

trading and profit and loss account

There is no effect on gross profit, so the details of the trading account are not shown here. The profit and loss account appears as shown below, with the depreciation amounts for the year included amongst the expenses, where they are shaded for illustrative purposes. Note that it is usual to show the separate amount of depreciation for each class of fixed asset (as below), rather than the total amount of depreciation.

PROFIT AND LOSS ACCOUNT OF WYVERN WHOLESALERS
FOR THE YEAR ENDED 31 DECEMBER 20-1

	£	£	£
Gross profit			99,750
Add Discount received			2,500
			102,250
Less expenses:			
Discount allowed		3,700	
Salaries		46,000	
Electricity and gas		3,250	
Rent and rates		1,900	
Sundry expenses		4,700	
Depreciation:			
premises		2,000	
equipment		3,000	
			64,550
Net profit			37,700

The effect of taking note of depreciation is to reduce net profit:

	£
Net profit (before adjustment for depreciation)	42,700 (see page 203)
Less depreciation £2,000 + £3,000	5,000
Net profit (after adjustment for depreciation)	37,700

balance sheet

The balance sheet is shown on the next page with the depreciation amounts shaded for illustrative purposes. Note that the deduction in the balance sheet is the amount of provision for depreciation to date (ie this year's depreciation, plus depreciation from previous years, if any). Cost, less provision for depreciation, equals the net book value (NBV) of the fixed asset. It is good practice when preparing balance sheets to total the first two columns and to sub-total the third, as illustrated on the next page.

BALANCE SHEET OF WYVERN WHOLESALERS AS AT 31 DECEMBER 20-1			
	£	£	£
Fixed Assets	Cost	Prov for dep'n	Net book value
Premises	100,000	2,000	98,000
Equipment	30,000	3,000	27,000
	130,000	5,000	125,000
Current Assets			
Stock		16,300	
Debtors		23,850	
Prepayment of expenses		100	
Cash		125	
		40,375	
Less Current Liabilities			
Creditors	12,041		
Accrual of expenses	250		
Bank	851		
		13,142	
Net Current Assets or Working Capital			27,233
			152,233
Less Long-term Liabilities			
Loan			11,500
NET ASSETS			140,733
FINANCED BY			
Capital			
Opening capital			113,475
Add net profit			*37,700
			151,175
Less drawings			10,442
			140,733

* see net profit calculations on previous page

depreciation: a non-cash expense

It is very important to realise that depreciation is a non-cash expense: unlike most of the other expenses in the profit and loss account, no cheque is written out, or cash paid, for depreciation. In cash terms, depreciation causes no outflow of money. Nevertheless, it is correct, in the final accounts of a business, to show an allowance for depreciation in the profit and loss account, and to reduce the value of the fixed asset in the balance sheet. This is because the business has had the use of the asset, and needs to record the fall in value as an expense in order to present a true picture of its financial state. Thus we are led back to the definition of depreciation as 'a measure of the amount of the fall in value of fixed assets over a time period', ie it is an accounting adjustment. As depreciation is shown as an expense in profit and loss account, it reduces net profit – a lower profit figure may discourage the owner from drawing too much cash from the business. The non-cash effect of depreciation is shown in the diagram on the next page.

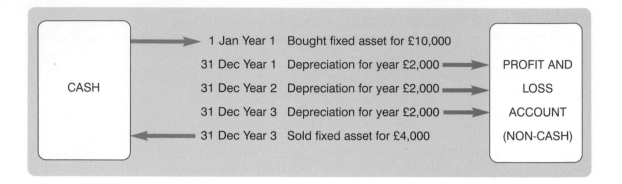

As depreciation is a non-cash expense, it should be noted that depreciation is not a method of providing a fund of cash which can be used to replace the asset at the end of its life.

BAD DEBTS

A bad debt is a debt owing to a business which it considers will never be paid.

Most businesses selling their goods and services to other businesses do not receive payment immediately. Instead, they often have to allow a period of credit and, until the payment is received, they have a current asset of debtors. Unfortunately, it is likely that not all debtors will eventually settle the amount they owe, ie the amounts are bad debts which have to be written off because the cost of their collection would be greater than the amount recovered.

Let us consider a business with debtors of £10,000. This total will, most probably, be made up of a number of debtors' accounts. At any one time, a few of these accounts will be bad, and therefore the amount is uncollectable: these are bad debts, and they need to be written off, ie the business will give up trying to collect the debt and will accept the loss. The one thing the business with debtors of £10,000 cannot do is to show this debtors' amount as a current asset in the balance sheet: to do so would be to imply that the full £10,000 is collectable. Instead, this gross debtors' figure might be reduced, for example, by writing off debtors' accounts with balances totalling £200.

Thus the debtors' figure becomes:

Gross debtors	£10,000
Less: bad debts	£200
Net debtors (recorded in balance sheet)	£9,800

Bad debts is an application of the accounting concept of prudence. By reducing the debtors' figure, through the profit and loss account and balance sheet, a more reliable view is shown of the amount that the business can expect to receive.

treatment of bad debts

Bad debts are written off when they become uncollectable. This means that all reasonable efforts to recover the amount owing have been exhausted, ie statements and letters have been sent to the debtor requesting payment, and legal action, where appropriate, or the threat of legal action has failed to obtain payment.

In writing off a debtor's account as bad, the business is bearing the cost of the amount due. The debtor's account is closed and the amount (or amounts, where a number of accounts are dealt with in this way) is debited to bad debts written off account. This account stores up the amounts of account balances written off during the year (in much the same way as an expense account). At the end of the financial year, the balance of the account is transferred to profit and loss account, where it is described as bad debts written off.

In terms of book-keeping, the transactions are:

- debit bad debts written off account
- credit debtor's account

with the amount of the bad debt.

At the end of the financial year, bad debts written off account is transferred to profit and loss account:

- debit profit and loss account
- credit bad debts written off account

with the total of bad debts written off for the year.

WORKED EXAMPLE: TREATMENT OF BAD DEBTS

The following debtor's account is in the sales ledger:

Dr			T Hughes			Cr
20-1		£	20-1	£		
5 Jan	Sales	55	8 May	Bank		25
			6 Jul	Cash		5

It is now 15 December 20-1 and you are reviewing the debtors' accounts before the end of the financial year on 31 December. Your business has sent statements and 'chaser' letters to T Hughes – the last letter was dated 30 September, and was returned marked 'gone away, not known at this address'. Nothing further has been heard from T Hughes. You take the decision to write off this account as a bad debt; the account will be closed off as follows:

Dr		T Hughes				Cr
20-1			£	20-1		£
5 Jan	Sales		55	8 May	Bank	25
				6 Jul	Cash	5
				15 Dec	Bad debts written off	25
			55			55

The balance is transferred to the 'holding' account, bad debts written off (in the general ledger), together with other debtors' accounts written off. At the end of the financial year, the total of this account is transferred to profit and loss account:

Dr		Bad Debts Written Off Account			Cr
20-1		£	20-1		£
15 Dec	T Hughes	25	31 Dec	Profit and loss account	200
15 Dec	A Lane	85			
15 Dec	A Harvey	90			
		200			200

In final accounts, the effect of writing off debts as bad is to reduce the previously reported profit – in the example above, by £200. Note that:

- If you are preparing final accounts and the figure for bad debts is shown in the trial balance (debit side), simply record the amount as an expense in profit and loss account – the debtors' figure has been reduced already.

- If the bad debts figure is not already shown in the trial balance, and a note tells you to write off a certain debt as bad, you need to list the amount as an expense in profit and loss account and reduce the debtors' figure for the balance sheet.

BAD DEBTS IN THE FINAL ACCOUNTS

We will now focus on how the amounts for bad debts are shown in the profit and loss account and balance sheet. We will continue with the final accounts of Wyvern Wholesalers (see pages 208 and 209) where the owner tells you that there is £250 to be written off the debtors figures as bad debts.

trading and profit and loss account

There is no effect on gross profit, so the details of the trading account are not shown here. The profit and loss account appears as shown on the next page, with the bad debts written off amount for the year included amongst the expenses, where it is shaded for illustrative purposes.

PROFIT AND LOSS ACCOUNT OF WYVERN WHOLESALERS
FOR THE YEAR ENDED 31 DECEMBER 20-1

	£	£	£
Gross profit			99,750
Add Discount received			2,500
			102,250
Less expenses:			
Discount allowed		3,700	
Salaries		46,000	
Electricity and gas		3,250	
Rent and rates		1,900	
Sundry expenses		4,700	
Depreciation:			
premises		2,000	
equipment		3,000	
Bad debts		250	
			64,800
Net profit			37,450

The effect of taking note of bad debts written off is to reduce net profit:

Net profit (before adjustment for bad and doubtful debts)	£37,700 (see page 208)
Less bad debts written off	£250
Net profit (after adjustment for bad debts)	£37,450

balance sheet

The balance sheet is shown on the next page with the debtors amount shaded for illustrative purposes. The amount of bad debts of £250 has been deducted before debtors are recorded in the balance sheet, ie £23,850 – £250 written off = £23,600.

BALANCE SHEET OF WYVERN WHOLESALERS
AS AT 31 DECEMBER 20-1

	£	£	£
Fixed Assets	Cost	Prov for dep'n	Net book value
Premises	100,000	2,000	98,000
Equipment	30,000	3,000	27,000
	130,000	5,000	125,000
Current Assets			
Stock		16,300	
Debtors 23,850 – 250		23,600	
Prepayment of expenses		100	
Cash		125	
		40,125	
Less Current Liabilities			
Creditors	12,041		
Accrual of expenses	250		
Bank	851		
		13,142	
Net Current Assets or Working Capital			26,983
			151,983
Less Long-term Liabilities			
Loan			11,500
NET ASSETS			140,483
FINANCED BY			
Capital			
Opening capital			113,475
Add net profit			*37,450
			150,925
Less drawings			10,442
			140,483

* see net profit calculations on previous page

PRIVATE EXPENSES AND GOODS FOR OWN USE

Adjustments also have to be made in the final accounts for the amount of any business facilities that are used by the owner for private purposes. These adjustments are for private expenses and goods for own use.

private expenses

Sometimes the owner of a business uses business facilities for private purposes, eg telephone, or car. The owner will agree that part of the expense shall be charged to him or her as drawings, while the other part represents a business expense.

For example, telephone expenses for the year amount to £600, and the owner agrees that this should be split as one-quarter private use, and three-quarters to the business. This is recorded in the final accounts as:

- £450 (three-quarters) in profit and loss account as a business expense
- £150 (one-quarter) is added to the owner's drawings

goods for own use

When the owner of a business takes some of the goods in which the business trades for his or her own use, the amount is:

- deducted from purchases
- added to the owner's drawings

The reason for reducing purchases is to ensure that only those purchases used in the business are recorded; these are then matched to the sales derived from them.

INSURANCE CLAIMS

When a business loses stock as a result of causes such as fire, theft, water damage, a claim is made to the insurance company for the cost of the insured stock. The insurance company will then need to agree the amount of the claim and will make payment to the business.

In the final accounts of a business that has agreed an insurance claim, but where payment has not yet been received from the insurance company, the adjustments are:

- reduce the figure for purchases in the trading account by the amount of the claim
- show the amount of the agreed claim due from the insurance company as a current asset in the balance sheet

INCOME AND EXPENDITURE ACCOUNTING

In this chapter we have made adjustments for accruals and prepayments to ensure that the profit and loss account shows the correct amount of expenses for the financial year, ie what should have been paid, instead of what has actually been paid. In doing this we are adopting the principle of income and expenditure accounting. If we simply used the trial balance figures, we would be following the principle of receipts and payments accounting, ie comparing money coming in, with money going out: this would usually give a false view of the net profit for the year.

The principle of income and expenditure accounting is applied in the same way to purchases and sales, although no adjustments are needed because of the way in which these two are handled in the accounting records. For purchases, the amount is entered into the accounts when the supplier's invoice is received, although the agreement to buy will be contained in the legal contract which exists between buyer and seller. From the accounting viewpoint, it is receipt of the supplier's invoice that causes an accounting entry to be made; the subsequent payment is handled as a different accounting transaction. A business could have bought goods, not paid for them yet, but will have a purchases figure to enter into the trading account. Doubtless the creditors will soon be wanting payment!

Sales are recorded in a similar way – when the invoice for the goods is sent, rather than when payment is made. This applies the principle of income and expenditure accounting. In this way, a business could have made a large amount of sales, which will be entered in the trading account, but may not yet have received any payments.

The way in which accounts are adjusted to take note of adjustments such as expenses accruals and prepayments, depreciation of fixed assets, and bad debts, is formally recognised in the accruals (or matching) concept, which is discussed in more detail in AS Unit 2, Chapter 14.

CHAPTER SUMMARY

- Final accounts are prepared on the income and expenditure basis, rather than the receipts and payments basis.

- An adjustment should be made at the end of the financial year in respect of expense accruals and prepayments.

- In the final accounts, accrued expenses are:
  - added to the expense in the trial balance
  - shown as a current liability in the balance sheet

- In the final accounts, prepaid expenses are:
  - deducted from the expense in the trial balance
  - shown as a current asset in the balance sheet

- Depreciation is a measure of the amount of the fall in value of fixed assets over a time period.

- A common method of calculating depreciation is the straight-line method.

- The depreciation amount for each class of fixed asset is included amongst the expenses in profit and loss account, while the value of the asset, as shown in the balance sheet, is reduced by the same amount.

- Depreciation is a non-cash expense.

- A bad debt is a debt owing to a business which it considers will never be paid.

- In the profit and loss account a bad debt written off is charged as an expense, and in the balance sheet a net debtors' figure is shown.

- Adjustments also need to be made in the final accounts for:
  - private expenses
  - goods for own use

This chapter completes your studies for AS Unit 1. However, in AS Unit 2 you will continue to study further aspects of the preparation of final accounts – both of sole traders and limited companies.

QUESTIONS

An asterisk (*) after the question number means that the answer is given at the end of this book.

12.1 Explain how the following would be dealt with in the profit and loss account, and balance sheet of a business with a financial year end of 31 December 20-2:

(a) Wages and salaries paid to 31 December 20-2 amount to £55,640. However, at that date, £1,120 is owing: this amount is paid on 4 January 20-3.

(b) Rates totalling £3,565 have been paid to cover the period 1 January 20-2 to 31 March 20-3.

(c) A computer is rented at a cost of £150 per month. The rental for January 20-3 was paid in December 20-2 and is included in the total payments during 20-2 which amount to £1,950.

12.2 The following information has been extracted from the accounts of Southtown Supplies, a wholesaling business, for the year ended 31 December 20-9:

	£
Sales	420,000
Purchases	280,000
Stock at 1 January 20-9	70,000
Stock at 31 December 20-9	60,000
Rent and rates	10,250
Electricity	3,100
Telephone	1,820
Salaries	35,600
Vehicle expenses	13,750

Notes: at 31 December 20-9:
- rent prepaid is £550
- salaries owing are £450

You are to prepare the trading and profit and loss account of Southtown Supplies for the year ended 31 December 20-9.

12.3* Susan Harper has produced a draft profit and loss account for the year ended 31 December 20-8. As yet no entries have been made in the profit and loss account for the following information:

	£
Payments for business rates during the year	2,250
Payments for rent of premises during the year	5,300

Additional information	Year ended 31 December 20-7		Year ended 31 December 20-8	
		£		£
Payment for business rates	in advance	110	in arrears	150
Payment for rent of premises	in arrears	250	in advance	400

REQUIRED

Calculate the amounts to be entered in the profit and loss account for the year ended 31 December 20-8. Indicate in the table below the amount and whether it should be subtracted from or added to the profit of the business.

	Amount to be subtracted from draft net profit £	Amount to be added to draft net profit £
Business rates		
Rent of premises		

12.4* The following trial balance has been extracted by the book-keeper of Don Smith, who runs a wholesale stationery business, at 31 December 20-8:

	Dr	Cr
	£	£
Debtors	24,325	
Creditors		19,684
Capital		30,000
Bank		1,083
Rent and rates	10,862	
Electricity	2,054	
Telephone	1,695	
Salaries	55,891	
Vehicles	22,250	
Office equipment	7,500	
Vehicle expenses	10,855	
Drawings	15,275	
Discount allowed	478	
Discount received		591
Purchases	138,960	
Sales		257,258
Stock at 1 January 20-8	18,471	
	308,616	308,616

Notes at 31 December 20-8:
- stock was valued at £14,075
- rates are prepaid £250
- electricity owing £110
- salaries are owing £365

REQUIRED

(a) Prepare the rent and rates, electricity and salaries accounts to record the balances shown by the above trial balance, the amounts to be transferred to the profit and loss account and the balances to be carried forward to next year.

(b) Prepare the trading and profit and loss account of Don Smith for the year ended 31 December 20-8, together with his balance sheet at that date.

12.5* Martin Hough, sole owner of Juicyburger, a fast food shop, operating from leased premises in the town, is suspicious of his accountant, Mr S Harris, whom he claims doesn't really understand the food business. On the telephone he asks Mr Harris why depreciation is charged on a rigid formula, as surely no-one really knows how much his equipment is worth, and in fact he might not get anything for it. Draft a reply to Mr Hough from Mr Harris explaining the importance of depreciation and its application to final accounts.

12.6* David Evans started in business on 1 July 20-1 with a financial year end of 30 June. On 1 July 20-1 he bought fixed assets at a cost of £50,000. The fixed assets have an expected useful life of 10 years at the end of which they will have a nil scrap value.

David has decided to use the straight-line method of depreciating his fixed assets at an annual rate of 10%.

David's profits for his first two years in business *before* depreciation of fixed assets were £18,700 for 20-2 and £33,100 for 20-3.

REQUIRED

(a) Calculate David's net profit after depreciation of fixed assets.

	year ended 30 June 20-2 £	year ended 30 June 20-3 £
Net profit before depreciation	18,700	33,100
Depreciation on fixed assets	....	....
Net profit after depreciation	....	....

(b) Prepare a balance sheet extract showing David's fixed assets after allowing for provision for depreciation.

	as at 30 June 20-2 £	as at 30 June 20-3 £
Fixed assets at cost	50,000	50,000
Less provision for depreciation to date	....	....
Net book value	....	....

12.7 The following trial balance has been extracted by the book-keeper of Hazel Harris at 31 December 20-4:

	Dr £	Cr £
Bank loan		75,000
Capital		125,000
Purchases and sales	465,000	614,000
Building repairs	8,480	
Vehicles at cost	12,000	
Provision for depreciation on vehicles		2,400
Vehicle expenses	2,680	
Freehold land at cost	100,000	
Bank overdraft		2,000
Furniture and fittings at cost	25,000	
Provision for depreciation on furniture and fittings		2,500
Wages and salaries	86,060	
Discounts	10,610	8,140
Drawings	24,000	
Rates and insurance	6,070	
Debtors and creditors	52,130	41,850
General expenses	15,860	
Stock at 1 January 20-4	63,000	
	870,890	870,890

Notes at 31 December 20-4:

- Stock was valued at £88,000
- Wages and salaries outstanding: £3,180
- Rates and insurance paid in advance: £450
- Depreciate vehicles at 20 per cent using the straight-line method
- Depreciate furniture and fittings at 10 per cent using the straight-line method
- The freehold land is not to be depreciated

REQUIRED

You are to prepare the trading and profit and loss account of Hazel Harris for the year ended 31 December 20-4, together with her balance sheet at that date.

12.8* You are the book-keeper at Waterston Plant Hire. At 31 December 20-8, the end of the financial year, the business has gross debtors of £20,210. The owner decides to write off, as bad debts, the accounts of:

P Ross	£55
J Ball	£105
L Jones	£50

You are to:

(a)   show the bad debts written off account in the general ledger for the financial year

(b)   explain the effect of this write off on the final accounts at the end of the financial year

12.9 The following trial balance has been extracted by the book-keeper of Beth Davis, a shopkeeper, after the preparation of her trading account for the year ended 31 December 20-8.

	Dr £	Cr £
Gross profit		95,374
Wages and salaries	55,217	
Heating and lighting	1,864	
Rent and rates	5,273	
Advertising	2,246	
Bad debts written off	395	
General expenses	783	
Shop fittings at cost	12,000	
Provision for depreciation on shop fittings		2,400
Stock at 31 December 20-8	28,176	
Debtors	3,641	
Creditors		10,290
Bank		3,084
Cash	163	
Capital		20,806
Drawings	22,196	
	131,954	131,954

Notes at 31 December 20-8:
- rent prepaid £310
- accrued general expenses £85
- depreciate shop fittings at 20% per annum, using the straight-line method

You are to prepare the profit and loss account of Beth Davis for the year ended 31 December 20-8, together with her balance sheet at that date.

12.10

The owner of Beta Batteries is completing his final accounts for the year ended 31 May 2007. The following information for telephone charges has been extracted from the books of account and from information supplied.

	£
Amounts paid during the year ended 31 May 2007	2,400
Amounts owed for telephone calls at 31 May 2007	130
Telephone rental paid in advance at 31 May 2007	210

REQUIRED

(a)   Complete the ledger account below. Balance the account, carrying down any balances.

Telephone Account

Date	Details	£	Date	Details	£

J Booth, a customer of Beta Batteries, has been declared bankrupt owing the business £350. The owner of Beta Batteries is of the opinion that none of this amount will be recovered.

(b)   Write a memorandum to the owner of Beta Batteries explaining how this debt should be dealt with in the ledger accounts. Explain the effect it will have on **both** the profit **and** on the entries in the balance sheet.

Assessment and Qualifications Alliance (AQA), Specimen Paper for 2009

12.11* Mike Barnett owns a shop selling bicycles. the following balances have been extracted from the books of account at 31 May 2007.

	£	£
Bank overdraft		21,690
Capital		62,100
Carriage inwards	540	
Carriage outwards	1,270	
Discounts allowed	1,410	
Discounts received		2,090
Drawings	24,180	
Equipment:		
at cost	67,360	
provision for depreciation		16,840
Mortgage on premises (repayable 2022)		20,000
Motor expenses	15,430	
Premises at cost	50,000	
Purchases	132,700	
Returns inwards	630	
Returns outwards		1,310
Sales		266,300
Shop expenses	21,380	
Stock at 1 June 2006	35,820	
Trade creditors		9,210
Trade debtors	2,490	
Wages	46,330	
	399,540	399,540

Additional information

(1) Stock at 31 May 2007 was £29,700

(2) Motor expenses paid in advance at 31 May 2007 were £250

(3) Wages unpaid at 31 May 2007 amounted to £840

(4) Equipment is to be depreciated at 12.5% per annum using the straight-line method

REQUIRED

(a) Prepare a trading and profit and loss account for the year ended 31 May 2007.

(b) Prepare a balance sheet at 31 May 2007.

Assessment and Qualifications Alliance (AQA), Specimen Paper for 2009

AS Accounting Unit 2

Financial and Management Accounting

This Unit for AQA AS Accounting develops your knowledge and understanding of financial accounting and introduces some of the ways in which financial accounting can provide valuable information for monitoring business performance and for planning future business operations. AS Unit 2 covers:

- types of business organisation

- accounting concepts

- further aspects of the preparation of the final accounts of sole traders

- financial accounts of limited companies for internal use

- ratio analysis and the assessment of business performance

- an introduction to budgeting and budgetary control

- the impact of computer technology in accounting

13 BUSINESS ORGANISATIONS

In AS Unit 1 we have prepared the final accounts of sole traders. A sole trader is a person who sets up in business on his or her own.

In this chapter we look at two further types of business organisation – partnerships and limited companies – and compare the advantages of the three types of ownership.

Later on in AS Unit 2, in Chapter 17, we will prepare the final accounts of limited companies for internal use.

PRIVATE SECTOR ORGANISATIONS

Sole traders, partnerships and limited companies are all private sector organisations – as distinct from public sector organisations (such as local authorities, central government, the National Health Service) and not-for-profit organisations (such as societies and charities). The following diagram illustrates the types of private sector organisations:

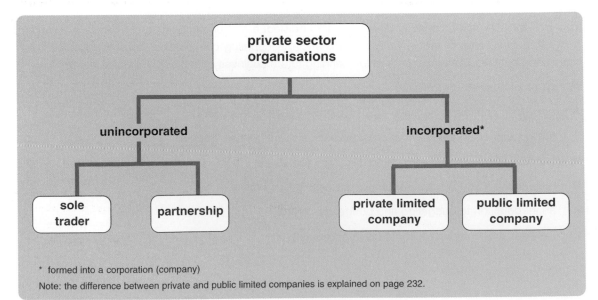

* formed into a corporation (company)

Note: the difference between private and public limited companies is explained on page 232.

In terms of accounting, we have already prepared the final accounts of sole traders in AS Unit 1. The transition from sole trader to partnership final accounts is not too big a step. In a partnership, instead of one person owning the business, there will be two or more owners.

The step from sole traders and partnerships to limited companies is rather greater, as a limited company is an incorporated business ('incorporated' means 'formed into a company'), where the owners are members (shareholders) of the company. The limited company final accounts you will study in this AS Unit are for internal use by the owners and managers of the business. They are covered in Chapter 17.

Each of the three types of business organisation – sole trader, partnership, and limited company – is discussed in more detail in the rest of this chapter. The following table illustrates the key differences between them:

	sole trader	*partnership*	*limited company*
ownership	• owned by the sole trader	• owned by the partners	• owned by the shareholders
legal status	• the sole trader is the business	• the partners are the business	• separate legal entity from its owners
members	• one	• between 2 and 20 (normal maximum)	• minimum of one shareholder; no maximum
liability	• unlimited liability, for debts of business	• partners normally liable for entire partnership debt	• shareholders can lose their investment
legislation	• none	• Partnership Act 1890	• Companies Act 2006
regulation	• none	• written or oral partnership agreement	• Articles of Association
taxation	• as an individual on profit	• each partner as an individual on share of profit	• company pays tax on profit
management	• owner takes all decisions	• all partners normally take an active part	• directors and authorised employees
final accounts	• private – not available to the public	• private – not available to the public	• must be filed at Companies House where they are available to the public

SOLE TRADERS

A sole trader is a person who is in business on his or her own. Sole traders run shops, travel agencies, garages, local franchises, and so on. The businesses are generally small because the owner usually has a limited amount of capital to invest. All the profit belongs to the sole trader; some of it will be taken out as drawings and the rest ploughed back into expanding the business.

People set up as sole traders for various reasons:

* the owner has independence and can run the business, by and large without the need to involve others in decision-making
* in a small business with few, if any, employees, the owner is able to give personal service and supervise all areas of the business
* the business is easy to establish legally – either using the owner's name, or a trading name such as 'Wyvern Plumbing Services'

The disadvantages of a sole-trader business are:

* the owner has unlimited liability for the debts of the business – this means that if the sole trader should become bankrupt (unable to pay debts when they are due), the owner's personal assets may be sold to pay creditors
* expansion is limited because it can be achieved only by the owner ploughing back profits, or by borrowing from a lender such as a bank
* the owner usually has to work long hours and it may be difficult to find time to take holidays; if the owner should become ill the work of the business may either slow down or stop altogether

final accounts of a sole trader

The final accounts of a sole trader comprise:

* trading and profit and loss account, which shows the profit or loss of the business
* balance sheet, which shows the assets and liabilities of the business together with the owner's capital

These final accounts can be produced more often than once a year in order to give information to the owner on how the business is progressing. However, it is normal to produce annual accounts for the benefit of HM Revenue and Customs (the tax authorities, who will wish to see that tax due – income tax and VAT – has been paid), providers of finance (such as the bank), and other stakeholders.

PARTNERSHIPS

The Partnership Act of 1890 defines a partnership as:

the relation which subsists between persons carrying on a business in common with a view of profit

Normally, partnerships consist of between two and twenty partners. Exceptions to this include large professional firms, eg solicitors and accountants, who often set what are known as 'limited liability partnerships' (LLPs). Partnerships are often larger businesses than sole traders because, as there is more than one owner, there is likely to be more capital. A partnership may be formed to set up a new business or it may be the logical growth of a sole trader taking in partners to increase the capital.

advantages and disadvantages

Partnerships are cheap and easy to set up; their advantages are:

- there is the possibility of increased capital
- individual partners may be able to specialise in particular areas of the business
- with more people running the business, there is more cover for illness and holidays

The disadvantages are:

- as there is more than one owner, decisions may take longer because other partners may need to be consulted
- there may be disagreements amongst the partners
- each partner is liable in law for the dealings and business debts of the whole firm – unless it is a limited liability partnership (LLP) set up under the Limited Liability Partnerships Act 2000
- the retirement or death of one partner may adversely affect the running of the business

accounting requirements of a partnership

The accounting requirements of a partnership are:

- either to follow the rules set out in the Partnership Act 1890
- or – and more likely – for the partners to agree amongst themselves, by means of a partnership agreement, to follow different accounting rules

Unless the partners agree otherwise, the Partnership Act 1890 states the following accounting rules:

- profits and losses are to be shared equally between the partners
- no partner is entitled to a salary
- partners are not entitled to receive interest on their capital
- interest is not to be charged on partners' drawings
- when a partner contributes more capital than agreed, he or she is entitled to receive interest at five per cent per annum on the excess

As noted above, the partners may well decide to follow different accounting rules – these will be set out in a partnership agreement:

- division of profits and losses between partners
- partners' salaries
- whether interest is to be allowed on capital and at what rate
- whether interest is to be charged on partners' drawings, and at what rate

final accounts of a partnership

A partnership prepares the same type of final accounts as a sole trader business:

* trading and profit and loss account
* balance sheet

The main difference is that, immediately after the trading and profit and loss account, follows an appropriation section (often described as an appropriation account). This shows how the net profit from profit and loss account is shared amongst the partners.

LIMITED COMPANIES

A limited company is a separate legal entity, owned by shareholders and run by directors.

Many people in business as sole traders often consider converting to a limited company. Read the following Case Study about a sole trader business and the discussions that take place between the sole trader and her accountant:

Case Study: conversion to a limited company

Veta Bix has been trading very successfully for the last three years running her bodycare products business as a sole trader. At the moment she has three shops and an online business trading under the 'BodyZone' name. She has plans, as she says to her accountant:

'I've big plans for expansion and have identified suitable sites for new shops in the south east, nearer to London. My problem, though, is finance; I will need a lot more capital. As a sole trader, it is difficult to see how I can raise the money I will need. I am also concerned about my unlimited liability for the debts of the business.'

Veta's accountant suggests that she consider forming a private limited company which will enable her to issue shares to family, friends and to local investors. As the accountant says:

'We aren't talking about a company quoted on the Stock Exchange – although some small businesses have made it to that stage. Instead, forming a private limited company should enable you to raise the finance you need and you will still be able to retain control of the business.'

The accountant suggests she calls the company BodyZone Limited. He comments:

'Forming a company is a big change from a sole trader business as it must be registered at Companies House. The company will have to produce formal annual accounts, which have to be filed at Companies House. The way you draw income from the company will also be different – a mix of salary and dividend payments. In terms of cost, it is quite an expensive option, but it would give you the added protection of limited liability.'

People choose to run a business as a limited company for a number of reasons:

limited liability

The shareholders (members) of a limited company can lose only the amount of their investment, being the money paid already, together with any money unpaid on their shares (unpaid instalments on new share issues, for example). Thus, if the company became insolvent (went 'bust'), shareholders would have to pay any unpaid instalments to help pay the creditors. As this happens very rarely, shareholders are usually in a safe position: their personal assets are not available to the company's creditors – ie they have **limited liability**.

separate legal entity

A limited company is a separate legal entity from its owners. Anyone taking legal action proceeds against the company and not the individual shareholders.

ability to raise finance

A limited company can raise substantial funds from outside sources by the issue of shares:

* for the larger public company – from the public and investing institutions on the Stock Exchange or similar markets
* for the smaller company – privately from venture capital companies, relatives and friends

Companies can also raise finance by means of debentures, which are formal certificates issued by companies raising long-term finance from lenders and investors.

membership

A member of a limited company is a person who owns at least one share in that company. A member of a company is the same as a shareholder. All ordinary shareholders have voting rights, so a sole trader who has converted to limited company status may lose some control of the business if some of the shares are held by other investors.

other factors

A limited company may be a much larger business unit than a sole trader. This gives the company a higher standing and status in the business community, allowing it to benefit from economies of scale, and making it of sufficient size to employ specialists for functions such as production, marketing, finance and human resources.

On the negative side, there is more documentation – eg the preparation of formal annual accounts – for a company to produce than for a sole trader business. The costs of administering a company are higher than for a sole trader.

running the company

As noted in the definition, a limited company is owned by its shareholders but is run by the directors. Under the Companies Act 2006, the company's *Articles of Association* provides the constitution of the company, regulates the affairs of the company to the outside world, and sets out the rules for running the company – including the powers of directors and the holding of company meetings. (Note that companies formed prior to the Companies Act 2006 will have an additional governing document, a *Memorandum of Association*.)

the Companies Act

Limited companies are regulated by the Companies Act 2006. Under the terms of the Act there are two main types of limited company: the larger **public limited company** (abbreviated to 'Plc') and the smaller company, traditionally known as a **private limited company** (abbreviated to 'Ltd'). A further type of company is limited by guarantee.

public limited company (Plc)

A company may become a public limited company if it has:

- issued share capital of over £50,000
- at least two members (shareholders) and at least two directors

A public limited company may raise capital from the public on the Stock Exchange or similar markets; however, a plc does not have to issue shares on the stock markets, and not all do so.

private limited company (Ltd)

The private limited company is the most common form of limited company and is defined by the Act as 'any company that is not a public company'. Many private limited companies are small companies, often in family ownership. A private limited company has:

- no minimum requirement for issued share capital
- at least one member (shareholder) and at least one director who may be the sole shareholder

The shares are not traded publicly, but are transferable between individuals, although valuation will be more difficult for shares not quoted on the stock markets.

company limited by guarantee

A company limited by guarantee does not have share capital, but relies on the guarantee of its members to pay a stated amount in the event of the company's insolvency. Examples of such companies include charities, and artistic and educational organisations.

final accounts of a limited company

For internal use, a limited company prepares the same type of final accounts as a sole trader and partnership business:

- trading and profit and loss account
- balance sheet

The main difference is that a limited company follows the trading and profit and loss with an appropriation section (or profit and loss appropriation account). This shows how the net profit is distributed to the tax authorities (for the amount of tax due on the profits of the company) and to shareholders (who receive dividends on the shares they hold).

Every limited company is required by law to produce final accounts – or financial statements – which are also available for anyone to inspect if they so wish. Such 'published accounts' are those which are required to be produced under company law, and a copy is sent to Companies House (a Government Agency). The level of detail contained in the published accounts is set out in company law and varies depending on the size of the company – for example, small and medium-sized private companies file modified accounts containing much less detail than public companies.

In Chapter 17 of this book we will prepare the final accounts of limited companies for internal use.

accounting personnel of a limited company

There are a number of different staff who may be involved in the accounting function. A large limited company, for example, may employ a book-keeper, financial accountant, cost and management accountant, and internal and external auditors, as shown in the diagram below.. A small limited company, on the other hand may have only have a few employees carrying out these functions.

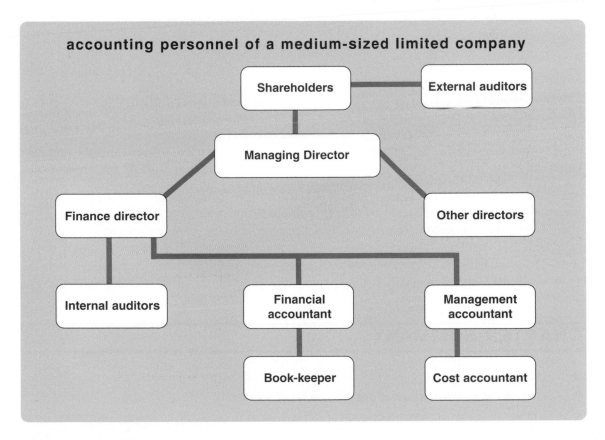

financial accountant

The function of the financial accountant is to take further the information prepared by the book-keeper. This includes the preparation of final accounts both for internal use, and published accounts which comply with the requirements of the Companies Act 2006. This Act requires the directors of a company to report annually to shareholders, with certain minimum financial accounting information being disclosed.

The financial accountant may be required to negotiate with the tax authorities on the amount of tax to be paid on the profits of the company. The financial accountant usually reports to the finance director.

cost and management accountants

The cost accountant obtains information about the recent costs of the company, eg raw materials and labour, and estimates costs for the future. Often the cost accountant reports to the management accountant who prepares budgets and reports, and makes recommendations to the directors or managers of the company. The management accountant usually reports to the finance director.

The work of the cost and management accountants includes the preparation of budgets and the exercise of budgetary control – see Chapter 19.

auditors

Auditors are accountants whose role is to check that accounting procedures have been followed correctly. There are two types of auditors:

- external auditors
- internal auditors

External auditors are independent of the firm whose accounts are being audited. The most common type of audit carried out by external auditors is the statutory audit for larger limited companies. In this, the auditors are reporting directly to the shareholders of the company, stating that the legal requirements laid down in the Companies Acts 2006 have been complied with, and that the accounts represent a 'true and fair view' of the state of the business. External auditors are usually appointed by the shareholders at the Annual General Meeting of the company.

Internal auditors are employees of the company which they audit. They are concerned with the internal checking and control procedures of the company: for example, procedures for the control of cash, authorisation of purchases, and disposal of property. The nature of their work requires that they should have a degree of independence within the company and they usually report directly to the finance director or to the company's audit committee.

CHAPTER SUMMARY

- Sole traders, partnerships and limited companies are private sector organisations.
- A sole trader is a person who is in business on his or her own.
- A partnership is formed when two or more (usually up to a maximum of twenty) people set up in business.
- The Partnership Act of 1890 defines a partnership as 'the relation which subsists between persons carrying on a business in common with a view of profit.'
- The Partnership Act 1890 states certain accounting rules, principally that profits and losses must be shared equally.
- Many partnerships over-ride the accounting rules of the Act by making a partnership agreement which covers:
  - division of profits and losses between partners
  - partners' salaries
  - whether interest is to be allowed on capital, and at what rate
  - whether interest is to be charged on partners' drawings, and at what rate

- A limited company has a separate legal entity from its owners.

- A limited company is regulated by the Companies Act 2006, and is owned by shareholders and managed by directors.

- A limited company may be either a public limited company or a private limited company.

- The liability of shareholders is limited to the amount of their investment and any money unpaid on their shares.

QUESTIONS

visit
www.osbornebooks.co.uk
to take an online test

An asterisk (*) after the question number means that the answer is given at the end of this book.

13.1* Karen, a friend of yours, is keen to set up in business running a sandwich and coffee shop on her own. She will call the business 'Karen's Katering'. Point out to her the advantages and disadvantages of a sole trader business and indicate possible future developments in the business organisation that she might consider.

13.2 What final accounts are produced at the end of each financial year for a sole trader business? Explain the main sections contained within the final accounts.

13.3 (a) Define a partnership.

(b) State three accounting provisions from the Partnership Act 1890 which will apply to a partnership where no partnership agreement exists.

13.4* Paging Systems plc wishes to prepare a handout for new staff explaining some facts about limited companies.

REQUIRED

(a) Who owns Paging Systems plc?

(b) Who is responsible for the day-to-day running of Paging Systems plc?

(c) What is the meaning of limited liability?

Assessment and Qualifications Alliance (AQA), 2003

13.5 Prepare a five-minute talk on the types of companies and the advantages of forming a limited company. The talk is to form part of your local radio station's business programme entitled 'Business Matters'. To accompany your talk, prepare an information sheet which can be put on the station's website.

14 ACCOUNTING CONCEPTS AND STOCK VALUATION

In this chapter we will explain how accounting concepts – or principles – are applied when preparing final accounts. If the same concepts are followed, then comparisons can be made between the final accounts of different businesses.

Later in the chapter we see how the accounting concepts are applied to the valuation of the stock of goods which a business holds for resale.

ACCOUNTING CONCEPTS

There are a number of generally applied **accounting concepts** – or principles of accounting – which underlie the preparation of final accounts. These concepts help to make final accounts relevant and reliable to stakeholders, and also enable them to be comparable and understandable.

The accounting concepts – which apply equally to sole trader, partnership and limited company businesses – are illustrated in the diagram below.

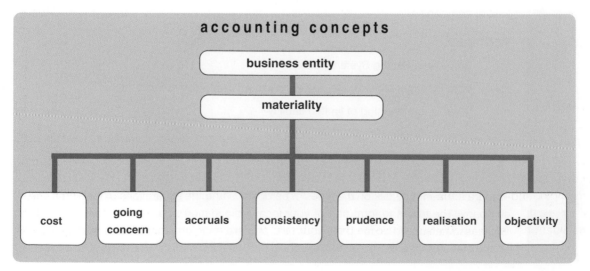

The two 'gateway' concepts of business entity and materiality apply to all aspects of final accounts – if information is not dealt with correctly under these two concepts it could have consequences for stakeholders who make decisions on the basis of the final accounts.

business entity

This refers to the fact that final accounts record and report on the activities of a particular business. They do not include the assets and liabilities of people who play a part in owning or running the business. For example, the personal assets and liabilities of the owner of a sole trader business are kept separate from those of the business. The main links between the business and the owner's personal funds are capital and drawings.

materiality

Some items in accounts have such a low monetary (money) value that it is not worthwhile recording them separately, ie they are not 'material'. Examples of this include:

- Small expense items, such as donations to charities, the purchase of plants for the office, window cleaning, etc, may not justify their own separate expense account; instead they are grouped together in a sundry expenses account.

- End-of-year stocks of office stationery, eg paper clips, staples, photocopying paper, etc, are often not valued for the purpose of final accounts, because the amount is not material and does not justify the time and effort involved. This does mean, however, that the cost of all stationery purchased during the year is charged as an expense to profit and loss account – this is technically wrong, but is not material enough to affect the final accounts significantly.

- Low-cost fixed assets are often charged as an expense in profit and loss account, eg a stapler, waste-paper basket, etc. Theoretically, these should be treated as fixed assets and depreciated each year over their estimated life; in practice, because the amounts involved are not material, they are treated as profit and loss account expenses.

Materiality depends very much on the size of the business. A large company may consider that items of less than £1,000 are not material; a smaller business will usually use a much lower figure. What is material and what is not becomes a matter of judgement and will vary from business to business.

cost

Assets and liabilities are recorded in the final accounts at historical cost, ie the actual amount of the transaction involved. The benefit of this is that the balance sheet valuations are objective – there can be no dispute about the amounts shown. However, as time passes, historical cost valuations become out-of-date and some businesses do adopt a policy of regular revaluation of assets. For example, freehold land and buildings bought, say, 20 years ago will have a much higher value today than their cost price. Thus it makes sense to carry out revaluations from time-to-time. However, such revaluations are invariably subjective, ie they represent the views of the valuer (who may well be a professional person), but there is no certainty that the asset could be sold at the revalued amount.

Generally, then, it can be said that the cost concept applies to all assets and liabilities unless there are sound reasons for using a different valuation.

going concern

This presumes that the business to which the final accounts relate will continue to trade in the foreseeable future. The trading and profit and loss account and balance sheet are prepared on the basis that there is no intention to reduce significantly the size of the business or to liquidate the business. If the business was not a going concern, assets would have very different values, and the balance sheet would be affected considerably. For example, a large, purpose-built factory has considerable value to a going concern business but, if the factory had to be sold, it is likely to have a limited use for other industries, and therefore will have a lower market value. The latter case is the opposite of the going concern concept and would be described as a 'gone concern'. Also, in a gone concern situation, extra depreciation would need to be charged as an expense to profit and loss account to allow for the reduced value of fixed assets. Stock valuation (see page 241), which is usually on a going concern basis, would normally be much lower on a gone concern basis.

accruals (or matching)

This means that expenses and income for goods and services are matched to the same time period. We have already put this concept into practice in Chapter 12 (AS Unit 1), where expenses and income were adjusted to take note of prepayments and accruals. The trading and profit and loss account shows the amount of the expense that should have been incurred, and the amount of income that should have been received. This is the principle of income and expenditure accounting, rather than using receipts and payments as they are received and paid.

Further examples of the accruals concept in accounting are:

* debtors
* creditors
* depreciation of fixed assets
* bad debts written off
* provision for doubtful debts (see Chapter 15)
* opening and closing stock adjustments in the trading account

consistency

This requires that, when a business adopts particular accounting policies, it should continue to use such policies consistently. For example, a business that decides to make a provision for depreciation on machinery at ten per cent a year, using the straight-line method, should continue to use that percentage and method for future final accounts for this asset. Of course, having once chosen a particular policy, a business is entitled to make changes provided there are good reasons for so doing, and a note to the final accounts would explain what has happened. By applying the consistency concept, direct comparison between the final accounts of different years can be made. Further examples of the use of the consistency concept are:

*   stock valuation (see page 241)
*   the application of the materiality concept

prudence

This concept, also known as conservatism in accounting, requires that final accounts should always, where there is any doubt, report a conservative (lower) figure for profit and the valuation of assets. To this end, profits are not to be anticipated and should only be recognised when it is reasonably certain that they will be actually made; at the same time all known liabilities should be provided for. 'Anticipate no profit, but anticipate all losses' is a summary of the concept which, in its application, prevents an over-optimistic presentation of a business through the final accounts.

Examples of the use of the prudence concept in accounting are:

*   accrual of expenses and income, where an estimate is made of the amount
*   prepayment of expenses and income, where an estimate is made of the amount
*   stock valuation (see page 241)
*   depreciation of fixed assets
*   bad debts written off
*   provision for doubtful debts (see Chapter 15)

realisation

This concept states that business transactions are recorded in the final accounts when the legal title (ownership in law) passes between buyer and seller. This may well not be at the same time as payment is made. For example, credit sales are recorded at the time the sale is made (which is when legal title passes to the buyer), but payment will be made at a later date.

objectivity

This requires that the presentation of final accounts should be objective, rather than subjective, and is not influenced by the opinions or personal expectations of the owner of the business concerned, or the accountant preparing the accounts. As far as possible, objectivity is supported by business documents. As an example, the owner of a business says that she has just invented a new product that will make 'millions of pounds of profit' and wants to put it on the balance sheet as an asset of £5m, the concept of objectivity says that this cannot be done – only time will tell what the effect will be on profits.

application of accounting concepts

The diagram on the next page shows how the accounting concepts link to the adjustments which are made in order to improve the relevance and reliability of final accounts in showing the profit, assets and liabilities of the business.

the application of accounting concepts

concept / application	business entity	materiality	cost	going concern	accruals	consistency	prudence	realisation	objectivity
accruals of expenses and income					✓		✓		
prepayments of expenses, and income					✓		✓		
depreciation of fixed assets		✓				✓	✓		
bad debts written off							✓	✓	✓
provision for doubtful debts							✓		
stock valuation		✓		✓	✓	✓	✓		✓
asset valuation		✓	✓	✓		✓	✓		✓
asset revaluation				✓					
business will continue to trade				✓					
accounts prepared on same principles						✓			
business separate from owner	✓								
capital and drawings	✓								
goods for own use taken by owner	✓								

ACCOUNTING POLICIES

Accounting policies are the methods used by an individual business to show in its accounts the effect of transactions, and record assets and liabilities. For example, straight-line and reducing balance (see Chapter 15) are two ways of recording depreciation in the accounts: a business will select, as its accounting policy, a particular method for each class of fixed asset to be depreciated. A business selects its accounting policies to fit in with the objectives of:

- relevance – the financial information is useful to users of accounts
- reliability – the financial information can be depended upon by users
- comparability – financial information can be compared with that from previous accounting periods
- understandability – users can understand the financial information provided

ACCOUNTING STANDARDS

Over the last thirty years or so, accounting standards have been developed to provide the rules, or framework, of accounting. The intention has been to reduce the variety of alternative accounting treatments. For larger companies this framework for accounting is represented by **International Financial Reporting Standards** (IFRSs). The International Accounting Standards Board is the organisation responsible for these rules of accounting. Its aims are to establish and improve standards of financial accounting and reporting.

VALUATION OF STOCK

The control and valuation of stock is an important aspect in the efficient management of a business. Manual or computer records are used to show the amount of stock held and its value at any time during the year. However, at the end of the financial year it is essential for a business to make a physical stock-take for use in the final accounts. This involves stock control personnel going into the stores, the shop, or the warehouse and counting each item. The counted stock for each type of stock held is then valued as follows:

number of items held x stock valuation per item = stock value

The auditors of a business may make random checks to ensure that the stock value is correct.

The value of stock at the beginning and end of the financial year is used in the calculation for cost of sales. Therefore, the stock value has an effect on profit for the year.

Stock is valued at:

- either what it cost the business to buy the stock (including additional costs to bring the product or service to its present location and condition, such as delivery charges)

- or the net realisable value – the actual or estimated selling price (less any further costs, such as repairs and replacement parts, selling and distribution)

The stock valuation is often described as being **at the lower of cost and net realisable value** and is an application of the prudence concept. It is illustrated as follows:

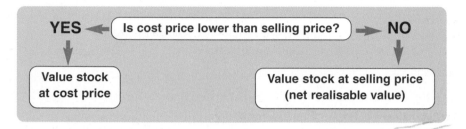

Thus two different stock values are compared:

- cost, including additional costs such as delivery charges
- net realisable value, which is the selling price of the goods, less any expenses incurred in getting the stock into a saleable condition, such as repairs and replacement parts, selling and distribution costs

Sometimes very large businesses use replacement cost – the cost of replacing stock that has been sold – as a further stock valuation. However, replacement cost applies only to raw materials, such as oil, that are traded on world markets. Unless you are told otherwise, the stock valuation rule of the lower of cost and net realisable value should be used at all times.

WORKED EXAMPLE: STOCK VALUATION

situation

Andrew Williams runs an electrical shop. He asks for your advice on the valuation of the following items of stock:

ITEM	COST £	NET REALISABLE VALUE £	COMMENTS
washing machine	220	350	
dishwasher	300	280	the replacement cost is £290
TV	250	325	the case is badly scratched and will need to be replaced at a cost of £90 before the television can be sold
DVD recorder	75	125	the remote control has been lost; a new one will cost £20

You are to advise Andrew of the valuations for each item.

solution

The principle of lower of cost and net realisable value applies here as follows:

- **washing machine**
  - the cost price of £220 is used, being lower than the net realisable value of £350

- **dishwasher**
  - the net realisable value of £280 is used, being lower than cost price
  - replacement cost of £290 is not used as it does not apply to the stock values of this type of business

- **TV**
  - replacement parts are needed before the item can be sold
  - the rule to follow is to deduct the cost of replacement parts/repairs from net realisable value, and then to compare with cost
  - here it is £325 – £90 = £235, compared with cost of £250
  - the net realisable value of £235 is used, being lower than cost price of £250

- **DVD recorder**
  - as with the television, money needs to be spent before this item can be sold
  - £125 – £20 = £105, compared with cost of £75
  - the cost price of £75 is used, being lower than the net realisable value less expenses, of £105

CHAPTER SUMMARY

- Accounting concepts – or principles – underlie the preparation of final accounts.

- Business entity concept – final accounts record and report on the activities of one particular business.

- Materiality concept – items with a low value are not worthwhile recording in the accounts separately.

- Cost concept – assets and liabilities are recorded in the final accounts at historical cost.

- Going concern concept – the presumption that the business to which the final accounts relate will continue to trade in the foreseeable future.

- Accruals concept – expenses and income for goods and services are matched to the same time period.

- Consistency concept – when a business adopts particular accounting policies, it should continue to use such policies consistently.

- Prudence concept – final accounts should always, where there is any doubt, report a conservative figure for profit or the valuation of assets.

- Realisation concept – business transactions are recorded in the final accounts when the legal title (ownership) passes between buyer and seller.

- Objectivity concept – the presentation of final accounts should be objective rather than subjective.

- The usual valuation for stock is at the lower of cost and net realisable value.

- Net realisable value is the selling price of the goods, less any expenses incurred in getting the stock into a saleable condition.

In the next chapter we return to the preparation of the final accounts – trading and profit and loss account and balance sheet – of sole traders. We will study further aspects including making provisions for doubtful debts, and the use of reducing balance depreciation.

QUESTIONS

visit
www.osbornebooks.co.uk
to take an online test

An asterisk (*) after the question number means that the answer is given at the end of this book.

14.1   The accounting concepts applied when preparing accounts include:

- the going concern concept

- the accruals concept

- the materiality concept

- the business entity concept

You are to explain each of these concepts, giving in each case an example to illustrate an application of the concept.

14.2   When preparing the final accounts of a business, the concepts and principles of accounting should be applied.

REQUIRED

(a)   Explain the concept of prudence.

....

....

....

....

(b)   Explain, giving **one** example, how prudence is applied.

....

....

....

(c)   Explain the concept of consistency.

....

....

....

(d)   Explain, giving **one** example, how consistency is applied.

....

....

....

Assessment and Qualifications Alliance (AQA), 2007

14.3*   **REQUIRED**

(a)   Daniel has included £720 sales to Bill Brown in October 2004 in the total sales for the year ended 31 December 2004. Bill has yet to pay for the goods.

This is an example of the .... concept.

(b)   Daniel owns a delivery van which belonged to his grandfather and has great sentimental value. He recently refused an offer of £4,000 for it from a heritage museum. Daniel shows the van on his balance sheet at cost £650.

This is an example of the .... concept.

Assessment and Qualifications Alliance (AQA), 2005

14.4*   Antonio owns and runs an Italian restaurant. He bought the business premises ten years ago at a cost of £100,000. A regular customer, Francesca, who is an estate agent's receptionist, tells him that the premises ought now to fetch £250,000 if he sold them.

REQUIRED

(a)   Advise Antonio how he should value the premises on his balance sheet at the end of the current financial year.

(b)   Identify the concepts that he uses to come to the balance sheet valuation.

14.5 Dimitri sells electrical goods. At his financial year end, he is unsure how to value an electric kettle that he has in stock.

The kettle cost £18. It will sell for £31.

Before it can be sold, the kettle requires a repair which will cost £15.

REQUIRED

(a) Calculate the value of the kettle to be included as part of Dimitri's closing stock.

The kettle should be valued at £...

Workings ....

....

....

(b) Complete the following sentences.

Stock should be valued at ....

or .... whichever is lower.

This is an example of using the .... concept.

Assessment and Qualifications Alliance (AQA), 2005

14.6* A discussion is taking place between Jane Smith, a sole trader, who owns a furniture shop, and her husband, John, who solely owns an engineering business. The following points are made:

(a) At the end of her financial year, Jane comments that the stock of her shop had cost £10,000. She says that, as she normally adds 50 per cent to cost price to give the selling price, she intends to put a value of £15,000 for closing stock in the final accounts.

(b) John's car is owned by his business but he keeps referring to it as my car. Jane reminds him that it does not belong to him, but to the firm. He replies that of course it belongs to him and, furthermore, if the firm went bankrupt, he would be able to keep the car.

(c) John's business has debtors of £30,000. He knows that, included in this figure is a bad dobt of £2,500. He wants to show £30,000 as debtors in the year end balance sheet in order to have a high figure for current assets.

(d) On the last day of her financial year, Jane sold a large order of furniture, totalling £3,000, to a local hotel. The furniture was invoiced and delivered from stock that day, before year end stocktaking commenced. The payment was received early in the new financial year and Jane now asks John if she will be able to put this sale through the accounts for the new year, instead of the old, but without altering the figures for purchases and closing stock for the old year.

(e)   John says that his accountant talks of preparing his accounts on a going concern basis. John asks Jane if she knows of any other basis that can be used, and which it is usual to follow.

You are to take each of the points and state the correct accounting treatment, referring to appropriate accounting concepts.

14.7*   Given below are three *unconnected* proposals for three *different* businesses.

1.   Ben Chan has always depreciated his fixed assets at the rate of 20% on cost. He thinks that he may sell his business next year so he has proposed changing the rate of depreciation to 5% this year as this will increase his profits.

2.   Lotte Betz's drawings have increased this year to £36,000. Lotte's drawings normally average £18,000 per annum. She is proposing to charge the usual £18,000 to drawings and include £18,000 as business expenses.

3.   Harry Jones has his financial year end on 30 June 2001. He has been negotiating to supply ski jackets to Pierre Duval in August 2001. Pierre will sign the contract on 5 July 2001 when he returns from a business trip to Austria. Harry proposes to include the selling price of the jackets, £9,700, in his sales figure for the year ending 30 June 2001.

REQUIRED

Identify which generally accepted accounting concepts should have been applied and the correct treatment for each proposal. Proposal 1 has been answered for you.

Proposal	Concept	Action
1.	Consistency	Continue to depreciate at 20%
2.		
3.		

Assessment and Qualifications Alliance (AQA), 2001

14.8

Bert's profits are less than they have been in previous years. In order to improve his profitability he has included the following in this year's final accounts.

1. Bert delayed paying the annual rent of £4,000 on his premises until after his financial year end. He has not recorded this in any way.

2. Bert has always calculated his depreciation on equipment at 25% per annum on cost. This year he has charged £10,000 depreciation which is only 10% on cost.

3. The closing stock at the financial year end cost £30,000. Bert has valued this stock at £48,000 which is cost plus 60% to increase his profits.

4. The anticipated increase in profits meant that Bert was able to take a family holiday cruise in the Caribbean. The holiday which cost £13,000 has been charged to his profit and loss account. "The rest did me good and made me more effective in my business", he said.

REQUIRED

Using the table below, identify the concept involved in each of the notes above. Show the effect that any corrective treatment will have. The first one has been done for you as an example.

	Concept	Gross Profit	Net Profit	Current Assets	Current Liabilities	Capital
1.	Accruals	no change	decrease £4,000	no change	increase £4,000	decrease £4,000
2.						
3.						
4.						

Assessment and Qualifications Alliance (AQA), 2001

14.9* The accountant of Wyvern Garden Centre has valued the year end stock at £35,500. The three items below have not been included in the stock valuation and the accountant provides you with the following information:

item	cost	net realisable value	replacement cost
	£	£	£
lawnmower	220	430	200
conservatory	800	750	850
greenhouse	300	290	320

The accountant explains that he has not included the above items in the stock valuation as he was not sure which value to use for each.

REQUIRED

(a) You are to calculate the total value of Wyvern Garden Centre's stock at the year-end.

(b) Which concept should be used in the valuation of the three items listed above?

(c) What is meant by the term 'net realisable value'?

14.10 Roger Dunn runs a clothes and accessories shop. He asks you for advice on the valuation of the following items of stock:

item	cost	net realisable value	comments
	£	£	
jacket	40	75	the replacement cost is £35
shirt	30	25	
suit	80	150	there is a fault in the material, so Roger will sell the suit for £120
trousers	20	35	the stitching needs repairing at a cost of £10, after which the trousers will be sold for £25
electric trouser press	80	155	the electric plug and wiring is damaged and replacements will cost £15, after which the press will be sold for £130

REQUIRED

(a) Advise Roger on the value of each item of stock.

(b) How is the concept of prudence applied to stock valuation and why is it necessary to apply it?

15 FURTHER ASPECTS OF FINAL ACCOUNTS

This chapter develops the preparation of final accounts of sole traders from what has been covered already in AS Unit 1 (Chapters 9 and 12). In particular, in this chapter, we describe the further adjustments for:

- accruals and prepayments of income
- bad debts recovered
- provision for doubtful debts
- provision for depreciation of fixed assets

The ledger entries for these adjustments will be shown, together with the way in which the final accounts are affected by each.

The next chapter continues the theme of these adjustments by applying them to a practical worked example of the final accounts of a sole trader.

INTRODUCTION TO FURTHER ASPECTS OF FINAL ACCOUNTS

In AS Unit 1 (Chapter 12) we made a number of adjustments to final accounts in order to improve the relevance and reliability of the accounts. In this chapter we take those adjustments further as follows:

- **adjusting for accruals of income** – showing income due in an accounting period which has not been received at the end of that period (see page 251)

- **adjusting for prepayments of income** – showing income paid in advance of the accounting period to which it relates (see page 251)

- **bad debts recovered** – recording money received from a former debtor whose account has been previously written off as a bad debt (see page 255)

- **provision for doubtful debts** – making provisions for debtors who may not pay (see page 257)

- **provision for depreciation of fixed assets** – writing down the value of fixed assets over their useful economic lives (see page 263)

We have already seen the principles of depreciation of fixed assets in AS Unit 1 (Chapter 12) and, in particular, application of the straight-line method. In this chapter we look at a further method of depreciation – the reducing balance method – and make comparisons between the two, as well as understanding the reasons for providing for depreciation (see pages 263 to 270).

In the next chapter we will use a practical worked example of sole trader final accounts which applies these adjustments.

Also, in this chapter, we see how to account for fixed assets when they are disposed of at the end of their useful economic lives and are removed from the ledger accounts – see pages 271 to 274.

ACCRUALS AND PREPAYMENTS OF INCOME

In Chapter 12 of AS Unit 1 we saw how expenses can be accrued or prepaid at the end of a financial year. In the same way, income amounts – such as rent income and commission income – can also be accrued or prepaid. Note that sales, which is usually the main item of income for a business, are already dealt with on an accruals basis because sales are recorded when legal title passes to the buyer, whether or not payment has been received – this is the reason why we use accounts for debtors.

Amounts of income from sources other than sales – which is shown in the trading account – are listed in the profit and loss account where they are added to gross profit.

accrual of income

An accrual of income is an amount due in an accounting period which has not been received at the end of that period.

With accrual of income, an amount due to a business has not been received at the end of the financial year. For example, commission income might have been earned, but the payment is received after the end of the financial year to which it relates.

In the final accounts, accrual of income is:

- added to the income in the trial balance before listing it in the profit and loss account
- shown as a current asset in the year end balance sheet

prepayment of income

A prepayment of income is a payment received in advance of the accounting period to which it relates.

With prepayment of income, an amount of income of a business has been received in advance. For example, the rent income account for the financial year includes an advance payment received from a tenant in respect of the next financial year.

In the final accounts, prepayment of income is:

- deducted from the income in the trial balance before listing it in the profit and loss account
- shown as a current liability in the year end balance sheet

The objective of taking note of accruals and prepayments of income is to ensure that the amount of income stated in the profit and loss account relates to the period covered by that account. This is the application of the accruals concept.

WORKED EXAMPLE: ACCRUALS AND PREPAYMENTS OF INCOME

situation

The book-keeper of Corley Carpets asks for your assistance in calculating the amount of income to show in the profit and loss account for the year ended 31 December 20-8. The following information is available:

	£
Receipts from Zelah Limited for commission received during the year	700
Receipts received during the year from advertising board in shop window	320
Receipts received during the year from tenants for rent of the flats above the shop	15,720

Details of accruals and prepayments of income are:

	year ended 31 December 20-7		year ended 31 December 20-8	
		£		£
Commission income from Zelah Limited	–		in arrears	20
Income from advertising board	–		in advance	40
Income from tenants for rent	in advance	200	in advance	400
	in arrears	125	in arrears	75

solution

To calculate the correct amount for profit and loss, we must take account of accruals and prepayments of income.

accrual of income – the book-keeping records

In the double-entry records, accruals of income are shown as an amount due to the business at the end of the financial year. Thus the account for commission income in the records of Corley Carpets is as follows:

Dr		**Commission Income Account**				Cr
20-8		£	20-8			£
31 Dec	Profit and loss account	720	31 Dec	Bank/Cash		700
				(receipts for year)		
			31 Dec	Balance c/d		20
				(accrual of income)		
		720				720
20-9			20-9			
1 Jan	Balance b/d	20				
	(accrual of income)					

Notes:

- The amount of commission received during the year, £700, is shown on the credit side.

- As £20 of commission due to the business has not been received at the end of the year, the income transferred to profit and loss account is the amount that should have been received during the year, ie £700 + £20 accrued income = £720.

- The balance remaining on the account – a debit balance of £20 – is the amount of the accrual of income, which is shown on the balance sheet at 31 December 20-8 as a current asset.

- Later on, for example on 10 January, the commission is paid by cheque and the account is as follows:

Dr			Commission Income Account			Cr
20-9		£	20-9			£
1 Jan	Balance b/d	20	10 Jan	Bank		20

- Note that, applying the concept of prudence, accruals of income should be made only when the amount is expected to be received – if there is any doubt, then the accrual of income should not be made.

- The effect on profit of taking note of the accrual of income is to increase a previously reported net profit – income has been increased, so net profit is higher.

prepayment of income – the book-keeping records

In the double-entry records, prepayments of income are shown as a liability of the business at the end of the financial year – in effect the business owes the amount back to the payer. Thus the account for income from the advertising board in the records of Corley Carpets is as follows:

Dr			Advertising Income Account			Cr
20-8		£	20-8			£
31 Dec	Profit and loss account	280	31 Dec	Bank/Cash		320
31 Dec	Balance c/d	40		(receipts for year)		
	(prepayment of income)					
		320				320
20-9			20-9			
			1 Jan	Balance b/d		40
				(prepayment of income)		

Notes:

- The amount of advertising received during the year, £320, is shown on the credit side.

- As £40 of advertising receipts is a prepayment, the income transferred to profit and loss account is the amount due for the year, ie £320 – £40 prepayment of income = £280.

- The balance remaining on the account – a credit balance of £40 – is the amount of the prepayment of income, which is shown on the balance sheet at 31 December 20-8 as a current liability.

- The credit balance of £40 on 1 January 20-9 will be included in the advertising income for 20-9 and will be transferred to profit and loss account on 31 December 20-9.

- The effect on profit of taking note of the prepayment of income is to reduce a previously reported net profit – income has been reduced, so net profit is lower.

dealing with opening and closing balances

So far we have taken note of accruals and prepayments of income which take place at the end of a financial year. But what happens when there are also accruals and prepayments of income at the *beginning* of the year? In the Worked Example, this happens with the rent income from tenants of the flats above Corley Carpets' shop.

The rules for dealing with opening and closing balances in the income account are as follows:

> start of year
> + prepayments of income
> – accruals of income
> end of year
> – prepayments of income
> + accruals of income
> = amount of income to profit and loss account

For the rent income of Corley Carpets the calculations are:

	£
received in year	15,720
+ prepayment at start of year	200
– accrual at start of year	125
– prepayment at end of year	400
+ accrual at end of year	75
= amount of income to profit and loss account	15,470

In the double-entry records of Corley Carpets, the account for rent income is as follows:

Dr			Rent Income Account			Cr
20-8		**£**		**20-8**		**£**
1 Jan	Balance b/d (accrual of income)	125		1 Jan	Balance b/d (prepayment of income)	200
31 Dec	Profit and loss account	15,470		31 Dec	Bank/Cash (receipts for year)	15,720
31 Dec	Balance c/d (prepayment of income)	400		31 Dec	Balance c/d (accrual of income)	75
		15,995				15,995
20-9				**20-9**		
1 Jan	Balance b/d (accrual of income)	75		1 Jan	Balance b/d (prepayment of income)	400

The balance sheet at 31 December 20-8 will show a current asset for the accrual of income of £75, and a current liability for the prepayment of income of £400.

BAD DEBTS RECOVERED

A bad debt recovered is when a former debtor, whose account has been written off as a bad debt, makes a payment.

In Chapter 12 (AS Unit 1) we saw how bad debts can arise as a result of allowing customers a period of credit before they pay. A bad debt is a debt owing to a business which it considers will never be paid.

To recap, the book-keeping entries to write off a bad debt are:

– debit bad debts written off account

– credit debtor's account

with the amount of the debt. At the end of the financial year, the balance of bad debts written off account is debited to profit and loss account as an expense, so reducing profit for the year.

From time-to-time, a former debtor whose account has been written off as bad may make a payment – either voluntarily, or as a result of debt collection procedures. For such a bad debt recovered the book-keeping entries are:

– debit cash/bank account (with the amount of the recovery)

– credit bad debts recovered account

The effect on final accounts is to record the amount recovered during the year as income – this is added to gross profit and described as 'bad debts recovered'. Note that the payment received – either in cash or by cheque – is debited to cash/bank account and credited to bad debts recovered account; when preparing final accounts in an examination question, unless told otherwise, there will be no need to adjust cash/bank account.

Having recovered payment from a former debtor, if the customer now wishes to buy goods or services, it is prudent to insist on cash payment for some time to come!

WORKED EXAMPLE: BAD DEBTS RECOVERED

situation

T Hughes is a former debtor of Pershore Packaging. The balance of £25 on T Hughes' account was written off as a bad debt on 15 December 20-1.

Today, on 15 April 20-3, T Hughes wishes to pay off the amount of the debt – with a cheque for £25.

solution

The book-keeping entries to record the bad debt recovered on 15 April 20-3 are as follows:

Dr		Bank Account			Cr
20-3		£	20-3		£
15 Apr	Bad debts recovered	25			

Dr		Bad Debts Recovered Account			Cr
20-3		£	20-3		£
			15 Apr	Bank (T Hughes)	25

Bad debts recovered account is a 'holding account' to which any other recoveries can be credited. At the end of the financial year, the total of the account is transferred to profit and loss account:

Dr		Bad Debts Recovered Account			Cr
20-3		£	20-3		£
31 Dec	Profit and loss account	25	15 Apr	Bank (T Hughes)	25

In final accounts, the effect of bad debts recovered is to increase the previously reported profit – by £25 in this case. It is recorded in the profit and loss account (extract) as follows:

Profit and loss account (extract) for the year ended 31 December 20-3

	£	£
Gross profit		x
Add income:		
Bad debts recovered		25
		x
Less expenses:	x	
	x	
		x
Net profit		x

For the preparation of final accounts note that:

- if a figure for bad debts recovered is shown in the trial balance (credit side), simply record the amount as income in the profit and loss account, as above; do not alter the cash/bank account

- if there is no figure for bad debts recovered shown in the trial balance, and a note says that an amount has recently been recovered but has not been recorded in the book-keeping, you need to increase cash/bank with the amount of the recovery and to record the income in profit and loss account.

PROVISION FOR DOUBTFUL DEBTS

A provision for doubtful debts is an estimate by a business of the likely percentage of its debtors which may go bad during any one accounting period.

Making a provision for doubtful debts is a further aspect of bad debts. However, it is different from writing off a bad debt because we are allowing for the possibility – not the certainty – of future bad debts. The debtors' figure (after bad debts, if any, have been written off) is reduced either by totalling the balances of the accounts that may not pay or, more likely, by applying a percentage to the total figure for debtors. The percentage chosen will be based on past experience and will vary from business to business – for example, a hire purchase company may well use a higher percentage than a bank.

The book-keeping entries for doubtful debts make use of a **provision for doubtful debts account**, which records the accumulated total of the provision.

initial creation of a provision for doubtful debts

The procedure for the provision for doubtful debts comes after writing off bad debts (if any). The steps are:

1 A business, with debtors of £10,000 at the end of the financial year, estimates that five per cent of its debtors may go bad

2 The provision is calculated (eg £10,000 x 5% = £500)

3 The provision is recorded in the book-keeping system:

   – debit profit and loss account

   – credit provision for doubtful debts account

   The provision for doubtful debts account holds the total of the provision, which is deducted from debtors in the balance sheet (see below), and represents the realistic estimate of debtors who may not pay

4 In the final accounts, the amount of the provision is:

   • listed in the profit and loss account as an expense described as 'increase in provision for doubtful debts'

   • deducted from the debtors' figure in the current assets section of the balance sheet, as here:

	£	£	£
Current Assets			
Stock		X	
Debtors	10,000		
Less provision for doubtful debts	500		
		9,500	
Prepayments		X	
Bank		X	
Cash		X	
		X	

Note that, by creating a provision for doubtful debts, the business is following the accounting concept of prudence in the realistic estimate of its debtor position.

adjustments to provision for doubtful debts

Once a provision for doubtful debts has been created, the only adjustments that need to be made to the provision for doubtful debts are as a result of:

• a policy change in the provision, eg a decrease in the fixed percentage from 5% to 3%

• an arithmetic adjustment in the provision as a result of a change in the total of debtors, eg increase in debtors of £5,000 will require a higher provision

When either or both of these two situations arises, the adjustment to the existing position will be:

• either upwards (increase in provision percentage, or increase in debtor figure)

• or downwards (decrease in provision percentage, or decrease in debtor figure)

An **increase in the provision** is recorded in the book-keeping system as follows:

– debit profit and loss account

– credit provision for doubtful debts account

with the amount of the increase

For the final accounts the amount of the increase is:

- listed in the profit and loss account as an expense described as 'increase in provision for doubtful debts'

- shown in the balance sheet where the amount of the increase is added to the existing provision to give a new figure for provision for doubtful debts (which is deducted from the debtors' figure)

A **decrease in the provision** is recorded in the book-keeping system as follows:

– debit provision for doubtful debts account

– credit profit and loss account

with the amount of the decrease

For the final accounts the amount of the decrease is:

- added to gross profit in the profit and loss account as income, and described as 'reduction in provision for doubtful debts'

- shown in the balance sheet at the lower amount, ie the existing provision less amount of decrease

Note that making a provision for doubtful debts is a completely separate adjustment from writing off a bad debt: the two should not be confused. It is quite usual to see in a profit and loss account entries for both bad debts (written off) and provision for doubtful debts (the creation or adjustment of provision for bad debts).

WORKED EXAMPLE: PROVISION FOR DOUBTFUL DEBTS

situation

A business decides to create a provision for doubtful debts of five per cent of its debtors. After writing off bad debts, the debtors figures at the end of each of three years are:

20-1	£10,000
20-2	£15,000
20-3	£12,000

solution

Creating the provision (20-1)

– debit profit and loss account

– credit provision for doubtful debts account

with £10,000 x 5% = £500

Increasing the provision (20-2)

> – debit profit and loss account
>
> – credit provision for doubtful debts account
>
> with £5,000 (increase in debtors) x 5% = £250

Decreasing the provision (20-3)

> – debit provision for doubtful debts account
>
> – credit profit and loss account
>
> with £3,000 (decrease in debtors) x 5% = £150

The provision for doubtful debts account is as follows:

Dr			**Provision for Doubtful Debts Account**		Cr
20-1		£	20-1		£
31 Dec	Balance c/d	500	31 Dec	Profit and loss account	500
20-2			20-2		
31 Dec	Balance c/d	750	1 Jan	Balance b/d	500
			31 Dec	Profit and loss account	250
				(increase in provision)	
		750			750
20-3			20-3		
31 Dec	Profit and loss account	150	1 Jan	Balance b/d	750
	(decrease in provision)				
31 Dec	Balance c/d	600			
		750			750
20-4			20-4		
			1 Jan	Balance b/d	600

the final accounts

The effect of the above transactions on the final accounts is shown in the following table:

Year	Profit and loss account		Balance sheet		
	Expense	Income	Debtors	Less provision for doubtful debts	Net debtors
	£	£	£	£	£
20-1	500	-	10,000	500	9,500
20-2	250	-	15,000	750	14,250
20-3	-	150	12,000	600	11,400

The profit and loss account and balance sheet extracts for each year are as follows:

20-1   **Profit and loss account (extract) for the year ended 31 December 20-1**

	£	£
Gross profit		x
Less expenses:		
Provision for doubtful debts	500	

Balance sheet (extract) as at 31 December 20-1

	£	£	£
Current Assets			
Stock		x	
Debtors	10,000		
Less provision for doubtful debts	500		
		9,500	

20-2   **Profit and loss account (extract) for the year ended 31 December 20-2**

	£	£
Gross profit		x
Less expenses:		
Increase in provision for doubtful debts	250	

Balance sheet (extract) as at 31 December 20-2

	£	£	£
Current Assets			
Stock		x	
Debtors	15,000		
Less provision for doubtful debts	750		
		14,250	

20-3   **Profit and loss account (extract) for the year ended 31 December 20-3**

	£	£
Gross profit		x
Add income:		
Reduction in provision for doubtful debts		150

Balance sheet (extract) as at 31 December 20-3

	£	£	£
Current Assets			
Stock		x	
Debtors	12,000		
Less provision for doubtful debts	600		
		11,400	

Note:

When preparing final accounts in an examination question, there will be a note to the trial balance telling you to make an adjustment to the provision for doubtful debts. Sometimes you will be told a percentage figure, eg 'provision for doubtful debts is to be maintained at five per cent of debtors'; alternatively, you may be told the new provision figure (be careful of the wording – make sure you distinguish between 'increase the provision **to** £750' and 'increase the provision **by** £750').

MINIMISING THE RISK OF BAD DEBTS

Having studied the technicalities of accounting for bad debts in Chapter 12, and creating a provision for doubtful debts in this chapter, it is appropriate to look at ways in which businesses selling on credit can minimise the risks. The following are some of the procedures that can be followed:

- When first approached by an unknown business wishing to buy goods on credit, the seller should ask for references. One of these should be the buyer's bank, and the others should be from traders (at least two) with whom the buyer has previously done business.

- The seller, before supplying goods on credit, should take up the references and obtain satisfactory replies.

- Once satisfactory replies have been received, a credit limit for the customer should be established, and an account opened in the sales ledger. The amount of the credit limit will depend very much on the expected amount of future business – for example, £2,000 might be appropriate. The credit limit should not normally be exceeded – the firm's credit controller or financial accountant will approve any transactions above the limit.

- Invoices and month end statements of account should be sent out promptly; invoices should state the terms of trade and statements should analyse the balance to show how long it has been outstanding, eg 'over 30 days, over 60 days, over 90 days' – computer-produced statements can show this automatically.

- If a customer does not pay within a reasonable time, the firm should follow established procedures in order to chase up the debt promptly. These procedures are likely to include 'chaser' letters, the first of which points out that the account is overdue, with a later letter threatening legal action. Whether or not legal action is taken will depend on the size of the debt – for a small amount the costs and time involved in taking legal action may outweigh the benefits of recovering the money.

the use of an aged schedule of debtors

To help with credit control, many firms produce an aged schedule of debtors at the end of each month. This analyses individual debtor balances into the time that the amount has been owing. Thus it shows the long outstanding debts that are, potentially, bad debtors, against whom early action is necessary. An aged schedule is easily produced using a computer accounting system (see page 384).

An aged schedule of debtors can also be used to calculate the provision for doubtful debts. For example, a business has the following schedule of debtors at the end of its financial year:

Days outstanding	Debtors
	£
Current (up to 30 days)	50,000
31 to 60	26,000
61 to 90	10,000
91 and over	4,000
	90,000

Provision for doubtful debts is to be calculated by providing for 25% on debts which have been outstanding for 91 days and over, 10% on debts outstanding for 61-90 days, and 2% on debts outstanding for 31-60 days. No provision is to be made on current debts.

Provision for doubtful debts is calculated as:

			£
Current	£50,000 (no provision)	=	nil
31-60 days	£26,000 x 2%	=	520
61-90 days	£10,000 x 10%	=	1,000
91 days and over	£4,000 x 25%	=	1,000
Provision for doubtful debts to be created (or adjusted) to			2,520

DEPRECIATION OF FIXED ASSETS

Depreciation is a measure of the amount of the fall in value of fixed assets over a time period.

We have already seen this definition of depreciation in AS Unit 1 (Chapter 12) when the straight-line method of depreciation was studied. In AS Unit 2, the topic of depreciation is taken further by studying the reducing balance method and making a comparison between the two. Also, in this section, we see the accounting entries for the disposal of fixed assets (including the calculation of any profit or loss on sale).

To recap on the basics of depreciation:

- the expense of depreciation is an estimate of both the fall in value of the fixed asset and the passage of time
- the estimate is linked to the cost price of the asset
- depreciation is an application of the accruals concept – the recognition of the timing difference between payment for the fixed asset and the asset's fall in value
- the main factors which cause fixed assets to depreciate are
  - wearing out through use
  - passage of time
  - using up of the asset
  - economic reasons, such as obsolescence and inadequacy
- depreciation is a non-cash expense – there is no outflow of money from the bank account

Remember that all fixed assets – even buildings – are depreciated over their useful economic life. The only exception is freehold land which, because it is a non-wasting asset, does not normally depreciate (unless it is a quarry or a mine, when it will have a limited useful economic life). Freehold land and buildings are sometimes increased in value from time-to-time, ie a revaluation takes place, and this is recorded in the accounts (see Chapter 17, page 320).

METHODS OF CALCULATING DEPRECIATION

All depreciation methods are estimates, and it is only when the asset is sold or scrapped that we will know the accuracy of the estimate (see page 271). The two most common methods of calculating depreciation are:

- straight-line method
- reducing balance method

For the calculations of depreciation amounts we will use the following data:

MACHINE	
Cost price on 1 January 20-1	£2,000
Estimated life	4 years
Estimated scrap value at end of four years	£400

straight-line method

With this method, a fixed percentage is written off the original cost of the asset each year. The depreciation percentage will be decided by a business on the basis of what it considers to be the useful economic life of the asset.

Different classes of fixed assets are often depreciated at different rates, eg vehicles may be depreciated at a different rate to office equipment. It is important that, once a particular method and rate of depreciation has been selected, the concept of consistency should be applied, ie depreciation methods and rates are not changed from year-to-year without good reason.

The method of calculating straight-line depreciation, taking into account the asset's estimated sale proceeds (if any) at the end of its useful economic life, is:

$$\frac{\text{cost of asset} - \text{estimated residual (scrap or salvage) sale proceeds}}{\text{number of years' expected use of asset}}$$

For example, the machine is expected to have a residual (scrap or salvage) value of £400, so the depreciation amount will be:

$$\frac{£2,000 - £400}{4 \text{ years}} = £400 \text{ per year (ie 20\% per annum on cost)}$$

reducing balance method

With this method, a fixed percentage is written off the reduced balance each year. The reduced balance is cost of the asset less depreciation to date. For example, the machine is to be depreciated by 33.3% (one-third) each year, using the reducing balance method. The depreciation amounts for the four years of ownership are:

Original cost	£2,000
20-1 depreciation: 33.3% of £2,000	£667
Value at end of 20-1	£1,333
20-2 depreciation: 33.3% of £1,333	£444
Value at end of 20-2	£889
20-3 depreciation: 33.3% of £889	£296
Value at end of 20-3	£593
20-4 depreciation: 33.3% of £593	£193
Value at end of 20-4	£400

Note that the figures have been rounded to the nearest £, and year 4 depreciation has been adjusted by £5 to leave a residual value of £400.

Although you will not need to use it in your examination, you may be interested in the formula to calculate the percentage of reducing balance depreciation:

$$r = 1 - \sqrt[n]{\frac{s}{c}}$$

In this formula:

r = percentage rate of depreciation

n = number of years

s = salvage (residual) value

c = cost of asset

In the example above the 33.3% is calculated as:

$$r = 1 - \sqrt[4]{\frac{400}{2,000}}$$

$$r = 1 - \sqrt[4]{0.2}$$ (to find the fourth root press the square root key on the calculator twice)

$$r = 1 - 0.669$$

$$r = 0.331 \text{ or } 33.1\% \text{ (which is close to the 33.3\% used above)}$$

straight-line and reducing balance methods compared

When selecting a method of depreciation, the main consideration must be how the value of the asset reduces within the business. For example, vehicles lose a large amount of their value in the first two years of ownership – therefore it is appropriate to use the reducing balance method of depreciation. The diagram on the next page makes a comparison between the two main methods of depreciation.

The following comparison tables use the depreciation amounts calculated above.

	straight-line depreciation			
	1	*2*	*3*	*4*
Year	Original cost	Depreciation for year	Provision for depreciation	Net book value (ie column 1-3)
	£	£	£	£
20-1	2,000	400	400	1,600
20-2	2,000	400	800	1,200
20-3	2,000	400	1,200	800
20-4	2,000	400	1,600	400

Note: Net book value is cost, less provision for depreciation, ie column 1, less column 3.

These calculations will be used in the final accounts as follows: taking 20-2 as an example, the profit and loss account will be charged with £400 (column 2) as an expense, while the balance sheet will record £1,200 (column 4) as the net book value.

reducing balance depreciation				
Year	*1* Original cost	*2* Depreciation for year	*3* Provision for depreciation	*4* Net book value (ie column 1-3)
	£	£	£	£
20-1	2,000	667	667	1,333
20-2	2,000	444	1,111	889
20-3	2,000	296	1,407	593
20-4	2,000	193	1,600	400

In the final accounts, using 20-3 as an example, £296 (column 2) will be charged as an expense in profit and loss account, while £593 (column 4) is the net book value that will be shown in the balance sheet.

Using these tables, we will now see how the two methods compare:

	straight-line method	reducing balance method
depreciation amount	Same money amount each year – see chart below	Different money amounts each year: more than straight-line in early years, less in later years – see chart below
depreciation percentage	Lower depreciation percentage required to achieve same residual value	Higher depreciation percentage required to achieve same residual value – but can never reach a nil value
suitability	Best used for fixed assets likely to be kept for the whole of their expected lives, eg machinery, office equipment, fixtures and fittings	Best used for fixed assets which depreciate more in early years and which are not kept for the whole of expected lives, eg vehicles

The year-by-year depreciation amounts of the machine in the example are shown on the following bar chart:

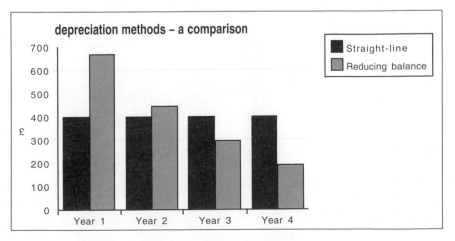

BOOK-KEEPING ENTRIES FOR DEPRECIATION

Once the amounts of depreciation have been calculated, they can be recorded in the book-keeping system. The procedure is to use two accounts for each class of fixed assets:

- fixed asset account, which records the cost price of the asset
- provision for depreciation account, which records the amount of depreciation for the asset

example book-keeping entries

A machine is purchased for £2,000 on 1 January 20-1. It is decided to depreciate it at twenty per cent each year, using the straight-line method. The firm's financial year runs from 1 January to 31 December. The accounting records for the first four years will be:

Dr			Machinery Account			Cr
20-1			£	20-1		£
1 Jan	Bank		2,000			

This account remains with the balance of £2,000, which is the cost price of the machine. The other transaction on 1 January 20-1 is to bank account – this has not been shown.

The double-entry book-keeping for each year's depreciation is:

- debit profit and loss account
- credit provision for depreciation account

Dr		Provision for Depreciation Account – Machinery			Cr
20-1		£	20-1		£
31 Dec	Balance c/d	400	31 Dec	Profit and loss account	400
20-2			20-2		
31 Dec	Balance c/d	800	1 Jan	Balance b/d	400
			31 Dec	Profit and loss account	400
		800			800
20-3			20-3		
31 Dec	Balance c/d	1,200	1 Jan	Balance b/d	800
			31 Dec	Profit and loss account	400
		1,200			1,200
20-4			20-4		
31 Dec	Balance c/d	1,600	1 Jan	Balance b/d	1,200
			31 Dec	Profit and loss account	400
		1,600			1,600
20-5			20-5		
			1 Jan	Balance b/d	1,600

The provision for depreciation account stores up the amounts of depreciation year by year. Notice that, while the asset account of machinery has a debit balance, provision for depreciation has a credit balance. The difference between the two balances at any time will tell us the net book value of the asset, ie what it is worth according to our accounting records. For example, at 31 December 20-3, the net book value of the machine is £800 (£2,000 cost, less £1,200 depreciation to date).

When a business owns several fixed assets of the same class, eg several machines, it is usual practice to maintain only one asset account and one provision for depreciation account for that class. This does mean that the calculation of amounts of depreciation can become quite complex – particularly when assets are bought and sold during the year. It may be helpful, in an examination question, to calculate the separate depreciation amount for each machine, or asset, before amalgamating the figures as the year's depreciation charge.

We will look at how to deal with the sale of an asset on page 271.

DEPRECIATION AND FINAL ACCOUNTS

profit and loss account

The depreciation amount calculated for each class of asset is listed amongst the expenses. For example, for the machine being depreciated by the straight-line method (see table on page 266), the profit and loss account will show 'depreciation: machinery £400' as an expense for each of the years 20-1 to 20-4. If the machine is being depreciated by the reducing balance method, the profit and loss account for 20-1 will show 'depreciation: machinery £667' as an expense. In subsequent years the amounts will be £444 in 20-2, £296 in 20-3, and £193 in 20-4.

balance sheet

Each class of fixed asset should be shown at cost price (or revaluation – see Chapter 17, page 320), less the amount of provision for depreciation to date (ie this year's depreciation, plus depreciation from previous years if any). The resulting figure is the net book value of the fixed asset.

The usual way of setting these out in a balance sheet (using the first year figures for the machine being depreciated by the straight-line method) is:

Balance sheet (extract) as at 31 December 20-1

	£	£	£
	Cost	Prov for dep'n	Net book value
Fixed Assets			
Machinery	2,000	400	1,600
Vehicles, etc	x	x	x
	x	x	x

Note that the figures for the balance sheet come from columns 1, 3 and 4 from the table on page 266. Where there is only one class of fixed asset, eg machinery, the balance sheet extract can be set out in a simpler layout, as follows:

Balance sheet (extract) as at 31 December 20-1

	£
Fixed Assets	
Machinery at cost	2,000
Less provision for depreciation	400
Net book value	1,600

At the end of the second year, the machine is shown in the balance sheet as follows:

Balance sheet (extract) .... **as at 31 December 20-2**

	£ Cost	£ Prov for dep'n	£ Net book value
Fixed Assets			
Machinery	2,000	800	1,200
Vehicles, etc	X	X	X
	X	X	X

Notice, from the above, how provision for depreciation increases with the addition of each further year's depreciation. At the same time, the net book value figure reduces – it is this net book value figure which is added to the other fixed assets to give a sub-total for this section of the balance sheet.

depreciation policies of a business

In examination questions, information will be given – where it is needed – on the depreciation policies of the business whose accounts you are preparing. In particular, the information will be given on what to do when a fixed asset is bought part of the way through a firm's financial year. The choices here will be to allocate depreciation for the part of the year that it is owned; alternatively the firm may choose to provide for depreciation for the whole year on assets held at the end of the year.

SALE OF FIXED ASSETS

When a fixed asset is sold or disposed, it is necessary to bring together:

- the original cost of the fixed asset
- provision for depreciation over the life of the fixed asset
- sale proceeds

These figures are transferred from the appropriate accounts in the book-keeping system to a disposals account (also known as a sale of assets account). The disposals account will enable us to calculate the 'profit' or 'loss' on sale of the asset (more correctly the terms are 'over-provision' and 'under-provision' of depreciation, respectively). The book-keeping entries are:

- **original cost of the asset**

  – debit disposals account

  – credit fixed asset account

  with the cost price of the fixed asset now sold

- **depreciation provided to date**

  – debit provision for depreciation account

  – credit disposals account

  with depreciation provided over the life of the asset

  Note that the amount of depreciation provided to date may need to be calculated for the correct period, eg if disposal takes place part of the way through a financial year and the firm's policy is to charge part-years.

- **sale proceeds**

  – debit bank/cash account

  – credit disposals account

  with the sale proceeds of the asset

- **loss on sale**

  – debit profit and loss account

  – credit disposals account

  with the amount of under-provision of depreciation

- **profit on sale**

  – debit disposals account

  – credit profit and loss account

  with the amount of over-provision of depreciation

Small adjustments for under- or over-provision of depreciation will usually be needed because it is impossible, at the start of an asset's life, to predict exactly what it will sell for in a number of years' time.

WORKED EXAMPLE: SALE OF A FIXED ASSET

situation

To illustrate the calculation of profit or loss on sale, we will use the machine purchased for £2,000 on 1 January 20-1, which is depreciated at twenty per cent each year, using the straight-line depreciation method. On 31 December 20-3, the machine is sold for £600; the company's accounting policy is to depreciate assets in the year of sale.

solution

The calculations are

		£
	original cost of machine	2,000
less	provision for depreciation to date	1,200
equals	net book value at date of sale	800
less	sale proceeds (or part-exchange – see page 274)	600
equals	loss on sale	200

The book-keeping entries (excluding bank account) are:

Dr			**Machinery Account**			Cr
20-1			£	20-3		£
1 Jan	Bank		2,000	31 Dec Disposals		2,000

Dr		**Provision for Depreciation Account – Machinery**			Cr
20-1		£	20-1		£
31 Dec	Balance c/d	400	31 Dec Profit and loss account		400
20-2			20-2		
31 Dec	Balance c/d	800	1 Jan Balance b/d		400
			31 Dec Profit and loss account		400
		800			800
20-3			20-3		
31 Dec	Disposals	1,200	1 Jan Balance b/d		800
			31 Dec Profit and loss account		400
		1,200			1,200

Dr		Disposals Account – Machinery		Cr
20-3		£	20-3	£
31 Dec	Machinery	2,000	31 Dec Provision for depreciation	1,200
			31 Dec Bank	600
			31 Dec Profit and loss account (loss on sale)	200
		2,000		2,000

Profit and loss account (extract) for the year ended 31 December 20-3

	£	£
Gross profit		x
Less expenses:		
Provision for depreciation: machinery	400	
Loss on sale of machinery	200	

Notes on these entries:

● In the machinery account, which is always kept 'at cost', the original price of the asset is transferred at the date of sale to disposals account. In this example, a nil balance remains on machinery account; however it is quite likely that the machinery account includes several machines, only one of which is being sold – in this case, there would be a balance on machinery account comprising the cost prices of the remaining machines.

● In provision for depreciation account, the amount of depreciation relating to the machine sold is transferred to disposals account. In this example, as only one machine is owned, the whole balance is transferred. However, if there were machines remaining, only part of the balance would be transferred – the amount remaining on the account relates to remaining machines.

● Disposals account would balance without the need for a profit and loss account transfer if the depreciation rate used reflected exactly the fall in value of the machine. In practice, this is unlikely to happen, so a transfer to profit and loss account must be made. In this example, it is an under-provision of depreciation (loss on sale), and the profit and loss account lists an extra expense. If there had been an over-provision of depreciation (profit on sale), an item of additional income would be shown in profit and loss account.

part-exchange of a fixed asset

Instead of selling a fixed asset for cash, it is quite common to part-exchange it for a new asset. This is exactly the same as if a person trades in an old car for a new (or newer) one. Once the part-exchange allowance has been agreed, the book-keeping entries for disposal are as detailed earlier except that, instead of sale proceeds, there will be entries for the part-exchange amount:

– debit fixed asset account

– credit disposals account

The remainder of the purchase cost of the new fixed asset paid by cheque is debited to fixed asset account and credited to bank account in the usual way.

For example, the machine referred to earlier in this section is part-exchanged on 31 December 20-3 at an agreed value of £600 for a new machine costing £2,500. The balance is paid by cheque. Machinery account will now be shown as:

Dr				Machinery Account			Cr
20-1			£	20-3			£
1 Jan	Bank		2,000	31 Dec	Disposals		2,000
20-3							
31 Dec	Disposals (part-exchange allowance)		600	31 Dec	Balance c/d		2,500
31 Dec	Bank (balance paid by cheque)		1,900				
			2,500				2,500
20-4							
1 Jan	Balance b/d		2,500				

Notes:
* This gives two debits (£600 and £1,900) in machinery account for a single machine.
* Disposals account will be unchanged, except that the description for the credit transaction of £600 will be machinery account, instead of bank.

CHAPTER SUMMARY

● An adjustment should be made at the end of the financial year to allow for accruals and prepayments of income.

● In the final accounts, accruals of income are:
* added to the income in the trial balance
* shown as a current liability in the balance sheet

- In the final accounts, prepayments of income are:
  - deducted from the income in the trial balance
  - shown as a current liability in the balance sheet

- A bad debt recovered is when a former debtor, whose account has been written off as a bad debt, makes a payment – either voluntarily, or as a result of debt collection procedures.

- A bad debt recovered is recorded as income, and the book-keeping entries are:
  - debit cash/bank account
  - credit bad debts recovered account

- In final accounts, the amount of any bad debts recovered during the year is recorded as income and added below the gross profit figure.

- A provision for doubtful debts is an estimate by a business of the likely percentage of its debtors which may go bad during any one accounting period.

- In the final accounts:
  - an increase or decrease in provision for doubtful debts is shown in profit and loss account
  - the provision for doubtful debts is deducted from the debtors' figure in the current assets section of the balance sheet

- Having created a provision for doubtful debts, it will either be increased or decreased from year-to-year in line with the change in the level of provision and/or the level of debtors.

- Depreciation is a measure of the amount of the fall in value of fixed assets over a time period.

- Two common methods of calculating depreciation are the straight-line method and the reducing balance method.

- The depreciation amount for each class of fixed asset being depreciated is included amongst the expenses in profit and loss account, while the value of the asset, as shown in the balance sheet, is reduced by the same amount.

- When a fixed asset is sold, it is necessary to make an adjustment in respect of any under-provision (loss on sale) or over-provision (profit on sale) of depreciation during the life of the asset. The amount of profit or loss is calculated using a disposals account, and is then transferred to profit and loss account.

- Instead of selling a fixed asset for cash, it is quite common to part-exchange it for a new asset.

In the next chapter we continue the theme of these adjustments by applying them in a practical worked example of final accounts of a sole trader. We also see how, when preparing final accounts, it is important to distinguish between capital expenditure and revenue expenditure.

QUESTIONS

An asterisk (*) after the question number means that the answer is given at the end of this book.

15.1* Martin Ostrowski is about to prepare his final accounts for the year ended 31 December 20-8.

The flat above Martin's business premises is let to a tenant at a rent of £400 per calendar month. On 1 December 20-8 the tenant paid Martin £800 to cover the rent for December 20-8 and January 20-9.

You are to:

(a) state how Martin should treat the tenant's rent payment of £800 on 1 December 20-8 in his final accounts

(b) identify the accounting concept that should be applied in this situation

15.2 You are the book-keeper of Pershore Products. You are calculating the amount of income to be shown in the profit and loss account for the year ended 31 December 20-7. The following information is available to you:

	£
Receipts from Aggie Surf Limited for commission received during the year	1,250
Receipts from advertising on the company website received during the year	2,720
Receipts from tenants for rent of the flats owned by the business received during the year	18,290

Details of accruals and prepayments are:

	year ended 31 December 20-6		year ended 31 December 20-7	
		£		£
Commission income from Aggie Surf Limited	in arrears	100		–
Income from website advertisements	in arrears	150	in arrears	250
Income from tenants for rent	in advance	850	in arrears	120

You are to:

(a)   write up the accounts, below, for

- commission income

- advertising income

- rent income

to show the transfer to profit and loss account for the year ended 31 December 20-7.

Dr		Commission Income Account		Cr
20-7	£	20-7		£

Dr		Advertising Income Account		Cr
20-7	£	20-7		£

Dr	Rent Income Account			Cr
20-7	£	20-7		£

15.3* The accounts supervisor at the firm where you work hands you a cheque for £50 received from a former debtor, James Abel, whose account was written off as bad last year. The cheque is in part settlement of the amount owed by James Abel.

You are to write up the following accounts using today's date for the transactions:

Dr	Bank Account		Cr
	£		£

Dr	Bad Debts Recovered Account		Cr
	£		£

15.4 You are the book-keeper of Wyvern Traders. At 31 December 20-9, the end of the financial year, the business has gross debtors of £40,420. The owner decides to:

- write off, as bad debts, the accounts of:

    Webster Limited   £110

    T Smith   £210

    Khan and Company   £100

- make a provision for doubtful debts of 2.5% of debtors (after writing off the above bad debts)

You are to:

(a)   show the bad debts written off account in the general ledger for the financial year

(b)   show the provision for doubtful debts account in the general ledger for the financial year

(c)   explain the effect of these transactions on the final accounts at the end of the financial year

15.5* Ross Engineering has an existing provision for doubtful debts of £300, based on 5 per cent of debtors. After writing off bad debts, the amounts of debtors at the end of the next two financial years are found to be:

    30 June 20-1   £8,000

    30 June 20-2   £7,000

The business continues to keep the provision for doubtful debts equal to 5 per cent of debtors.

As an accounts assistant at Ross Engineering, you are to show:

(a)   the adjustments to the provision for doubtful debts at the end of the financial years ended 30 June 20-1 and 30 June 20-2

(b)   how the provision for doubtful debts will be recorded in the final accounts at the end of each of the two financial years.

15.6 You are the book-keeper at Enterprise Trading Company. The following information is available for the financial years ending 31 December 20-5, 20-6, 20-7:

                                                                                                            £

- Debtor balances at 31 December 20-5, before writing off bad debts   105,200
- Bad debts written off on 31 December 20-5   1,800
- 2.5% provision for doubtful debts created at 31 December 20-5

- Debtor balances at 31 December 20-6, before writing off bad debts   115,600
- Bad debts written off on 31 December 20-6   2,400
- 2.5% provision for doubtful debts adjusted in line with the change in the level of debtors at 31 December 20-6
- Bad debt recovered on 15 June 20-7   150
- Debtor balances at 31 December 20-7, before writing off bad debts   110,200
- Bad debts written off on 31 December 20-7   1,400
- 2.5% provision for doubtful debts adjusted in line with the change in the level of debtors at 31 December 20-7

You are to record the effect of these transactions in the appropriate columns of the following table:

YEAR	PROFIT AND LOSS ACCOUNT				BALANCE SHEET		
	Expense		Income				
	Bad debts written off	Increase in provision for doubtful debts	Bad debts recovered	Decrease in provision for doubtful debts	Debtors (after bad debts written off)	Less prov for doubtful debts	Net debtors
	£	£	£	£	£	£	£
20-5							
20-6							
20-7							

15.7* The following balances were extracted from the books of account of Josh Porter, a trader, as at 31 March 2001.

	Dr £	Cr £
Provision for doubtful debts		700
Debtors	10,000	
Bad debts written off during the year	178	
Bad debts recovered during the year		261

It has always been Josh's policy to provide for doubtful debts at the rate of 5% on debtors outstanding at his financial year end.

The net profit earned in the year ended 31 March 2001 was £18,090.

The net profit and the debtors' figures have been arrived at *before* taking into account any bad debts, any bad debts recovered and any adjustments to the provision for doubtful debts.

REQUIRED

Analyse the effect that the information outlined above would have had on Josh's:

(a)   net profit

(b)   working capital (or net current assets)

(c)   bank balance

Assessment and Qualifications Alliance (AQA), 2001

15.8   Cindy Fireplace wishes to improve her reported business profits and cash balances. She has purchased a new computer system for her business at a cost of £6,000. She will use the system for two years and then replace it. At the end of the two years the system will have no scrap value.

She will depreciate her computer system by using
either   the straight-line method
or   the reducing-balance method using 60% per annum

She is unsure which method will increase her reported profits and her cash balances over the two years.

REQUIRED

(a)   Calculate the charge to the profit and loss account for each year for each method.

	Straight-line method £	Reducing-balance method £
Year 1		
Year 2		

(b)   Discuss how charging depreciation will affect Cindy's cash flow.

Assessment and Qualifications Alliance (AQA), 2003

15.9* Jack Myers sold a van for £3,500.

The van had been used in Jack's business for four years. The van had cost £18,000 and had been depreciated at 20% per annum using the straight-line method.

REQUIRED

(a) Calculate the profit or loss on disposal of the van.

....

....

Workings ....

....

....

....

....

(b) State how the answer to (a) should be treated in the profit and loss account.

....

....

....

Assessment and Qualifications Alliance (AQA), 2004

15.10* On 1 January 20-1, Martin Jackson bought a car for £12,000. In his final accounts, which have a year-end of 31 December, he has been depreciating it at 25 per cent per annum using the reducing balance method. On 31 December 20-3 he sells the car for £5,500 (cheque received). His accounting policy is to depreciate assets in the year of sale.

You are to show:

(a) The provision for depreciation account for 20-1, 20-2 and 20-3.

(b) The balance sheet extract at 31 December 20-1 and 20-2.

(c) The asset disposal account.

Round your answer down to whole £s where appropriate.

15.11 Rachael Hall's financial year runs to 31 December. On 1 January 20-8 her accounts show that she owns a car with an original cost of £12,000 and depreciation to date of £7,200.

On 1 October 20-8, Rachael bought a new car at a cost of £15,000. She traded in the old car at a part-exchange value of £5,500 and paid the balance by cheque.

Rachael depreciates vehicles at 20 per cent per year using the straight-line method. Her accounting policy is to charge a full year's depreciation in the year of purchase, but none in the year of sale.

You are to show the following for the year ended 31 December 20-8:

(a)   vehicles account

(b)   provision for depreciation account – vehicles

(c)   disposals account – vehicles

(d)   balance sheet extract at 31 December 20-8

15.12 On 1 January 20-9 the following information is taken from the accounting system of Lisa Hall.

		£
•	Vehicle (registration number VU54 UUF) at cost	20,000
•	Provision for depreciation of Vehicle VU54 UUF	12,500

Lisa purchased a new vehicle (registration number VK09 PZV) on 15 March 20-9 at a cost of £25,000. The garage gave Lisa a trade in allowance of £4,000 on vehicle VU54 UUF. Lisa's financial year ends on 31 December. She depreciates vehicles at 12.5% per annum using the straight-line method. Depreciation is calculated on vehicles held at the end of the financial year.

REQUIRED

(a)   Calculate the profit or loss made on the disposal of vehicle VU54 UUF.

(b)   Prepare the balance sheet extract as at 31 December 20-9 of Lisa Hall, showing entries arising from the above transactions.

15.13 The following is an extract from the business balance sheet of Gorg Hammann as at 31 December 2002.

Fixed assets	£	£
Machinery at cost	170,000	
Depreciation to date	105,000	65,000

On 31 December 2003 Gorg purchased a new machine.

The cost of the machine was £30,000. To be settled as follows:

	£
Old machine trade-in	8,000
Deposit paid on 31 December 2003	11,000
Instalment to be paid on 31 May 2004	11,000

The old machine cost £24,000 on 1 January 2001 and had been depreciated by £18,000 up to 31 December 2003.

REQUIRED

(a)   Calculate the profit or loss on disposal of the old machine.

....

Workings ....

....

....

....

....

(b)   Prepare a balance sheet extract as at 31 December 2003 showing **all** items relating to machinery. (No depreciation is to be charged on the new machine.)

Gorg Hammann

Balance sheet extract as at 31 December 2003

....

....

....

....

....

....

....

....

Assessment and Qualifications Alliance (AQA), 2004

15.14* Howard and Son, a joinery business, depreciates its machinery at the rate of 10% per annum, using the straight line method. Depreciation is calculated on assets held at the end of the financial year.

The following information was extracted from Howard and Son's general ledger.

	1 January 2010
	£
Machinery at cost	100,000
Provision for depreciation of machinery	60,000

On 2 January 2010 an additional machine was purchased at a cost of £30,000.

In November 2010 machine VM/3, which had been purchased on 1 January 2004 at a cost of £18,000, was sold for £4,000 cash. The aggregate depreciation on the machine amounted to £10,800.

REQUIRED

(a) Calculate the profit or loss made on the sale of machine VM/3.

(b) Prepare an extract from the balance sheet as at 31 December 2010, of Howard and Son, showing entries arising from the above transactions.

Assessment and Qualifications Alliance (AQA), 2001 (with dates amended)

15.15* The following information has been extracted from the books of Cora Smythe after preparing her draft final accounts

	£
Net profit for the year ended 31 December 2003	21,630
Net current assets as at 31 December 2003	4,260

She has not yet made **any** entries to record the following:

	£
Bad debts written off during the year	420
Increase in provision for doubtful debts at 31 December 2003	85
Wages owing at 31 December 2003	720
Insurance premiums paid in advance at 31 December 2003	135
Cash withdrawn for private use on 31 December 2003	210

REQUIRED

(a)   Calculate the corrected net profit for the year ended 31 December 2003 after recording the above entries. Show **all** the adjustments.

	£
Draft net profit for the year ended 31 December 2003	21,630

Corrected net profit for the year ended 31 December 2003

(b)   Calculate the corrected total of net current assets as at 31 December 2003 after recording the above entries. Show **all** the adjustments.

	£
Draft net current assets as at 31 December 2003	4,260

Corrected net current assets as at 31 December 2003

Assessment and Qualifications Alliance (AQA), 2004

15.16 Thomas Salmon provides the following information for his business for the year ended 30 November 2004.

	£
Wages	26,320
Drawings	18,560
Bad debts	340
Rent and rates	4,630
Other expenses	21,435
Discount allowed	286
Discount received	119
Rent receivable	720
Gross profit for the year	68,772

Additional information	As at 1 December 2003	As at 30 November 2004
	£	£
Provision for depreciation of fixed assets	27,000	30,000
Provision for doubtful debts	890	1,120

During the year ended 30 November 2004, a delivery van which had originally cost £8,000 had been sold for £1,900. The depreciation on the van was £6,000.

REQUIRED

Prepare a profit and loss account for the year ended 30 November 2004.

....

....

....

....

....

....

....

....

....

....

....

....

Assessment and Qualifications Alliance (AQA), 2005

16 PREPARING SOLE TRADER FINAL ACCOUNTS

This chapter brings together all that has been studied on the preparation of final accounts of sole traders – in AS Unit 1, Chapters 9 and 12, and AS Unit 2, Chapter 15.

When preparing final accounts it is important to distinguish between capital expenditure and revenue expenditure. We begin this chapter by looking at the differences between these, and why they are important to final accounts.

We then see how the adjustments to final accounts are applied by looking at a practical worked example of sole trader final accounts.

CAPITAL EXPENDITURE AND REVENUE EXPENDITURE

When preparing final accounts it is important to distinguish between capital expenditure and revenue expenditure.

capital expenditure

Capital expenditure is expenditure incurred on the purchase, alteration or improvement of fixed assets.

Included in capital expenditure are such costs as:

- delivery of fixed assets
- installation of fixed assets
- improvement (but not repair) of fixed assets
- legal costs of buying property

A common example of capital expenditure is the purchase of a car for use in the business.

Note that we use the word 'capitalised' to mean that an item has been treated as capital expenditure.

Capital expenditure is subject always to the application of the accounting concept of materiality (see page 237) – when items in accounts have a low monetary value and it is not worthwhile recording them separately.

revenue expenditure

Revenue expenditure is expenditure incurred on running expenses.

Included in revenue expenditure are the costs of:

* maintenance and repair of fixed assets
* administration of the business
* selling and distributing the goods or products in which the business trades

An example of revenue expenditure is the cost of petrol or diesel for the car used in the business.

capital expenditure and revenue expenditure – the differences

Capital expenditure is shown on the balance sheet, while revenue expenditure is an expense in the profit and loss account. It is important to classify these types of expenditure correctly in the accounting system. For example, if the cost of the car was shown as an expense in profit and loss account, then net profit would be reduced considerably, or even a net loss recorded; meanwhile, the balance sheet would not show the car as a fixed asset – clearly this is incorrect as the business owns the asset.

Study the following examples and the table on the next page; they both show the differences between capital expenditure and revenue expenditure.

● **cost of building an extension to the factory £30,000, which includes £1,000 for repairs to the existing factory**
  – capital expenditure, £29,000
  – revenue expenditure, £1,000 (because it is for repairs to an existing fixed asset)

● **a plot of land has been bought for £20,000, the legal costs are £750**
  – capital expenditure £20,750 (the legal costs are included in the capital expenditure, because they are the cost of acquiring the fixed asset, ie the legal costs are capitalised)

● **the business' own employees are used to install a new air conditioning system: wages £1,000, materials £1,500**
  – capital expenditure £2,500 (an addition to the property); note that, in cases such as this, revenue expenditure, ie wages and materials purchases, will need to be reduced to allow for the transfer to capital expenditure

● **own employees used to repair and redecorate the premises: wages £500, materials £750**
  – revenue expenditure £1,250 (repairs and redecoration are running expenses)

● **purchase of a new machine £10,000, payment for installation and setting up £250**
  – capital expenditure £10,250 (costs of installation of a fixed asset are capitalised)

Only by allocating capital expenditure and revenue expenditure correctly between the balance sheet and the profit and loss account can the final accounts report reliably on the financial state of the business. The chart on the next page shows the main items of capital expenditure and revenue expenditure associated with three classes of fixed assets – buildings, vehicles and machinery/computers/office equipment.

	capital expenditure	revenue expenditure
buildings	• cost of building • cost of extension • carriage on raw materials used • legal fees • labour cost of own employees used on improving the building • installation of utilities, eg gas, water, electricity • installation of air conditioning	• insurance of building • general maintenance • repairs • redecoration
vehicles	• cost of vehicle, including any optional extras • delivery costs • number plates • changes to the vehicle	• fuel • tax disc • extended warranty • painting company logo • insurance of vehicle • servicing and repairs
machinery/ computers/ office equipment	• cost of asset • installation and testing • modifications to meet specific needs of business • installation of special wiring, etc • staff training (where directly related to new equipment) • computer programs (but can be classified as revenue expenditure if cost is low and will have little impact on final accounts – the accounting concept of materiality)	• insurance of asset • servicing and repairs • consumables – such as paper, ink cartridges, etc • computer programs (or can be classified as capital expenditure if cost is high and will have a large impact on final accounts)

FINAL ACCOUNTS: INTRODUCING THE WORKED EXAMPLE

Many AQA examination questions focus on aspects of the preparation of final accounts – for example, asking you to prepare a trading and profit and loss account, or a balance sheet. Some questions will also require the preparation of the full final accounts – trading and profit and loss account, together with a balance sheet.

Examination questions often include a number of adjustments which need to be incorporated into the final accounts. The diagram on the next page summarises the adjustments and their effect on the final accounts. Remember that the adjustments are made in order to apply the accounting concepts – the diagram already seen in Chapter 14 (on page 240) links the adjustments to the accounting concepts. The objective of making adjustments is to improve the relevance and reliability of final accounts in showing the profit, and the assets and liabilities of the business.

The Worked Example on the next page brings together all of the adjustments that we have seen previously in AS Unit 1, Chapters 9 and 12, and AS Unit 2, Chapter 15. Although in total the Worked Example is more complex than would be required in an examination, it does provide a useful reference point which shows how all the adjustments are incorporated into the final accounts of a sole trader.

The examination questions at the end of this chapter are based on the preparation of final accounts – either from a trial balance or a list of balances – and provide practice to help with your studies.

SUMMARY OF ADJUSTMENTS FOR FINAL ACCOUNTS		
ADJUSTMENT	**TRADING AND PROFIT AND LOSS ACCOUNT**	**BALANCE SHEET**
closing stock	• deduct from purchases in trading account	• current asset
accrual of expenses	• add to expense in profit and loss account	• current liability
prepayment of expenses	• deduct from expense in profit and loss	• current asset
accrual of income	• add to income in profit and loss account	• current asset
prepayment of income	• deduct from income in profit and loss account	• current liability
provision for depreciation of fixed assets	• expense in profit and loss account	• fixed assets reduced by provision for depreciation to date
bad debts written off	• expense in profit and loss account	• deduct from debtors
bad debts recovered	• income in profit and loss account	• add to bank/cash
creation of, or increase in, provision for doubtful debts	• expense in profit and loss account	• debtors' figure reduced by total amount of provision
decrease in provision for doubtful debts	• income in profit and loss account	• debtors' figure reduced by total amount of provision
goods taken by the owner for own use	• deduct from purchases in trading account	• add to drawings

WORKED EXAMPLE: PREPARING SOLE TRADER FINAL ACCOUNTS

situation

You are the accountant to Olivia Boulton, a sole trader, who runs a kitchen and cookware shop in Brighton. Her book-keeper has just extracted the year end trial balance from the books of account, as follows:

Trial balance of Olivia Boulton as at 31 December 20-2

	Dr £	Cr £
Stock at 1 January 20-2	50,000	
Purchases	420,000	
Sales		557,500
Shop expenses	6,200	
Shop wages	33,500	
Telephone expenses	500	
Interest paid	8,000	
Travel expenses	550	
Discounts allowed	450	
Discounts received		900
Rents received		2,350
Commission received		500
Bad debts recovered		250
Premises at cost	250,000	
Shop fittings at cost	40,000	
Provision for depreciation of premises at 1 Jan 20-2		10,000
Provision for depreciation of shop fittings at 1 Jan 20-2		8,000
Debtors	10,100	
Provision for doubtful debts		200
Bank	5,850	
Cash	50	
Capital		125,000
Drawings	24,000	
Loan from bank (repayable in 20-9)		130,000
Creditors		14,500
	849,200	849,200

You are to prepare the final accounts for Olivia and, to help with this, she gives you the following information:

- after a stock take at the end of December, closing stock was valued at £42,000
- a telephone bill received on 5 January 20-3 showed calls for £100 in 20-2
- in December Olivia paid shop wages of £200 in advance for January
- in December Olivia received rent of £200 from her tenant in advance for January
- commission income of £100 is owing and was received on 10 January

- depreciation on premises is at the rate of 2% per annum, using the straight-line method
- depreciation on shop fittings is at the rate of 25% per annum, using the reducing balance method
- Olivia has incurred bad debts of £100 during 20-2 which she wishes to write off
- a provision for doubtful debts is to be 2.5% of debtors
- goods costing £1,000 were taken by Olivia for her own use

Note: In making adjustments in the final accounts for the above information we are ensuring that the accounts are more relevant and reliable to stakeholders. The adjustments are based on the application of accounting concepts (see page 236) – the concepts applied here include cost, accruals, consistency and prudence.

solution

The final accounts incorporating these adjustments are shown on the next two pages. A summary of the effect of each adjustment is given below.

closing stock

The adjustment for closing stock is to:

- deduct £42,000 from purchases in the trading account
- show stock valued at £42,000 as a current asset in the balance sheet

accrual of expenses

For the telephone expenses accrued:

- increase the profit and loss account expense by £100 to £600 (ie £500 from the trial balance, plus £100 expenses accrued)
- show £100 accrual of expenses as a current liability in the balance sheet

prepayment of expenses

For the shop wages prepaid:

- reduce the profit and loss account expense by £200 to £33,300 (ie £33,500 from the trial balance, less £200 expenses prepaid)
- show £200 prepayment of expenses as a current asset in the balance sheet

prepayment of income

For the prepaid rent received:

- reduce the profit and loss account income by £200 to £2,150 (ie £2,350 from the trial balance, less £200 income prepaid)
- show £200 prepayment of income as a current liability in the balance sheet

accrual of income

For the accrued commission income:

- increase the profit and loss account income by £100 to £600 (ie £500 from the trial balance, plus £100 income accrual)
- show £100 accrual of income as a current asset in the balance sheet

depreciation of fixed assets

The depreciation amounts are:

- premises: 2% per annum straight-line, ie £250,000 x 2% = £5,000
- shop fittings: 20% per annum reducing balance,
  ie (£40,000 – £8,000 provision for depreciation to date) x 20% = £6,400

The depreciation is shown in the final accounts as follows:

- in the profit and loss account show (as expenses) provision for depreciation amounts for premises £5,000, and shop fittings £6,400
- in the balance sheet show provision for depreciation amounts being deducted from fixed assets to give net book values as follows:

	£	£	£
	Cost	Prov for dep'n	Net book value
Premises	250,000	15,000	235,000
Shop fittings	40,000	14,400	25,600
	290,000	29,400	260,600

Remember that the provision for depreciation column in the balance sheet comprises depreciation from previous years, plus this year's depreciation (just calculated). For premises, provision for depreciation is the trial balance figure of £10,000, plus £5,000 for this year; for shop fittings, it is £8,000 from the trial balance, plus £6,400 for this year.

bad debts written off

The adjustment to write off bad debts in the final accounts is as follows:

- record bad debts written off of £100 as an expense in profit and loss account
- reduce the debtors' figure by £100 to £10,000 and show this latter figure as a current asset in the balance sheet

provision for doubtful debts

A provision for doubtful debts of £200 (see trial balance) is already in existence. As the provision is to be maintained at 2.5% of debtors, the provision at the end of the year is £10,000 debtors (see above) x 2.5% = £250. Thus an increase of £50 (from £200 to £250) is required; this is shown in the final accounts as follows:

- in profit and loss account record the £50 amount of the increase in provision for doubtful debts as an expense
- in the balance sheet deduct £250 from the debtors' figure of £10,000 to give net debtors of £9,750 – it is this amount that is added in to current assets

Note that, where an existing provision for doubtful debts is to be reduced, show the amount of the reduction as income in profit and loss account; the balance sheet deduction from debtors is the total amount of the provision remaining, ie existing provision less reduction.

goods for own use

As Olivia has taken goods in which the business trades for her own use, the adjustment is:

- deduct £1,000 from purchases in the trading account to give a purchases figure of £419,000
- add £1,000 to owner's drawings in the balance sheet to give a drawings figure of £25,000

final accounts

The final accounts of Olivia Boulton, incorporating the above adjustments, are shown below

OLIVIA BOULTON

TRADING AND PROFIT AND LOSS ACCOUNT FOR THE YEAR ENDED 31 DECEMBER 20-2

	£	£
Sales		557,500
Opening stock (1 January 20-2)	50,000	
Purchases	419,000	
	469,000	
Less Closing stock (31 December 20-2)	42,000	
Cost of sales		427,000
Gross profit		130,500
Add income:		
Discounts received		900
Rent received		2,150
Commission received		600
Bad debts recovered		250
		134,400
Less expenses:		
Shop expenses	6,200	
Shop wages	33,300	
Telephone	600	
Interest paid	8,000	
Travel expenses	550	
Discounts allowed	450	
Provision for depreciation: premises	5,000	
shop fittings	6,400	
Bad debts written off	100	
Increase in provision for doubtful debts	50	
		60,650
Net profit		73,750

BALANCE SHEET AS AT 31 DECEMBER 20-2

	£	£	£
Fixed Assets	Cost	Prov for dep'n	Net book value
Premises	250,000	15,000	235,000
Shop fittings	40,000	14,400	25,600
	290,000	29,400	260,600
Current Assets			
Stock		42,000	
Debtors	10,000		
Less provision for doubtful debts	250		
		9,750	
Prepayment of expenses		200	
Accrual of income		100	
Bank		5,850	
Cash		50	
		57,950	
Less Current Liabilities			
Creditors	14,500		
Accrual of expenses	100		
Prepayment of income	200		
		14,800	
Net Current Assets or Working Capital			43,150
			303,750
Less Long-term Liabilities			
Loan from bank			130,000
NET ASSETS			173,750
FINANCED BY			
Capital			
Opening capital			125,000
Add Net profit			73,750
			198,750
Less Drawings			25,000
			173,750

Tutorial note:

The only adjustment omitted from this Worked Example is the sale of fixed assets, and the resultant calculation of any profit or loss on sale. This topic has been covered already in the previous chapter and there are questions incorporating the sale of fixed assets at the end of both this chapter and the previous one (Chapter 15).

CHAPTER SUMMARY

- Capital expenditure is expenditure incurred on the purchase, alteration or improvement of fixed assets.

- Revenue expenditure is expenditure incurred on running expenses.

- Adjustments are made to final accounts in order to apply the accounting concepts.

- The objective of making adjustments is to improve the relevance and reliability of final accounts.

In the last two chapters we have looked at preparing sole trader final accounts, together with a number of adjustments, in some detail. In the next chapter we turn our attention to the final accounts of limited companies.

QUESTIONS

visit
www.osbornebooks.co.uk
to take an online test

An asterisk (*) after the question number means that the answer is given at the end of this book.

16.1 Tara Kassir has bought a new delivery van for use in her business. The invoice received from the garage for the van includes the following items:

	£
Cost of van	11,650
Air conditioning	550
Fitted shelving	350
Tax disc	165
Cost of extended warranty	220
Tank of fuel	40
Insurance premium	450

REQUIRED

(a) calculate the total amount of capital expenditure incurred by Tara

(b) calculate the total amount of revenue expenditure incurred by Tara

16.2*

The following trial balance has been extracted by the book-keeper of John Barclay at 30 June 20-3:

	Dr	Cr
	£	£
Sales		864,321
Purchases	600,128	
Sales returns	2,746	
Purchases returns		3,894
Office expenses	33,947	
Salaries	122,611	
Vehicle expenses	36,894	
Discounts allowed	3,187	
Discounts received		4,951
Commission received		1,245
Rent received		3,350
Debtors	74,328	
Creditors		58,821
Stock at 1 July 20-2	63,084	
Vehicles	83,500	
Office equipment	23,250	
Land and buildings	100,000	
Bank loan (repayable in 20-9)		75,000
Bank	1,197	
Capital		155,000
Drawings	21,710	
	1,166,582	1,166,582

Notes at 30 June 20-3:
- stock was valued at £66,941
- vehicle expenses owing £1,250
- office expenses prepaid £346
- commission income owing £150
- rent received prepaid £200
- goods costing £250 were taken by John Barclay for his own use

REQUIRED

You are to prepare the trading and profit and loss account of John Barclay for the year ended 30 June 20-3, together with his balance sheet at that date.

16.3* The following list of balances has been extracted by the book-keeper of Southtown Supplies, a wholesaling business, at 31 December 20-4:

	£
Opening stock	70,000
Purchases	280,000
Sales	420,000
Sales returns	6,000
Purchases returns	4,500
Rent received	2,500
Commission received	1,250
Discounts received	750
Discounts allowed	500
Electricity	13,750
Salaries	35,600
Post and packing	1,400
Premises	120,000
Fixtures and fittings	45,000
Debtors	55,000
Creditors	49,250
Bank balance	5,000
Capital	195,000
Drawings	41,000

Notes at 31 December 20-4:

- stock was valued at £60,000; this figure excludes goods which were damaged by a burst water pipe and have been scrapped (no sale proceeds); Wyvern Insurance has agreed to cover the loss of £500 incurred in writing off the goods

- commission income owing £200

- rent received prepaid £300

- electricity owing £350

- salaries prepaid £400

REQUIRED

You are to prepare the trading and profit and loss account of Southtown Supplies for the year ended 31 December 20-4, together with a balance sheet at that date.

16.4

The following trial balance was extracted from the books of Abel Brown as at 31 December 2001.

	Dr £	Cr £
Capital 1 January 2001		78,570
Fixed assets	150,000	
Provision for depreciation of fixed assets 1 January 2001		90,000
Purchases	153,900	
Sales		278,400
Wages	74,750	
Rent	2,500	
Other expenses	25,120	
Debtors	16,100	
Creditors		8,400
Bank balance	1,700	
Drawings	18,600	
Stock 1 January 2001	12,700	
	455,370	455,370

At 31 December 2001 the following additional information was available:
• stock in trade was valued at £14,100
• one week's wages £650 was owed to staff
• two weeks' rent amounting to £220 had been paid in advance
• depreciation is provided on fixed assets at the rate of 10% per annum on cost using the straight line method

REQUIRED

(a) Prepare a trading and profit and loss account for the year ended 31 December 2001 for Abel Brown.

(b) Abel is considering changing his method of providing depreciation on fixed assets from the straight line method to the reducing (diminishing) balance method.
What would Abel's net profit for the year ended 31 December 2001 have been if he had used the reducing balance method of providing for depreciation on fixed assets at 20% per annum instead of using the straight line method?

Assessment and Qualifications Alliance (AQA), 2002

16.5   The following list of balances has been extracted from the books of John Henson at 31 December 20-8:

	£
Purchases	71,600
Sales	122,000
Stock at 1 January 20-8	6,250
Vehicle running expenses	1,480
Rent and rates	5,650
Office expenses	2,220
Discounts received	285
Wages and salaries	18,950
Office equipment	10,000
Vehicle	12,000
Debtors	5,225
Creditors	4,910
Capital	20,000
Drawings for the year	13,095
Cash at bank	725

REQUIRED

You are to prepare the trading and profit and loss account of John Henson for the year ended 31 December 20-8, together with his balance sheet at that date, taking into account:

- closing stock of £8,500

- office expenses prepaid £120

- vehicle running expenses owing £230

- depreciation of office equipment for the year £1,000

- depreciation of vehicle for the year £3,000

16.6

The following information has been extracted from the ledgers of Ken Tucky at 31 March 2006.

Purchases	£280,797	Bad debts	£1,368
Sales	£587,461	General expenses	£33,713
Returns inwards	£837	Premises at cost	£145,000
Stock 1 April 2005	£39,771	Equipment at cost	£11,400
Wages	£128,528	Motor vehicles at cost	£42,000
Motor expenses	£47,870	Provisions for depreciation at 1 April 2005:	
Rates	£7,810	Premises	£46,400
Insurance	£7,780	Equipment	£6,840
		Motor vehicles	£26,880

Additional information at 31 March 2006:

(1) Stock was valued at £40,135.

(2) A motor van purchased during the year for £18,500 has been included in the motor expenses account.

(3) Wages remaining unpaid amounted to £1,383.

(4) Insurances paid in advance amounted to £286.

(5) Ken took goods to the value of £2,170 from the business for his own personal use.

(6) Depreciation is to be charged at the following rates:

Premises at 2% per annum using the straight-line method;

Equipment at 10% per annum using the straight-line method;

Motor vehicles at 40% per annum using the reducing balance method.

It is Ken's policy to charge a full year's depreciation on all assets held at the end of the financial year.

REQUIRED

(a) Prepare a trading and profit and loss account for the year ended 31 March 2006.

(b) Explain your treatment of Additional information (4) and (5). Make reference to appropriate concepts that you have used.

Ken has recently seen an increase in the number of customers' debts that need to be written off as bad.

REQUIRED

(c) Advise Ken why he should create a provision for doubtful debts.

Assessment and Qualifications Alliance (AQA), 2006

16.7* The following balances have been extracted from the books of Rachel Sorcim at 31 March 2005.

	£	£
Capital		86,048
Sales		81,643
Purchases	38,642	
Office wages	21,347	
Rent, rates and insurances	4,990	
General expenses	16,281	
Bad debts	137	
Provision for doubtful debts 1 April 2004		100
Bad debts recovered		88
Premises at cost	70,000	
Equipment at cost	28,000	
Provisions for depreciation 1 April 2004:		
Premises		16,800
Equipment		16,530
Debtors and creditors	1,360	981
Stock at 1 April 2004	1,487	
Drawings	16,500	

Additional information at 31 March 2005 not yet included by Rachel:

(1) Closing stock £1,638.

(2) Wages accrued £412.

(3) Insurance paid in advance £146.

(4) During the year, Rachel took goods to the value of £1,200 from the business for her private use.

(5) Rachel maintains a provision for doubtful debts of 5% of debtors outstanding at the year end.

(6) Rachel provides for depreciation of fixed assets as follows:

premises at 2% per annum on cost using the straight-line method;

equipment 20% per annum using the reducing balance method.

REQUIRED

(a) Prepare a trading and profit and loss account for the year ended 31 March 2005.

(b) Prepare an extract from the balance sheet as at 31 March 2005 showing the capital section only.

Assessment and Qualifications Alliance (AQA), 2005

16.8 The following trial balance has been extracted from the books of account of Siobhan Huggett on 30 April 2004.

	£	£
Vehicles at cost	160,000	
Fixtures and fittings at cost	85,000	
Provisions for depreciation		
vehicles		80,400
fixtures and fittings		21,000
Provision for doubtful debts		310
Stock 1 May 2003	7,800	
Debtors and creditors	9,000	7,150
Purchases and sales	149,400	293,100
Wages and general expenses	116,200	
Business rates	13,510	
Bad debts	750	
Bank balance		11,450
Drawings	18,500	
Capital		146,750
	560,160	560,160

Additional information and instructions

(1) At 30 April 2004 stock had been valued at cost, £8,700. However, Siobhan believes that it could be sold for £11,500.

(2) No adjustment has been made for goods taken from the business by Siobhan, cost price £3,000, for her private use.

(3) On 17 January 2004 Siobhan purchased fixtures for £23,000. This amount is included in the purchases figure on the trial balance.

(4) Wages and general expenses accrued and due at 30 April 2004 amounted to £1,600.

(5) Business rates paid in advance on 30 April 2004 amounted to £180.

(6) Depreciation is to be provided on the value of fixed assets held at the financial year end as follows:

fixtures and fittings 10% straight line;

vehicles 40% reducing balance.

(7) Provision for doubtful debts is to be maintained at 3% on debtors outstanding at the financial year end.

REQUIRED

(a)   Prepare a trading and profit and loss account for the year ended 30 April 2004.

(b)   Identify one example of capital expenditure and one example of revenue expenditure from the final accounts of Siobhan.

(c)   Explain why it is important to distinguish between capital and revenue expenditure when preparing a set of final accounts.

Assessment and Qualifications Alliance (AQA), 2004

16.9   The following information has been extracted from the books of account of Wullie McDuff at 30 September 2005.

	£	£
Gross profit for the year		807,850
Wages	748,432	
Rent and rates	12,460	
General expenses	36,980	
Bad debts written off during year	760	
Bad debts recovered during year		100
Trade debtors	35,000	
Trade creditors		27,000
Premises	120,000	
Vehicles	60,000	
Provision for depreciation		
Premises		21,600
Vehicles		30,000
Provision for doubtful debts		940

Additional information

(1)   General expenses remaining unpaid at 30 September 2005 amounted to £918.

(2)   Rent paid for October 2005 amounted to £320.

(3)   Depreciation is to be provided at the following rates:

Premises at 2% using the straight-line method;

Vehicles at 25% using the reducing balance method.

(4)   The provision for doubtful debts is to be maintained at 2.5% of debtors outstanding at the financial year-end.

(5)   During the year, a vehicle that cost £20,000 was sold for £4,800 cash. The vehicle had been depreciated by £15,000 over its lifetime. This transaction has been recorded, but the profit or loss on the disposal has yet to be calculated.

REQUIRED

(a)   Prepare a profit and loss account for the year ended 30 September 2005.

> Wullie's sister, Morag, has told him that she thinks that it may be to his advantage if he changes his business into a private limited company.

REQUIRED

(b)   Advise Wullie whether it would be to his advantage to change his business into a private limited company.

Assessment and Qualifications Alliance (AQA), 2006

16.10*   The following trial balance has been extracted by the book-keeper of James Jenkins, who owns a patisserie and coffee lounge, as at 30 June 20-9:

	Dr £	Cr £
Capital		36,175
Drawings	19,050	
Purchases and sales	105,240	168,432
Stock at 1 July 20-8	9,427	
Debtors and creditors	3,840	4,226
Returns	975	1,237
Commission received		2,350
Discounts	127	243
Wages and salaries	30,841	
Vehicle expenses	1,021	
Rent and rates	8,796	
Heating and lighting	1,840	
Telephone	355	
General expenses	1,752	
Bad debts recovered		210
Bad debts written off	85	
Vehicle at cost	8,000	
Provision for depreciation on vehicle		3,500
Shop fittings at cost	6,000	
Provision for depreciation on shop fittings		2,400
Provision for doubtful debts		150
Cash	155	
Bank	21,419	
	218,923	218,923

Notes at 30 June 20-9:
* stock was valued at £11,517
* commission income owing £160
* vehicle expenses owing £55
* rent prepaid £275
* depreciate the vehicle at 25 per cent per annum, using the reducing balance method
* depreciate shop fittings at 10 per cent per annum, using the straight-line method
* the provision for doubtful debts is to be equal to 2.5 per cent of debtors

You are to prepare the trading and profit and loss account of James Jenkins for the year ended 30 June 20-9, together with his balance sheet at that date.

16.11* Samina Hussein is a trader. She provides the following information for the year ended 31 December 2006:

	£
Gross profit	110,707
Wages	62,400
Rent and rates	8,430
General expenses	9,477
Discounts received	388
Discounts allowed	307
Debtors at 31 December 2006	27,000
Equipment at cost at 31 December 2006	12,000
Provision for doubtful debts at 1 January 2006	700
Provision for depreciation on equipment at 1 January 2006	4,800

Additional information not yet recorded in the accounts at 31 December 2006:

(1) Rates paid in advance amounted to £120.

(2) Rent owing amounted to £600.

(3) Samina maintains a provision for doubtful debts of 2.5% of debtors outstanding at year end.

(4) Samina provides for depreciation on equipment at 10% per annum using the straight-line method.

(5) During the year ended 31 December 2006, Samina took goods from the business for her own use valued at cost price £2,783.

REQUIRED

Prepare a profit and loss account for the year ended 31 December 20-6.

Assessment and Qualifications Alliance (AQA), 2007

Tutorial note: before preparing the profit and loss account, gross profit should be adjusted for goods taken for Samina's own use (note 5).

17 FINAL ACCOUNTS OF LIMITED COMPANIES

In the last few chapters we have looked at a number of adjustments made to the final accounts of sole traders in order to improve their relevance and reliability. In this chapter we turn our attention to limited companies and their final accounts, including:

- the differences between ordinary shares and preference shares
- the use of loans and debentures to raise finance
- the concept of reserves, and the differences between capital reserves and revenue reserves
- the layout of a company's trading, profit and loss, and profit and loss appropriation accounts, and balance sheet for internal use
- recording the revaluation of freehold land and buildings
- recording bonus issues and rights issues on company balance sheets

COMPANIES ACT 2006

The Companies Act 2006 requires that companies produce sets of accounts and states the detailed information that must be disclosed. For larger companies the accounts are audited by external auditors – this is a costly and time-consuming exercise (smaller companies are often exempt from audit). Nevertheless, the audit process enhances the reliability of the accounts for stakeholders – such as shareholders, creditors and lenders. The accounts must be sent to Companies House, where they are available for public inspection. The accounts are available to all shareholders, together with a report on the company's activities during the year.

In this chapter we will study the 'internal use' accounts, rather than being concerned with the accounting requirements of the Companies Act 2006.

Before we examine the final accounts in detail we will examine first the principal ways in which a company raises finance by the issue of shares. There are different types of shares which appear in a company's balance sheet as the company's share capital.

Shares Issued by Limited Companies

limited liability

One of the benefits of owning shares in a limited company is that the shareholders (members) of a company can only lose the amount of their investment. In the event of the company becoming insolvent (going 'bust'), the shareholders' personal assets are not available to the company's creditors because the shareholders have limited liability.

The amount of a shareholder's investment comprises the money paid for the shares, together with any money unpaid on their shares (unpaid instalments on new share issues, for example). This means that, if the company became insolvent, shareholders would have to pay any unpaid instalments to help pay the creditors. As this happens very rarely, shareholders are usually in a safe position.

authorised capital

Many companies have a stated amount of **authorised share capital** which is the maximum share capital that the company is allowed to issue. For companies formed prior to the Companies Act 2006, the statement of authorised share capital is given in a governing document of the company called the Memorandum of Association. Under the terms of the Companies Act 2006 there is no requirement for a company to have authorised capital – however, the majority of existing companies will have been formed under earlier company legislation.

Where a company has an amount stated for authorised capital, it can increase the amount by passing a resolution at a general meeting of the shareholders. This will enable a company that has already issued the amount of the authorised capital to expand the business by issuing more shares.

Authorised capital can be shown on the balance sheet ('financed by' section) – or as a note for information – but is not added into the balance sheet total, as it may not be for the same amount as the issued capital (see below).

issued capital

The **issued share capital** is the amount of share capital that the company has issued. Note that, where a company has authorised capital, the issued capital cannot exceed the amount authorised. Another name for issued capital is **called up share capital**.

Share capital – authorised and issued – may be divided into a number of classes or types of share; the main types are **ordinary shares** and, less commonly, **preference shares**.

The issued share capital – showing the classes and number of shares that have been issued – forms part of the 'financed by' section of the balance sheet of a limited company.

ordinary (equity) shares

Ordinary shares – often called 'equities' – are the most commonly issued class of share which carry the main 'risks and rewards' of the business. The risks are of losing part or all of the value of the shares if the business loses money or becomes insolvent; the rewards are that they take a share of the profits – in the form of **dividends** – after allowance has been made for all expenses of the business, including loan and debenture interest (see page 312), taxation, and after preference dividends (if any). Amounts paid as dividends to ordinary shareholders will vary: when a company makes large profits, it will have the ability to pay higher dividends to the ordinary shareholders; when losses are made, the ordinary shareholders may receive no dividend.

Often dividends are paid twice a year to shareholders. An **interim dividend** is paid just over half-way through the company's financial year and is based on the profits made during the first half of the year. A **final dividend** is paid early in the next financial year and is based on the profits made for the full year. Until the final dividend is paid, it is shown as a current liability in the balance sheet. Note that dividends are expressed as either pence per share or a percentage (based on the nominal value of the shares). For example, 5 pence per share is the same as a 5 per cent dividend for shares that have a nominal value of £1; 3 pence per share is the same as a 6 per cent dividend for shares that have a nominal value of 50 pence.

Companies rarely pay out all of their profits in the form of dividends; most retain some profits as reserves. These can always be used to enable a dividend to be paid in a year when the company makes little or no profit, always assuming that the company has sufficient cash in the bank to make the payment. Ordinary shareholders, in the event of the company becoming insolvent, will be the last to receive any repayment of their investment: other creditors will be paid off first.

Ordinary shares carry voting rights – thus shareholders have a say at the annual general meeting and at any other shareholders' meetings.

Ordinary shares are not normally repayable, so the company will have the finance for the foreseeable future.

preference shares

Whereas ordinary share dividends will vary from year-to-year, preference shares usually carry a fixed percentage rate of dividend – for example, "5 per cent preference shares" will receive a dividend of five per cent of nominal value (see next page). Their dividends are paid in preference to those of ordinary shareholders; but they are only paid if the company makes profits. In the event of the company ceasing to trade, the preference shareholders will also receive repayment of capital before the ordinary shareholders. Sometimes preference shares are issued as **redeemable** – this means that they are repayable at some date in the future.

Preference shares do not carry voting rights.

advantages and disadvantages of shares

To the company raising finance, the advantages and disadvantages of issuing ordinary and preference shares need to be considered.

ordinary shares

advantages to the company:

- ordinary shares are not normally repayable
- a variable dividend is paid, which is dependent on profits
- if profits are low and a dividend is not paid in one year, the dividend is not carried forward
- in the event of insolvency of the company, ordinary shareholders will be paid off last

disadvantage to the company:

- ordinary shareholders can speak and vote at the annual general meeting of the company, and each share carries one vote; this could be a problem to the company if the shareholders are dissatisfied

preference shares

advantages to the company:

- the dividend is fixed so, if profits of the company increase, more profit is retained in the company
- preference shareholders cannot vote at meetings of the company, so they have little control over the company

disadvantages to the company:

- preference dividends are usually cumulative, that is they must be paid each year; if not, they have to be carried forward to the next year

  shareholders can attend meetings of the company (but cannot vote)
- preference shares may be redeemable (repayable) in the future
- in the event of insolvency of the company, preference shareholders must be repaid in full before any money can be paid to ordinary shareholders

nominal value of shares

Each share has a nominal value – or face value – which is entered in the accounts. Shares may be issued with nominal values of 5p, 10p, 25p, 50p or £1, or indeed for any amount. Thus a company with an issued share capital of £100,000 might divide this up into:

100,000 ordinary shares of 50p each	£50,000
50,000 five per cent preference shares of £1 each	£50,000
	£100,000

market value of shares

The market value is the price at which issued – or 'secondhand' – shares are traded. For ordinary shares this value can go up or down depending on, amongst other things, the success of the company – the 'risks and rewards' of equity shares. The market value usually bears little relationship to the nominal value. Note that only a small number of limited companies have their shares bought and sold on the Stock Exchange (eg Tesco, BT); the very large majority of companies are much smaller and are not quoted on the stock market and will only need to be valued if the company is up for sale.

issue price

This is the price at which shares are issued to shareholders by the company – either when the company is being set up, or at a later date when it needs to raise more funds. The issue price is either 'at par' (ie the nominal value), or above nominal value. In the latter case, the amount of the difference between issue price and nominal value is known as a **share premium** (see page 320): for example – nominal value £1.00; issue price £1.50; therefore share premium is 50p per share. Share premium often comes about when established companies issue additional shares – the new shareholders are paying extra to buy a stake in a profitable business.

LOANS AND DEBENTURES

In addition to money provided by shareholders, who are the owners of the company, further funds can be obtained by borrowing **loan capital**, usually in the form of loans or debentures.

loans

Loans are money borrowed by companies from lenders (such as banks) and investors on a medium or long-term basis. Generally repayments are made throughout the period of the loan, but can often be tailored to suit the needs of the borrower. Lenders often require security for loans so that, if the loan is not repaid, the lender has an asset – such as the company's premises – that can be sold.

Smaller companies are sometimes also financed by directors' loans.

debentures

Debentures are formal certificates issued by companies raising long-term finance from lenders and investors. Debenture certificates issued by large public limited companies are often traded on the Stock Exchange. Most debentures state the date they will be repaid, for example, "debentures 2020-2025" means that repayment will be made by the issuer between the years 2020 and 2025, at a date to be decided by the issuer. Debentures are commonly secured against assets such as property so that, in the event of the company ceasing to trade, the assets could be sold and used to repay the debenture holders.

Loans and debentures usually carry fixed rates of interest – for example, "5 per cent debentures" – that must be paid, just like other business expenses, whether a company makes profits or not. As loan and debenture interest is a business expense, this is shown in the profit and loss account along with all other expenses. In the event of the company ceasing to trade, loan and debenture-holders would be repaid before any shareholders.

A major advantage to a company of raising finance by means of loans and debentures is that the lender receives interest payments at an agreed rate and, if profits increase, more profit is retained in the company. However the disadvantage is that, if profits fall, interest payments must still be made and the company may cut dividends to ordinary shareholders; at worst the company could become insolvent.

SHARES OR LOAN CAPITAL? – AN INVESTMENT CHOICE

A person who has money to invest in a company is faced with the dilemma of whether to buy ordinary shares, preference shares, or loans/debentures. To make the decision, much depends on the 'risk profile' of the investor – is he/she prepared to take risks (a risk taker), or is he/she a more cautious person (risk averse)? Then there is the question of how much income the investor wants from the shares or loans, and whether he/she wants to receive a regular income.

Bearing these points in mind, the main advantages and disadvantages to the investor of ordinary shares, preference shares, and loans/debentures are:

ordinary shares

advantages to the investor:

- ordinary shareholders can speak and vote at the annual general meeting of the company, and each share carries one vote
- if the company prospers, there is the potential for shares to increase in value giving the shareholder capital growth
- if the company makes high profits, there is the possibility of the shareholder receiving high dividends

disadvantages to the investor:

- there is the risk of losing some or all of the money invested if the share price falls
- the dividend will vary, being dependent on profits
- if a dividend is not paid in one year, it is not carried forward
- in the event of insolvency of the company, ordinary shareholders will be paid off last

preference shares

advantages to the investor:

- the dividend is paid at a fixed rate which will not go down if the general level of interest rates falls
- preference dividends are usually cumulative, that is they must be paid each year or, if not, they have to be carried forward to the next year
- less risky than ordinary shares
- in the event of insolvency of the company, preference shareholders must be repaid in full before any money can be paid to ordinary shareholders
- preference shareholders can attend meetings of the company (but, generally, cannot vote)

disadvantages to the investor:

- generally, preference shareholders do not have voting rights
- the dividend rate is fixed, so there can be no growth in dividends if the company prospers
- there are fewer capital growth prospects than with ordinary shares

loans/debentures

advantages to the investor:

- where a fixed rate of interest is paid, this will not go down if the general level of interest rates falls
- the interest must be paid by the company each year
- loans and debentures are are a much safer investment than shares because they are often backed by the security of the company's assets
- in the event of insolvency of the company, loan and debenture holders will look firstly to their security backing; in any case, they must be repaid in full before anything is paid to shareholders
- altogether, loans and debentures are a much safer investment than shares

disadvantages to the investor:

- where a fixed rate of interest is paid, loan and debenture holders will not receive any benefit from any increase in the general level of interest rates
- there are no prospects for capital growth

the gearing ratio

In order to check the long-term financial stability of a company we use an accounting ratio called **gearing** (see Chapter 18 for more on ratios). Gearing measures the balance of the company's financing between share capital and loan capital as follows:

$$\frac{\text{Loan capital} + \text{preference shares}}{\text{Share capital (ordinary shares} + \text{reserves)}}$$

Gearing can be expressed as either a ratio or a percentage (to get a percentage multiply the ratio by 100). The higher the gearing, the less secure will be the company. This is because loan capital can be costly in terms of interest payments (if a company's profit falls, or a loss is made, interest on loan capital must still be paid).

It is difficult to set an acceptable standard for gearing – much depends on the individual company. However, in general, investors would not wish to see gearing exceeding a ratio of 1:1 (a percentage of 100%). At this level, the loan capital is the same as the ordinary shareholders' stake in the company. Experience shows that this is the point beyond which a company will have difficulty in making interest payments on its loan capital – a failure to keep up with interest payments often leads to insolvency of the company.

We will look more at the gearing ratio in the next chapter.

TRADING AND PROFIT AND LOSS ACCOUNT

A limited company uses the same form of final accounts as a sole trader. However there are two expense items commonly found in the profit and loss account of a limited company that are not found in those of other business types:

- **directors' remuneration** – ie amounts paid to directors; as directors are employed by the company, their pay appears amongst the profit and loss expenses of the company – this contrasts with the drawings taken by a sole trader which appear in the balance sheet
- **loan/debenture interest** – as already noted, when loan capital is issued by companies, the interest is shown as an expense in profit and loss account

Note that a figure is shown in the profit and loss account for **operating profit** after the deduction of expenses, but before the deduction of finance costs (such as debenture interest, bank and loan interest). The operating profit of a company is important to investors, lenders and other stakeholders because it shows them the profit made after deduction of the operating – or running – expenses (such as distribution costs, administrative expenses) but before finance costs are deducted, ie it shows them the ability of the company to generate profits from its day-to-day activities.

A limited company follows the profit and loss account with an **appropriation section**. This shows how net profit has been distributed and includes:

- corporation tax – the tax payable on company profits
- dividends paid and proposed – on both ordinary and preference shares, including interim dividends (usually paid just over half-way through the financial year) and final dividends (proposed at the end of the year, and paid early in the next financial year)
- transfers to and from reserves – see below

The diagram on pages 316 and 317 shows an example of the internal use trading and profit and loss account of a limited company. Explanations are set out on the left-hand page.

BALANCE SHEET

Balance sheets of limited companies follow the same layout as those we have seen earlier, but the capital section is more complex because of the different classes of shares that may be issued, and the various reserves. The diagram on pages 318 and 319 shows an example of the internal use balance sheet of a limited company. Explanations are set out on the left-hand page. Note that proposed dividends and corporation tax due are shown as current liabilities.

SHAREHOLDERS' FUNDS

On a company balance sheet, the total of the 'financed by' section is described as **shareholders' funds**. This amount represents the stake of the shareholders in the company and comprises:

- issued ordinary shares
- issued preference shares
- capital reserves (see page 320)
- revenue reserves (see page 321)

Shareholders' funds in a company balance sheet is the same concept as the owner's capital in a sole trader balance sheet.

The **appropriation section** (or account) is the part of the profit and loss account which shows how net profit is distributed. It includes corporation tax, dividends paid and proposed, and transfers to and from reserves.

The company has recorded an **operating profit** of £49,000, before deduction of finance costs (such as debenture interest, bank and loan interest).

The company has recorded a **net profit before taxation** of £46,000 in its profit and loss account – this is brought into the appropriation section.

Corporation tax, the tax that a company has to pay, based on its profits, is shown in the appropriation section. While we will not be studying the calculations for corporation tax in this book, we do need to know how the tax is recorded in the final accounts.

The company has already paid **interim dividends** on the two classes of shares it has in issue (ordinary shares and preference shares); these would, most probably, have been paid just over half-way through the company's financial year. The company also proposes to pay a **final dividend** to its shareholders: these will be paid in the early part of the next financial year. Note that a dividend is often expressed as an amount per share, based on the nominal value, eg 5p per £1 nominal value share (which is the same as a five per cent dividend).

Part of the profit is transferred to **general reserve**, which is a revenue reserve of the company.

Added to profit is a **balance of retained profits** of £38,000. This represents profits of the company from previous years that have not been distributed as dividends. Note that the appropriation section shows a balance of retained profits at the year end of £45,000. Such retained profits form a revenue reserve of the company.

MAX MUSIC LIMITED
TRADING AND PROFIT AND LOSS ACCOUNT
for the year ended 31 December 20-8

	£	£
Sales		725,000
Opening stock	45,000	
Purchases	<u>381,000</u>	
	426,000	
Less closing stock	<u>50,000</u>	
Cost of sales		<u>376,000</u>
Gross profit		349,000
Less expenses:		
Directors' remuneration	75,000	
Other expenses	<u>225,000</u>	
		<u>300,000</u>
Operating profit		49,000
Less finance costs (eg debenture interest)		<u>3,000</u>
Net profit before taxation		46,000
Less corporation tax		<u>15,000</u>
Profit for year after taxation		31,000
Less interim dividends paid		
ordinary shares	5,000	
preference shares	2,000	
final dividends proposed		
ordinary shares	10,000	
preference shares	<u>2,000</u>	
		<u>19,000</u>
		12,000
Less transfer to general reserve		<u>5,000</u>
Retained profit for year		7,000
Add balance of retained profits at beginning of year		<u>38,000</u>
Balance of retained profits at end of year		<u>45,000</u>

Limited company balance sheets usually distinguish between:

intangible fixed assets, which do not have material substance but belong to the company and have value, eg goodwill (the amount paid for the reputation and connections of a business that has been taken over), patents and trademarks; intangible fixed assets are amortised (depreciated) in the same way as tangible fixed assets.

tangible fixed assets, which have material substance, such as land and buildings, equipment, machinery, vehicles, fixtures and fittings.

Note that fixed assets, such as freehold land and buildings, may be revalued (revaluation) upwards (with an effect on revaluation reserve); other assets will be reduced in value by depreciation.

As well as the usual **current liabilities**, for limited companies, this section also contains the amount of proposed dividends (but not dividends that have been paid in the year) and the amount of corporation tax to be paid within the next twelve months. The amounts for both of these items are also included in the appropriation section of the profit and loss account.

Long-term liabilities are those that are due to be repaid more than twelve months from the date of the balance sheet, eg loans and debentures.

Authorised share capital (if applicable) is included on the balance sheet 'for information', but is not added into the balance sheet total, as it may not be the same amount as the issued share capital.

Issued share capital shows the classes and number of shares that have been issued. In this balance sheet, the shares are described as being fully paid, meaning that the company has received the full amount of the value of each share from the shareholders. Sometimes shares will be partly paid, eg ordinary shares of £1, but 75p paid. This means that the company can make a call on the shareholders to pay the extra 25p to make the shares fully paid.

Capital reserves are created as a result of non-trading profit, or may be unrealised profit.

Revenue reserves are profits generated from trading activities.

The total for **shareholders' funds** represents the stake of the shareholders in the company. It comprises issued share capital (ordinary and preference shares), plus reserves (capital and revenue reserves).

MAX MUSIC LIMITED
BALANCE SHEET AS AT 31 DECEMBER 20-8

Fixed Assets	Cost/Reval'n	Prov for dep'n	Net book value
	£	£	£
Intangible			
Goodwill	50,000	20,000	30,000
Tangible			
Freehold land and buildings	410,000	110,000	300,000
Fixtures and fittings	100,000	25,000	75,000
	560,000	155,000	405,000

Current Assets			
Stock		60,000	
Debtors		53,000	
Bank		32,000	
Cash		2,000	
		147,000	

Less Current Liabilities			
Creditors	25,000		
Proposed dividends	12,000		
Corporation tax	15,000		
		52,000	
Net Current Assets or Working Capital			95,000
			500,000

Less Long-term Liabilities			
5% debentures, 2020-2025			60,000
NET ASSETS			440,000

FINANCED BY
Authorised Share Capital

100,000 5% preference shares of £1 each	100,000
600,000 ordinary shares of £1 each	600,000
	700,000

Issued Share Capital

80,000 5% preference shares of £1 each, fully paid	80,000
300,000 ordinary shares of £1 each, fully paid	300,000
	380,000

Capital Reserve

Share premium account	10,000

Revenue Reserves

General reserve	5,000
Profit and loss account	45,000
SHAREHOLDERS' FUNDS	440,000

RESERVES

A limited company rarely distributes all its profits to its shareholders. Instead, it will often keep part of the profits earned each year in the form of reserves. There are two types of reserves:

- capital reserves, which are created as a result of a non-trading profit, or may be unrealised profits
- revenue reserves, which are retained profits from profit and loss account

capital reserves

Capital reserves are created as a result of a non-trading profit, or may be unrealised profit. Note that capital reserves cannot be used to fund dividend payments.

Examples of capital reserves include:

- **Revaluation reserve.** This occurs when a fixed asset, most probably freehold land and buildings, is revalued (in an upwards direction) in the balance sheet. The amount of the revaluation is placed in a revaluation reserve where it increases the value of the shareholders' investment in the company.

  In the example below a company revalues its freehold land upwards by £250,000 from £500,000 to £750,000.

BALANCE SHEET (EXTRACTS)	
Before revaluation	£
Fixed asset: freehold land at cost	500,000
Share capital: ordinary shares of £1 each	500,000
After revaluation	
Fixed asset: freehold land at revaluation	750,000
Share capital: ordinary shares of £1 each	500,000
Capital reserve: revaluation reserve	250,000
	750,000

  The book-keeping entry for this revaluation transaction is:
  - debit freehold land account £250,000
  - credit revaluation reserve account £250,000

  Note that this is purely a 'book' adjustment – no cash has changed hands.

- **Share premium account.** An established company may issue additional shares to the public at a higher amount than the nominal value. For example, a company seeks finance for further expansion by issuing additional ordinary shares. The shares have a nominal value of £1 each, but, because it is a well-established company, the shares are issued at £1.50 each. Of this amount, £1 is recorded in the issued share capital section, and the extra 50p is the share premium.

revenue reserves

Revenue reserves are profits from trading activities which have been retained in the company to help build the company for the future. Revenue reserves include the balance of the appropriation section of the profit and loss account: this balance is commonly described as 'profit and loss account' or 'balance of retained profits'. Alternatively, a transfer may be made from the appropriation section to a named revenue reserve account, such as general reserve, or a revenue reserve for a specific purpose, such as reserve for the replacement of machinery. Transfers to or from these named revenue reserve accounts are made in the appropriation section of the profit and loss account.

As revenue reserves have been created from the trading activities of the company, they are available to fund dividend payments (as we have seen on page 315, dividends are deducted in the appropriation section of the profit and loss account). A further use of revenue reserves is to provide bonus shares for shareholders (see below).

reserves: profits not cash

It should be noted that reserves – both capital and revenue – are not cash funds to be used whenever the company needs money, but are in fact represented by assets shown on the balance sheet. The reserves record the fact that the assets belong to the shareholders via their ownership of the company.

BONUS ISSUES AND RIGHTS ISSUES

Limited companies – and particularly public limited companies – quite often increase their capital by means of either **bonus issues** or **rights issues** of shares. Whilst both of these have the effect of increasing the number of shares in issue, they have quite different effects on the structure of the company balance sheet.

bonus issues

A bonus issue is made when a company issues free shares to existing shareholders; it does this by using reserves that have built up and capitalising them (ie they are turned into permanent share capital). The bonus issue is distributed on the basis of existing shareholdings – for example, one bonus share for every two shares already held.

With a bonus issue no cash flows in or out of the company. The shareholders are no better off: with more shares in issue the stock market price per share will fall in proportion to the bonus issue, ie the company's net assets are now spread among a greater number of shares.

Bonus issues are made in order to acknowledge the fact that reserves belong to shareholders. Often a build-up of reserves occurs because a company hasn't the cash to pay dividends, so a bonus issue is a way of passing the reserves to shareholders.

Note that capital or revenue reserves can be used for bonus issues. If there is a choice, then capital reserves are used first – this is because it is one of the few uses of a capital reserve, which cannot be used to fund the payment of dividends.

rights issues

A rights issue is used by a company seeking to raise further finance through the issue of shares. Instead of going to the considerable expense of offering additional shares to the public, it is cheaper to offer shares to existing shareholders at a favourable price (a little below the current market value). As with a bonus issue the extra shares are offered in proportion to the shareholders' existing holding. The shareholder may take up the rights by subscribing for the shares offered; alternatively the rights can often be sold on the stock market.

WORKED EXAMPLE: BONUS ISSUES AND RIGHTS ISSUES

situation

The following are the summary balance sheets of Severn plc and Wye plc:

	Severn £	Wye £
Fixed assets	300,000	300,000
Current assets (including bank)	100,000	100,000
	400,000	400,000
Ordinary shares of £1 each	200,000	200,000
Reserves (capital and revenue)	200,000	200,000
	400,000	400,000

Severn is planning a one-for-two bonus issue.

Wye is seeking finance for a major expansion programme through a one-for-two rights issue at a price of £1.80 per share.

solution

After the issues, the balance sheets appear as:

	Severn £	Wye £
Fixed assets	300,000	300,000
Current assets (including bank)	100,000	280,000
	400,000	580,000
Ordinary shares of £1 each	300,000	300,000
Share premium account (capital reserve)	–	80,000
Reserves	100,000	200,000
	400,000	580,000

The changes are:

Severn   Reserves are reduced by £100,000, whilst share capital is increased by the same amount; the ordinary share capital is now more in balance with fixed assets; no cash has been received.

Wye   The bank balance has increased by £180,000, being 100,000 shares (assuming that all shareholders took up their rights) at £1.80; share capital has increased by £100,000, whilst 80p per share is the share premium, ie £80,000 in total. The company now has the money to finance its expansion programme. There are also significant reserves which could be used for a bonus issue in the future.

differences between a bonus issue and a rights issue

bonus issue	rights issue
• additional shares given free to existing shareholders	• additional shares offered for sale to existing shareholders in proportion to their holdings
• the capitalisation of reserves into share capital	• offer price is below the current market value
• distributed in proportion to existing shareholdings	• shareholders can either buy the additional shares or can sell the rights on the stock market
• no payment made for shares	• company receives payment from shares sold
• stock market price of shares falls in proportion to bonus issue	• stock market price of shares may fall slightly (because offer price is below current market price)

CHAPTER SUMMARY

● Shareholders have limited liability, but will be liable for any money unpaid on their shares.

● The main types of shares that may be issued by companies are ordinary shares and preference shares.

● Loan capital in the form of loans and debentures is a further source of finance.

● The gearing ratio is used to check the long-term financial stability of a company.

● The final accounts of a company include an appropriation section, which follows the profit and loss account.

● The balance sheet of a limited company includes a shareholders' funds section which states the ownership of the company by its shareholders:

  – ordinary shares and preference shares issued

  – capital reserves and revenue reserves

● Capital reserves are created as a result of a non-trading profit, or may be unrealised profits, and cannot be used to fund dividend payments.

● Revenue reserves are profits from trading activities.

● A bonus issue is the capitalisation of reserves – either capital or revenue – in the form of free shares issued to existing shareholders in proportion to their holdings; no cash flows into the company.

● A rights issue is the raising of cash by offering shares to existing shareholders, in proportion to their holdings, at a favourable price.

In the next chapter we look at how we can assess business performance by interpreting and analysing the financial statements. To help us in this we shall be calculating ratios, percentages and other performance indicators.

QUESTIONS

visit
www.osbornebooks.co.uk
to take an online test

An asterisk (*) after the question number means that the answer is given at the end of this book.

17.1 Distinguish between:
  (a)   ordinary shares and preference shares
  (b)   nominal value and market value of shares
  (c)   capital reserves and revenue reserves
  (d)   a bonus issue and a rights issue

17.2 Explain where the following items appear in a limited final accounts:
  (a)   debenture interest
  (b)   directors' remuneration
  (c)   corporation tax
  (d)   dividends proposed
  (e)   revaluation reserve
  (f)   goodwill

17.3* Chapelporth Limited has made a pre-tax profit of £135,000 for the year ended 30 June 20-8. The following interim dividends for the half-year ended 31 December 20-7 were paid in February 20-8:

	£
interim ordinary dividend	21,000
interim preference dividend	8,000

The directors of Chapelporth Limited wish to provide for the following at the year end on 30 June 19-8:

	£
corporation tax	48,000
final ordinary dividend	29,000
final preference dividend	8,000

You are to prepare the profit and loss appropriation account of Chapelporth Limited for the year ended 30 June 20-8.

17.4 Mason Motors Limited is a second-hand car business. The following information is available for the year ended 31 December 20-1:

- balance of retained profits from previous years stands at £100,000

- net profit for the year was £75,000

- it has been agreed that a transfer to a general reserve of £20,000 is to be made

- corporation tax of £20,050 is to be paid on the year's profit

- it has been agreed that a final dividend of 10% is to be paid on the issued share capital of £100,000

You are to

(a) Set out the appropriation section of the profit and loss account for Mason Motors Limited for the year ended 31 December 20-1.

(b) State how you would reply to one of the directors of the company who asks if the £20,000 being transferred to general reserve could be used to rebuild the garage forecourt.

17.5* The following figures are taken from the accounting records of Jobseekers Limited, a recruitment agency, at the end of the financial year on 31 December 20-6:

	£
Issued share capital (£1 ordinary shares)	100,000
Premises at cost	175,000
Depreciation of premises to date	10,500
Office equipment at cost	25,000
Depreciation of office equipment to date	5,000
Goodwill at cost	20,000
Amortisation* of goodwill to date	6,000
Stock at 31 December 20-6	750
Debtors	42,500
Creditors	7,250
Bank overdraft	13,950
Bank loan	55,000
Net profit for year before taxation	68,200
Corporation tax owing for the year	14,850
Interim ordinary dividend paid	10,000
Final ordinary dividend proposed	40,000
Retained profit at 1 January 20-6	7,350

* amortisation is similar to depreciation

You are to prepare the appropriation section of the profit and loss account (starting with net profit) for the year ended 31 December 20-6, together with a balance sheet at that date.

17.6* Jill and her brother Jack have recently inherited £10,000 each. They wish to invest all of their inheritance in Multar plc.

They could invest in one of the following:

> ordinary shares
>
> 7% preference shares
>
> 6% debentures

Jill does not mind taking risks with any money she has whereas her brother is a much more cautious person. He is looking for an investment which will give him a steady income.

REQUIRED

(a)   State **one** advantage **and one** disadvantage of each type of investment.

Ordinary shares

Advantage ....

....

Disadvantage ....

....

7% preference shares

Advantage ....

....

Disadvantage ....

....

6% debentures

Advantage ....

....

Disadvantage ....

....

(b)   Advise Jill which type of investment she should choose.

....

....

....

(c)   Advise Jack which type of investment he should choose.

....

....

....

Assessment and Qualifications Alliance (AQA), 2003

17.7

(a) The draft profit for the year ended 31 May 2003 of Srian plc is £12,000,000. The following information for the year has not been taken into account.

	£
Ordinary dividends – paid	800,000
proposed	1,300,000
Directors' fees	1,500,000
Provision for corporation tax	2,600,000
Debenture interest	1,200,000
Transfer to general reserve	1,000,000

REQUIRED

Prepare the profit and loss appropriation account for the year ended 31 May 2003.

(b) The following has been extracted from the balance sheet of Srian plc as at 31 May 2003.

	£
Ordinary shares of £1 each fully paid	25,000,000
6% Debentures	20,000,000

The directors have seen an opportunity to expand the company's operation. They need to raise £30,000,000.

The directors are considering raising the whole amount by

either an issue of 20,000,000 ordinary shares at £1.50 each

or an issue of £30,000,000 6% debentures.

REQUIRED

Evaluate the two methods of raising finance being considered by the directors of the company.

Assessment and Qualifications Alliance (AQA), 2003

Tutorial note: part (b) of the question requires an evaluation of two ways in which Srian plc could finance an expansion scheme; your evaluation should include a written comment on the advantages and disadvantages of ordinary shares and debentures, together with a calculation and comment on the gearing ratio under each option.

17.8*

The following is the summarised draft balance sheet of Vlasmin plc as at 31 March 2002.

	Cost	Depreciation	Net
	£000	£000	£000
Fixed assets	1,000	620	380
Current assets		420	
Less Current liabilities		360	60
			440
Ordinary share capital			200
Profit and loss account			240
			440

Depreciation has been charged on all fixed assets at 20% per annum using the straight-line method.

After preparing the draft balance sheet the directors of Vlasmin plc have decided to incorporate the following changes in the final accounts.

(a) Wages due but unpaid at the year end amounted to £12,000.

(b) Depreciation on all fixed assets is to be charged at 15% per annum using the straight-line method.

(c) A transfer of £25,000 to a general reserve.

(d) A final dividend on the ordinary share capital of £43,000.

REQUIRED

Using the table below show the effect that any amendments resulting from notes (a) to (d) above will have on the balance sheet of Vlasmin plc.

If you believe that there is no amendment necessary write *no change*.

Note (a) has been completed as an example.

Note	Net profit before appropriations	Retained profits	Shareholders' funds	Current assets	Current liabilities
(a)	decrease £12,000	decrease £12,000	decrease £12,000	no change	increase £12,000
(b)					
(c)					
(d)					

Assessment and Qualifications Alliance (AQA), 2002

17.9

The directors of Stoulby Ltd provided the following information before the preparation of the final accounts for the year ended 31 December 2006.

	£
Authorised capital – 10,000,000 ordinary shares of 50 pence each	5,000,000
Issued capital – 4,000,000 ordinary shares of 50 pence each	2,000,000
Profit and loss account	410,000
General reserve	300,000
Share premium account	500,000
Ordinary dividend paid on 3 August 2006	63,000

Additional information

(1)   Net profit for the year ended 31 December 2006 was £650,000.

(2)   The directors wish to transfer £120,000 to the general reserve and propose a final dividend of 2.5 pence per share.

(3)   The corporation tax charge for the year is expected to be £155,000.

REQUIRED

(a)   Prepare a profit and loss appropriation account for the year ended 31 December 2006.

(b)   Prepare the share capital and reserves section of the balance sheet at 31 December 2006.

(c)   Explain the term 'revenue reserve'.

(d)   Identify **one** example of a revenue reserve from the information given for Stoulby Ltd.

(e)   Explain **one** way in which a revenue reserve may be used.

Assessment and Qualifications Alliance (AQA), 2007

17.10 The following is the summarised draft balance sheet as at 31 December 2002 for David Mark Ltd.

	£	£
Fixed assets		700,000
Current assets		
Stock	85,000	
Debtors	60,000	
Bank	17,000	
	162,000	
Less Current liabilities		
Trade creditors	37,000	125,000
		825,000
Share capital and reserves		
Ordinary shares of 50 pence each		250,000
8% preference shares of £1 each		100,000
Profit and loss account		400,000
General reserve		75,000
		825,000

The company's retained profit for the year, before appropriations, was £150,000, which has been included in the profit and loss account figure shown in the balance sheet above.

Additional information:

The following have **not** yet been taken into consideration

- Transfer from profit and loss account to the general reserve £45,000
- A proposed final dividend on preference shares of £4,000
- A proposed final dividend on ordinary shares of 7 pence per share
- An issue of 200,000 ordinary shares of 50 pence each at 75 pence per share.

    (*Note*: these shares are not eligible for dividend in the year ended 31 December 2002)

REQUIRED

(a) Starting with the retained profit of £150,000 from the draft accounts, calculate the retained profit for the year ended 31 December 2002 after appropriations.

(b) Prepare the summarised balance sheet as at 31 December 2002 as it would appear, after taking into account the additional information listed above.

(c) State the type of business ownership that would have "Ltd" as part of its name.

(d) Assess the importance of the term "Ltd" to an ordinary shareholder in David Mark Ltd.

Assessment and Qualifications Alliance (AQA), 2003

17.11* The chief accountant of Srewolf Ltd has been ill. During her absence, one of her assistants has produced the following balance sheet, which failed to balance by £280,000.

Srewolf Ltd
Summarised Balance Sheet at 30 April 2006

	£	£
Fixed assets		1,270,000
Current assets	355,000	
Creditors	31,000	
		324,000
		1,594,000
Capital and reserves		
Ordinary shares of £1 each		750,000
General reserve		100,000
Profit and loss account at 1 May 2005		77,000
Net profit for this year before appropriations		387,000
Suspense account (difference in balance sheet totals)		280,000
		1,594,000

On her return, the chief accountant discovered the following:

(1) An issue of 200,000 ordinary shares was made in October 2005 at £1.40 per share. Although the monies received had been correctly entered in the cash book, no other entries had been made in the company's books of account.

(2) The following items have been proposed by the company directors but have yet to be taken into account:

(i) a final dividend of 4p per share on all shares held at the year-end;

(ii) a transfer to general reserve of £50,000;

(iii) a provision for corporation tax of £110,000.

REQUIRED

(a) Prepare a profit and loss appropriation account for the year ended 30 April 2006.

(b) Prepare a corrected summarised balance sheet at 30 April 2006.

Assessment and Qualifications Alliance (AQA), 2006

17.12

The following information has been extracted from the books of account of Leroy McDade plc as at 31 December 2001.

	£
Issued share capital:	
ordinary shares of 50p each, fully paid	1,600,000
7% debentures (2020 - 2025)	200,000
Share premium account	800,000
Profit and loss account balance 1 January 2001	612,000
General reserve	150,000
Interim ordinary dividend paid 4 August 2001	40,000
Trade creditors	78,200
Directors' fees	117,000
Provision for corporation tax due	180,000

Additional information:

- Net profit for the year after interest but before taxation was £546,000.

- Debenture interest is payable half-yearly to 30 June and 31 December. It is paid to debenture holders on 27 July and 27 January each year.

- The directors propose a transfer to general reserve of £50,000 and a final ordinary dividend of 5p per share.

REQUIRED

(a) Prepare the profit and loss appropriation account for the year ended 31 December 2001 of Leroy McDade plc.

(b) Prepare balance sheet extracts as at 31 December 2001 for Leroy McDade plc showing the sections for:

(i) the capital and reserves, and

(ii) current liabilities.

(c) Discuss the advantages and disadvantages that an investor should consider when deciding whether to invest in debentures or ordinary shares.

Assessment and Qualifications Alliance (AQA), 2002

17.13* The following balances have been extracted from the books of account of Pafftol Ltd after a draft trading and profit and loss account was prepared for the year ended 31 March 2004.

	£
Issued share capital:	
ordinary shares £1 each fully paid	500,000
7% debentures (2015-2018)	400,000
Plant and machinery at cost	1,420,000
Vehicles at cost	710,000
Provisions for depreciation:	
plant and machinery	192,000
vehicles	150,000
Net profit for the year	676,000
Profit and loss account 1 April 2003	439,000
Bank balance (debit)	113,600
General reserve	250,000
Share premium account	100,000
Stock 31 March 2004	211,000
Debtors	24,900
Creditors	16,500
Interim ordinary dividend paid	30,000

Additional information and instructions

The following have not been included in the balances shown above:

(1) directors' fees £200,000;

(2) debenture interest paid £14,000;

(3) debenture interest accrued £14,000;

(4) proposed ordinary dividend £60,000;

(5) corporation tax payable £102,000;

(6) transfer to general reserve £50,000.

REQUIRED

(a)   Prepare a profit and loss appropriation account for the year ended 31 March 2004.

(b)   Prepare a balance sheet as at 31 March 2004.

The directors of Pafftol Ltd wish to raise £600,000 additional capital. They are unsure whether to:

(1)   issue a further 200,000 ordinary shares with a nominal value of £1 each at a premium of £2 each;

or

(2)   issue 6% debentures.

REQUIRED

(c)   Advise the directors which of the two options would be the most beneficial to the company.

Assessment and Qualifications Alliance (AQA), 2004

Tutorial note: in part (a), net profit for the year from the list of balances needs adjusting for certain profit and loss expenses which are given in the 'additional information'.

17.14   The following are the summary balance sheets of Avon plc and Teme plc:

	Avon	Teme
	£	£
Fixed assets	300,000	400,000
Current assets (including bank)	200,000	200,000
	500,000	600,000
Ordinary shares of £1 each	300,000	400,000
Reserves (capital and revenue)	200,000	200,000
	500,000	600,000

Avon is planning a one-for-three bonus issue.

Teme is seeking finance for a major expansion programme through a one-for-two rights issue at a price of £2.50 per share.

You are to show the balance sheets of Avon plc and Teme plc after the issues have taken place (assume that the issues have been taken up fully).

18 RATIO ANALYSIS

Ratio analysis is the technique of interpreting the final accounts of businesses in order to assess strengths and weaknesses. A business needs to be performing well in areas of profitability, liquidity, and capital structure.

In this chapter we examine:

- the importance of interpretation of final accounts
- the main accounting ratios and performance indicators
- the difference between profit and cash
- a commentary on trends shown by the main accounting ratios
- how to report on the overall financial situation of a business
- limitations in the use of ratio analysis

INTERESTED PARTIES

The use of ratio analysis to interpret accounts is not always made by an accountant; interested parties (stakeholders) include:

- **managers** or **owners** of the business, who need to make financial decisions affecting the future development of the business
- **banks**, who are being asked to lend money to finance the business
- **creditors**, suppliers who want to know if they are likely to get paid
- **customers**, who wish to be assured of continuity of supplies in the future
- **shareholders** of a limited company, who wish to be assured that their investment is sound
- prospective **investors** in a limited company, who wish to compare comparative strengths and weaknesses
- the **owner** of a business, who wishes to make comparisons with other businesses
- **employees** and **trade unions**, who wish to check on the financial prospects of the business
- **government** and **government agencies**, eg HM Revenue & Customs, that wants to check it is receiving the amount due for VAT and the tax payable on the profits of the business

In all of these cases, the interested parties will be able to calculate the main ratios, percentages and performance indicators. By doing this, the strengths and weaknesses of the business will be highlighted and appropriate conclusions can be drawn as to whether or not the business is meeting the expectations of stakeholders.

Types of Accounting Ratios and Performance Indicators

The general term 'accounting ratios' is usually used to describe the calculations aspect of interpretation of accounts. The term ratio is, in fact, partly misleading because the performance indicators include percentages, time periods, as well as ratios in the strict sense of the word.

The main themes covered by ratio analysis are:

- profitability – the relationship between profit and sales turnover, assets and capital employed
- liquidity – the stability of the business on a short-term basis
- capital structure – the stability of the business on a long-term basis

Making Use of Ratio Analysis

It is important when examining a set of final accounts and using ratio analysis to relate them to reference points or standards. These points of reference might be to:

- establish trends from past years, so providing a standard of comparison
- compare against other businesses in the same industry
- compare with standards assumed to be satisfactory by the interested party, eg a bank

Above all, it is important to understand the relationships between ratios: one ratio may give an indication of the state of the business but, before drawing conclusions, this needs to be supported by other ratios. Ratios can highlight symptoms, but the cause will then need to be investigated.

Another use of ratios is to estimate the likely future profit or balance sheet of a business. For example, it might be assumed that the same gross profit percentage as last year will also apply next year; thus, given an estimated increase in sales, it is a simple matter to estimate gross profit. In a similar way, by making use of ratios, net profit and the balance sheet can be forecast.

Now study the illustration on the next two pages. It shows the ways in which the profitability of a business is assessed. The first page sets out the calculation of the ratios and the next page highlights the figures that are used in calculating them. Then read the section 'Profitability' which follows on page 340.

PROFITABILITY RATIOS

Gross profit margin = $\dfrac{\text{Gross profit}}{\text{Sales turnover}} \times \dfrac{100}{1}$

Gross profit mark-up = $\dfrac{\text{Gross profit}}{\text{Cost of sales}} \times \dfrac{100}{1}$

Overheads/turnover = $\dfrac{\text{Overheads (expenses)}}{\text{Sales turnover}} \times \dfrac{100}{1}$

Net profit margin = $\dfrac{\text{Net profit*}}{\text{Sales turnover}} \times \dfrac{100}{1}$

* use operating profit (ie profit before interest) if the figure is available

Return on capital employed = $\dfrac{\text{Net profit*}}{\text{Capital employed†}} \times \dfrac{100}{1}$

* use operating profit (ie profit before interest) if the figure is available

† for limited companies: this is ordinary share capital + reserves + preference share capital + loan capital;
 for sole traders, capital employed is the owner's capital in the business

Mithian Trading Company Limited

TRADING AND PROFIT AND LOSS ACCOUNT

for the year ended 31 December 20-7

	£000s	£000s
Sales/turnover		1,430
Opening stock	200	
Purchases	1,000	
	1,200	
Less Closing stock	240	
Cost of sales		960
Gross profit		470
Less **expenses/overheads**:		
Selling expenses	160	
Administration expenses	135	
		295
Operating profit		175
Less finance costs (debenture interest)		5
Net profit before taxation		170
Less: Corporation tax		50
Profit for year after taxation		120
Less:		
preference dividend paid	25	
ordinary dividend proposed	75	
		100
Retained profit for the year		20
Add balance of retained profits at beginning of year		180
Balance of retained profits at end of year		200

BALANCE SHEET (extract)

	£000s
Capital employed (share capital + reserves + long-term liabilities)	1,550

Notes: Items used in the ratios on the opposite page are shown in bold type on a blue background

PROFITABILITY

One of the main objectives of a business is to make a profit. Profitability ratios examine the relationship between profit and sales turnover, and capital employed. Before calculating the profitability ratios, it is important to read the profit and loss account in order to review the figures.

The key profitability ratios are illustrated on the previous two pages. We will be calculating the accounting ratios from these figures in a Worked Example (pages 348 - 353).

gross profit margin

$$\frac{\text{Gross profit}}{\text{Sales turnover}} \quad \times \frac{100}{1}$$

This ratio expresses, as a percentage, the gross profit (sales minus cost of sales) in relation to sales turnover. For example, a gross profit margin of 20 per cent means that for every £100 of sales made, the gross profit is £20.

The gross profit margin should be similar from year-to-year for the same business. It will vary between different types of businesses, eg the gross profit margin on jewellery is considerably higher than that on food. A significant change from one year to the next, particularly a fall in the percentage, requires investigation into the buying and selling prices.

Gross profit margin and mark-up (see below) – and also net profit margin (see next page) – need to be considered in context. For example, a supermarket may well have a lower gross profit margin than a small corner shop but, because of the supermarket's much higher sales turnover, the amount of profit will be much higher. Whatever the type of business, gross profit – both as an amount and a percentage – needs to be sufficient to cover the overheads (expenses), and then to give an acceptable return on capital employed (see page 342).

gross profit mark-up

$$\frac{\text{Gross profit}}{\text{Cost of sales}} \quad \times \frac{100}{1}$$

This ratio expresses, as a percentage, the gross profit in relation to cost of sales. For example, a gross profit mark-up of 25 per cent means that for every £100 of purchases made, the gross profit is £25. Gross profit mark-up should be similar from year-to-year for the same business, although it will vary between different types of businesses. Any significant change needs investigation into the buying and selling prices.

It is quite common for a business to establish its selling price by reference to either a margin or a mark-up. The difference between the two is that:

- margin is a percentage profit based on the selling price
- mark-up is a profit percentage added to buying or cost price

For example, a product is bought by a retailer for £100; the retailer sells it for £125, ie

cost price	+	gross profit	=	selling price
£100	+	£25	=	£125

The **margin** is:

$$\frac{\text{gross profit}}{\text{selling price}} \times \frac{100}{1} = \frac{£25}{£125} \times \frac{100}{1} = \textbf{20\%}$$

The **mark-up** is:

$$\frac{\text{gross profit}}{\text{cost price}} \times \frac{100}{1} = \frac{£25}{£100} \times \frac{100}{1} = \textbf{25\%}$$

Notice here that gross profit margin and mark-up look at the same information, but from a different viewpoint: with margin, it is the gross profit related to the selling price; with mark-up, it is the gross profit related to the buying price (cost of sales).

overheads/turnover margin

$$\frac{\textbf{Overheads/expenses}}{\textbf{Sales turnover}} \times \frac{\textbf{100}}{\textbf{1}}$$

Here the overheads (expenses) of a business are expressed as a percentage of sales turnover. The ratio should fall as sales turnover increases – this is because not all overheads are variable, ie increase in direct proportion to the increase in sales turnover.

Note that each overhead or expense falls into one of three categories of cost:

- fixed costs, eg rent, council tax
- variable costs, eg commission
- semi-variable costs, eg car hire, telephone expenses

Fixed costs remain constant despite other changes. Variable costs alter with changed circumstances, such as increased sales. Semi-variable costs combine both a fixed and a variable element, eg hire of a car at a basic (fixed) cost, with a variable cost per mile. It is important to appreciate the nature of costs when interpreting accounts: for example, if sales this year are twice last year's figure, not all expenses will have doubled.

Any overhead item from profit and loss account can be expressed as a percentage of sales turnover. For example, if advertising is £50,000 and turnover is £500,000 then the percentage is 10 per cent; if it is found to be 20 per cent next year then this could indicate that an increase in advertising has failed to produce a proportionate increase in sales.

net profit margin

$$\frac{\textbf{Net profit*}}{\textbf{Sales turnover}} \times \frac{\textbf{100}}{\textbf{1}}$$

* *use operating profit (ie profit before interest), if it is available*

As with gross profit margin, the net profit margin should be similar from year-to-year for the same business, and should also be comparable with other firms in the same line of business. Net profit margin should, ideally, increase from year-to-year, which indicates that the profit and loss account expenses are being kept under control. Any significant fall should be investigated to see if it has been caused by

- a fall in gross profit margin
- and/or an increase in expenses, eg wages and salaries, advertising, etc

return on capital employed (ROCE)

This compares the net profit of a business with the amount of capital invested in the business by the owner. The percentage return is best thought of in relation to other investments, eg a bank might offer a return of five per cent on a savings account. A person running a business is investing a sum of money in that business, and the profit is the return that is achieved on that investment. However, it should be noted that the risks in running a business are considerably greater than depositing the money with a bank, and an additional return to allow for the extra risk is needed.

For limited companies, the calculation of return on capital employed must take note of their methods of financing. It is necessary to distinguish between the ordinary shareholders' investment (the equity) and the capital employed by the company, which includes preference shares and loan capital, such as debentures/long-term loans:

	Ordinary share capital
add	Reserves (capital and revenue)
equals	Equity
add	Preference share capital
add	Loan capital (including debentures)
equals	Capital Employed

The reason for including preference shares and loan capital in the capital employed is that the company has the use of the money from these contributors for the foreseeable future, or certainly for a fixed time period. Note that a bank overdraft is not included in the capital employed – this is because it is a current liability which is likely to be repaid sooner than loan capital.

The calculation of return on capital employed is:

Net profit* $\quad$ **x 100**

Capital employed† $\quad$ **1**

  * *use operating profit (ie profit before interest) if it is available*

  † *for limited companies: this is ordinary share capital + reserves + preference share capital + loan capital;*
    for sole traders, capital employed is the owner's capital in the business

the difference between profit and cash

This section has looked at the profitability of a business, ie the ability of the business to generate profit. Many people who use accounts are also interested in cash flows – the ability to generate cash.

There is an important difference between profit and cash – it is possible to have a highly profitable company that is using more cash than it is generating so that its bank balance is falling (or its overdraft is increasing). Liquidity (which we shall be looking at in the next section) is important: it is often a lack of cash (a lack of liquidity) that causes most businesses to fail.

To distinguish between cash and profit:

- **cash** is the actual amount of money held in the bank or as cash
- **profit** is a calculated figure which shows the surplus of income over expenditure for the year; it takes note of adjustments for accruals and prepayments and non-cash items such as depreciation and provision for doubtful debts.

Various transactions have an unequal effect on cash and profit as shown by the examples in the following diagram:

Effect on profit		Transaction	Effect on cash	
increase	decrease		increase	decrease
		• purchase of fixed assets		✓
	✓	• depreciation of fixed assets		
		• issue of new shares	✓	
		• payment of dividends		✓
		• raising of a loan	✓	
		• repayment of a loan		✓
✓		• increase in stock		✓
	✓	• decrease in stock	✓	
		• increase in debtors		✓
		• decrease in debtors	✓	
	✓	• increase in provision for doubtful debts		
✓		• reduction in provision for doubtful debts		
		• increase in creditors	✓	
		• decrease in creditors		✓

LIQUIDITY

Liquidity ratios measure the financial stability of the business, ie the ability of the business to operate on a short-term basis. For this we focus our attention on the current assets and current liabilities sections of the balance sheet.

The key liquidity ratios are shown linked to the balance sheet of Mithian Trading Company Limited on the next two pages. The ratios are calculated in the Worked Example on pages 348 - 353.

explanation continued on page 346

LIQUIDITY RATIOS

Net current asset ratio* =

$$\frac{\text{Current assets}}{\text{Current liabilities}}$$

* also known as the current ratio, or working capital ratio

Liquid capital ratio* =

$$\frac{\text{Current assets} - \text{Stock}}{\text{Current liabilities}}$$

* also known as the acid test or quick ratio

Stock turnover (days) =

$$\frac{\text{Average stock*}}{\text{Cost of sales}} \times 365 \text{ days}$$

* usually taken as: (opening stock + closing stock) ÷ 2;
alternatively, if opening stock figure not available, use closing
stock from the balance sheet in the calculation

Debtor collection period (days) =

$$\frac{\text{Debtors}}{\text{Credit sales}} \times 365 \text{ days}$$

Creditor payment period (days) =

$$\frac{\text{Trade creditors}}{\text{Credit purchases}} \times 365 \text{ days}$$

CAPITAL STRUCTURE

Gearing ratio* =

$$\frac{\text{Loan capital} + \text{preference shares (if any)}}{\text{Capital (ordinary shares} + \text{reserves)}}$$

* also known as capital gearing ratio, or debt/equity ratio;
for a percentage multiply the ratio by 100

Mithian Trading Company Limited
BALANCE SHEET
as at 31 December 20-7

Fixed Assets	Cost	Prov for dep'n	Net book value
	£000s	£000s	£000s
Premises	950	100	850
Fixtures and fittings	300	120	180
Vehicles	350	100	250
	1,600	320	1,280

Current Assets

Stock		240
Debtors		150
Bank/cash		135
		525

Less **Current Liabilities**

Creditors	130	
Proposed ordinary dividend	75	
Corporation tax	50	
		255

Net Current Assets or Working Capital		270
		1,550

Less Long-term Liabilities

5% Debentures		100
NET ASSETS		1,450

FINANCED BY

Issued Share Capital

1,000,000 ordinary shares of £1 each, fully paid	1,000
250,000 10% preference shares of £1 each, fully paid	250
	1,250

Revenue Reserve

Profit and loss account	200
SHAREHOLDERS' FUNDS	1,450

PROFIT AND LOSS ACCOUNT (extract)

	£000s
Cost of sales	960
Credit sales	1,430
Credit purchases	1,000

Note: Items used in ratios are shown in bold type with a blue background.

net current assets

Net current assets = Current assets – Current liabilities

Net current assets, or working capital, is needed by all businesses in order to finance day-to-day trading activities. Sufficient net current assets enables a business to hold adequate stocks, allow a measure of credit to its customers (debtors), and to pay its suppliers (creditors) as payments fall due.

net current asset ratio (or current ratio, or working capital ratio)

Net current asset ratio =   Current assets : Current liabilities

Net current asset ratio uses figures from the balance sheet and measures the relationship between current assets and current liabilities. Although there is no ideal net current asset ratio, an acceptable ratio is about 2:1, ie £2 of current assets to every £1 of current liabilities. However, a business in the retail trade may be able to work with a lower ratio, eg 1.5:1 or even less, because it deals mainly in sales for cash and so does not have a large figure for debtors. A net current asset ratio can be too high: if it is above 3:1 an investigation of the make-up of current assets and current liabilities is needed: eg the business may have too much stock, too many debtors, or too much cash at the bank.

liquid capital ratio (or acid test, or quick ratio)

$$\text{Liquid capital ratio} = \frac{\text{Current assets} - \text{Stock}}{\text{Current liabilities}}$$

The liquid capital ratio uses the current assets and current liabilities from the balance sheet, but stock is omitted. This is because stock is the most illiquid current asset: it has to be sold, turned into debtors, and then the cash has to be collected from the debtors. Thus the liquid capital ratio provides a direct comparison between debtors/cash/bank and short-term liabilities. The balance between liquid assets, that is debtors and cash/bank, and current liabilities should, ideally, be about 1:1, ie £1 of liquid assets to each £1 of current liabilities. This means that a business is expected to be able to pay its current liabilities from its liquid assets; a figure below 1:1, eg 0.75:1, indicates that the firm would have difficulty in meeting pressing demands from creditors. However, as with the net current asset ratio, some businesses are able to operate with a lower liquid capital ratio than others.

stock turnover

$$\frac{\text{Average stock}}{\text{Cost of sales}} \quad \text{x} \quad \text{365 days}$$

Stock turnover is the number of days' stock held on average. This figure will depend on the type of goods sold by the business. For example, a market trader selling fresh flowers, who finishes each day when sold out, will have a stock turnover of one day. By contrast, a jewellery shop – because it may hold large stocks of jewellery – will have a much slower stock turnover, perhaps sixty or ninety days, or longer. Nevertheless, stock turnover must not be too long, bearing in mind the type of business. A business which is improving will seek to reduce the number of days' stock it holds, when comparing one year with the previous one, or with the stock turnover of similar businesses. This indicates that it is more efficient at managing its stocks.

Stock turnover can also be expressed as number of times per year:

Stock turnover (times per year) = $\dfrac{\textbf{Cost of sales}}{\textbf{Average stock}}$

A stock turnover of, say, twelve times a year means that about thirty days' stock is held. Note that stock turnover can only be calculated where a business buys and sells goods; it cannot be used for a business that provides a service.

debtor collection period

$\dfrac{\textbf{Debtors}}{\textbf{Credit sales}}$ x   **365 days**

This calculation shows how many days, on average, debtors take to pay for goods sold to them by the business. The figure of credit sales for the year may not be disclosed in the trading account, in which case the sales turnover figure should be used. Some businesses make the majority of their sales on credit but others, such as shops, will have a considerably lower proportion of credit sales.

The debtor collection time can be compared with that for the previous year, or with that of a similar business. In Britain, most debtors should make payment within about 30 days; however, sales made abroad will take longer for the proceeds to be received. Over time, a business will seek to reduce the debtor collection period, showing that it is more efficient at collecting the money that is due to it.

creditor payment period

$\dfrac{\textbf{Trade creditors}}{\textbf{Credit purchases}}$ x   **365 days**

This calculation is the opposite aspect to that of debtors: here we are measuring the speed it takes to pay creditors. While creditors can be a useful temporary source of finance, delaying payment too long may cause problems, such as stopping the delivery of supplies. This ratio is most appropriate for businesses that buy and sell goods; it cannot be used for a business that provides a service; it is also difficult to interpret when a business buys in some goods and, at the same time, provides a service, eg an hotel. Generally, though, we would expect to see the creditor days period longer than the debtor days, ie money is being received from debtors before it is paid out to creditors. Over time, a business should seek to maintain the same creditor payment period, and possibly increase it slightly if better terms can be negotiated with the creditors.

Tutorial note: instead of being stated in days, stock turnover, debtor collection and creditor payment periods can also be calculated in weeks or months. Instead of multiplying by 365, use 52 for weeks, or 12 for months.

CAPITAL STRUCTURE

Capital structure focuses on the long-term financing of the business – contained in the balance sheet sections for long-term liabilities and shareholders' funds (the 'financed by' section).

gearing ratio (or capital gearing, or debt/equity ratio)

Gearing ratio   =   Loan capital + preference shares (if any)   or   Debt

Capital (ordinary shares + reserves)   Equity

Whilst the net current asset and liquid capital ratios focus on whether the business can pay its way in the short-term, gearing is concerned with long-term financial stability. Here we measure how much of the business is financed by debt (including preference shares) against capital (ordinary shares plus reserves) – gearing is often referred to as the debt/equity ratio. The higher the gearing, the less secure will be the ordinary share capital of the business and, therefore, the future of the business. This is because debt is costly in terms of interest payments (particularly if interest rates are variable). It is difficult to set a standard for an acceptable gearing ratio: in general terms most investors (or lenders) would not wish to see debt exceeding equity (ordinary shares + reserves): thus a gearing ratio of greater than 1:1 is undesirable.

Gearing can also be expressed as a percentage – a gearing ratio of 1:1 is a percentage of 100%.

In Chapter 17 (page 314) we have already seen how the gearing ratio is used to guide a business seeking to expand. The business usually has to make a choice between ordinary shares, or loans – the gearing ratio gives an assessment of the effects on long-term financial stability of each course of action.

Note that an alternative calculation for gearing is to measure debt in relation to the capital employed of the company:

Gearing ratio   =   Debt (loan capital + preference shares if any)

Capital employed (see page 342)

This calculation always gives a lower gearing ratio than debt/equity when using the same figures. Accordingly, a gearing ratio of 0.5:1 (50%) would be a normal maximum when calculated in this way.

WORKED EXAMPLE: RATIO ANALYSIS

Ratio analysis is the calculation of a number of accounting ratios. Interpretation of accounts involves the analysis of the relationships between the figures in the accounts and the presentation of the information gathered in a meaningful way to interested parties.

In the Worked Example which follows, we will look at the set of accounts of a limited company. For clarity, one year's accounts are given although, in practice, more than one year's accounts should be used. The comments given indicate what should be looked for when analysing and interpreting a set of accounts.

situation

The following are the accounts of Mithian Trading Company Limited. The business trades in office supplies and sells to the public through three retail shops in its area; it also delivers direct to businesses in the area from its modern warehouse on a local business park.

Using ratio analysis to analyse the final accounts, prepare a report for a potential investor in the company.

Mithian Trading Company Limited
TRADING AND PROFIT AND LOSS ACCOUNT
for the year ended 31 December 20-7

	£000s	£000s
Sales/turnover		1,430
Opening stock	200	
Purchases	1,000	
	1,200	
Less Closing stock	240	
Cost of sales		960
Gross profit		470
Less expenses/overheads:		
Selling expenses	160	
Administration expenses	135	
		295
Operating profit		175
Less finance costs (debenture interest)		5
Net profit before taxation		170
Less: Corporation tax		50
Profit for year after taxation		120
Less:		
preference dividend paid	25	
ordinary dividend proposed	75	
		100
Retained profit for the year		20
Add balance of retained profits at beginning of year		180
Balance of retained profits at end of year		200

Mithian Trading Company Limited
BALANCE SHEET
as at 31 December 20-7

Fixed Assets

	Cost £000s	Prov for dep'n £000s	Net book value £000s
Premises	950	100	850
Fixtures and fittings	300	120	180
Vehicles	350	100	250
	1,600	320	1,280

Current Assets

Stock		240	
Debtors		150	
Bank/cash		135	
		525	

Less Current Liabilities

Creditors	130		
Proposed ordinary dividend	75		
Corporation tax	50		
		255	

Net Current Assets or Working Capital		270
		1,550

Less Long-term Liabilities

5% debentures		100
NET ASSETS		1,450

FINANCED BY
Issued Share Capital

1,000,000 ordinary shares of £1 each, fully paid	1,000
250,000 10% preference shares of £1 each, fully paid	250
	1,250

Revenue Reserve

Profit and loss account	200
SHAREHOLDERS' FUNDS	1,450

solution

REPORT

To: Potential investor
From: Student Accountant
Date: Today
Subject: Mithian Trading Company Limited – report on final accounts

I have used accounting ratios to analyse the final accounts using the main themes of profitability, liquidity and capital structure.

Please note that all money amounts shown are in £000s.

PROFITABILITY

Gross profit margin

$$\frac{£470}{£1,430} \qquad x \qquad \frac{100}{1} \qquad\qquad = \quad 32.87\%$$

Gross profit mark-up

$$\frac{£470}{£960} \qquad x \qquad \frac{100}{1} \qquad\qquad = \quad 48.96\%$$

Overheads/turnover margin

$$\frac{£295}{£1,430} \qquad x \qquad \frac{100}{1} \qquad\qquad = \quad 20.63\%$$

Net profit margin

$$\frac{£175*}{£1,430} \qquad x \qquad \frac{100}{1} \qquad\qquad = \quad 12.24\%$$

Return on capital employed

$$\frac{£175*}{£1,000 + £250 + £200 + £100} \qquad x \qquad \frac{100}{1} \qquad\qquad = \quad 11.29\%$$

* *operating profit*

The gross profit margin and mark-up, and net profit margin seem to be acceptable figures for the type of business, although comparisons should be made with those of the previous accounting period. A business should always aim at least to hold its margin and mark-up with, ideally, a small improvement. A significant fall may indicate a poor buying policy, poor pricing (perhaps caused by competition), and the causes should be investigated.

Overheads seem to be quite a high percentage of sales turnover – comparisons need to be made with previous years to see if they are increasing. As they are likely to be a relatively fixed cost, it would seem that the business could increase sales turnover without a corresponding increase in overheads.

Return on capital employed is satisfactory, but could be better. At 11.29% return on capital employed is only just over one percentage point above the ten per cent cost of the preference shares.

LIQUIDITY

Net current asset ratio

$$\frac{£525}{£255} \qquad = 2.06:1$$

Liquid capital ratio

$$\frac{(£525 - £240)}{£255} \qquad = 1.12:1$$

Stock turnover

$$\frac{(£200 + £240) \div 2 \times 365}{£960} \qquad = 83.6 \text{ days (or 4.36 times per year)}$$

Debtor collection period

$$\frac{£150 \times 365}{£1,430} \qquad = 38.3 \text{ days}$$

Creditor payment period

$$\frac{£130 \times 365}{£1,000} \qquad = 47.5 \text{ days}$$

The net current asset and liquid capital ratios are excellent: they are slightly higher than the expected 'norms' of 2:1 and 1:1 respectively (although many companies operate successfully with lower ratios).

The stock, debtor and creditor ratios show up the main weakness of the company: not enough business is passing through for the size of the company. Stock turnover is very low for an office supplies business: the stock is turning over only every 83 days – surely it should be faster than this. Debtor collection period is acceptable on the face of it – 30 days would be better – but quite a volume of the sales will be made through the retail outlets in cash. This amount should, if known, be deducted from the sales turnover before calculating the debtor collection period: thus the collection period is, in reality, longer than that calculated. Creditor payment period is quite leisurely for this type of business – long delays could cause problems with suppliers in the future.

CAPITAL STRUCTURE

Gearing ratio

$$\frac{£100 + £250*}{£1,000 + £200} \qquad = 0.29:1 \text{ or } 29\%$$

* preference shares

The gearing ratio is low: anything up to 1:1 (100%) could be seen. With a low ratio of 0.29:1 this indicates that the company could borrow more money if it wished to finance expansion plans. There are plenty of fixed assets for a lender – such as a bank – to take as security for a loan.

CONCLUSION

This appears to be a profitable business, although there may be some scope for cutting down somewhat on the profit and loss account expenses. The business offers a reasonable return on capital employed, although things could be improved.

The company is liquid and has good net current asset and liquid capital ratios. The main area of weakness is in the use of stocks, debtors and creditors. It appears that the company could do much to reduce the days for stock turnover and the debtor collection period; at the same time creditors could be paid faster.

Gearing is low – a good sign during times of variable interest rates – and there is scope for borrowing more money to finance expansion plans.

It does seem that there is much scope for expansion within the structure of the existing company. As the benefits of expansion flow through to the final accounts, the ratios will show an improvement from their present leisurely performance.

A potential investor must consider whether the directors of Mithian Trading Company Limited have the ability to focus on the weaknesses shown by ratio analysis and take steps to improve the business.

LIMITATIONS IN THE USE OF RATIO ANALYSIS

Although ratio analysis can usefully highlight strengths and weaknesses, it should always be considered as a part of the overall assessment of a business, rather than as a whole. We have already seen the need to place ratios in context and relate them to a reference point or standard. The limitations of ratio analysis should always be borne in mind.

retrospective nature of ratio analysis

Accounting ratios are usually retrospective, based on previous performance and conditions prevailing in the past. They may not necessarily be valid for making forward projections: for example, a large customer may become insolvent, so threatening the business with a bad debt, and also reducing sales in the future.

differences in accounting policies

When the accounts of a business are compared, either with previous years' figures, or with figures from a similar business, there is a danger that the comparative accounts are not drawn up on the same basis as those currently being worked on. Different accounting policies, in respect of depreciation and stock valuation for instance, may well result in distortion and invalid comparisons.

inflation

Inflation may prove a problem, as most financial statements are prepared on an historic cost basis, that is, assets and liabilities are recorded at their original cost. As a result, comparison of figures from one year to the next may be difficult. In countries where inflation is running at high levels any form of comparison becomes practically meaningless.

reliance on standards

We have already mentioned guideline standards for some accounting ratios, for instance 2:1 for the net current asset ratio. There is a danger of relying too heavily on such suggested standards, and ignoring other factors in the balance sheet. An example of this would be to criticise a business for having a low net current asset ratio when the business sells the majority of its goods for cash and consequently has a very low debtors figure: this would in fact be the case with many well-known and successful retail companies.

other considerations

Economic: The general economic climate and the effect this may have on the nature of the business, eg in an economic downturn retailers are usually the first to suffer, whereas manufacturers feel the effects later.

State of the business: The director's report for a limited company should be read in conjunction with the final accounts to ascertain an overall view of the state of the business. Of great importance are the products of the company and their stage in the product life cycle, eg is a car manufacturer relying on old models, or is there an up-to-date product range which appeals to buyers?

Comparing like with like: Before making comparisons between 'similar' businesses we need to ensure that we are comparing 'like with like'. Differences, such as the acquisition of assets – renting premises compared with ownership, leasing vehicles compared with ownership – will affect the profitability of the business and the structure of the balance sheet; likewise, the long-term financing of a business – the balance between debt and equity – will also have an effect.

CHAPTER SUMMARY

The key accounting ratios are summarised in this chapter on pages 338 and 344.

- Ratio analysis uses numerical values – percentages, time periods, ratios – extracted from the final accounts of businesses.

- Accounting ratios can be used to measure:
  - profitability
  - liquidity
  - capital structure

- Comparisons need to be made with previous final accounts, or those of similar businesses.

- There are a number of limitations to be borne in mind when drawing conclusions from accounting ratios:
  - retrospective nature, based on past performance
  - differences in accounting policies
  - effects of inflation when comparing year-to-year
  - reliance on standards
  - economic and other factors

QUESTIONS

visit
www.osbornebooks.co.uk
to take an online test

An asterisk (*) after the question number means that the answer is given at the end of this book.

18.1* The following information is taken from the profit and loss accounts of two plcs:

	Amero plc	Britz plc
	£m	£m
Sales	55.7	32.3
Cost of sales	(49.1)	(20.2)
GROSS PROFIT	6.6	12.1
Expenses/overheads	(5.0)	(7.4)
NET PROFIT BEFORE TAX	1.6	4.7
Note: Capital employed	£8.8m	£34.3m

You are to calculate, for each company:
- gross profit margin
- gross profit mark-up
- overheads/turnover
- net profit margin
- return on capital employed

18.2* The following is taken from the balance sheets of two plcs:

	Cawston plc	Dunley plc
	£m	£m
Stock	3.8	4.1
Debtors	4.5	0.7
Bank/(bank overdraft)	(0.4)	6.3
Creditors	5.1	10.7
Long-term loan capital	3.2	2.1
Ordinary share capital	4.5	8.4
Reserves	1.4	4.7
Notes:		
Sales for year	43.9	96.3
Purchases for year	32.4	85.1
Cost of sales for year	33.6	84.7

(a) You are to calculate, for each company:
- net current asset (current) ratio
- liquid capital (acid test) ratio
- debtor collection period

- creditor payment period
- stock turnover
- gearing ratio

(b)   One company runs department stores, the other is a chemical manufacturer. Which is which? Why is this?

18.3   The following information relates to two businesses, Exton and Frimley:

	Exton £000s	Frimley £000s
PROFIT AND LOSS ACCOUNT (EXTRACTS)		
Sales	3,057	1,628
Cost of sales	2,647	911
Gross profit	410	717
Expenses/overheads	366	648
Net profit	44	69

	Exton £000s	£000s	Frimley £000s	£000s
SUMMARISED BALANCE SHEETS				
Fixed Assets		344		555
Current Assets				
Stock	242		237	
Debtors	6		269	
Bank	3		1	
	251		507	
Less Current Liabilities	195		212	
Net Current Assets or Working Capital		56		295
NET ASSETS		400		850
FINANCED BY				
Capital		400		850

One business operates a supermarket; the other is an engineering company. You are to calculate the following accounting ratios for both businesses:

(a)   gross profit margin

(b)   gross profit mark-up

(c)   overheads/turnover

(d)   net profit margin

(e)   stock turnover (use balance sheet figure as average stock)

(f)   net current asset (current) ratio

(g)   liquid capital (acid test) ratio

(h)   debtor collection period

(i)   return on capital employed

Indicate which business you believe to be the supermarket and which the engineering company. Briefly explain the reasons for your choice based on the ratios calculated and the accounting information.

18.4 Distinguish between the following terms:

(a)   gross profit margin and gross profit mark-up

(b)   net current assets and liquid capital

(c)   cash and profit

(d)   return on capital employed and gearing

18.5* The following figures are extracted from the trial balance of Haque Limited as at 31 December 20-8:

	Dr	Cr
	£	£
Credit sales		96,000
Credit purchases	56,000	
Stock at 1 January 20-8	8,400	
Debtors	10,250	
Trade creditors		6,000
Bank		1,865
Cash	450	

Notes:

*   Stock at 31 December 20-8 was valued at £5,200

*   A debtor who owes £2,450 has gone into liquidation and is not expected to be able to pay off any of the debt. No adjustment has been made for this in the above figures.

REQUIRED

(a)   Define the terms:

*   net current assets

*   liquid capital

(b)   State the formula to be used for:
  • net current asset ratio
  • liquid capital ratio
  • debtor collection period
  • creditor payment period

(c)   Calculate the following for Haque Limited (showing your workings to two decimal places):
  • net current asset (current) ratio
  • liquid capital (acid test) ratio
  • debtor collection period
  • creditor payment period

(d)   Assess the effect on the liquidity and liquidity ratios of Haque Limited of
  • writing off the debt for £2,450
  • reducing the value of stock over the year

18.6   Season Suppliers Ltd sell Christmas gifts. The following information is available for the last two years.

	As at 31 October 2001	As at 31 October 2002
	£	£
Trade debtors	43,000	32,550
Trade creditors	28,500	38,500

	For the year ended 31 October 2001	For the year ended 31 October 2002
Credit sales	680,000	660,000
Credit purchases	520,000	540,000

REQUIRED

(a)   State the formula for the debtor collection period.

(b)   State the formula for the creditor payment period.

(c)   Calculate the debtor collection periods in days for the years ended 31 October 2001 and 31 October 2002. Show your workings.

(d)   Calculate the creditor payment periods in days for the years ended 31 October 2001 and 31 October 2002. Show your workings.

(e)   Briefly evaluate Season Suppliers Ltd's management of credit control. Base your answers on your calculations from (c) and (d).

Assessment and Qualifications Alliance (AQA), 2003

18.7 The following accounting ratios have been calculated for two different businesses for the year ended 30 June 20-7:

	Green Ltd	Hawke Ltd
Net current asset (current) ratio	1.1:1	1.8:1
Liquid capital (acid test) ratio	0.6:1	0.9:1
Net profit margin	3%	12%
Stock turnover	20 times	5 times
Return on capital employed	3%	6%

One business is a supermarket; the other is a furniture store.

REQUIRED

(a) State the formula used to calculate each accounting ratio.

(b) Indicate which business you believe to be the supermarket and which the furniture store. Briefly explain the reasons for your choice based on the ratio analysis.

(c) Write a note to the owner of Green Limited suggesting two ways in which the performance of the business could be improved.

18.8* Susie Ng owns a small manufacturing business. Information for the years ended 31 December 2004 and 31 December 2005 is as follows:

	2004	2005
	£	£
Sales	320,000	280,000
Cost of sales	160,000	160,000
Overheads	140,000	90,000
Current assets	420,000	360,000
Current liabilities	140,000	180,000

REQUIRED

(a) Calculate a relevant ratio to show the liquidity of the business for each of the two years. State the formula used.

(b) Calculate **one** relevant ratio to show the profitability of the business for **each** of the two years. State the formula used.

(c) Write a report to Susie explaining the significance of the ratios calculated.

Assessment and Qualifications Alliance (AQA), 2006

18.9* The following information is available for Eurometics Ltd.

	Year ended 30 April 2003		Year ended 30 April 2004	
	£	£	£	£
Turnover		300,000		400,000
Opening stock	40,000		50,000	
Purchases	250,000		340,000	
	290,000		390,000	
Closing stock	50,000		60,000	
Cost of sales		240,000		330,000
Gross profit		60,000		70,000

REQUIRED

(a) Calculate the rate of stock turnover for each year. State the formula used.

(b) Calculate the gross profit margin for each year. State the formula used.

(c) Assess the profitability of Eurometics Ltd, by comparing the performance for the years ended 30 April 2003 and 30 April 2004.

Assessment and Qualifications Alliance (AQA), 2004

18.10 The following information relates to Aaron and Associates Ltd as at 31 December 2004.

	£
Ordinary shares of £1 each	200,000
Share premium	40,000
Retained earnings as at 31 December 2004	140,000

During the next financial year the business intends to expand.

The directors are considering two proposals to raise finance:

Proposal 1 – to issue 100,000 ordinary shares of £1 each at a price of £2.20 per share

or Proposal 2 – to arrange a long-term bank loan of £160,000 and an overdraft of £60,000.

The forecast net profit for the year ending 31 December 2005 is £30,000.

REQUIRED

(a) State the formula used to calculate the Return on Capital Employed (ROCE).

(b) Calculate the Return on Capital employed (ROCE) for **each** of the proposals.

(c) Write a report to an existing shareholder of Aaron and Associates Ltd analysing the effects of each proposal.

Assessment and Qualifications Alliance (AQA), 2005

18.11

The following trial balance has been extracted from the books of account of Falcon Ltd at 31 March 2007 **after** the preparation of the profit and loss appropriation account.

	Dr	Cr
	£	£
Bank	1,058	
Debenture (2011 - 2013)		28,000
Fixtures and fittings – net book value	17,500	
Issued ordinary shares of £1 each, fully paid		50,000
Premises – net book value	80,000	
Proposed dividends		2,500
Provision for corporation tax		5,400
Retained profits at 31 March 2007		19,832
Share premium account		5,000
Stock at 31 March 2007	14,560	
Trade creditors		7,842
Trade debtors	5,456	
	118,574	118,574

The following adjustments need to be made before the preparation of a balance sheet.

1. The directors have had the premises valued and wish to include the revaluation in the final accounts. The premises are to be valued at £200,000.

2. The directors made a rights issue of ordinary shares, at a premium of 20p, on the basis of 1 new share for every 2 shares held. The rights issue was fully subscribed.

REQUIRED

(a) Prepare a balance sheet at 31 March 2007 after making any necessary adjustments.

(b) Calculate the gearing ratio **before** and **after** making any necessary adjustments. State the formula used.

(c) Assess the impact of the rights issue and the revaluation of the premises on the gearing of Falcon Ltd.

Assessment and Qualifications Alliance (AQA), Specimen Paper for 2009

18.12

A friend of yours, Samantha Smith, owns a shop selling children's clothes. You are helping Samantha to understand her year end accounts which have been prepared by her accountant. She says to you: "I cannot understand why my bank overdraft has increased in a year when I have made such a good profit."

REQUIRED

(a) Explain to Samantha the difference between profit and cash.

(b) Give two examples to explain how a business can make a good profit during a year when the bank balance reduces or the bank overdraft increases.

19 BUDGETING AND BUDGETARY CONTROL

Budgeting is used by businesses as a method of financial planning for the future. Budgets are prepared for main areas of the business – purchases, sales, production, labour, debtors, creditors, cash – and provide detailed plans of the business for the next three, six or twelve months. The focus of this chapter is the cash budget.

In this chapter we shall be examining:

- the benefits of budgets and budgetary control
- the limitations of budgets and budgetary control
- the preparation and use of cash budgets

INTRODUCTION TO BUDGETS

Businesses need to plan for the future. In large businesses such planning is very formal while, for smaller businesses, it will be less formal. Planning for the future falls into three time scales:

- **long-term**: from about three years up to, sometimes, as far as twenty years ahead
- **medium-term**: one to three years ahead
- **short-term**: for the next year

Clearly, planning for these different time scales needs different approaches: the further on in time, the less detailed are the plans. In the medium and longer term, a business will establish broad **business objectives**. Such objectives do not have to be formally written down, although in a large business they are likely to be. In smaller businesses, objectives will certainly be considered and discussed by the owners or managers. Planning takes note of these broader business objectives and sets out how these are to be achieved in the form of detailed plans known as **budgets**.

In this chapter we are concerned with planning for the more immediate future, ie the next financial year.

What is a Budget?

A budget is a financial plan for a business, prepared in advance.

A budget may be set in money terms, eg a sales budget of £500,000, or it can be expressed in terms of units, eg a purchases budget of 5,000 units to be bought.

Budgets can be **income** budgets for money received, eg a sales budget, or **expenditure** budgets for money spent, eg a purchases budget.

The budget we shall be focusing on in this chapter is the **cash budget**, which combines both income and expenditure, estimating what will happen to the bank balance during the time period of the budget.

Most budgets are prepared for the next financial year (the **budget period**), and are usually broken down into shorter time periods, commonly four-weekly or monthly. This enables **budgetary control** to be exercised over the budget: the actual results can be monitored against the budget, and discrepancies between the two can be investigated and corrective action taken where appropriate.

Benefits of Budgets and Budgetary Control

Budgets provide benefits both for the business, and also for its managers and other staff:

the budget assists planning

By formalising objectives through a budget, a business can ensure that its plans are achievable. It will be able to decide what is needed to produce the output of goods and services, and to make sure that everything will be available at the right time.

the budget communicates and co-ordinates

Because a budget is agreed by the business, all the relevant managers and staff will be working towards the same end.

When the budget is being set, any anticipated problems should be resolved and any areas of potential confusion clarified. All departments should be in a position to play their part in achieving the overall goals.

the budget helps with decision-making

By planning ahead through budgets, a business can make decisions on how much output – in the form of goods or services – can be achieved. At the same time, the cost of the output can be planned and changes can be made where appropriate.

the budget can be used to monitor and control

An important reason for producing a budget is that management is able to use budgetary control to monitor and compare the actual results (see diagram below). This is so that action can be taken to modify the operation of the business as time passes, or possibly to change the budget if it becomes unachievable.

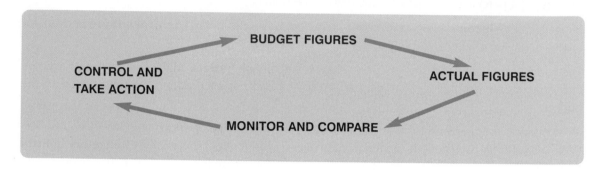

the budget can be used to motivate

A budget can be part of the techniques for motivating managers and other staff to achieve the objectives of the business. The extent to which this happens will depend on how the budget is agreed and set, and whether it is thought to be fair and achievable. The budget may also be linked to rewards (for example, bonuses) where targets are met or exceeded.

LIMITATIONS OF BUDGETS AND BUDGETARY CONTROL

Whilst most businesses will benefit from the use of budgets, there are a number of limitations of budgets to be aware of:

the benefit of the budget must exceed the cost

Budgeting is a fairly complex process and some businesses – particularly small ones – may find that the task is too much of a burden in terms of time and other resources, with only limited benefits. Nevertheless, many lenders – such as banks – often require the production of budgets as part of the business plan. As a general rule, the benefit of producing the budget must exceed its cost.

budget information may not be accurate

It is essential that the information going into budgets should be as accurate as possible. Anybody can produce a budget, but the more inaccurate it is, the less use it is to the business as a planning and control mechanism. Great care needs to be taken with estimates of sales – often the starting point of the budgeting process – and costs. Budgetary control is used to compare the budget against what actually happened – the budget may need to be changed if it becomes unachievable.

the budget may demotivate

Employees who have had no part in agreeing and setting a budget which is imposed upon them, will feel that they do not own it. As a consequence, the staff may be demotivated. Another limitation is that employees may see budgets as either a 'carrot' or a 'stick', ie as a form of encouragement to achieve the targets set, or as a form of punishment if targets are missed.

budgets may lead to disfunctional management

A limitation that can occur is that employees in one department of the business may over-achieve against their budget and create problems elsewhere. For example, a production department might achieve extra output that the sales department finds difficult to sell. To avoid such disfunctional management, budgets need to be set at realistic levels and linked and co-ordinated across all departments within the business.

budgets may be set at too low a level

Where the budget is too easy to achieve it will be of no benefit to the business and may, in fact, lead to lower levels of output and higher costs than before the budget was established. Budgets should be set at realistic levels, which make the best use of the resources available.

WHAT BUDGETS ARE PREPARED?

Budgets are planned for specific sections of the business: these budgets can then be controlled by a **budget holder**, who may be the manager or supervisor of the specific section. Such budgets include:

- purchases budget – what the business needs to buy to make/supply the goods it expects to sell
- sales budget – what the business expects to sell
- production budget – how the business will make/supply the goods it expects to sell
- labour budget – the cost of employing the people who will make/supply the goods
- debtor budget – how much the business will receive from credit sales
- creditor budget – how much the business will pay for credit purchases
- cash budget – how much money will be flowing in and out of the bank account

The end result of the budgeting process is often the production of a **master budget**, which takes the form of forecast operating statements – forecast trading and profit and loss account – and forecast balance sheet. The master budget is the 'master plan' which shows how all the other budgets 'work together'.

Note that, in this chapter, we focus our attention on the cash budget; you will examine the other budgets, including the master budget, if you go on to study A2 Accounting.

BUDGETARY PLANNING

Many large businesses take a highly formal view of planning the budget and make use of:

- a **budget manual**, which provides a set of guidelines as to who is involved with the budgetary planning and control process, and how the process is to be conducted

- a **budget committee**, which organises the process of budgetary planning and control; this committee brings together representatives from the main functions of the business – eg production, sales, administration – and is headed by a budget co-ordinator whose job is to administer and oversee the activities of the committee

In smaller businesses, the process of planning the budget may be rather more informal, with the owner or manager overseeing and budgeting for all the business functions.

Whatever the size of the business it is important, though, that the planning process begins well before the start of the budget period; this then gives time for budgets to be prepared, reviewed, redrafted, and reviewed again before being finally agreed and submitted to the directors or owners for approval. For example, the planning process for a budget which is to start on 1 January might commence in the previous June, as follows:

- June   Budget committee meets to plan next year's budgets
- July   First draft of budgets prepared
- August   Review of draft budgets
- September   Draft budgets amended in light of review
- October   Further review and redrafting to final version
- November   Budgets submitted to directors or owners for approval
- December   Budgets for next year circulated to managers
- January   Budget period commences

CASH BUDGET

A cash budget sets out the expected cash/bank receipts and payments, usually on a month-by-month basis, for the next three, six or twelve months, in order to show the estimated bank balance at the end of each month throughout the period.

From the cash budget, the managers of a business can decide what action to take when a surplus of cash is shown to be available or, as is more likely, when a bank overdraft needs to be arranged.

layout of a cash budget

A suitable format for a cash budget, with sample figures, is set out on the next page.

Name ....Cash Budget for the .... months ending				
	Jan	Feb	Mar	Apr
	£000	£000	£000	£000
Receipts				
eg from debtors	150	150	161	170
cash sales	70	80	75	80
Total receipts for month (A)	220	230	236	250
Payments				
eg to creditors	160	165	170	170
expenses	50	50	50	60
fixed assets		50		
Total payments for month (B)	210	265	220	230
Net cash flow (Receipts less Payments, ie A–B)	10	(35)	16	20
Add bank balance at beginning of month	10	20	(15)	1
Bank balance (overdraft) at end of month	20	(15)	1	21

sections of a cash budget

A cash budget consists of three main sections:

- receipts for the month
- payments for the month
- summary of bank account

Receipts are analysed to show the amount of money that is expected to be received from cash sales, debtors, sale of fixed assets, capital introduced/issue of shares, loans received etc.

Payments show how much money is expected to be paid in respect of cash purchases, creditors, expenses (often described in cash budgets as operating expenses), purchases of fixed assets, repayment of capital/shares and loans. Note that non-cash expenses (such as depreciation and doubtful debts) are not shown in the cash budget.

The **summary of the bank account** at the bottom of the cash budget shows **net cash flow** (total receipts less total payments) added to the bank balance at the beginning of the month, and resulting in the estimated closing bank balance at the end of the month. An overdrawn bank balance is shown in brackets.

The main difficulty in the preparation of cash budgets lies in the **timing** of receipts and payments – for example, debtors may pay two months after date of sale, or creditors may be paid by the business one month after date of purchase: it is important to ensure that such receipts and payments are recorded in the correct month column.

Remember that the cash budget, as its name suggests, deals only in cash/bank transactions; thus non-cash items, such as depreciation, are never shown. Where cash discounts are allowed or received, only the actual amount of money expected to be received or paid is recorded. Similarly, where a business incurs bad debts, only the amount of money expected to be received from good debtors is recorded in the cash budget.

WORKED EXAMPLE: CASH BUDGET

situation

A friend of yours, Mike Anderson, has recently been made redundant from his job as a sales representative for an arts and crafts company. Mike has decided to set up in business on his own selling art supplies to shops and art societies. He plans to invest £20,000 of his savings into the new business. He has a number of good business contacts, and is confident that his firm will do well. He thinks that some additional finance will be required in the short term and plans to approach his bank for this.

Mike asks for your assistance in producing a cash budget for his new business for the next six months.

He provides the following information:

- The business, which is to be called 'Art Supplies' will commence in January 20-8.

- Fixed assets costing £8,000 will be bought in early January. These will be paid for immediately and are expected to have a five-year life, at the end of which they will be worthless.

- An initial stock of goods costing £5,000 will be bought and paid for at the beginning of January.

- Monthly purchases of stocks will then be made at a level sufficient to replace forecast sales for that month, ie the goods he expects to sell in January will be replaced by purchases made in January, and so on.

- Forecast monthly sales are:

January	February	March	April	May	June
£3,000	£6,000	£6,000	£10,500	£10,500	£10,500

- The selling price of goods is fixed at the cost price plus 50 per cent; for example, the goods he expects to sell in January for £3,000 will have cost him £2,000 (two-thirds of the selling price), ie his mark-up is 50%.

- To encourage sales, he will allow two months' credit to customers; however, only one month's credit will be received from suppliers of stock (but the initial stock will be paid for immediately).

- Operating expenses of the business, including rent of premises, but excluding depreciation of fixed assets, are estimated at £1,600 per month and are paid for in the month in which they are incurred.

- Mike intends to draw £1,000 each month in cash from the business.

You are asked to prepare a cash budget for the first six months of the business.

solution

<table>
<tr><th colspan="7">Mike Anderson, trading as 'Art Supplies'
Cash budget for the six months ending 30 June 20-8</th></tr>
<tr><th></th><th>Jan
£</th><th>Feb
£</th><th>Mar
£</th><th>Apr
£</th><th>May
£</th><th>Jun
£</th></tr>
<tr><td>**Receipts**</td><td></td><td></td><td></td><td></td><td></td><td></td></tr>
<tr><td>Capital introduced</td><td>20,000</td><td></td><td></td><td></td><td></td><td></td></tr>
<tr><td>Debtors</td><td>–</td><td>–</td><td>3,000</td><td>6,000</td><td>6,000</td><td>10,500</td></tr>
<tr><td>Total receipts for month</td><td>20,000</td><td>–</td><td>3,000</td><td>6,000</td><td>6,000</td><td>10,500</td></tr>
<tr><td>**Payments**</td><td></td><td></td><td></td><td></td><td></td><td></td></tr>
<tr><td>Fixed assets</td><td>8,000</td><td></td><td></td><td></td><td></td><td></td></tr>
<tr><td>Stock</td><td>5,000</td><td></td><td></td><td></td><td></td><td></td></tr>
<tr><td>Creditors</td><td>–</td><td>2,000</td><td>4,000</td><td>4,000</td><td>7,000</td><td>7,000</td></tr>
<tr><td>Operating expenses</td><td>1,600</td><td>1,600</td><td>1,600</td><td>1,600</td><td>1,600</td><td>1,600</td></tr>
<tr><td>Drawings</td><td>1,000</td><td>1,000</td><td>1,000</td><td>1,000</td><td>1,000</td><td>1,000</td></tr>
<tr><td>Total payments for month</td><td>15,600</td><td>4,600</td><td>6,600</td><td>6,600</td><td>9,600</td><td>9,600</td></tr>
<tr><td>Net cash flow</td><td>4,400</td><td>(4,600)</td><td>(3,600)</td><td>(600)</td><td>(3,600)</td><td>900</td></tr>
<tr><td>Add bank balance (overdraft)
at beginning of month</td><td>–</td><td>4,400</td><td>(200)</td><td>(3,800)</td><td>(4,400)</td><td>(8,000)</td></tr>
<tr><td>Bank balance (overdraft) at end
of month</td><td>4,400</td><td>(200)</td><td>(3,800)</td><td>(4,400)</td><td>(8,000)</td><td>(7,100)</td></tr>
</table>

Reminder: No depreciation – a non-cash expense – is shown in the cash budget.

Notes:

- purchases are two-thirds of the sales values (because selling price is cost price plus 50 per cent)

- customers pay two months after sale, ie debtors from January settle in March

- suppliers are paid one month after purchase, ie creditors from January are paid in February

The cash budget shows that there is a need, in the first six months at least, for a bank overdraft. An early approach to the bank needs to be made.

The total net cash outflow for the six month period is £7,100 (ie from a nil opening balance to £7,100 overdraft at 30 June).

advantages of a cash budget

The use of a cash budget enables a business to:

- identify any possible bank overdraft in advance and take steps to minimise the borrowing (so saving interest payable)
- consider rescheduling payments to avoid bank borrowing, eg delay purchase of fixed assets, agreement to pay rises, payment of drawings/dividends
- arrange any possible bank finance well in advance
- identify any possible cash surpluses in advance and take steps to invest the surplus on a short-term basis (so earning interest)

CHAPTER SUMMARY

- A budget is a financial plan for a business, prepared in advance.

- Budgets are used to plan and control the business.

- Budgets – for income or expenditure – are prepared for each section of the business – purchases, sales, production, labour, debtors, creditors, cash

- Budgetary planning is the process of setting the budget for the next period.

- Budgetary control uses the budgets to monitor actual results with budgeted figures.

- Responsibility for budgets is given to managers and supervisors – the budget holders.

- A cash budget sets out the expected cash/bank receipts and payments expected to pass through the bank account, usually on a month-by-month basis.

- A cash budget enables the managers of a business to take action when a surplus of money is shown to be available or when a bank overdraft needs to be arranged.

The next chapter looks at the way in which computers are used to handle accounting transactions and the benefits they bring.

QUESTIONS

visit
www.osbornebooks.co.uk
to take an online test

An asterisk (*) after the question number means that the answer is given at the end of this book.

19.1 Classic Furniture is a manufacturer of reproduction antique furniture. It is owned by Helen Sutton as a sole trader business. There are four employees and annual sales turnover is approximately £200,000 per year.

REQUIRED

(a) Explain two benefits of budgetary control to Helen Sutton.

(b) Suggest three budgets which Helen could use in the business to provide an adequate system of budgetary control.

(c) Advise Helen of the relevant factors to consider when implementing budgetary control.

19.2* N Kayali, the assistant accountant at Strudwick Stationers Ltd, has obtained the following information for the seven months ending 30 September 2002. This information is to be used to prepare a cash budget for the four months ending 31 August 2002.

1. Actual sales were £44,000 and £46,000 for March and April 2002 respectively.

2. Total forecast sales at the end of each of the next five months are expected to be:

		2002		
May	June	July	Aug	Sep
£	£	£	£	£
44,000	46,000	42,000	44,000	48,000

   80% of each month's total forecast sales are expected to be for cash. The debtors are expected to pay one month in arrears.

3. Purchases are expected to be 70% of the following month's total forecast sales value and are paid for two months in arrears.

4. The following costs are expected to be paid for in the month in which they occur:

   Wages   £9,000 per month to 31 July 2002 and £9,500 per month thereafter

   Fixed Costs   £3,000 per month

   Variable costs being 10% of each month's total forecast sales

5. The bank balance as at 1 May 2002 was £12,100.

REQUIRED

(a)   Prepare a cash budget for each of the four months ending 31 August 2002.

Strudwick Stationers Ltd

Cash Budget for four months ending 31 August 2002

Details	May £000	June £000	July £000	Aug £000

Tutorial note: In the layout provided by this question you need to fill in the details of receipts and payments – use the guidance of the sample layout shown on page 367 to assist you.

(b)   N Kayali is unsure of the benefits of producing a cash budget for a four month period. Explain one benefit to Strudwick Stationers Ltd of completing a four month cash budget.

....

....

....

....

Assessment and Qualifications Alliance (AQA), 2002

19.3 Sunshine Ltd sells beach buckets and spades.

The forecast information for the six months ending 31 October 2002 is:

	May	June	July	August	September	October
	£000	£000	£000	£000	£000	£000
Sales	16	20	26	28	24	20
Purchases	12	16	18	14	12	10
Overheads	4	8	8	8	8	4

Additional information

1. On average 20% of each month's sales is expected to be for cash. A further 60% will be given one month's credit. The rest will be given two months' credit. All monies should be received when due.

2. The increase in overheads arises from the employment of casual staff. The overheads are paid in the month in which they occur.

3. Suppliers are expected to allow one month's credit.

4. The cash at bank balance as at 1 July 2002 is £7,200 overdrawn.

REQUIRED

(a) Prepare a detailed forecast month by month cash budget for the four months ending 31 October 2002.

Sunshine Ltd

Cash budget for four months ending 31 October 2002

	July £000	Aug £000	Sept £000	Oct £000
Sales – cash				
– 1 month				
– 2 months				
Purchases				
Overheads				
Net inflow/outflow				
Opening balance				
Closing balance				

(b) (i) Assess the cash position of Sunshine Ltd as at 31 October 2002.

    (ii) Recommend one way the company could improve its cash position.

Assessment and Qualifications Alliance (AQA), 2001

19.4* Carolanne wishes to open up a launderette. She is applying for an overdraft facility and the bank requires a cash budget for the first four months of business.

The following additional information is available:

1. She intends to start her business with £2,000 in the business bank account.

2. The launderette will open 24 days a month.

3. Sales will be:

Month 1	200 washes
Months 2 and 3	400 washes per month
Month 4	700 washes

Carolanne charges £2 per wash and £1 for drying. 80% of washes will be dried on the premises.

4. In months 1, 2 and 3, advertising costs will be £30 per month.

5. In month 4, she will employ a part-time assistant at an expected cost of £20 per morning.

6. Washing powder and other washing materials will cost £15 per day.

7. The launderette's fixed costs will be £300 per month.

8. The total cost of the washing machines and dryers will be £18,000. These costs will be paid for in equal monthly instalments over two years.

9. Each month, Carolanne will withdraw for personal use £150 or 10% of the gross monthly revenue, whichever is the greater amount.

REQUIRED

(a) Prepare a cash budget for Carolanne for each of the first four months.

Cash budget for Carolanne for four months

	Month 1 £	Month 2 £	Month 3 £	Month 4 £

(b)　Explain two benefits to Carolanne of drawing up this cash budget.

Benefit 1 ....

....

....

Benefit 2 ....

....

....

Assessment and Qualifications Alliance (AQA), 2005

19.5　The accountant of Hawk Ltd is preparing information for the next Directors' meeting. She has calculated that the net profit for the next six months will be: £36,000.

She has also prepared the cash budget for the five months July to November and provided the following information relating to December.

The cash from debtors figure is calculated on the following basis:

　　　20% of cash from sales is received in the current month, with customers taking 2% cash discount;

60% is received in the month following the sale;

20% is received two months after the sale is made.

The forecast sales are:

	October	November	December
	£	£	£
	30,000	50,000	60,000

The following payments are forecast for December:

payments to creditors	£12,500
operating expenses	£12,000
purchase of fixed assets	£19,510
repayment of loan	£20,000

REQUIRED

(a)   Make the entry for December in the cash budget below.

	Jul £	Aug £	Sep £	Oct £	Nov £	Dec £
Income						
Cash from debtors	20,000	24,000	28,500	32,500	38,500	
Expenditure						
Payments to creditors	10,000	11,000	14,000	18,000	24,500	
Operating expenses	12,000	12,000	12,000	12,000	12,000	
Purchase of fixed assets		8,500				
Repayment of loan						
	22,000	31,500	26,000	30,000	36,500	
Net cash flow	(2,000)	(7,500)	2,500	2,500	2,000	
Opening balance	980	(1,020)	(8,520)	(6,020)	(3,520)	(1,520)
Closing balance	(1,020)	(8,520)	(6,020)	(3,520)	(1,520)	

(b) Calculate the total net cash outflow for the six months.

(c) Write a memorandum to the Directors explaining three reasons why Hawk Ltd could make a profit but have a bank overdraft.

(d) Explain two benefits of using a spreadsheet* to prepare a cash budget.

* see Chapter 20.

Assessment and Qualifications Alliance (AQA), Specimen Paper for 2009

19.6* You are preparing the cash budget of Wilkinson Limited for the first six months of 20-8. The following budgeted figures are available:

	Sales	Purchases	Wages and salaries	Other expenses
	£	£	£	£
January	65,000	26,500	17,500	15,500
February	70,000	45,000	18,000	20,500
March	72,500	50,000	18,250	19,000
April	85,000	34,500	18,500	18,500
May	65,000	35,500	16,500	20,500
June	107,500	40,500	20,000	22,000

The following additional information is available:

• Sales income is received in the month after sale, and sales for December 20-7 amounted to £57,500

• 'Other expenses' each month includes an allocation of £1,000 for depreciation; all other expenses are paid for in the month in which they are incurred

• Purchases, and wages and salaries are paid for in the month in which they are incurred

• The bank balance at 1 January 20-8 is £2,250

REQUIRED

(a) Prepare a month-by-month cash budget for the first six months of 20-8, using the layout on the next page.

(b) Calculate the total net cash outflow for the six months.

Wilkinson Limited
Cash budget for the six months ending 30 June 20-8

	Jan £	Feb £	Mar £	Apr £	May £	Jun £
Receipts						
....						
....						
Total receipts for month						
Payments						
....						
....						
....						
....						
....						
Total payments for month						
Net cash flow						
Add bank balance (overdraft) at beginning of month						
Bank balance (overdraft) at end of month						

19.7 Jim Smith has recently been made redundant; he has received a redundancy payment and this, together with his accumulated savings, amounts to £10,000. He has decided to set up his own business selling computer stationery and this will commence trading with an initial capital of £10,000 on 1 January. On this date he will buy a van for business use at a cost of £6,000. He has estimated his purchases, sales, and expenses for the next six months as follows:

	Purchases £	Sales £	Expenses £
January	4,500	1,250	750
February	4,500	3,000	600
March	3,500	4,000	600
April	3,500	4,000	650
May	3,500	4,500	650
June	4,000	6,000	700

He will pay for purchases in the month after purchase; likewise, he expects his customers to pay for sales in the month after sale. All expenses will be paid for in the month they are incurred.

REQUIRED

(a)   Jim realises that he may need a bank overdraft before his business becomes established. Prepare a month-by-month cash budget for the first six months of Jim Smith's business, using the layout below.

(b)   What is the maximum bank overdraft shown by the cash budget? Suggest two ways in which Jim Smith could amend his business plans in order to avoid the need for a bank overdraft.

Jim Smith

Cash budget for the six months ending 30 June 20--

	Jan £	Feb £	Mar £	Apr £	May £	Jun £
Receipts						
....						
....						
Total receipts for month						
Payments						
....						
....						
....						
....						
....						
Total payments for month						
Net cash flow						
Add bank balance (overdraft) at beginning of month						
Bank balance (overdraft) at end of month						

20 THE IMPACT OF COMPUTER TECHNOLOGY IN ACCOUNTING

Although some businesses, particularly small ones, still use paper-based accounting systems, an increasing number are now operating computerised accounting systems. Small and medium-sized businesses can buy 'off-the-shelf' accounting programs – such as Sage – while larger businesses often have custom-designed programs.

Accounting programs carry out functions such as invoicing, dealing with payments, paying wages and providing regular accounting reports, for example debtor analysis, stock reports and trial balances.

Businesses also make considerable use of computer spreadsheets, particularly for preparing budgets and for reporting purposes.

COMPUTER TECHNOLOGY AND ACCOUNTING

ICT

The commonly used abbreviation 'ICT' stands for 'Information and Communication Technology'. It represents the coming together of computer ('IT') and communication technologies. A definition of ICT is:

a range of technologies which gather, store, retrieve, process, analyse and communicate information

ICT very much relates to accounting, which involves the recording and processing of financial data (eg sales, purchases, payments) and the communication of the analysis of that information.

the 'pros' and 'cons'

The impact of the introduction of ICT in accounting has brought about significant advantages, such as speed and accuracy in processing accounting data and the ease with which a computer system can produce and report information to the managers and other employees within businesses.

There are inevitably certain disadvantages, such as cost and training needs, which the management of a business must take into account before introducing a computerised accounting system. The rapid growth of computerised accounting systems is a clear sign that the advantages outweigh the disadvantages, as we will see towards the end of this chapter.

FEATURES OF COMPUTER ACCOUNTING

facilities

Computer accounting programs, such as the widely-used Sage systems, offer a range of facilities:

- on-screen input and printout of sales invoices and automatic updating of customer accounts
- recording of suppliers' invoices and automatic updating of suppliers' accounts
- recording of bank receipts and payments
- automatic updating of stock records

The processing of wages can also be computerised – often using a separate 'payroll' program.

computer accounting – ledger system

The 'ledger' – which basically means 'the books of the business' – is a term used to describe the way the accounts of a business are grouped into different sections:

- **sales ledger**, containing the accounts of debtors (customers)
- **purchases ledger**, containing the accounts of creditors (suppliers)
- **general ledger** (also called nominal ledger) containing the remaining accounts, eg expenses (including purchases), income (including sales), assets (including the main cash book), loans, stock

The screens of a ledger computer accounting system are designed to be user-friendly. Study the toolbar of the opening screen of a Sage accounting system shown below and the notes printed underneath. Note that the terminology used in Sage may differ slightly from what you are used to, eg general ledger is referred to as 'nominal' ledger.

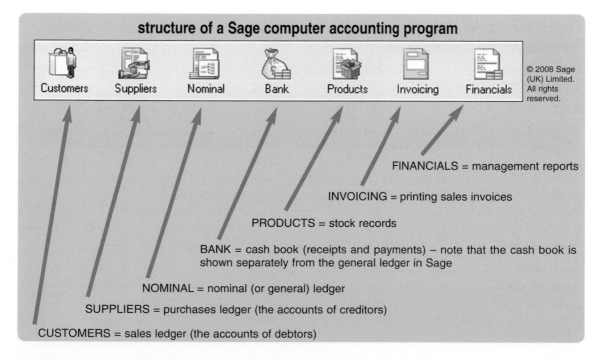

structure of a Sage computer accounting program

Customers Suppliers Nominal Bank Products Invoicing Financials

© 2008 Sage (UK) Limited. All rights reserved.

FINANCIALS = management reports

INVOICING = printing sales invoices

PRODUCTS = stock records

BANK = cash book (receipts and payments) – note that the cash book is shown separately from the general ledger in Sage

NOMINAL = nominal (or general) ledger

SUPPLIERS = purchases ledger (the accounts of creditors)

CUSTOMERS = sales ledger (the accounts of debtors)

using a computer accounting system

Computer input screens are designed to be easy to use. Their main advantage is that each transaction needs to be input once only, unlike in a manual double-entry system where normally two entries are required. In the example below, payment is made for copy paper costing £45.50. The input line includes the account number of bank account (nominal code 1200), the date of payment, the cheque number (234234), and the account code for stationery expenses (nominal code 7500). The net amount of £45.50 is entered and the computer automatically transfers the amounts to bank account and stationery expenses account.

Bank Payments									
Bank	Bank current account						Tax Rate		17.50
N/C Name	Stationery						Batch Total		53.46

Bank	Date	Ref	N/C	Dept	Details	Net	Tc	Tax	
1200	1/4/2008	234234	7500	3	Copy paper	45.50	T1	7.96	
							45.50		7.96

The screen below shows an invoice input screen. In this example 20 Enigma 35s are being invoiced to R Patel & Co in Salisbury. The computer will in due course print the invoice, which will contain the name of the seller as well as all the customer details held in the accounting program's database.

R Patel & Co			Invoice No.	27398
Phoenix Business Park			Invoice Date	1/4/2008
Southampton Road			Order No.	SA 234
Salisbury			A/C Ref	997
Wilts				
SN1 9LX				

Product Code	Description	Qty	Net	V.A.T.
EDB	Enigma 35	20.00	119.00	20.83
		Totals	119.00	20.83
Item 2 of 2		Carriage	0.00	0.00
		Gross		139.83

computerised ledgers – an integrated system

A computerised ledger system is **fully integrated**. This means that when a business transaction is input on the computer it is recorded in a number of different accounting records at the same time. For example, when the sales invoice on the previous page is entered on the screen and the ledgers are 'updated' an integrated program will:

- record the amount of the invoice in the debtor account, R Patel & Co, in the sales ledger
- record the amount of the invoice in sales account in the general ledger
- reduce the stock of goods held (in this case Enigma 35s) in the stock records

The diagram below shows how the three 'ledgers' can link with the general (nominal) ledger, which is the centre of the accounting system. You can see how an account in the general ledger is affected by each of these three transactions. This is the double-entry book-keeping system at work. The advantage of the computer system is that in each case only one entry has to be made.

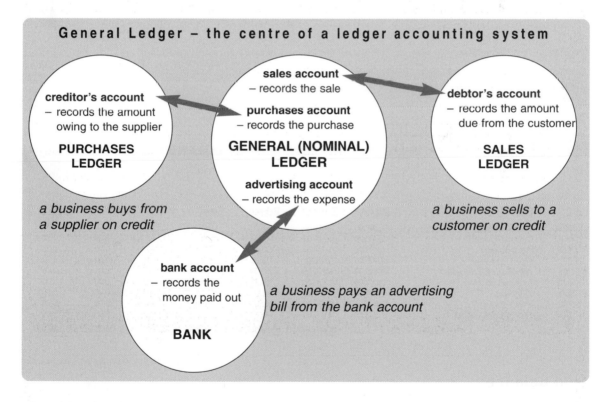

management reports

A computer accounting program can provide instant reports for management, for example:

- aged debtors analysis
- trial balance
- stock records

These are illustrated on the next two pages.

aged debtors analysis

An aged debtors analysis shows the amount owing by each customer and splits it up according to the length of time it has been outstanding. The aged debtors analysis will be printed out from the computer and passed to the person dealing with credit control, ie the person who monitors payments received from debtors and who has the job of chasing up overdue debts. A sample aged debtors analysis produced by a Sage system is illustrated below. The columns show (from left to right):

- the debtor account number and name

- the credit limit (the maximum amount of credit allowed on the account)

- the turnover (total sales for each customer in the current financial year)

- the balance (the current balance on the debtor's account)

- any transactions due in future months

- 'current' invoices are invoices less than 30 days old, period 1 is 30 to 59 days, period 2 is 60 to 89 days, and so on

This is an extremely useful report. It can be produced rapidly by the computer and, by highlighting possible bad payers, can save the business money through efficient debt collection and by speeding up the flow of cash into the business bank account.

Aged Debtors Analysis (Summary)

A/C	Name	Crd Limit	Turnover	Balance	Future	Current	Period 1	Period 2
CH001	Charisma Design	5,000.00	2,416.00	18.80	0.00	18.80	0.00	0.00
CR001	Crowmatic Limited	5,000.00	3,334.00	117.50	0.00	117.50	0.00	0.00
DB001	David Boossey	5,000.00	3,400.00	235.00	0.00	235.00	0.00	0.00
FE001	French Emporium	10,000.00	5,960.00	470.00	0.00	470.00	0.00	0.00
JB001	John Butler & Associates	10,000.00	6,020.00	611.00	0.00	611.00	0.00	0.00
JG001	Jo Green Systems	5,000.00	3,728.00	310.20	0.00	310.20	0.00	0.00
KD001	Kay Denz	10,000.00	6,620.00	6,641.00	0.00	141.00	6,500.00	0.00
LG001	L Garr & Co	15,000.00	8,680.00	211.50	0.00	211.50	0.00	0.00
PT001	Prism Trading Limited	5,000.00	2,906.00	376.00	0.00	376.00	0.00	0.00
	Totals:		43,064.00	8,991.00	0.00	2,491.00	6,500.00	0.00

trial balance

As you will know from your studies of AS Unit 1, a trial balance lists and totals all debit and credit balances of a double-entry book-keeping system in separate columns. If a manual accounting system is being used, the totals may differ if there is an error. In a computer accounting system, however, the totals will agree because the debit and credit entries are always generated from a single figure entered on the system. This is another efficiency of a computer-based system. A trial balance produced by the Sage system is shown on the next page.

Period Trial Balance

To Period: Month 2, February

N/C	Name	Debit	Credit
0020	Plant and Machinery	35,000.00	
0030	Office Equipment	15,760.00	
0040	Furniture and Fixtures	25,000.00	
1100	Debtors Control Account	8,991.00	
1200	Bank Current Account	19,224.35	
2100	Creditors Control Account		11,797.00
2200	Sales Tax Control Account		18,242.70
2201	Purchase Tax Control Account	28,266.35	
2300	Loans		35,000.00
3000	Ordinary Shares		75,000.00
4000	Computer hardware sales		86,040.00
4001	Computer software sales		15,564.00
4002	Computer consultancy		2,640.00
5000	Materials Purchased	77,862.00	
6201	Advertising	12,400.00	
7000	Gross Wages	16,230.00	
7100	Rent	4,500.00	
7103	General Rates	450.00	
7200	Electricity	150.00	
7502	Telephone	275.00	
7504	Office Stationery	175.00	
	Totals:	**244,283.70**	**244,283.70**

stock records

Another benefit of a computer accounting system is that a business can set up stock records which provide the business with details such as:

- product details (eg stock code, description, price, reorder level and quantity) and the number of items in stock (which changes each time a sale or purchase is made)
- the value of the items in stock

This information is very useful because a business is able to see from computer reports when it needs to re-order stock and how much stock is needed. Also, a stock valuation figure can be automatically produced. This figure, as you will know, is needed in the preparation of the trading and profit and loss account and balance sheet. A Sage screen showing the 'Enigma 35' product is illustrated below.

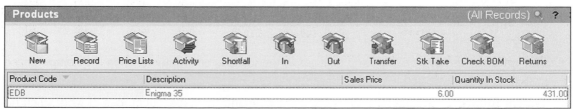

the 'pros' and 'cons' of computer accounting systems

Any business introducing a computer accounting system will need to weigh up carefully the 'pros and cons'. This is an area which has featured in past examinations. We will now look at these advantages and disadvantages and then see, in a Worked Example, the effect on employees of the introduction of a new computer accounting system.

advantages of computer accounting systems

The main advantages of using a computer accounting program such as Sage include:

- **speed** – data entry on the computer with its formatted screens and built-in databases of customer and supplier details and stock records can be carried out far more quickly than any manual processing, and normally only one entry is needed for input of the data

- **automatic document production** – fast and accurate invoice and credit note printing, statement runs, payroll (wages) processing

- **accuracy** – there is less room for error as only one account entry is needed for each transaction rather than the two normally required in a manual double-entry system; also all calculations are carried out automatically and correctly

- **up-to-date information** – the accounting records are updated automatically and so account balances (eg customer accounts) will always be up-to-date

- **availability of information** – the data can be made available to different users at the same time

- **management information** – reports can be produced which will help management monitor and control the business, for example the aged debtors analysis, trial balance, trading and profit and loss account and balance sheet

- **legibility** – the onscreen and printed data should always be legible and so will avoid errors caused by poor figures

- **efficiency** – better use is made of resources and time

- **staff motivation** – the system requires staff to be trained to use new skills, which can make them feel more valued; it may also improve their salaries and employment prospects

disadvantages of computer accounting systems

The main disadvantages of using computer accounting programs include:

- **cost of installation** – the hardware and software need to be budgeted for, not only as 'one-off' expenditure but also as recurrent costs, as and when they need replacing and updating

- **cost of training** – employees will need to be trained in the use of the hardware and software

- **staff opposition** – motivation may suffer as some employees may not like computers; also there may be staff redundancies, which may create bad feeling

- **disruption** – loss of work time and changes in the working environment when the computerised system is first introduced

- **system failure** – the danger of the system crashing and the subsequent loss of work when no back-ups have been made

- **back-up requirements** – the need to keep regular and secure back-ups in case of system failure

- **breaches of security** – the danger of people hacking into the system from outside, the danger of viruses, the incidence of staff fraud

- **health** dangers – the problems of bad backs, eyestrain and muscular complaints such as RSI (Repetitive Strain Injury)

- **errors** – there is still the danger of errors of omission (data entry not made at all), errors of original entry (the wrong figure is entered), errors of principle (the entry is in the wrong type of account) and mispost (entry is in the wrong person's account)

WORKED EXAMPLE

situation

Stitch-in-time Limited is an old-fashioned company which manufactures sewing machines. The Finance Director, Charles Cotton, is considering the introduction of a computer accounting system which will completely replace the existing manual double-entry system.

He is worried because he knows that the proposition will not go down very well with employees who have been with the company for a long time.

He asks you to prepare notes in which you are to set out:

(a)   the benefits to staff of the new scheme

(b)   the likely causes of staff dissatisfaction with the new scheme

solution

(a)   **potential benefits to staff**

- the staff will be able to update their skills

- they will receive training

- they may get an increase in pay

- the training will increase their career prospects and future employability

- they will be motivated

- they will get job satisfaction

(b)   **causes of staff dissatisfaction**

- staff prefer doing the job in a way which is familiar to them

- they may not like computers

- they may see their jobs threatened as they worry that redundancies will occur

- they do not look forward to the disruption at the time of the changeover

- they worry about the possible bad effects to their health, having heard about RSI (Repetitive Strain Injury) and eye strain from computer screens

- they will be demotivated as they consider the new system 'mechanical' – they will have to sit in front of a computer for hours at a time and not be able to communicate so well with their colleagues as they have in the past

COMPUTER SPREADSHEETS

A spreadsheet is a grid of boxes – 'cells' – set up on the computer, organised in rows and columns into which you can enter text and numbers.

A spreadsheet enables you to set up formulas in the cells so that the figures can be used to carry out calculations. For example, columns can be totalled and percentages worked out. The computer program works out the calculations automatically. A commonly used spreadsheet program is Microsoft Excel.

Spreadsheets are used for a variety of functions in business:

- producing invoices and credit notes
- producing a trial balance in situations where a computer accounting program is not being used
- preparing budgets for future income and expenditure

advantages of using a computer spreadsheet

There are a number of benefits of using a spreadsheet:

- speed of calculation, and therefore . . .
- saving of time . . . and money
- accuracy of calculation
- ease of updating, eg if a figure, which forms the basis of a complex calculation, changes
- it enables 'what-if' calculations to be carried out quickly, eg 'what what would be the effect on profit if our sales increased by 10%, 30% or 50%'

disadvantages of using a computer spreadsheet

There are not many drawbacks of using a spreadsheet, but . . .

- the result of the calculation is only accurate if the initial figures used are also accurate (the 'garbage in, garbage out' principle)
- for a quick 'one-off' calculation spreadsheets can take time to set up and so the 'saving of time' benefit may be lost
- spreadsheet data, like any computer data, may become corrupted, and if there is no back-up, a great deal of time (and data) may be lost

a cash budget on a spreadsheet

A common example of a computer spreadsheet used in the accounting process is a form of budget known as a **cash budget** (see Chapter 19). This is a projection of the cash income and cash expenditure of a business over a period of months. Study the example shown on the next page.

Each month the spreadsheet calculates the total income (receipts) and total expenditure (payments). It then deducts total expenditure from total income to calculate the net cashflow.

This net cashflow figure is then added to the opening bank balance (second line from the bottom) to calculate the projected 'closing' bank balance of the business (shown on the bottom line). If this figure is negative – see the figure for April below – it shows that the business will need to request an overdraft from the bank.

The great advantage of using a spreadsheet is that if the business wishes to change any of the projected income or expenditure amounts – eg if the sales receipts are likely to increase – then the cash budget figures can be be recalculated automatically, potentially saving hours of work.

The cash budget features in Chapter 19, and you may find that a spreadsheet is a useful way of processing your figures. The spreadsheet below is shown both with the formulas that are needed (top spreadsheet) and also with a set of data that has been input (bottom spreadsheet).

	A	B	C	D	E	F	G
1	ENIGMA LIMITED						
2	CASH BUDGET for January - June						
3		JANUARY	FEBRUARY	MARCH	APRIL	MAY	JUNE
4		£	£	£	£	£	£
5	*Income*						
6							
7	Receipts from debtors	30000	30000	40000	42000	45000	40000
8	Cash sales	500	600	500	650	550	500
9							
10							
11	TOTAL INCOME	=SUM(B6:B10)	=SUM(C6:C10)	=SUM(D6:D10)	=SUM(E6:E10)	=SUM(F6:F10)	=SUM(G6:G10)
12							
13							
14	*Expenditure*						
15							
16	Payments to creditors	25000	25000	30000	35000	40000	35000
17	Purchase of fixed assets				8500		
18	Operating expenses	2000	3000	3000	3500	3000	3500
19	Loan repayment			10000			
20							
21							
22							
23	TOTAL EXPENDITURE	=SUM(B16:B22)	=SUM(C16:C22)	=SUM(D16:D22)	=SUM(E16:E22)	=SUM(F16:F22)	=SUM(G16:G22)
24	NET CASHFLOW	=SUM(B11-B23)	=SUM(C11-C23)	=SUM(D11-D23)	=SUM(E11-E23)	=SUM(F11-F23)	=SUM(G11-G23)
25	Opening Balance	551	=SUM(B26)	=SUM(C26)	=SUM(D26)	=SUM(E26)	=SUM(F26)
26	Closing Balance	=SUM(B24:B25)	=SUM(C24:C25)	=SUM(D24:D25)	=SUM(E24:E25)	=SUM(F24:F25)	=SUM(G24:G25)

	A	B	C	D	E	F	G
1	ENIGMA LIMITED						
2	CASH BUDGET for January - June						
3		JANUARY	FEBRUARY	MARCH	APRIL	MAY	JUNE
4		£	£	£	£	£	£
5	*Income*						
6							
7	Receipts from debtors	30,000	30,000	40,000	42,000	45,000	40,000
8	Cash sales	500	600	500	650	550	500
9							
10							
11	TOTAL INCOME	30,500	30,600	40,500	42,650	45,550	40,500
12							
13							
14	*Expenditure*						
15							
16	Payments to creditors	25,000	25,000	30,000	35,000	40,000	35,000
17	Purchase of fixed assets				8,500		
18	Operating expenses	2,000	3,000	3,000	3,500	3,000	3,500
19	Loan repayment			10,000			
20							
21							
22							
23	TOTAL EXPENDITURE	27,000	28,000	43,000	47,000	43,000	38,500
24	NET CASHFLOW	3,500	2,600	- 2,500	- 4,350	2,550	2,000
25	Opening Balance	551	4,051	6,651	4,151	- 199	2,351
26	Closing Balance	4,051	6,651	4,151	- 199	2,351	4,351

CHAPTER SUMMARY

- The letters 'ICT" stand for 'Information and Communication Technology', which is often incorporated into modern accounting systems.

- Computer accounting systems save businesses time and money by automating many accounting processes, including the production of reports for management.

- Most computer accounting programs are based on the ledger system and integrate a number of different functions – one transaction will change accounting data in a number of different parts of the system.

- The different functions can include: sales ledger, purchases ledger, general (nominal) ledger, cash and bank receipts and payments, stock control, invoicing, report production.

- It is common for a payroll (wages) processing program to be linked to the general (nominal) ledger of a computer accounting program.

- A business must consider carefully all the advantages and disadvantages of computer accounting before installing a computerised system. The main advantages are speed, accuracy, availability of up-to-date information; the main disadvantages are cost, security implications and possible opposition from employees.

- Computer spreadsheets are often used to carry out individual functions in an accounting system, for example the creation of cash budgets.

QUESTIONS

visit
www.osbornebooks.co.uk
to take an online test

An asterisk (*) after the question number means that the answer is given at the end of this book.

20.1* Explain **two** advantages to a business of using a computer accounting system to record financial transactions.

20.2* Describe **two** advantages of using a computer spreadsheet for a document such as a cash budget.

20.3* What is meant by 'ICT'? Explain how **three** different areas of the accounting system might benefit from the introduction of computer accounting.

20.4* A business is planning to introduce a computer accounting system and holds an employee meeting to explain the implications of the change. One employee asks 'I have heard that there are all sorts of risks to the computer data which could cause us to lose the lot.' Describe **two** of the main risks to the security of computer data.

20.5* You are the Accounts Manager of a large company which imports and supplies computer games to UK retailers. You want to introduce an integrated computer accounting system throughout the company.

Explain the advantages you would point out to the line manager of the Sales Ledger section to persuade her that the new system would help her staff in processing orders and producing financial documents.

20.6 John Wilson, Managing Director of Flexman Limited, is considering investing in a computerised accounting system to replace a manual system. He asks you to prepare him a set of briefing notes explaining:

(a) two ways in which the use of a computer system can improve the speed with which the book-keeping processes are carried out

(b) two ways in which the accuracy of the book-keeping will be improved

(c) two types of error which a computer book-keeping system may not be able to eliminate

20.7* Gerry Mann is the Finance Director of Colourways Limited, a design company. He wants to introduce a computer accounting system into the business, but is encountering opposition from Helen Baxill, an active trade union member, who works in the Finance Department.

Describe:

(a) the objections relating to staff working conditions and welfare that Helen is likely to raise to try and block the introduction of a computer system

(b) the advantages to staff of a computer system that Gerry could use to persuade Helen to accept its introduction

Answers to Selected Questions

Answers to asterisked (*) questions follow in chapter order over the next thirty pages. Answers are given in fully displayed form; this will assist by showing the correct layouts, which is important in accounting.

Where answers are given to questions from the past examination papers, these answers are the responsibility of the author and not of the examining board. They have not been provided by or approved by AQA and may not necessarily constitute the only possible solutions.

Answers to the remaining questions (without asterisks) are available to tutors direct from Osborne Books. Please call 01905 748071 (Customer Services) for further details.

1.1

(a)	ledger	(f)	general (nominal) ledger
(b)	debtor	(g)	assets – liabilities = capital
(c)	creditor	(h)	business entity
(d)	sales day book		
(e)	cash book		

1.8

capital	£20,000
capital	£10,000
liabilities	£7,550
assets	£14,100
liabilities	£18,430
assets	£21,160

1.9

(a)	Owner started in business with capital of £10,000 in the bank
(b)	Bought office equipment for £2,000, paying by cheque
(c)	Received a loan of £6,000 by cheque
(d)	Bought a van for £10,000, paying by cheque
(e)	Owner introduces £2,000 additional capital by cheque
(f)	Loan repayment of £3,000 made by cheque

CHAPTER 2 Double-entry book-keeping: first principles

2.2

Bank Account

Dr		£	20-2		Cr £
20-2					
1 May	Capital	6,000	4 May	Machinery	3,500
12 May	L Warner: loan	1,000	6 May	Office equipment	2,000
17 May	Commission rec'd	150	10 May	Rent paid	350
			15 May	Wages	250
			20 May	Drawings	85
			25 May	Wages	135

Capital Account

Dr		£	20-2		Cr £
20-2			1 May	Bank	6,000

Machinery Account

Dr		£	20-2	Cr £
20-2				
4 May	Bank	3,500		

Office Equipment Account

Dr		£	20-2	Cr £
20-2				
6 May	Bank	2,000		

Rent Paid Account

Dr		£	20-2	Cr £
20-2				
10 May	Bank	350		

Lucy Warner: Loan Account

Dr		£	20-2		Cr £
20-2			12 May	Bank	1,000

Wages Account

Dr		£	20-2	Cr £
20-2				
15 May	Bank	250		
25 May	Bank	135		

Commission Income Account

Dr		£	20-2		Cr £
20-2			17 May	Bank	150

Drawings Account

Dr		£	20-2	Cr £
20-2				
20 May	Bank	85		

2.4

Bank Account

Dr		£	20-2		Cr £
20-2			20-2		
1 Mar	Capital	6,500	4 Mar	Office equipment	1,000
5 Mar	Bank loan	2,500	7 Mar	Wages	250
8 Mar	Commission rec'd	150	10 Mar	Rent paid	200
			12 Mar	Drawings	175
			15 Mar	Van	6,000

Capital Account

Dr		£	20-2		Cr £
20-2			1 Mar	Bank	6,500

Office Equipment Account

Dr		£	20-2	Cr £
20-2				
4 Mar	Bank	1,000		

Bank Loan Account

Dr		£	20-2		Cr £
20-2			5 Mar	Bank	2,500

Wages Account

Dr		£	20-2	Cr £
20-2				
7 Mar	Bank	250		

Commission Income Account

Dr			Cr
20-2		20-2	£
		8 Mar Bank	150

Rent Paid Account

Dr		£	Cr
20-2		20-2	£
10 Mar	Bank	200	

Drawings Account

Dr		£	Cr
20-2		20-2	£
12 Mar	Bank	175	

Van Account

Dr		£	Cr
20-2		20-2	£
15 Mar	Bank	6,000	

3.2

Bank Account

Dr		£		Cr	£
20-1			20-1		
1 Feb	Capital	3,000	3 Feb	Purchases	100
2 Feb	Sales	250	5 Feb	Wages	150
7 Feb	Sales	300	12 Feb	Purchases	200
15 Feb	J Walters: loan	1,000	20 Feb	Computer	1,950
25 Feb	Sales	150	27 Feb	Wages	125

Capital Account

Dr			Cr	£
20-1		20-1		
		1 Feb	Bank	3,000

Sales Account

Dr			Cr	£
20-1		20-1		
		2 Feb	Bank	250
		7 Feb	Bank	300
		25 Feb	Bank	150

Purchases Account

Dr		£	Cr
20-1			20-1
3 Feb	Bank	100	
12 Feb	Bank	200	

Wages Account

Dr		£	Cr
20-1			20-1
5 Feb	Bank	150	
27 Feb	Bank	125	

J Walters: Loan Account

Dr		£	Cr	£
20-1			20-1	
			15 Feb Bank	1,000

Computer Account

Dr		£	Cr	£
20-1			20-1	
20 Feb	Bank	1,950		

3.3

Bank Account

20-1		Debit	Credit	Balance
		£	£	£
1 Feb	Capital	3,000		3,000 Dr
2 Feb	Sales	250		3,250 Dr
3 Feb	Purchases		100	3,150 Dr
5 Feb	Wages		150	3,000 Dr
7 Feb	Sales	300		3,300 Dr
12 Feb	Purchases		200	3,100 Dr
15 Feb	J Walters: loan	1,000		4,100 Dr
20 Feb	Computer		1,950	2,150 Dr
25 Feb	Sales	150		2,300 Dr
27 Feb	Wages		125	2,175 Dr

3.4

Purchases Account

Dr		£	Cr	£
20-1			20-1	
4 Jan	AB Supplies Ltd	250		
20 Jan	Bank	225		

AB Supplies Ltd

Dr		£	Cr	£
20-1			20-1	
15 Jan	Bank	250	4 Jan Purchases	250

Sales Account

Dr			Cr	£
20-1		20-1		
		5 Jan	Bank	195
		7 Jan	Cash	150
		17 Jan	L Lewis	145

Bank Account

Dr		£	Cr	£
20-1			20-1	
5 Jan	Sales	195	15 Jan AB Supplies Ltd	250
10 Jan	J Johnson: loan	1,000	20 Jan Purchases	225
29 Jan	L Lewis	145	31 Jan Mercia Office Supplies Ltd	160

Cash Account

Dr		£	Cr		£
20-1			20-1		
7 Jan	Sales	150	22 Jan	Wages	125

J Johnson: Loan Account

Dr		£	Cr		£
20-1			20-1		
			10 Jan	Bank	1,000

L Lewis

Dr		£	Cr		£
20-1			20-1		
17 Jan	Sales	145	29 Jan	Bank	145

Wages Account

Dr		£	Cr	£
20-1			20-1	
22 Jan	Cash	125		

Office Equipment Account

Dr		£	Cr	£
20-1			20-1	
26 Jan	Mercia O S Ltd	160		

Mercia Office Supplies Ltd

Dr		£	Cr		£
20-1			20-1		
31 Jan	Bank	160	26 Jan	Office equipment	160

CHAPTER 4   Business documents

4.1
(a) purchase order
(b) invoice
(c) cash discount
(d) trade discount
(e) net
(f) credit note
(g) statement of account

4.6 (a) (i) Trade discount is given, if prearranged:
– to businesses, often in the same trade (but not to the general public)
– for buying in bulk (this discount is also known as bulk discount)
– by wholesalers, as a discount off list price to retailers

(ii) Cash discount (also known as settlement discount) is given, for prompt payment, if prearranged, and indicated on the invoice

(b) Invoice total: £400.00
Workings:

£500 – 20% = £400

(c) Queenstown Retail will pay £380.00 (£400.00 x 95%) for settlement in full within 14 days

CHAPTER 5   Balancing accounts – the trial balance

5.3 (a)

LORNA FOX
Trial balance as at 31 March 20-2

	Dr £	Cr £
Purchases	96,250	
Sales		146,390
Sales returns	8,500	
Administration expenses	10,240	
Wages	28,980	
Telephone	3,020	
Interest paid	2,350	
Travel expenses	1,045	
Premises	125,000	
Machinery	40,000	
Debtors	10,390	
Bank overdraft		1,050
Cash	150	
Creditors		12,495
Loan from bank		20,000
Drawings	9,450	
Capital		155,440
	335,375	335,375

(b) See Chapters 2 and 3 and page 65. The explanation should be appropriate for someone who does not understand accounting.

5.4 (a) principle
(b) mispost
(c) original entry
(d) compensating
(e) reversal of entries
(f) omission

6.1 (a)

Purchases Day Book

Date	Details	Invoice	Reference	Amount
20-6				£
1 Feb	Flair Clothing			520
4 Feb	Modernwear			240
18 Feb	Quality Clothing			800
28 Feb	Flair Clothing			200
28 Feb	Total for month			1,760

Sales Day Book

Date	Details	Invoice	Reference	Amount
20-6				£
2 Feb	Wyvern Fashions			200
10 Feb	Zandra Smith			160
15 Feb	Just Jean			120
23 Feb	Zandra Smith			320
24 Feb	Wyvern Fashions			80
26 Feb	Mercian Models			320
28 Feb	Total for month			1,200

(b)

PURCHASES LEDGER

Flair Clothing

Dr					Cr
20-6	£		20-6		£
			1 Feb	Purchases	520
			28 Feb	Purchases	200

Modernwear

Dr					Cr
20-6	£		20-6		£
			4 Feb	Purchases	240

Quality Clothing

Dr					Cr
20-6	£		20-6		£
			18 Feb	Purchases	800

SALES LEDGER

Wyvern Fashions

Dr					Cr
20-6		£	20-6		£
2 Feb	Sales	200			
24 Feb	Sales	80			

Zandra Smith

Dr					Cr
20-6		£	20-6		£
10 Feb	Sales	160			
23 Feb	Sales	320			

Just Jean

Dr					Cr
20-6		£	20-6		£
15 Feb	Sales	120			

Mercian Models

Dr					Cr
20-6		£	20-6		£
26 Feb	Sales	320			

GENERAL LEDGER

Purchases Account

Dr					Cr
20-6		£	20-6		£
28 Feb	Purchases Day Book	1,760			

Sales Account

Dr					Cr
20-6		£	20-6		£
			28 Feb	Sales Day Book	1,200

6.4 (a)

Sales Day Book

Date	Details	Invoice	Reference	Amount
				£
20-2				
5 Jan	Mereford College	1093	SL 201	3,900.00
7 Jan	Carpminster College	1094	SL 202	8,500.00
14 Jan	Carpminster College	1095	SL 202	1,800.50
14 Jan	Mereford College	1096	SL 201	2,950.75
20 Jan	Carpminster College	1097	SL 202	3,900.75
22 Jan	Mereford College	1098	SL 201	1,597.85
31 Jan	Total for month			22,649.85

Purchases Day Book

Date	Details	Invoice	Reference	Amount
				£
20-2				
2 Jan	Macstrad plc	M1529	PL 101	2,900.00
3 Jan	Amtosh plc	A7095	PL 102	7,500.00
18 Jan	Macstrad plc	M2070	PL 101	1,750.00
19 Jan	Amtosh plc	A7519	PL 102	5,500.00
31 Jan	Total for month			17,650.00

Sales Returns Day Book

Date	Details	Credit Note	Reference	Amount
				£
20-2				
13 Jan	Mereford College	CN109	SL 201	850.73
27 Jan	Mereford College	CN110	SL 201	593.81
31 Jan	Total for month			1,444.54

Purchases Returns Day Book

Date	Details	Credit Note	Reference	Amount
				£
20-2				
10 Jan	Macstrad plc	MC105	PL 101	319.75
12 Jan	Amtosh plc	AC 730	PL 102	750.18
23 Jan	Macstrad plc	MC120	PL 101	953.07
31 Jan	Total for month			2,023.00

(b)

SALES LEDGER

Mereford College (account no 201)

Dr			£				Cr £
20-2				20-2			
1 Jan	Balance b/d		705.35	13 Jan	Sales Returns		850.73
5 Jan	Sales		3,900.00	27 Jan	Sales Returns		593.81
14 Jan	Sales		2,950.75	31 Jan	Balance c/d		7,709.41
22 Jan	Sales		1,597.85				
			9,153.95				9,153.95
1 Feb	Balance b/d		7,709.41				

Carpminster College (account no 202)

Dr			£				Cr £
20-2				20-2			
1 Jan	Balance b/d		801.97	31 Jan	Balance c/d		15,003.22
7 Jan	Sales		8,500.00				
14 Jan	Sales		1,800.50				
20 Jan	Sales		3,900.75				
			15,003.22				15,003.22
1 Feb	Balance b/d		15,003.22				

PURCHASES LEDGER

Macstrad plc (account no 101)

Dr		£				Cr £
20-2				20-2		
10 Jan	Purchases Returns	319.75		1 Jan	Balance b/d	1,050.75
23 Jan	Purchases Returns	953.07		2 Jan	Purchases	2,900.00
31 Jan	Balance c/d	4,427.93		18 Jan	Purchases	1,750.00
		5,700.75				5,700.75
				1 Feb	Balance b/d	4,427.93

Amtosh plc (account no 102)

Dr		£				Cr £
20-2				20-2		
12 Jan	Purchases Returns	750.18		1 Jan	Balance b/d	2,750.83
31 Jan	Balance c/d	15,000.65		3 Jan	Purchases	7,500.00
				19 Jan	Purchases	5,500.00
		15,750.83				15,750.83
				1 Feb	Balance b/d	15,000.65

6.7

	Transaction	Source Document	Subsidiary Book
(a)	Goods purchased on credit from a supplier	Purchase invoice	Purchases day book
(b)	Goods sold on credit to a customer	Sales invoice	Sales day book
(c)	Faulty goods returned to a supplier	Credit note received	Purchases returns (returns out) day book
(d)	Payment made by cheque to a supplier	Cheque counterfoil	Main cash book
(e)	Purchase of a new machine for use in the factory on credit	Purchase invoice	General journal, or analysed purchases day book
(f)	Faulty goods returned by a customer	Credit note issued	Sales returns (returns in) day book
(g)	Cheque received from a customer and paid into the bank	Paying-in slip counterfoil	Main cash book

6.9

	Source document	Subsidiary Book	Account to be debited	Account to be credited
(a)	invoice received	purchases day book	purchases	A Cotton
(b)	invoice issued	sales day book	D Law	sales
(c)	paying in slip counterfoil	main cash book	bank	
(d)	credit note received	purchases returns day book	A Cotton	purchases returns
(e)	cheque counterfoil	main cash book	gas	bank
(f)	credit note issued	sales returns day book	sales returns	D Law

GENERAL LEDGER

Sales Account

Dr				Cr
20-2	£	20-2		£
		31 Jan	Sales Day Book	22,649.85

Purchases Account

Dr				Cr
20-2		£	20-2	£
31 Jan	Purchases Day Book	17,650.00		

Sales Returns Account

Dr				Cr
20-2		£	20-2	£
31 Jan	Sales Returns Day Book	1,444.54		

Purchases Returns Account

Dr				Cr
20-2		£	20-2	£
			31 Jan Purchases Returns Day Book	2,023.00

6.6

(a) Credit note

(b) 8 x £50 = £400 – £80 (trade discount) = £320

(c) Sales returns/returns in day book

Amount £320

CHAPTER 7 The main cash book

7.1

Main responsibilities of the cashier

- Recording receipts and payments by cheque and in cash in the firm's cash book
- Issuing receipts for cash (and sometimes cheques) received
- Making authorised cash payments (except for low-value expenses payments)
- Preparing cheques and BACS payments for signature and authorisation
- Paying cash and cheques received into the bank
- Controlling the firm's cash, either in a cash till or cash box
- Ensuring that all transactions passing through the cash book are supported by documentary evidence
- Checking the accuracy of the cash and bank balances at regular intervals
- Liaising with the other accounts staff

Qualities of a cashier

- Accuracy – in writing up the cash book, in cash handling, and in ensuring that payments are made only against correct documents and appropriate authorisation
- Security – of cash and cheque books, and correct authorisation of payments
- Confidentiality – that all cash/bank transactions, including cash and bank balances, are kept confidential

7.2 (a)

Cash Book

Dr | | | | | | Cr

Date	Details	Ref	Discount allowed £	Cash £	Bank £	Date	Details	Ref	Discount received £	Cash £	Bank £
20-2						20-2					
1 Jun	Balance b/d			280	2,240	1 Jun	Balance b/d				2,240
3 Jun	G Wheaton		5		195	8 Jun	F Lloyd		10		390
5 Jun	T Francis		2	53		10 Jun	Wages			165	
16 Jun	Bank	C		200		12 Jun	A Morris		3	97	
18 Jun	H Watson		30		640	16 Jun	Cash	C			200
28 Jun	M Perry		6		234	20 Jun	R Marks				78
30 Jun	K Willis			45		24 Jun	D Farr		2		65
30 Jun	Balance c/d				1,904	26 Jun	Telephone			105	
						30 Jun	Balance c/d			211	
			43	578	2,973				15	578	2,973
1 Jul	Balance b/d			211		1 Jul	Balance b/d				1,904

(b)

Discount Allowed Account

Dr | | | Cr

20-2		£	20-2		£
30 Jun	Cash Book	43			

Discount Received Account

Dr | | | Cr

20-2		£	20-2		£
			30 Jun	Cash Book	15

7.5 (a)

Cash Book

Dr | | | | | | Cr

Date	Details	Discount allowed £	Cash £	Bank £	Date	Details	Discount received £	Cash £	Bank £
2002					2002				£
1 Jan	Balance b/d		50.00	136.98	1 Jan	Balance b/d			263.67
3 Jan	M S Supplies	4.67			3 Jan	J B Smith Ltd	4.00		120.00
4 Jan	J O Jones			246.89	4 Jan	A E Evans Ltd			146.59
7 Jan	Cash sales		467.23		5 Jan	K L M Spares	3.96		127.45
7 Jan	ABC Traders			120.56	6 Jan	PCB Ltd			45.67
7 Jan	Cash			400.23	7 Jan	Insurance			100.00
					7 Jan	Bank charges			23.98
					7 Jan	Bank interest			46.97
					7 Jan	Wages		40.00	
					7 Jan	Postage		27.00	
					7 Jan	Bank		400.23	
					7 Jan	Balance		50.00	30.33
		4.67	517.23	904.66			7.96	517.23	904.66
8 Jan	Balance b/d		50.00	30.33					

(b)

(i) Count the cash float or cash in the till and check to the book total.

(ii) Prepare a bank reconciliation statement (see Chapter 8)

	Source document	Subsidiary book	Ledger account to be debited	Ledger account to be credited
Sold goods on credit to a customer	Sales invoice	Sales day book	Debtors/Sales ledger control account*	Sales
Faulty goods returned to the supplier	Purchases credit note	Purchases returns day book	Creditors/Purchases ledger control account*	Purchases returns
Cash sales paid into the bank	Bank paying-in slip counterfoil	Cash book	Bank	Sales
Charges made by the bank	Bank statement	Cash book	Bank charges	Bank
Purchase of office stationery paid for by cheque	Cheque counterfoil/invoice	Cash book	Stationery	Bank

* see Chapter 11

8.4   (a) - (c)

CASH BOOK

Date	Details	Bank		Date	Cheque no	Details	Bank
20-4		£		20-4			£
1 May	Balance b/f	3,652		4 May	451762	Smith and Company	751
26 May	J Ackland	832		4 May	451763	Bryant Limited	268
28 May	Stamp Limited	1,119		7 May	451764	Curtis Cars	1,895
14 May	Perran Taxis	2,596		7 May	451765	Parts Supplies	1,045
				18 May		Wyvern Council	198
				20 May		A1 Insurance	1,005
				25 May		Okaro and Company	254
				25 May		Bank charges	20
				31 May		Balance c/d	2,763
		8,199					8,199
1 Jun	Balance b/d	2,763					

(d)

MILESTONE MOTORS

Bank Reconciliation Statement as at 31 May 20-4

		£	£
Balance at bank as per bank statement			2,707
Less:	unpresented cheque no 451764		1,895
			812
Add:	outstanding lodgements		
	J Ackland	832	
	Stamp Limited	1,119	
			1,951
Balance at bank as per cash book			2,763

CHAPTER 8   Bank reconciliation statements

8.1

TOM REID
BANK RECONCILIATION STATEMENT AS AT 31 DECEMBER 20-7

	£
Balance at bank as per cash book	200
Add: unpresented cheque	
B Kay cheque no. 345126	20
	220
Less: outstanding lodgement	
J Hill	13
Balance at bank as per bank statement	207

8.6 (a)

Cash Book

Dr					Cr		
Date	Details	£		Date	Details	£	
1 Dec	Balance b/d	430		2 Dec	F Banks	250	
7	Sales banked	380		18	H Wilton	470	
22	Sales banked	300		29	M Wall	140	
31	Sales banked	560		30	Wages	100	
18	J Ball C/T	240		12	British Gas S/O	200	
				30	Bank charges	20	
				30	B Brown - dishonoured cheque	150	
				31	Balance c/d	580	
		1,910				1,910	
1 Jan	Balance b/d	580					

(b)

KINGDOM CARPET FITTERS
BANK RECONCILIATION STATEMENT AS AT 31 DECEMBER 2005

	£	£
Balance at bank as per cash book		580
Add: unpresented cheques		
M Wall	140	
Wages	100	
		240
		820
Less: outstanding lodgement		
Sales banked		560
Balance at bank as per bank statement		260

(c)   A dishonoured cheque is one that has been refused payment by the debtor's bank due to insufficient funds in the debtor's bank account.

9.1

MATTHEW LLOYD
TRADING AND PROFIT AND LOSS ACCOUNT
FOR THE YEAR ENDED 31 DECEMBER 20-8

	£	£
Sales		125,890
Opening stock	–	
Purchases	94,350	
Less Closing stock	5,950	
Cost of sales		88,400
Gross profit		37,490
Less expenses:		
Rates	4,850	
Heating and lighting	2,120	
Wages and salaries	10,350	
		17,320
Net profit		20,170

BALANCE SHEET AS AT 31 DECEMBER 20-8

	£	£	£
Fixed Assets			
Office equipment			8,500
Vehicles			10,750
			19,250
Current Assets			
Stock		5,950	
Debtors		3,950	
Bank		4,225	
Cash		95	
		14,220	
Less Current Liabilities			
Creditors		1,750	
Net Current Assets or Working Capital			12,470
NET ASSETS			31,720
FINANCED BY			
Capital			
Opening capital			20,000
Add Net profit			20,170
			40,170
Less Drawings			8,450
			31,720

9.3

Business A:	gross profit £8,000, net profit £4,000
Business B:	gross profit £17,000, expenses £7,000
Business C:	sales £36,500, net profit £6,750
Business D:	purchases £25,500, expenses £9,800
Business E:	opening stock £8,350, net loss £1,700
Business F:	closing stock £4,600, expenses £15,000

JOHN ADAMS
TRADING AND PROFIT AND LOSS ACCOUNT
FOR THE YEAR ENDED 31 DECEMBER 20-7

	£	£
Sales		259,688
Opening stock	14,350	
Purchases	114,472	
	128,822	
Less Closing stock	16,280	
Cost of sales		112,542
Gross profit		147,146
Less expenses:		
Rates	13,718	
Heating and lighting	12,540	
Wages and salaries	42,614	
Vehicle expenses	5,817	
Advertising	6,341	81,030
Net profit		66,116

BALANCE SHEET AS AT 31 DECEMBER 20-7

	£	£
Fixed Assets		
Premises		75,000
Office equipment		33,000
Vehicles		21,500
		129,500
Current Assets		
Stock	16,280	
Debtors	23,854	
Bank	1,235	
Cash	125	
	41,494	
Less Current Liabilities		
Creditors	17,281	
Net Current Assets or Working Capital		24,213
		153,713
Less Long-term Liabilities		
Loan from bank		35,000
NET ASSETS		118,713
FINANCED BY		
Capital		
Opening capital		62,500
Add Net profit		66,116
		128,616
Less Drawings		9,903
		118,713

JAMES CADWALLADER
TRADING AND PROFIT AND LOSS ACCOUNT
FOR THE YEAR ENDED 31 DECEMBER 2002

	£	£
Sales		67,945
Less Returns inwards		2,945
Turnover/net sales		65,000
Opening stock		5,780
Purchases	34,981	
Carriage inwards	679	
Less Returns outwards	1,367	
Less Closing stock	34,293	
Cost of sales	6,590	
Gross profit		33,483
		31,517
Less expenses:		
Wages	12,056	
Carriage out	386	
Other expenses	4,650	
		17,092
Net profit		14,425

A to Z ENGINEERING SUPPLIES
BALANCE SHEET AS AT 31 MARCH 2003

	£	£
Fixed Assets		
Premises		50,000
Motor vehicles		14,560
		64,560
Current Assets		
Stock	14,905	
Debtors	6,500	
Cash	56	
	21,461	
Less Current Liabilities		
Creditors	4,590	
Overdraft	3,400	
	7,990	
		13,471
		78,031
Less Long-term Liabilities		
Mortgage on premises		25,000
		53,031
Capital		42,571
Add net profit		23,460
Less drawings		13,000
		53,031

10.1

Date	Details	Reference	Dr £	Cr £
20-8				
1 May	Vehicle	GL	6,500	
	Fixtures and fittings	GL	2,800	
	Stock	GL	4,100	
	Cash	GL	150	
	Loan from husband	GL		5,000
	Capital	GL		8,550
			13,550	13,550
	Assets and liabilities at the start of business			

10.3

	subsidiary book	debit	credit
(a)	purchases day book	purchases account	Temeside Traders
(b)	sales day book	Malvern Models	sales account
(c)	journal	office equipment account	A-Z Computers Ltd
(d)	sales returns day book	sales returns account	Johnson Bros
(e)	cash book	bank account	Melanie Fisher
(f)	cash book	cash account	sales account
(g)	cash book	drawings account	cash account
(h)	cash book	Stationery Supplies Ltd	bank account
(i)	journal	bad debts written off account	J Bowen
(j)	purchases returns day book	I Johnson	purchases returns account

10.5

	Date	Details	Reference	Dr £	Cr £
(a)		Office expenses	GL	85	
		Suspense	GL		85
		Omission of entry in office expenses account – payment made by cheque no .... on .....(date)			
(b)		Suspense	GL	78	
		Photocopying	GL		78
		Photocopying	GL	87	
		Suspense	GL		87
				165	165
		Payment for photocopying £87 (cheque no .... on ....) entered in photocopying account as £78 in error			
(c)		Suspense	GL	100	
		Sales returns	GL		100
		Overcast on ...(date)... now corrected			
(d)		Commission received	GL	25	
		Suspense	GL		25
		Commission received on .... entered twice in commission received account, now corrected			

Suspense Account

Dr		£	20-8		Cr £
20-8			20-8		
30 Sep	Trial balance difference	19	(a)	Office expenses	85
(b)	Photocopying	78	(b)	Photocopying	87
(c)	Sales returns	100	(d)	Commission received	25
		197			197

10.7

Suspense Account

Dr			Cr
Details	£	Details	£
Purchases	4,500	Opening balance (error)	5,669
Debtors	650	Rent payable	81
Discount received	300		
Discount received	300		
	5,750		5,750

Tutorial note: The mispost between Sunshine Products Ltd and Sunmaster Products needs to be corrected in the sales ledger, but has no effect on suspense account.

10.9 (a)

Suspense Account

Dr					Cr
Date	Details	£	Date	Details	£
2005			2005		
31 Mar	Sales	230	31 Mar	Trial balance difference	834
31 Mar	Wages	600	31 Mar	Postage	154
31 Mar	Discount received	79			
31 Mar	Discount received	79			
		988			988

(b)
- An error which affects both the debit and credit side of the trial balance by the same amount will not be revealed by the trial balance.
- Examples of errors not revealed by the trial balance (note: the question asks for one only):
  - error of omission
  - reversal of entries
  - mispost/error of commission
  - error of principle
  - error of original entry (or transcription)
  - compensating error

(c) The bank reconciliation statement:
- checks for errors and omissions (such as credit transfers and bank charges) in the bank columns of the cash book by making a comparison with the bank statement
- checks that entries such as standing orders and direct debits are correctly recorded on the bank statement and in the bank columns of the cash book

---

CHAPTER 11 Control accounts

11.1

Sales Ledger Control Account

Dr			£			Cr £
20-1				20-1		
1 Jun	Balances b/d		17,491	30 Jun	Sales returns	1,045
30 Jun	Credit sales		42,591	30 Jun	Payments received	39,024
				30 Jun	Cash discount allowed	593
				30 Jun	Bad debts written off	296
				30 Jun	Balances c/d	19,124
			60,082			60,082
1 Jul	Balances b/d		19,124			

11.2

Purchases Ledger Control Account

Dr		£			Cr £
20-2			20-2		
30 Apr	Purchases returns	653	1 Apr	Balances b/d	14,275
30 Apr	Payments made to creditors	31,074	30 Apr	Credit purchases	36,592
30 Apr	Cash discount received	1,048			
30 Apr	Set-off: sales ledger	597			
30 Apr	Balances c/d	17,495			
		50,867			50,867
			1 May	Balances b/d	17,495

11.4

(a) Benefits include:
- enabling the arithmetical accuracy of the ledgers to be checked
- making the preparation of final accounts easier
- disclosing errors
- supplying a figure of debtors' or creditors' totals quickly

(b)

Sales Ledger Control Account

Dr		£			Cr £
2000			2000		
31 Oct	Balance b/d	25,800	31 Oct	Discount	37
31 Oct	Sales	540	31 Oct	Adjustment to balance	720
31 Oct	Returns	100	31 Oct	Balance c/d	25,683
		26,440			26,440
1 Nov	Balance b/d	25,683			

(c) Certain errors are not revealed so users may believe it to be correct.

Examples include errors of omission, commission, compensating errors, original entry.

11.8 (a)

Sales Ledger Control Account

Date	Details	£	Date	Details	£
2007			2007		
1 Apr	Balance b/d	44,267	30 Apr	Sales returns 884+100	984
30 Apr	Sales 93,882–9	93,873	30 Apr	Bank 95,501+2,339	97,840
30 Apr	Bank (dishonoured		30 Apr	Set-off: purchases ledger	235
	cheque)	107	30 Apr	Bad debt written off	150
			30 Apr	Discount allowed	1,788
			30 Apr	Balance c/d	37,250
		138,247			138,247
1 May	Balance b/d	37,250			

Tutorial note:

- The cash sales amount of £2,276 is not entered into sales ledger control account because it has no effect on debtors' accounts.

(b) As well as assisting in the identification of errors, sales ledger control account:

- provides instant information, enabling the total debtors figure to be ascertained at a glance – useful management information and helping with the production of final accounts
- helps with prevention of fraud – managers have access to control accounts thus restricting the possibility of fraudulent transactions

(c) Types of errors not revealed by a control account (note: the question asks for two types):

- omission, where a transaction has been completely omitted from the accounting records
- mispost/error of commission, where a transaction is entered in the wrong person's account, but within the same ledger section
- original entry, where the wrong money amount has been entered into the accounting system
- compensating error, where one error is cancelled out by another error within the same ledger section

12.3

	Amount to be subtracted from draft net profit £	Amount to be added to draft net profit £
Business rates	2,510	
Rent of premises	4,650	

Workings:

Rates: £2,250 + £110 + £150

Rent: £5,300 – £250 – £400

12.4 (a)

Rent and Rates Account

Dr		£	Cr		£
20-8			20-8		
31 Dec	Balance b/d	10,862	31 Dec	Profit and loss account	10,612
			31 Dec	Balance c/d	250
		10,862			10,862
20-9			20-9		
1 Jan	Balance b/d	250			

Electricity Account

Dr		£	Cr		£
20-8			20-8		
31 Dec	Balance b/d	2,054	31 Dec	Profit and loss account	2,164
31 Dec	Balance c/d	110			
		2,164			2,164
20-9			20-9		
			1 Jan	Balance b/d	110

Salaries Account

Dr		£	Cr		£
20-8			20-8		
31 Dec	Balance b/d	55,891	31 Dec	Profit and loss account	56,256
31 Dec	Balance c/d	365			
		56,256			56,256
20-9			20-9		
			1 Jan	Balance b/d	365

(b)

DON SMITH
TRADING AND PROFIT AND LOSS ACCOUNT FOR THE YEAR ENDED 31 DECEMBER 20-8

	£	£
Sales		257,258
Opening stock (1 January 20-8)	18,471	
Purchases	138,960	
	157,431	
Less Closing stock (31 December 20-8)	14,075	
Cost of sales		143,356
Gross profit		113,902
Add Discount received		591
		114,493
Less expenses:		
Rent and rates	10,612	
Electr city	2,164	
Telephone	1,695	
Salaries	56,256	
Vehicle expenses	10,855	
Discount allowed	478	
		82,060
Net profit		32,433

BALANCE SHEET AS AT 31 DECEMBER 20-8

	£	£	£
Fixed Assets			
Vehicles			22,250
Office equipment			7,500
			29,750
Current Assets			
Stock		14,075	
Debtors		24,325	
Prepayment of expenses		250	
		38,650	
Less Current Liabilities			
Creditors	19,684		
Bank overcraft	1,083		
Accrual of expenses	475	21,242	
Net Current Assets or Working Capital			17,408
NET ASSETS			47,158
FINANCED BY			
Capital			
Opening capital			30,000
Add net profit			32,433
			62,433
Less drawings			15,275
			47,158

12.5 A letter incorporating the following points:

- Depreciation is a measure of the amount of the fall in value of fixed assets over a time period.
- It is a systematic method of charging against profits over the life of an asset.
- When the asset is sold, adjustments can be made for any inaccuracies in the estimates of depreciation.
- A recognised system which fits with the accounting concepts (see AS Unit 2, Chapter 14) of going concern, accruals, consistency and prudence.

12.6

(a)

	year ended	year ended
	30 June 20-2	30 June 20-3
	£	£
Net profit before depreciation	18,700	33,100
Depreciation on fixed assets	5,000	5,000
Net profit after depreciation	13,700	28,100

(b)

	as at	as at
	30 June 20-2	30 June 20-3
	£	£
Fixed assets at cost	50,000	50,000
Less provision for depreciation to date	5,000	10,000
Net book value	45,000	40,000

12.8 (a)

Bad Debts Written Off Account

Dr			£		Cr		£
20-8				20-8			
31 Dec	P Ross		55	31 Dec	Profit and loss account		210
31 Dec	J Ball		105				
31 Dec	L Jones		50				
			210				210

12.8 (b)

- Profit and loss account (expenses)
  debit bad debts written off £210
  Explanation: profit for the year is reduced by £210

- *Balance sheet*
  debtors £20,000
  workings: £20,210 – £210 bad debts = £20,000 net debtors
  Explanation: current assets are reduced by £210

12.11 (a)

MIKE BARNETT
TRADING AND PROFIT AND LOSS ACCOUNT FOR THE YEAR ENDED 31 MAY 2007

	£	£	£
Sales			266,300
Less Returns inwards			630
Net sales			265,670
Opening stock (1 June 2006)		35,820	
Purchases	132,700		
Carriage inwards	540		
Less Returns outwards	1,310		
Net purchases		131,930	
		167,750	
Less Closing stock (31 May 2007)		29,700	
Cost of sales			138,050
Gross profit			127,620
Add Discounts received			2,090
			129,710
Less expenses:			
Carriage out		1,270	
Discounts allowed		1,410	
Motor expenses 15,430 – 250		15,180	
Shop expenses		21,380	
Wages 46,330 + 840		47,170	
Equipment depreciation 67,360 x 12.5%		8,420	
			94,830
Net profit			34,880

(b)

BALANCE SHEET AS AT 31 MAY 2007

	Cost £	Prov for dep'n £	Net book value £
Fixed Assets			
Premises	50,000	–	50,000
Equipment	67,360	*25,260	42,100
	117,360	25,260	92,100
Current Assets			
Stock		29,700	
Trade debtors		2,490	
Prepayment of expenses		250	
		32,440	
Less Current Liabilities			
Trade creditors	9,210		
Bank overdraft	21,690		
Accrual of expenses	840		
		31,740	
Net Current Assets or Working Capital			700
			92,800
Less Long-term Liabilities			
Mortgage on premises			20,000
NET ASSETS			72,800
FINANCED BY			
Capital			
Opening capital			62,100
Add net profit			34,880
			96,980
Less drawings			24,180
			72,800

* prov for dep'n £16,840 + this year's dep'n £8,420 = £25,260

13.1 Advantages of a sole trader business:

- the owner has independence
- all profits belong to the owner
- personal service and supervision are available at all times
- the business is easy to establish legally

Disadvantages of a sole trader business:

- the owner has unlimited liability
- all losses are the owner's responsibility
- expansion is limited
- there may be limited access to finance
- the owner usually has to work long hours, with few holidays
- there may be limited expertise within the business
- if the owner becomes ill the business will be affected

Possible future developments:

- form a partnership
- form a private limited company

13.4 (a) The shareholders

(b) The directors

(c) If the company becomes insolvent (goes 'bust') the most the shareholders can lose is the amount of their investment, together with any money unpaid on their shares (unpaid instalments on new share issues, for example).

CHAPTER 14 Accounting concepts and stock valuation

14.3 (a) This is an example of the realisation concept (alternative answer: the accruals concept).

(b) This is an example of the cost concept (alternative answer: the objectivity concept).

14.4 (a) Antonio should value the premises on his balance sheet at £100,000.

(b) The concepts he uses are going concern, prudence, cost, objectivity.

14.6 (a) Prudence concept: stock valuation should be at lower of cost and net realisable value, ie £10,000 in this case.

(b) Business entity concept: car is an asset of John's firm, not a personal asset (in any case personal assets, for sole traders and partnerships, might well be used to repay debts of firm).

(c) Prudence concept: the bad debt should be written off as a bad debt in profit and loss account (so reducing net profit), and the balance sheet figure for debtors should be £27,500 (which is closer to the amount he can expect to receive from debtors).

(d) Accruals concept: expenses and income must be matched, therefore it must go through the old year's accounts.

(e) Going concern concept: presumes that business will continue to trade in the foreseeable future: alternative is 'gone concern' and assets may have very different values.

14.7

Proposal	Concept	Action
1	Consistency	Continue to depreciate at 20%
2	Business entity	The whole amount of £36,000 is drawings
3	Realisation or accruals (matching)	Do not include the sales in this year's accounts as this will anticipate profits

14.9 (a) £220 + £750 + £290 + £35,500 = £36,760

Note: replacement cost is not applicable here

(b) Prudence

(c) Net realisable value is the selling price of the goods, less any expenses incurred in getting the stock into a saleable condition

CHAPTER 15 Further aspects of final accounts

15.1 (a) • £400 is to be included as income, which is added to gross profit in the profit and loss account for the year ended 31 December 20-8.

• £400 will be included as income, which will be added to gross profit in the profit and loss account for the year ended 31 December 20-9.

• £400 is to be shown as a prepayment of income in the current liabilities section of the balance sheet as at 31 December 20-8.

(b) The accounting concept to be applied is accruals (or matching).

15.3

Dr	Bank Account		Cr
	£		£
Bad debts recovered	50		

Dr	Bad Debts Recovered Account		Cr
	£		£
		Bank	50

15.5

(a)

20-1 increasing the provision
- new provision is £8,000 x 5% = £400
- existing provision is £300
- therefore increase in provision is £100

20-2 decreasing the provision
- new provision is £7,000 x 5% = £350
- existing provision is £400
- therefore decrease in provision is £50

(b)

20-1 Extracts from final accounts produced for year ended 30 June:
- profit and loss account: expense of £100
- balance sheet: debtors £8,000 - £400 = £7,600

20-2 Extracts from final accounts produced for year ended 30 June:
- profit and loss account: income of £50
- balance sheet: debtors £7,000 - £350 = £6,650

15.7

(a)

net profit

	£
Reduction in provision for doubtful debts	200
Bad debts written off	(178)
Bad debts recovered	261
Change in net profit	283
Net profit is now £18,090 + £283 =	18,373

(b)

working capital (or net current assets)

	£
Debtors increase £200 – £178	
Bank increase	22
Working capital increase	261
	283

(c)

bank balance

Bank balance increases by £261 from the bad debts recovered

15.9

(a)

Loss on disposal of van =	£100

Workings

£18,000 – *£14,400 depreciation =   £3,600   net book value

* £18,000 x 20% x 4 years

	£
Net book value at date of sale	3,600
Sale proceeds	3,500
Loss on disposal	100

(b)

The loss on sale will be shown as an expense in profit and loss account, thus reducing profit by £100.

15.10

(a)

Provision for Depreciation Account – Car

Dr		£			£	Cr
20-1			20-1			
31 Dec	Balance c/d	3,000	31 Dec	Profit and loss account	3,000	
		3,000			3,000	
20-2			20-2			
31 Dec	Balance c/d	5,250	1 Jan	Balance b/d	3,000	
			31 Dec	Profit and loss account	2,250	
		5,250			5,250	
20-3			20-3			
31 Dec	Disposals account	6,937	1 Jan	Balance b/d	5,250	
			31 Dec	Profit and loss account	1,687	
		6,937			6,937	

(b)

BALANCE SHEET EXTRACT AS AT 31 DECEMBER 20-1

Fixed Assets	Cost	Prov for dep'n	Net book value
	£	£	£
Car	12,000	3,000	9,000

BALANCE SHEET EXTRACT AS AT 31 DECEMBER 20-2

Fixed Assets	Cost	Prov for dep'n	Net book value
	£	£	£
Car	12,000	5,250	6,750

(c)

Dr		Disposals Account – Car		Cr
	£			£
20-3		20-3		
31 Dec Car	12,000	31 Dec Provision for depreciation		6,937
31 Dec Profit and loss account (profit on sale)	437	31 Dec Bank		5,500
	12,437			12,437

15.14

(a)

	£
Net book value (£18,000 – £10,800)	7,200
Selling price	4,000
Loss on sale	3,200

(b)

BALANCE SHEET EXTRACT AS AT 31 DECEMBER 2010

Fixed Assets	£	
Machinery at cost	112,000	(£100,000 – £18,000 + £30,000)
Less prov for depreciation	60,400	(£60,000 – £10,800 + £11,200)
Net book value	51,600	

15.15

(a)

	£
Draft net profit for the year ended 31 December 2003	21,630
Bad debts written off	(420)
Increase in provision for doubtful debts	(85)
Wages accrued	(720)
Insurance premiums prepaid	135
Corrected net profit for the year ended 31 December 2003	20,540

(b)

	£
Draft net current assets as at 31 December 2003	4,260
Bad debts written off	(420)
Increase in provision for doubtful debts	(85)
Wages accrued	(720)
Insurance premiums prepaid	135
Drawings	(210)
Corrected net current assets as at 31 December 2003	2,960

CHAPTER 16 Preparing sole trader final accounts

16.2 JOHN BARCLAY

TRADING AND PROFIT AND LOSS ACCOUNT FOR THE YEAR ENDED 30 JUNE 20-3

	£	£	£
Sales			864,321
Less Sales returns			2,746
			861,575
Opening stock		63,084	
Purchases (less £250 goods for own use)	599,878		
Less Purchase returns	3,894		
		595,984	
		659,068	
Less Closing stock		66,941	
Cost of sales			592,127
Gross profit			269,448
Add income:			
Discounts received		4,951	
Commission received		1,395	
Rent received		3,150	
			278,944
Less expenses:			
Office expenses		33,601	
Salaries		122,611	
Vehicle expenses		38,144	
Discount allowed		3,187	
			197,543
Net profit			81,401

SOUTHTOWN SUPPLIES

TRADING AND PROFIT AND LOSS ACCOUNT FOR THE YEAR ENDED 31 DECEMBER 20-4

	£	£	£
Sales			420,000
Less Sales returns			6,000
			414,000
Opening stock		70,000	
Purchases 280,000 – 500*	279,500		
Less Purchases returns	4,500		
		275,000	
		345,000	
Less Closing stock		60,000	
Cost of sales			285,000
Gross profit			129,000
Add income:			
Discounts received			750
Rent received			2,200
Commission received			1,450
			133,400
Less expenses:			
Discounts allowed		500	
Electricity		14,100	
Salaries		35,200	
Post and packing		1,400	
			51,200
Net profit			82,200

* goods scrapped

BALANCE SHEET AS AT 30 JUNE 20-3

	£	£	£
Fixed Assets			
Land and buildings			100,000
Vehicles			83,500
Office equipment			23,250
			206,750
Current Assets			
Stock		66,941	
Debtors		74,328	
Prepayment of expenses		346	
Accrual of income		150	
Bank		1,197	
		142,962	
Less Current Liabilities			
Creditors	58,821		
Accrual of expenses	1,250		
Prepayment of income	200		
	60,271		
Net Current Assets or Working Capital		82,691	
		289,441	
Less Long-term Liabilities			
Bank loan		75,000	
NET ASSETS		214,441	
FINANCED BY			
Capital			
Opening capital		155,000	
Add Net profit		81,401	
		236,401	
Less Drawings (plus £250 goods for own use)		21,960	
		214,441	

BALANCE SHEET AS AT 31 DECEMBER 20-4

	£	£	£
Fixed Assets			
Premises		120,000	
Fixtures and fittings		45,000	
		165,000	
Current Assets			
Stock	60,000		
Debtors	55,000		
Prepayment of expenses	400		
Accrual of income	200		
Insurance claim*	500		
Bank	5,000		
	121,100		
Less Current Liabilities			
Creditors	49,250		
Accrual of expenses	350		
Prepayment of income	300		
	49,900		
Net Current Assets or Working Capital		71,200	
NET ASSETS		236,200	
FINANCED BY			
Capital			
Opening capital		195,000	
Add Net profit		82,200	
		277,200	
Less Drawings		41,000	
		236,200	

* for goods scrapped

16.7 (a)

RACHEL SORCIM

TRADING AND PROFIT AND LOSS ACCOUNT FOR THE YEAR ENDED 31 MARCH 2005

	£	£	£
Sales			81,643
Opening stock		1,487	
Purchases (less £1,200 goods for own use)		37,442	
		38,929	
Less Closing stock		1,638	
Cost of sales			37,291
Gross profit			44,352
Add income:			
Bad debts recovered			88
Reduction in provision for doubtful debts			32
			44,472
Less expenses:			
Office wages		21,759	
Rent, rates and insurance		4,844	
General expenses		16,281	
Bad debts written off		137	
Provision for depreciation:			
premises		1,400	
equipment		2,294	
			46,715
Net loss			2,243

Workings:

- Provision for doubtful debts: £1,360 debtors x 5% provision = £68, which is deducted from £100 existing provision = £32 reduction in provision for doubtful debts
- Office wages: £21,347 + £412 accrual = £21,759
- Rent, rates and insurance: £4,990 – £146 prepayment = £4,844
- Provision for depreciation of premises: £70,000 x 2% = £1,400
- Provision for depreciation of equipment: £28,000 – £16,530 depreciation to date = £11,470 x 20% = £2,294

(b) Capital

	£
Opening capital	86,048
Less Net loss	2,243
	83,805
Less Drawings (plus £1,200 goods for own use)	17,700
	66,105

JAMES JENKINS

TRADING AND PROFIT AND LOSS ACCOUNT FOR THE YEAR ENDED 30 JUNE 20-9

	£	£	£
Sales			168,432
Less Sales returns			975
			167,457
Opening stock		9,427	
Purchases	105,240		
Less Purchases returns	1,237	104,003	
		113,430	
Less Closing stock		11,517	
Cost of sales			101,913
Gross profit			65,544
Add income:			
Commission received			2,510
Discount received			243
Bad debts recovered			210
Reduction in provision for doubtful debts			54
			68,561
Less expenses:			
Discount allowed		127	
Wages and salaries		30,841	
Vehicle expenses		1,076	
Rent and rates		8,521	
Heating and lighting		1,840	
Telephone		355	
General expenses		1,752	
Bad debts written off		85	
Depreciation:			
vehicle		1,125	
shop fittings		600	
			46,322
Net profit			22,239

BALANCE SHEET AS AT 30 JUNE 20-9

	£	£	£
	Cost	Prov for dep'n	Net book value
Fixed Assets			
Vehicle	8,000	4,625	3,375
Shop fittings	6,000	3,000	3,000
	14,000	7,625	6,375
Current Assets			
Stock			11,517
Debtors	3,840		
Less Provision for doubtful debts	96		3,744
Accrual of income			160
Prepayment of expenses			275
Bank			21,419
Cash			155
			37,270
Less Current Liabilities			
Creditors	4,226		
Accrual of expenses	55	4,281	
Net Current Assets or Working Capital			32,989
NET ASSETS			39,364
FINANCED BY			
Capital			
Opening capital			36,175
Add Net profit			22,239
			58,414
Less Drawings			19,050
			39,364

Workings

- Provision for doubtful debts: £3,840 debtors x 2.5% provision = £96, which is deducted from £150 existing provision = £54 reduction in provision for doubtful debts
- Provision for depreciation of shop fittings: £6,000 x 10% = £600
- Provision for depreciation of vehicle: £8,000 – £3,500 depreciation to date = £4,500 x 25% = £1,125

SAMINA HUSSEIN
PROFIT AND LOSS ACCOUNT FOR THE YEAR ENDED 31 DECEMBER 2006

	£	£
Gross profit		113,490
Add income:		
Reduction in provision for doubtful debts		25
Discounts received		388
		113,903
Less expenses:		
Wages	62,400	
Rent and rates	8,910	
General expenses	9,477	
Discounts allowed	307	
Provision for depreciation: equipment	1,200	
		82,294
Net profit		31,609

Workings:

- Gross profit: £110,707 + £2,783 goods for own use = £113,490

- Provision for doubtful debts: £27,000 debtors x 2.5% provision = £675, which is deducted from £700 existing provision = £25 reduction in provision for doubtful debts

- Rent and rates: £8,430 – £120 prepayment + £600 accrual = £8,910

- Provision for depreciation: £12,000 x 10% = £1,200

17.3
CHAPELPORTH LIMITED
PROFIT AND LOSS APPROPRIATION ACCOUNT FOR THE YEAR ENDED 30 JUNE 20-8

	£	£	£
Net profit before taxation			135,000
Less corporation tax			48,000
Profit for year after taxation			87,000
Less interim dividends paid			
ordinary shares		21,000	
preference shares		8,000	
final dividends proposed			
ordinary shares		29,000	
preference shares		8,000	
			66,000
Retained profit for year			21,000

17.5
JOBSEEKERS LIMITED
PROFIT AND LOSS APPROPRIATION ACCOUNT
FOR THE YEAR ENDED 31 DECEMBER 20-6

	£	£
Net profit before taxation		68,200
Less corporation tax		14,850
Profit for year after taxation		53,350
Less ordinary dividends – interim paid	10,000	
– final proposed	40,000	
		50,000
Retained profit for year		3,350
Add balance of retained profits at beginning of year		7,350
Balance of retained profits at end of year		10,700

BALANCE SHEET AS AT 31 DECEMBER 20-6

Fixed Assets	Cost £	Prov for dep'n £	Net book value £
Intangible			
Goodwill	20,000	6,000	14,000
Tangible			
Premises	175,000	10,500	164,500
Office equipment	25,000	5,000	20,000
	220,000	21,500	198,500
Current Assets			
Stock		750	
Debtors		42,500	
		43,250	
Less Current Liabilities			
Creditors	7,250		
Bank overdraft	13,950		
Proposed dividends	40,000		
Corporation tax	14,850		
	76,050		
Net Current Assets or Working Capital		(32,800)	
			165,700
Less Long-term Liabilities			
Bank loan			55,000
NET ASSETS			110,700
FINANCED BY			
Issued Share Capital			
100,000 ordinary shares of £1 each			100,000
Revenue Reserve			
Profit and loss account			10,700
SHAREHOLDERS' FUNDS			110,700

17.6

(a)

Ordinary shares

Advantage
- Voting rights
- Potential capital growth
- High dividends in good years

Disadvantage
- Risk of losing money invested
- Low (or no) dividend in poor years

7% preference shares

Advantage
- Fixed rate of dividend which will not go down if interest rates fall
- Less risky than ordinary shares

Disadvantage
- Generally, no voting rights
- Fixed dividends, so no growth in dividends
- Fewer capital growth prospects than ordinary shares

6% debentures

Advantage
- Fixed rate of interest which will not go down if interest rates fall
- Loans rather than shares
- Less risky than shares

Disadvantage
- No capital growth prospects
- Fixed rate of interest, whatever may happen to interest rates

(b)

- Jill is probably better off investing in ordinary shares
- The risk is that she could lose the amount invested but, if the company does well, she could make large capital gains
- Her income – in the form of dividends – will vary from year-to-year, depending on how successful the company has been

(c)

- Jack is probably better off investing in debentures
- These are the safest form of investment for him and will give him an income of £600 per year
- If he wishes to take a slightly higher risk he could invest some or all of the money in preference shares; if all, then his income will be £700 per year
- With preference shares there could also be some capital growth
- Debentures offer the safest investment: in the event of the company going into liquidation, debentures will be repaid before the preference and ordinary shareholders

	Net profit before appropriations	Retained profits	Shareholders' funds	Current assets	Current liabilities
(a)	decrease £12,000	decrease £12,000	decrease £12,000	no change	increase £12,000
(b)	increase £50,000	increase £50,000	increase £50,000	no change	no change
(c)	no change	decrease £25,000	no change	no change	no change
(d)	no change	decrease £43,000	decrease £43,000	no change	increase £43,000

(b)

SUMMARISED BALANCE SHEET AS AT 30 APRIL 2006

	£	£	£	£
Fixed Assets				1,270,000
Current Assets			355,000	
Less Current Liabilities				
Creditors		31,000		
Corporation tax		110,000		
Proposed dividends		38,000		
			179,000	
Net Current Assets or Working Capital				176,000
NET ASSETS				1,446,000
FINANCED BY				
Issued Share Capital				
950,000 ordinary shares of £1 each				950,000
Capital Reserve				
Share premium account				*80,000
Revenue Reserves				
General reserve			**150,000	
Profit and loss account			266,000	
				416,000
SHAREHOLDERS' FUNDS				1,446,000

* 200,000 shares x 40p premium per share

** £100,000 + £50,000 transfer

17.11 (a)

SREWOLF LIMITED
PROFIT AND LOSS APPROPRIATION ACCOUNT FOR THE YEAR ENDED 30 APRIL 2006

	£
Net profit before taxation	387,000
Less corporation tax	110,000
Profit for year after taxation	277,000
Less ordinary dividend proposed	*38,000
	239,000
Less transfer to general reserve	50,000
Retained profit for year	189,000
Add balance of retained profits at beginning of year	77,000
Balance of retained profits at end of year	266,000

* ordinary shares 750,000 + new issue 200,000 = 950,000 x dividend of 4p per share

17.13 (a)

PAFFTOL LIMITED
PROFIT AND LOSS APPROPRIATION ACCOUNT FOR THE YEAR ENDED 31 MARCH 2004

	£	£
Net profit before taxation		*448,000
Less corporation tax		102,000
Profit for year after taxation		346,000
Less ordinary dividends – interim paid	30,000	
– final proposed	60,000	
		90,000
		256,000
Less transfer to general reserve		50,000
Retained profit for year		206,000
Add balance of retained profits at beginning of year		439,000
Balance of retained profits at end of year		645,000

	£	
* Net profit for year	676,000	
Less:		
directors' fees	200,000	
debenture interest	28,000	paid 14,000 + accrued 14,000
	448,000	
Net profit before taxation		

(b)

BALANCE SHEET AS AT 31 MARCH 2004

Fixed Assets	Cost	Prov for dep'n	Net book value
	£	£	£
Plant and machinery	1,420,000	192,000	1,228,000
Vehicles	710,000	150,000	560,000
	2,130,000	342,000	1,788,000
Current Assets			
Stock		211,000	
Debtors		24,900	
Bank		113,600	
		349,500	
Less Current Liabilities			
Creditors	16,500		
Proposed dividends	60,000		
Corporation tax	102,000		
Debenture interest	14,000		
		192,500	
Net Current Assets or Working Capital			157,000
			1,945,000
Less Long-term Liabilities			
7% debentures (2015-2018)			400,000
NET ASSETS			1,545,000
FINANCED BY			
Issued Share Capital			
500,000 ordinary shares of £1 each, fully paid			500,000
Capital Reserve			
Share premium account			100,000
Revenue Reserves			
General reserve		300,000	
Profit and loss account		645,000	
			945,000
SHAREHOLDERS' FUNDS			1,545,000

18.1

	Amero plc	Britz plc
• gross profit margin	11.85%	37.46%
• gross profit mark-up	13.44%	59.90%
• overheads/turnover	8.98%	22.91%
• net profit margin	2.87%	14.55%
• return on capital employed	18.18%	13.70%

18.2

(a)

	Cawston plc	Dunley plc
• net current asset ratio	1.51:1	1.04:1
• liquid capital ratio	0.82:1	0.65:1
• debtor collection period	37 days	3 days
• creditor payment period	57 days	46 days
• stock turnover	41 days	18 days
• gearing ratio	0.54:1	0.16:1

(b) Cawston plc is the chemical manufacturer, while Dunley plc runs department stores.

All of the ratios for Cawston are close to the benchmarks for a manufacturing business: eg net current asset and liquid capital ratios, although a little low, are near the 'accepted' figures of 2:1 and 1:1, respectively. Debtor, creditor and stock turnover show quite a high level of stock being held; debtor turnover indicates that most sales are on credit; creditor turnover is rather high. The gearing ratio is acceptable – medium geared.

For Dunley plc, the ratios indicate a business that sells most of its goods on cash terms: low net current asset and liquid capital ratios, with minimal debtor turnover. The stock turnover is speedy, whilst creditors are paid after 46 days (approximately one-and-a-half months). The gearing ratio is low, indicating that there is scope for future borrowing should it be required.

18.5

(a) *Net current assets*

Current assets – Current liabilities

Net current assets, or working capital, are needed by all businesses in order to finance day-to-day trading activities. Sufficient net current assets enable a business to hold adequate stocks, allow a measure of credit to debtors, and to pay creditors on time.

Liquid capital

(Current assets – Stock) – Current liabilities
Liquid capital is calculated in the same way as net current assets, except that stock is omitted. This is because stock is the most illiquid current asset. Liquid capital provides a direct comparison between the short-term assets of debtors/cash/bank and short-term liabilities.

(c) **Issue of ordinary shares**

Advantages

• Ordinary shares are not normally repayable, so the company will have the finance for the foreseeable future.

• A variable dividend is paid, which is dependent on profits.

• If profits are low and a dividend is not paid in one year, the dividend is not carried forward.

• In the event of insolvency of the company, ordinary shareholders will be paid off last.

• The company's gearing ratio will be improved by the issue of ordinary shares.

Disadvantages

• The new shareholders will have voting rights.

• The power of existing shareholders will be diluted because there will be more shares in issue.

Gearing ratio

$$\frac{£400,000}{*£1,545,000 + **£600,000} = \frac{£400,000}{£2,145,000} = 0.19:1 \text{ or } 19\%, \text{ ie low-geared}$$

* shareholders' funds
** 200,000 ordinary shares of £1 each + share premium of £2 each

Issue of debentures

Advantages

• Debentures do not carry voting rights so there will be no dilution of the power of existing shareholders.

• The interest rate is fixed, whatever may happen to the level of interest rates.

• The new debentures are at a rate of 6% which is lower than those currently in issue.

• The debt is not permanent and will be repaid at a date in the future.

Disadvantages

• The interest must be paid whether or not profits are made.

• A failure to pay interest could lead the company into insolvency.

• The company's gearing ratio will be worsened by the issue of debentures.

• Debenture holders may require security for their loan.

• Debentures will have a date in the future for repayment – cash will be needed for this.

Gearing ratio

$$\frac{*£400,000 + *£600,000}{**£1,545,000} = \frac{£1,000,000}{£1,545,000} = 0.65:1 \text{ or } 65\%, \text{ ie high-geared,}$$
but probably acceptable to lenders

* new debentures
** shareholders' funds

18.3

(a) *Formula*

Net current asset (current) ratio = Current assets : Current liabilities

Ratio calculations

2004	£420,000 : £140,000	= 3 : 1
2005	£360,000 : £180,000	= 2 : 1

(b) *Formula (Note: the question asks for one relevant ratio)*

Gross profit margin $=$ $\dfrac{\text{Gross profit}}{\text{Sales turnover}}$ $\times$ $\dfrac{100}{1}$

Net profit margin $=$ $\dfrac{\text{Net profit}}{\text{Sales turnover}}$ $\times$ $\dfrac{100}{1}$

Ratio calculations

2004

Gross profit margin $=$ $\dfrac{£160,000}{£320,000}$ $\times$ $\dfrac{100}{1}$ $=$ 50%

Net profit margin $=$ $\dfrac{£20,000}{£320,000}$ $\times$ $\dfrac{100}{1}$ $=$ 6.25%

2005

Gross profit margin $=$ $\dfrac{£120,000}{£280,000}$ $\times$ $\dfrac{100}{1}$ $=$ 42.86%

Net profit margin $=$ $\dfrac{£30,000}{£280,000}$ $\times$ $\dfrac{100}{1}$ $=$ 10.71%

(b)

• Net current asset ratio = Current assets : Current liabilities

• Liquid capital ratio = $\dfrac{(\text{Current assets} - \text{Stock})}{\text{Current liabilities}}$

• Debtor collection period = $\dfrac{\text{Debtors}}{\text{Credit sales}}$ × 365 days

• Creditor collection period = $\dfrac{\text{Trade creditors}}{\text{Credit purchases}}$ × 365 days

(c)

• Net current asset (current) ratio £13,450* : £7,865** = 1.71:1

  * (10,250 – 2,450) + 450 + 5,200
  ** 6,000 + 1,865

• Liquid capital (acid test) ratio = $\dfrac{£13,450 - £5,200 \text{ (stock)}}{£7,865}$ = 1.05:1

• Debtor collection period = $\dfrac{£7,800^*}{£96,000}$ × 365 days = 29.66 days

  * 10,250 – 2,450 (bad debt written off)

• Creditor collection period = $\dfrac{£6,000}{£56,000}$ × 365 days = 39.11 days

(d) *Writing off the debt for £2,450*

• Writing off the debt as bad has reduced debtors to £7,800, and current assets from £15,900 to £13,450.

• The effect of this is that the net current assets ratio has been reduced from 2.02:1 to 1.71:1.

• The effect on the liquid capital ratio has been a reduction from 1.36:1 to 1.05:1.

• By writing off the bad debt, liquidity ratios have reduced quite significantly.

Reducing the value of stock over the year

• Stock has reduced from £8,400 to £5,200.

• Had the higher level of stock been maintained, the net current asset ratio at the year's end would have been £16,650*:£7,865 = 2.12:1.

  * (10,250 – 2,450) + 450 + 8,400

• The liquid capital ratio would be unchanged – because stock is excluded.

• A change in the level of stock affects the net current asset ratio but has no effect on the liquid capital ratio.

(c)

Formula

$$\text{Gross profit margin} = \frac{\text{Gross profit}}{\text{Sales turnover}} \times \frac{100}{1}$$

Ratio calculations

2003

$$\frac{£60,000}{£300,000} \times \frac{100}{1} = 20\%$$

2004

$$\frac{£70,000}{£400,000} \times \frac{100}{1} = 17.5\%$$

(c)

Gross profit margin has fallen from 20% in 2003 to 17.5% in 2004. Despite this fall, gross profit has increased from £60,000 in 2003 to £70,000 in 2004. The explanation for this apparent contradiction is that sales turnover has increased from £300,000 to £400,000 – an increase of a third – perhaps as a result of reducing the selling prices. As gross profit margin has fallen, so cost of sales as a percentage of sales turnover has increased from 80% to 82.5%.

Stock turnover has improved – from 68.44 days in 2003 to 60.83 days in 2004. This indicates that, despite an increase of £10,000 in average stock, stock is moving more quickly – a good sign, which links in with the increase of one-third in sales turnover.

Overall, the business is increasing its sales turnover and gross profit – at the same time stock turnover is improving.

(c)

REPORT

To: Susie
From: Student Accountant
Date: Today
Subject: Explanation of the significance of the ratios calculated

Net current asset (current) ratio has deteriorated between 2004 and 2005. In 2004 there were £3 of current assets to each £1 of current liabilities; in 2005 the figure has fallen to £2 of current assets to each £1 of current liabilities. Whilst a 2:1 ratio is still satisfactory, if the downward trend continues, there will be liquidity problems in the future.

Gross profit margin has fallen from 50% in 2004 to 42.86% in 2005. This fall has been caused by either lower selling prices or higher buying prices from suppliers. The percentage is still high but the fall needs to be investigated.

Net profit margin has improved from 6.25% in 2004 to 10.71% in 2005 – this is a good sign. The most likely reason is that the overheads (expenses) have fallen – from 43.75% of sales in 2004 to 32.14% in 2005.

18.9 (a) *Formula*

$$\text{Stock turnover} = \frac{\text{Average stock}}{\text{Cost of sales}} \times 365 \text{ days} \quad \text{or} \quad \frac{\text{Cost of sales}}{\text{Average stock}}$$

Ratio calculations

2003

$$\frac{£45,000^*}{£240,000} \times 365 \text{ days} = 68.44 \text{ days} \quad \text{or} \quad \frac{£240,000}{£45,000} = 5.33 \text{ times per year}$$

* (£40,000 + £50,000) ÷ 2

2004

$$\frac{£55,000^*}{£330,000} \times 365 \text{ days} = 60.83 \text{ days} \quad \text{or} \quad \frac{£330,000}{£55,000} = 6 \text{ times per year}$$

* (£50,000 + £60,000) ÷ 2

19.2

(a)

Strudwick Stationers Ltd

Cash Budget for four months ending 31 August 2002

Details	May	June	July	Aug
	£000	£000	£000	£000
Receipts				
Cash sales	35.2	36.8	33.6	35.2
Credit sales	9.2	8.8	9.2	8.4
	44.4	45.6	42.8	43.6
Payments				
Purchases	32.2	30.8	32.2	29.4
Wages	9.0	9.0	9.0	9.5
Fixed costs	3.0	3.0	3.0	3.0
Variable costs	4.4	4.6	4.2	4.4
	48.6	47.4	48.4	46.3
Net cash flow	(4.2)	(1.8)	(5.6)	(2.7)
Add opening balance	12.1	7.9	6.1	0.5
Closing balance	7.9	6.1	0.5	(2.2)

(b)
- planning ahead – overdraft required in August (need to approach bank)
- monitoring and control of cash resources
- co-ordination of plans and resources – the pay rise might have been better offered in September
- communicating the budget to the directors and staff
- motivating staff to ensure that budget is met

19.4

(a)

Cash Budget for Carolanne for four months

	Month 1	Month 2	Month 3	Month 4
	£	£	£	£
Receipts				
Capital introduced	2,000			
Sales – wash	400	800	800	1,400
– dry	160	320	320	560
Total receipts for month	2,560	1,120	1,120	1,960
Payments				
Advertising	30	30	30	–
Assistant's wages	–	–	–	480
Washing powder, etc	360	360	360	360
Fixed costs	300	300	300	300
Washing machines and dryers	750	750	750	750
Drawings	150	150	150	196
Total payments for month	1,590	1,590	1,590	2,086
Net cash flow	970	(470)	(470)	(126)
Add bank balance (overdraft) at beginning of month	–	970	500	500
Bank balance (overdraft) at end of month	970	500	30	(96)

20.1 Explanation of two advantages out of the list on page 386. The most obvious advantages are speed of input, accuracy of transaction recording, accessibility of up-to-date information and document printing (eg invoices, credit notes and statements).

20.2 The main two advantages are that a spreadsheet saves time in calculation and secondly that if any of the figures should alter, the remaining dependent figures will automatically be recalculated.

20.3 ICT stands for "information and communication technology". ICT is significant to accounting in that it records, stores, processes and communicates accounting information. Three different areas could include: ledger accounting, eg sales ledger, purchases ledger, cash book; stock control; payroll processing; management reports, eg aged debtors analysis, trial balance, trading and profit and loss account and balance sheet.

20.4 Two from: hacking in from outside, hacking from the inside, theft from outside (or inside), computer breakdown when periodic back-ups have not been made, viruses, inefficient back-up policy.

20.5 The sales ledger function would benefit from: accuracy of input, up-to-date balances of account available to all authorised staff, aged debtors analysis produced automatically, automatic production of invoices, credit notes and statements.

20.7 (a) Objections might include dislike of change, dislike of computers, fear of redundancies, worries about health issues such as RSI, back strain and eye strain.
(b) Advantages include opportunities for staff training and promotion, motivation, job satisfaction and possibly higher pay

---

(b) Benefits of drawing up the cash budget:

- *Benefit 1*

  Carolanne can see that a bank overdraft will be needed at the end of month 4, so she can arrange an overdraft facility in advance – perhaps for both months 3 and 4.

- *Benefit 2*

  Carolanne may well be able to control her payments in order to avoid an overdraft – for example, if the assistant were to work for five fewer days in month 4, there would be no need for an overdraft.

19.6 (a)

Wilkinson Limited

Cash budget for the six months ending 30 June 20-8

	Jan £	Feb £	Mar £	Apr £	May £	Jun £
Receipts						
Debtors	57,500	65,000	70,000	72,500	85,000	65,000
Total receipts for month	57,500	65,000	70,000	72,500	85,000	65,000
Payments						
Creditors	26,500	45,000	50,000	34,500	35,500	40,500
Wages and salaries	17,500	18,000	18,250	18,500	16,500	20,000
Other expenses	14,500	19,500	18,000	17,500	19,500	21,000
Total payments for month	58,500	82,500	86,250	70,500	71,500	81,500
Net cash flow	(1,000)	(17,500)	(16,250)	2,000	13,500	(16,500)
Add bank balance (overdraft) at beginning of month	2,250	1,250	(16,250)	(32,500)	(30,500)	(17,000)
Bank balance (overdraft) at end of month	1,250	(16,250)	(32,500)	(30,500)	(17,000)	(33,500)

(b) £2,250 (opening balance 1 January) + £33,500 overdraft (closing balance 30 June) = £35,750 total net cash

Index